THIS QUIET DUST
And Other Writings

William Styron is the Pulitzer Prize-winning author of *The Long March*, *Lie Down in Darkness*, *Set This House on Fire*, *The Confessions of Nat Turner* and *Sophie's Choice*. He has also published *Darkness Visible*, the remarkable story of his descent into depression, a collection, *This Quiet Dust and Other Writings*, and, most recently, *A Tidewater Morning*. He lives in Roxbury, Connecticut, and Martha's Vineyard.

ALSO BY WILLIAM STYRON

The Long March
Lie Down in Darkness
Set This House on Fire
The Confessions of Nat Turner
Sophie's Choice
Darkness Visible
A Tidewater Morning

William Styron

THIS QUIET DUST
And Other Writings

V
VINTAGE

TO ROSE

Published by Vintage 2000

2 4 6 8 10 9 7 5 3 1

Copyright © William Styron, 1953, 1961, 1962, 1963, 1964,
1965, 1968, 1972, 1974, 1975, 1976, 1977, 1978, 1980, 1981, 1982, 1992.
Copyright renewed 1989, 1990, 1991, 1992 by William Styron

The right of William Styron to be identified as the author of this work has been asserted
by him in accordance with the Copyright, Designs and Patents Act, 1988

"The Aftermath of Benjamin Reid" and "Big Love" (originally published as
"Mrs Aadland's Little Girl, Beverly") were first published in *Esquire*.

Most of the essays in this book have been previously published by: the *American Scholar*,
Briarpatch Press, Duke *Encounters*, E. P. Dutton, Inc., *Geo: The Earth Diary*, Hampden-
Sydney College, *Harper's*, *Harper's Bazaar*, *Hartford Courant Magazine*, *Life*, *McCall's
Magazine*, the *Mississippi Quarterly*, *New York Magazine*, the *New York Review of Books*,
Oririna Press, Palaemon Press, the *South Atlantic Bulletin* and the *Washington Monthly*.

Grateful acknowledgement is made to the following for permission to reprint previously
published material: Little, Brown, and Company: the first four lines from "This Quiet
Dust" by Emily Dickinson from *The Collected Poems of Emily Dickinson*, edited by
Thomas H. Johnson. Copyright 1914, 1942, by Martha Dickinson Bianchi. Reprinted by
permission of Little, Brown & Company. The *New York Times*: "A Second Flowering,"
"The Joint," and "Calley" by William Styron. Copyright © 1971, 1973 by The New York
Times Company. Reprinted by permission.

First published in Great Britain in 1983 by Jonathan Cape

Vintage
Random House, 20 Vauxhall Bridge Road, London SW1V 2SA

Random House Australia (Pty) Limited
20 Alfred Street, Milsons Point, Sydney, New South Wales 2061, Australia

Random House New Zealand Limited
18 Poland Road, Glenfield, Auckland 10, New Zealand

Random House (Pty) Limited
Endulini, 5A Jubilee Road, Parktown 2193, South Africa

The Random House Group Limited Reg. No. 954009
www.randomhouse.co.uk

A CIP catalogue record for this book is available from the British Library

ISBN 0 09 928554 1

Papers used by Random House are natural, recyclable products made from
wood grown in sustainable forests. The manufacturing processes conform to
the environmental regulations of the country of origin

Printed and bound in Great Britain by
Cox & Wyman Limited, Reading, Berkshire

NOTE TO THE READER

As one who has primarily written fiction during his career as a writer, I have always considered the writing of prose other than fiction something of a sideline. This is not to say that I have assigned a greatly diminished value to the essays, essay-reviews and incidental pieces that make up the present collection. For better or for worse, I have applied as much effort and have spent as much time, proportionately, to the crafting of these pieces as I have to the writing of the novels. It is just that the shorter nonfiction works—perhaps because of their generally topical nature—seem to linger less reverberantly in one's own mind than the novels with their large scope and multiplicity of elements and the truly memorable demands they make upon one's stamina and patience as a writer. No doubt this is why I was taken a little by surprise when—after it was suggested that I put together this volume—I discovered that I had, in the past two decades, written a far greater amount in the essay form than I remembered. Certainly I have written enough of it to demonstrate that I harbor no disdain for literary journalism or just plain journalism, under whose sponsorship I have been able to express much that has fascinated me, or alarmed me, or amused me, or otherwise engaged my attention when I was not writing a book.

For this collection I have selected mainly those pieces which upon rereading seem to maintain their original integrity and interest, and have withstood the attrition of time. I think that it will be seen that this is a very personal book. The essays do not claim a great amplitude of range. Few are of an abstract or purely contemplative nature; virtually all of the pieces are the offshoot of either my occasional crotchets or perennial preoccupations. My preoccupations, of course, like those of all fiction writers, are embedded in my works of fiction. Therefore those readers who are familiar with my novels are likely to find here frequent echoes and reflections of the larger works. In helping me assemble this book, my editor, Robert Loomis, and my bibliographer, James West, made the happy discovery that the collection defined itself harmoniously in a couple of ways. First, some of my preoccupations—those having to do with such puzzles and mysteries as Southern life, criminal life and military life—could be arranged easily into categories, and they are so arranged here, following a logical rather than a chronological order. Whenever necessary or appropriate, I have added commentary at the beginning of these sections, or to certain individual pieces; but throughout I have changed or eliminated nothing from the original unless printing errors or annoying repetition made it unavoidable. Second, this book—besides being a chronicle of those matters which have either bedeviled or beguiled me in recent years—is held together by an autobiographical thread, sometimes barely seen but quite often plainly visible. This personal, binding strand is apparent everywhere, even in the most impersonal of the essays and reviews, but is quite clearly manifested toward the end of the collection, in the various portraits or sketches of people I have known, or in the final reminiscences. Thus *This Quiet Dust* is a collection of prose essays but a partial record of part of a life as well.

Aside from the gratitude I owe Messrs. Loomis and West, I want to express a word of thanks to my friend Michael J. Arlen, a superlative essayist and recorder of his own life. It was he who in a letter to me which attempted to suggest the tone I should adopt in this introductory note—and in the comments that will follow— perfectly described the way I now feel: "A patriarch introducing, with pleasure and assurance, his many children, all of whom he loves at least a little, though some of whose names have gotten a bit unclear."

W. S.

Roxbury, Connecticut
May 1982

CONTENTS

SOUTH

INTRODUCTION

It is beneath a writer's dignity to discuss his critics in print.
There is, I am sure, hardly a writer of any merit who does
not find the impulse nearly irresistible to reply to some of
those who have molested him—more often than not, professors
of English who are themselves authors of fiction of
undisputed harmlessness. Such an English professor with
a grudge against a particular writer can be more unrelenting
in his rage than a jilted lover, stalking him throughout his
career with a forlorn passion that is almost erotic. Although
one should never respond to criticism in general, I think I can
make an exception for myself in the case of *The Confessions
of Nat Turner*. I have no intention of opening old wounds
(especially my own) by taking up the fight again and
contriving a defensive reply to those antagonists of the 1960s.
But the controversy over *The Confessions of Nat Turner*
was a fascinating one, and now—fifteen years later—the
advantage of hindsight has enabled me to indulge in some
useful reflections. I do not appear often in public, but when
I do, some of the most frequently asked questions concern
Nat Turner and the storm that surrounded it. Thus what
follows is an abbreviated attempt to put my thoughts in order,
at last, about that strange and tumultuous time.

I recall a morning during the late summer of 1967—just a
couple of months before the publication of *Nat Turner*—
when I went on a fishing trip off Martha's Vineyard with two
black doctors. They were acquaintances of Jason Epstein,
the editor at Random House who had been one of the first to
read the manuscript of the book. Being most enthusiastic

about the work, he mentioned to the doctors—one a Harvard graduate and the other, I believe, from Cornell—that the subject of my novel was Nat Turner. I remember the unease I felt, and the consternation that Epstein later described feeling, when these two well-educated, worldly black men drew a total blank, declaring without any apparent embarrassment that neither of them had ever heard of Nat Turner in their lives. This was not, despite my suspicions, a put-on. Months later I finally became numb to the many particularities of the attack on me in the book called *William Styron's Nat Turner: Ten Black Writers Respond*, and managed to shrug off the charges of racism, distortion of the truth, and other derelictions laid against me by blacks everywhere. The one inference which continued to stick most undislodgeably in my craw was that I had maligned a hero universally known and revered throughout the black world in America. I have never professed to be more than an amateur historian, but it took very little professionalism to discover— as I discovered during my early research on Nat—that the writing done on the subject since that revolt in 1831 was skimpy indeed (and, when not skimpy, unreliable) and that with a single exception there had been no substantial work on Nat Turner which could be said to be the product of a professional historian.

Alas, the fiction still persists that Nat Turner was a vital figure in the black consciousness before 1967, studied and explicated by black scholars. As recently as March 1982, one of the more intelligent of my ten black respondents, the historian Vincent Harding, was quoted as saying that I had "ignored the work of black historians by taking credit for resurrecting a black hero." (To which one must ask: When were writers of historical novels obligated in any way to acknowledge the work of historians?) Claiming no credit really, even now, I still have to insist that prior to my own work there was no important study by any reputable scholar, black or white, with the sole exception of that of a white man, Herbert Aptheker, the Communist party theoretician, who covered the rebellion at some length in his *American Negro Slave Revolts*. (As if I didn't have enough trouble with the blacks, Aptheker became one of my fiercest adversaries and during that period denounced me both publicly and in print. Strange how the passing of time engenders charity. I bear no ill will against Aptheker and keep trying to remember—as it might behoove us all to do—that in the horrible dark night of racism at its worst in America, the 1930s, the Communists were among the few friends black people had.)

It was something of a phenomenon, all right. While, of course, many works of science or history or literature have elicited symposiumlike responses in the form of other books, *Nat Turner* was the first *novel* in the long annals of American publishing to evoke such an immediate, entirely hostile attack. There was no pretense at balance here, no observance of the gentlemanly rules of polemics or the usual admixture of pros and cons and the attempts to reconcile the bad and good. Justifying their lopsided animus by way of the dual complaint that my book had received unqualified praise in the white press (which was hardly true; it got some very poor reactions, among them a glibly contemptuous review on the front page of the *New York Times Book Review*) and that no black person had been invited to review it (again untrue; it was reviewed very favorably on the front page of the *Chicago Sunday Tribune* book section by John Hope Franklin, one of the country's most distinguished historians), the ten black writers let go an all-out assault. It contained such pitiless indictments of my artistry, my historical and social responsibility, my ethical stance ("morally senile" was the most memorable quote), and even my probable sexual inclinations, that the savagery was at first truly impossible to comprehend. As a matter of fact, though, it was a certain inability to comprehend on my part that enabled me to absorb the shock with less pain than I might have had the attack been more reasoned or temperate. Gradually it sank in that I was being subjected not even to discussible criticism but to the most intractable kind of hysteria—understandable perhaps, though no less ugly for being part of the chaotic racial politics of 1968.

Of course, I fretted and brooded a bit. No Southerner who had fought as hard as I had to free himself of the last clutches of the racial bugaboo wants to hear himself called "an unreconstructed white racist." Nonetheless, though many of my friends were horrified, I rather surprised myself by the equanimity with which I took this onslaught. (I had even begun to receive phone calls and mail heavy with threat.) Perhaps I simply knew, beleaguered as I was, that help was on its way. This help, I can now see, was essential, for while in my own mind I was guiltless of the atrocities it was claimed I committed, I knew that the general public could easily be bamboozled into thinking that the black writers had a valid case against me. My suspicions were confirmed in this regard when the *New York Times* daily book critic, who had given my book very favorable treatment in a two-part review, tendered equal time to the black writers, treating their charges with gravity and respect and leaving the impression that I might be every bit the honky trickster I was accused of being. Soon after this, two historians came to my rescue. Both of these scholars had excellent credentials not only as authorities in the field of American slavery but as men personally committed to the cause of civil rights. (The only flaw in their appearance on my behalf was, of course, that they were white.) Martin Duberman wrote a scathing review of the ten black writers in the *New York Times Book Review*, answering most of the accusations with great skill and a considerable show of contempt. But it was Eugene D. Genovese's long counterattack in the *New York Review of Books* that most effectively demolished my critics. His beautifully crafted essay, which point by point dealt inflexibly with all my alleged crimes, not only disposed of the case once and for all but did it with such lofty outrage that the effect was like that of catharsis. Unfortunately, though perhaps inevitably, his piece created its own pathos, for it seemed to say that if a hysterical assault on a novel like mine was all the American black intellectual community could muster, then the community was in a terrible shambles.

I have never ceased being a little surprised at the bustling cottage industry which *The Confessions of Nat Turner* spawned during the subsequent years. Shortly after its publication there appeared, aside from the *Ten Black Writers* and bushels of essays and reviews, two complete books devoted to my novel and the controversy surrounding it. Later, in the 1970s, at least two fat, sturdy volumes were written by historians on Nat Turner and his revolt. Each of

these writers had plainly worried about my *Nat Turner*
a lot. In one of the books the white author states explicitly
that he did not intend to either refute me or refute or defend
my critics, although his single reductive description of my
book ("depicts Nat as a celibate bachelor given to masturbating
about white women") I think more or less sums up his
attitude toward my work. He then goes on to say that "history
is largely an interpretive art, the best we can hope for is a
careful approximation of what really happened." To which,
of course, one must add that the historical novel, too, is
largely interpretive, and is an approximation of what really
happened—although the novelist should not (in fact, must
not) be very careful. It is his right and privilege to substitute
imagination for facts.

The other book—also by a white scholar—makes no bones
about being an attempt, at least in part, to refute my vision
of Nat Turner, and faults me constantly for having overlooked
numerous significant documents pertaining to the revolt.
That I did ignore or even willfully avoid certain information
which may have been available to me is true. Also, had I
been entirely meticulous, I should not have implied—as I
imply in this volume's first essay, "This Quiet Dust"—that
I examined every source of fact and data. There obviously
existed material which, had I been something more of a
scrounger, I might not have wanted to skip. However, I don't
see much importance in all of this. I am flattered that my
Nat Turner seems to have achieved such commanding prestige
as to provide historians with a touchstone to measure their
own notions of accuracy. But, really, how eager most
historians seem to be in their desire to preserve their insights
from the contamination of a novelist's insights! There are
few historians who appear capable of understanding that a
historical novel is in actual flight from facts and the restrictions
of pure data, and that the better the novel is—so long as it
does not seriously compromise the historical record—the less
likely it will show itself to be cluttered by the detritus of
fact. About Nat Turner—of whose departed flesh-and-blood
self so little is known, or ever will be known—I cared to
discover only so much as my instinct as a novelist told me to
care. In any case, I am pleased that *Nat Turner* has survived
so well, and that it is now even being read, occasionally, by

some intrepid black person of independent mind. I mean nothing supercilious about this last remark. Since the book invites the reader, black or white, merely to partake in an imagined vision within a vision, and claims for itself the quality of being "a meditation on history"—not the revealed truth—there should be nothing in it to fear or hate.

This Quiet Dust

You mought be rich as cream
And drive you coach and four-horse team,
But you can't keep de world from moverin' round
Nor Nat Turner from gainin' ground.

And your name it mought be Caesar sure
And got you cannon can shoot a mile or more,
But you can't keep de world from moverin' round
Nor Nat Turner from gainin' ground.

—OLD-TIME NEGRO SONG

MY NATIVE STATE of Virginia is, of course, more than ordinarily conscious of its past, even for the South. When I was learning my lessons in the mid-1930s at a grammar school on the banks of the James River, one of the required texts was a history of Virginia —a book I can recall far more vividly than any history of the United States or of Europe I studied at a later time. It was in this work that I first encountered the name Nat Turner. The reference to Nat was brief; as a matter of fact, I do not think it unlikely that it was the very brevity of the allusion—amounting almost to a quality of haste—which captured my attention and stung my curiosity. I can no longer quote the passage exactly, but I remember that it went something like this: "In 1831, a fanatical Negro slave named Nat Turner led a terrible insurrection in Southampton County, murdering many white people. The insurrection was immediately put down, and for their cruel deeds Nat Turner and most of the other Negroes involved in the rebellion were hanged." Give or take a few harsh adjectives, this was all the information on Nat Turner supplied by that forgotten historian, who hustled on to matters of greater consequence.

I must have first read this passage when I was ten or eleven years old. At that time my home was not far from Southampton County, where the rebellion took place, in a section of the Virginia Tidewater which is generally considered part of the Black Belt because of the predominance of Negroes in the population. (When I speak of the South and Southerners here, I speak of *this* South, where Deep South attitudes prevail; it would include parts of Maryland and East Texas.) My boyhood experience was the typically ambivalent one of most native Southerners, for whom the Negro is simultaneously taken for granted and as an object of unending concern. On the one hand, Negroes are simply a part of the landscape, an unexceptional feature of the local scenery, yet as central to its character as the pinewoods and sawmills and mule teams and sleepy river estuaries that give such color and tone to the Southern geography. Unnoticed by white people, the Negroes blend with the land and somehow melt and fade into it, so that only when one reflects upon their possible absence, some magical disappearance, does one realize how unimaginable this absence would be: it would be easier to visualize a South without trees, without *any* people, without life at all. Thus, at the same time, ignored by white people, Negroes impinge upon their collective subconscious to such a degree that it may be rightly said that they become the focus of an incessant preoccupation, somewhat like a monstrous, recurring dream populated by identical faces wearing expressions of inquietude and vague reproach. "Southern whites cannot walk, talk, sing, conceive of laws or justice, think of sex, love, the family, or freedom without responding to the presence of Negroes." The words are those of Ralph Ellison, and, of course, he is right.

Yet there are many Souths, and the experience of each Southerner is modified by the subtlest conditions of self and family and environment and God knows what else, and I have wondered if it has ever properly been taken into account how various this response to the presence of the Negroes can be. I cannot tell how typical my own awareness of Negroes was, for instance, as I grew up near my birthplace—a small seaside city about equally divided between black and white. My feelings seem to have been confused and blurred, tinged with sentimentality, colored by a great deal of folklore, and wobbling always between a patronizing affection, fostered by my elders, and downright hostility. Most importantly, my feelings were completely uninformed by that intimate knowledge of black people which Southerners claim as their special patent; indeed, they were based upon an almost total ignorance.

For one thing, from the standpoint of attitudes toward race, my upbringing was hardly unusual: it derived from the simple conviction that Negroes were in every respect inferior to white people and should be made to stay in their proper order in the scheme of things. At the same time, by certain Southern standards my family was enlightened: although my mother taught me firmly that the use of "lady" instead of "woman" in referring to a Negro female was quite improper, she writhed at the sight of the extremes of Negro poverty and would certainly have thrashed me had she ever heard me use the word "nigger." Yet outside the confines of family, in the lower-middle-class school world I inhabited every day, this was a word I commonly used. School segregation, which was an ordinary fact of life for me, is devastatingly effective in accomplishing something that it was only peripherally designed to do: it prevents the awareness even of the existence of another race. Thus, whatever hostility I bore toward the Negroes was based almost entirely upon hearsay.

And so the word "nigger," which like all my schoolmates I uttered so freely and so often, had even then an idle and listless ring. How could that dull epithet carry meaning and conviction when it was applied to a people so diligently isolated from us that they barely existed except as shadows which came daily to labor in the kitchen, to haul away garbage, to rake up leaves? An unremarked paradox of Southern life is that its racial animosity is really grounded not upon friction and propinquity, but upon an almost complete lack of contact. Surrounded by a sea of Negroes, I cannot recall more than once—and then briefly, when I was five or six—ever having played with a Negro child, or ever having spoken to a Negro, except in trifling talk with the cook, or in some forlorn and crippled conversation with a dotty old grandfather angling for hardshell crabs on a lonesome Sunday afternoon many years ago. Nor was I by any means uniquely sheltered. Whatever knowledge I gained in my youth about Negroes I gained from a distance, as if I had been watching actors in an all-black puppet show.

Such an experience has made me distrust any easy generalizations about the South, whether they are made by white sociologists or Negro playwrights, Southern politicians or Northern editors. I have come to understand at least as much about the Negro after having lived in the North. One of the most egregious of the Southern myths—one in this case propagated solely by Southerners—is that of the Southern white's boast that he "knows" the Negro. Certainly in many rural areas of the South the cultural climate has been such as to allow a mutual understanding, and even a kind of intimacy, to spring up between the races, at least in some individual instances. But my own boyhood surroundings, which were semi-urban (I suppose suburban is the best description, though the green little village on the city's outskirts where I grew up was a far cry from Levittown), and which have become the youthful environment for vast numbers of Southerners, tended almost totally to preclude any contact between black and white, especially when that contact was so sedulously proscribed by law.

Yet if white Southerners cannot "know" the Negro, it is for this very reason that the entire sexual myth needs to be re-examined. Surely a certain amount of sexual tension between the races does continue to exist, and the Southern white man's fear of sexual aggression on the part of the Negro male is still too evident to be ignored. But the nature of the growth of the urban, modern South has been such as to impose ever more effective walls between the races. While it cannot be denied that slavery times produced an enormous amount of interbreeding (with all of its totalitarianism, this was a free-for-all atmosphere far less self-conscious about carnal mingling than the Jim Crow era which began in the 1890s) and while even now there must logically take place occasional sexual contacts between the races—especially in rural areas where a degree of casual familiarity has always obtained—the monolithic nature of segregation has raised such an effective barrier between whites and Negroes that it is impossible not to believe that theories involving a perpetual sexual "tension" have been badly inflated. Nor is it possible to feel that a desire to taste forbidden fruit has ever really caused this barrier to be breached. From the standpoint of the Negro, there is indifference or uncomplicated fear; from that of the white—segregation, the law and, finally, indifference too. When I was growing up, the older boys might crack wan jokes about visiting the Negro whorehouse street (patronized entirely, I later discovered, by Negroes plus a few Scandinavian sailors), but to my knowledge none of them ever really went there. Like Negroes in general, Negro girls were to white men phantoms, shadows. To assume that anything more than a rare and sporadic intimacy on any level has existed in the modern South between whites and Negroes is simply to deny, with a truly willful contempt for logic, the monstrous effectiveness of that apartheid which has been the Southern way of life for almost three quarters of a century.

I have lingered on this matter only to try to underline a truth about Southern life which has been too often taken for granted, and which has therefore been overlooked or misinterpreted. Most Southern white people *cannot* know or touch black people and this is because of the deadly intimidation of a universal law. Certainly one feels the presence of this gulf even in the work of a writer as supremely knowledgeable about the South as William Faulkner, who confessed a hesitancy about attempting to "think Negro," and whose Negro characters, as marvelously portrayed as most of them are, seem nevertheless to be meticulously *observed* rather than *lived*. Thus, in *The Sound and the Fury*, Faulkner's magnificent Dilsey comes richly alive, yet in retrospect one feels this is a result of countless mornings, hours, days Faulkner had spent watching and listening to old Negro servants, and not because Dilsey herself is a being created from a sense of withinness: at the last moment Faulkner draws back, and it is no mere happenstance that Dilsey, alone among the four central figures from whose points of view the story is told, is seen from the outside rather than from that intensely "inner" vantage point, the interior monologue.

Innumerable white Southerners have grown up as free of knowledge of the Negro character and soul as a person whose background is rural Wisconsin or Maine. Yet, of course, there is a difference, and it is a profound one, defining the white Southerner's attitudes and causing him to be, for better or for worse, whatever it is he is to be. For the Negro is *there*. And he is there in a way he never is in the North, no matter how great his numbers. In the South he is a perpetual and immutable part of history itself, a piece of the vast fabric so integral and necessary that without him the fabric dissolves; his voice, his black or brown face passing on a city street, the sound of his cry rising from a wagonload of flowers, his numberless procession down dusty country roads, the neat white church he has built in some pine grove with its air of grace and benison and tranquillity, his silhouette behind a mule team far off in some spring field, the wail of his blues blaring from some jukebox in a backwoods roadhouse, the sad wet faces of nursemaids and cooks waiting in the evening at city bus stops in pouring rain—the Negro is always *there*.

No wonder then, as Ellison says, the white Southerner can do virtually nothing without responding to the presence of Negroes. No wonder the white man so often grows cranky, fanciful, freakish, loony, violent: how else respond to a paradox which requires, with the full majesty of law behind it, that he deny the very reality of a people whose multitude approaches and often exceeds his own; that he disclaim the existence of those whose human presence has marked every acre of the land, every hamlet and crossroad and city and town, and whose humanity, however inflexibly denied, is daily evidenced to him like a heartbeat in loyalty and wickedness, madness and hilarity and mayhem and pride and love? The Negro may feel that it is too late to be known, and that the desire to know him reeks of outrageous condescension. But to break down the old law, to come to *know* the Negro, has become the moral imperative of every white Southerner.

I I

I suspect that my search for Nat Turner, my own private attempt as a novelist to re-create and bring alive that dim and prodigious black man, has been at least a partial fulfillment of this mandate, although the problem has long since resolved itself into an artistic one—which is as it should be. In the late 1940s, having finished college in North Carolina and come to New York, I found myself again haunted by that name I had first seen in the Virginia history textbook. I had learned something more of Southern history since then, and I had become fascinated by the subject of Negro slavery. One of the most striking aspects of the institution is the fact that in the two hundred and fifty years of its existence in America, it was singularly free of organized uprisings, plots and rebellions. (It is curious that as recently as the late 1940s, scholarly insights were lagging, and I could only have suspected then what has since been made convincing by such historians as Frank Tannenbaum and Stanley Elkins:* that American Negro slavery, unique in its psychological oppressiveness—the worst the world has ever known—was simply so despotic and emasculating as to render organized revolt next to impossible.) There were three exceptions: a conspiracy by

* There are several references to Elkins in these essays. Elkins' work has undergone such severe revision by other historians as to make my own responses to his theories appear perhaps a bit simplistic. Nonetheless, his work remains important and most of his insights are still valid.—W. S. (1982)

the slave Gabriel Prosser and his followers near Richmond in the year 1800, the plot betrayed, the conspirators hanged; a similar conspiracy in 1822, in Charleston, South Carolina, led by a free Negro named Denmark Vesey, who also was betrayed before he could carry out his plans, and who was executed along with other members of the plot.

The last exception, of course, was Nat Turner, and he alone in the entire annals of American slavery—alone among all those "many thousand gone"—achieved a kind of triumph.

Even today, many otherwise well-informed people have never heard the name Nat Turner, and there are several plausible reasons for such an ignorance. One of these, of course, is that the study of our history—and not alone in the South—has been tendentious in the extreme and has often avoided even an allusion to a figure like Nat, who inconveniently disturbs our notion of a slave system which, though morally wrong, was conducted with such charity and restraint that any organized act of insurrectory and murderous violence would be unthinkable. But a general ignorance about Nat Turner is even more understandable in view of the fact that so little is left of the actual record. Southampton County, which even now is off the beaten track, was at that period the remotest backwater imaginable. The relativity of time allows us elastic definitions: 1831 was yesterday. Yet the year 1831, in the presidency of Andrew Jackson, lay in the very dawn of our modern history, three years before a railroad ever touched the soil of Virginia, a full fifteen years before the use of the telegraph. The rebellion itself was of such a cataclysmic nature as practically to guarantee confusion of the news, distortion, wild rumors, lies and, finally, great areas of darkness and suppression; all of these have contributed to Nat's obscurity.

As for the contemporary documents themselves, only one survives: "The Confessions of Nat Turner," a brief pamphlet of some five thousand words, transcribed from Nat's lips as he awaited trial, by a somewhat enigmatic lawyer named Thomas Gray, who published the "Confessions" in Baltimore and then vanished from sight. There are several discrepancies in Gray's transcript but it was taken down in haste, and in all major respects it seems completely honest and reliable. Those few newspaper accounts of the time, from Richmond and Norfolk, are sketchy, remote, filled with conjecture, and are thus virtually worthless. The existing county court records of Southampton remain brief and unilluminating, dull lists, a dry catalogue of names in fading ink: the white people slain, the Negroes tried and transported south, or acquitted, or convicted and hanged.

Roughly seventy years after the rebellion (in 1900, which by coincidence was the year Virginia formally adopted its first Jim Crow laws), the single scholarly book ever to be written on the affair was published—*The Southampton Insurrection*, by a Johns Hopkins Ph.D. candidate named William S. Drewry, who was an unreconstructed Virginian of decidedly pro-slavery leanings and a man so quaintly committed to the *ancien régime* that, in the midst of a description of the ghastliest part of the uprising, he was able to reflect that "slavery in Virginia was not such to arouse rebellion, but was an institution which nourished the strongest affection and piety in slave and owner, as well as moral qualities worthy of any age of civilization." For Drewry, Nat Turner was some sort of inexplicable aberration, like a man from Mars. Drewry was close enough to the event in time, however, to be able to interview quite a few of the survivors, and since he also possessed a bloodthirsty relish for detail, it was possible for him to reconstruct the chronology of the insurrection with what appears to be considerable accuracy. Drewry's book (it is of course long out of print) and Nat's "Confessions" remain the only significant sources about the insurrection. Of Nat himself, his background and early years, very little can be known. This is not disadvantageous to a novelist, since it allows him to speculate—with a freedom not accorded the historian—upon all the intermingled miseries, ambitions, frustrations, hopes, rages and desires which caused this extraordinary black man to rise up out of those early mists of our history and strike down his oppressors with a fury of retribution unequaled before or since.

He was born in 1800, which would have made him at the time of the insurrection thirty-one years old—exactly the age of so many great revolutionaries at the decisive moment of their insurgency: Martin Luther,* Robespierre, Danton, Fidel Castro. Thomas Gray,

* See Erik Erikson's *Young Man Luther* for a brilliant study of the development of the revolutionary impulse in a young man, and the relationship of this impulse to the father figure. Although it is best to be wary of any heavy psychoanalytical emphasis, one cannot help believing that Nat Turner's relationship with his father (or his surrogate father, his master) was tormented and complicated, like Luther's.

in a footnote to the "Confessions," describes him as having the "true Negro face" (an offhand way of forestalling an assumption that he might have possessed any white blood), and he adds that "for natural intelligence and quickness of apprehension he is surpassed by few men I have ever seen"—a lofty tribute indeed at that inflammatory instant, with ante-bellum racism at its most hysteric pitch. Although little is known for certain of Nat's childhood and youth, there can be no doubt that he was very precocious and that he not only learned to read and write with ease—an illustrious achievement in itself, when learning to read and write was forbidden to Negroes by law—but at an early age acquired a knowledge of astronomy, and later on experimented in making paper and gunpowder. (The resemblance here to the knowledge of the ancient Chinese is almost too odd to be true, but I can find no reason to doubt it.)

The early decades of the nineteenth century were years of declining prosperity for the Virginia Tidewater, largely because of the ruination of the land through greedy cultivation of tobacco—a crop which had gradually disappeared from the region, causing the breakup of many of the big old plantations and the development of subsistence farming on small holdings. It was in these surroundings—a flat pastoral land of modest farms and even more modest homesteads, where it was rare to find a white man prosperous enough to own more than half a dozen Negroes, and where two or three slaves to a family was the general rule—that Nat was born and brought up, and in these surroundings he prepared himself for the apocalyptic role he was to play in history. Because of the failing economic conditions it was not remarkable that Nat was purchased and sold several times by various owners (in a sense, he was fortunate in not having been sold off to the deadly cotton and rice plantations of South Carolina and Georgia, which was the lot of many Virginia Negroes of the period); and although we do not know much about any of these masters, the evidence does not appear to be that Nat was ill-treated, and in fact one of these owners (Samuel Turner, brother of the man whose property Nat was born) developed so strong a paternal feeling for the boy and such regard for Nat's abilities that he took the fateful step of encouraging him in the beginnings of an education.

The atmosphere of the time and place was fundamentalist and devout to a passionate degree, and at some time during his twenties Nat, who had always been a godly person—"never owning a dollar, never uttering an oath, never drinking intoxicating liquors, and never committing a theft"—became a Baptist preacher. Compared to the Deep South, Virginia slave life was not so rigorous; Nat must have been given considerable latitude and found many opportunities to preach and exhort the Negroes. His gifts for preaching, for prophecy, and his own magnetism seem to have been so extraordinary that he grew into a rather celebrated figure among the Negroes of the county, his influence even extending to the whites, one of whom—a poor, half-cracked overseer named Brantley—he converted to the faith and baptized in a millpond in the sight of a multitude of the curious, both black and white. (After this no one would have anything to do with Brantley, and he left the county in disgrace.)

At about this time Nat began to withdraw into himself, fasting and praying, spending long hours in the woods or in the swamp, where he communed with the Spirit and where there came over him, urgently now, intimations that he was being prepared for some great purpose. His fanaticism grew in intensity, and during these lonely vigils in the forest he began to see apparitions:

> I saw white spirits and black spirits engaged in battle, and the sun was darkened; the thunder rolled in the heavens and blood flowed in streams . . . I wondered greatly at these miracles, and prayed to be informed of a certainty of the meaning thereof; and shortly afterwards, while laboring in the fields, I discovered drops of blood on the corn as though it were dew from heaven. For as the blood of Christ had been shed on this earth, and had ascended to heaven for the salvation of sinners, it was now returning to earth again in the form of dew . . . On the twelfth day of May, 1828, I heard a loud noise in the heavens, and the Spirit instantly appeared to me and said the Serpent was loosened, and Christ had laid down the yoke he had borne for the sins of men, and that I should take it on and fight against the Serpent, for the time was fast approaching when the first should be last and the last should be first . . .

Like all revolutions, that of Nat Turner underwent many worrisome hesitations, false starts, procrastinations, delays (with appropriate irony, Independence Day 1830 had been one of the original dates selected, but Nat fell sick and the moment was put off again); finally, however, on the night of Sunday, August 21, 1831, Nat, together with five other Negroes in whom he had placed his confidence and trust, assembled in the woods near the home of his owner of the time, a carriage maker named Joseph Travis, and commenced to carry out a plan of total annihilation. The penultimate goal was the capture of the county seat, then called Jerusalem (a connotation certainly not lost on Nat, who, with the words of the prophets roaring in his ears, must have felt like Gideon himself before the extermination of the Midianites); there were guns and ammunition in Jerusalem, and with these captured it was then Nat's purpose to sweep thirty miles eastward, gathering black recruits on the way until the Great Dismal Swamp was reached—a snake-filled and gloomy fastness in which, Nat believed, with probable justification, only Negroes could survive and no white man's army could penetrate. The immediate objective, however, was the destruction of every white man, woman and child on the ten-mile route to Jerusalem; no one was to be spared; tender infancy and feeble old age alike were to perish by the axe and the sword. The command, of course, was that of God Almighty, through the voice of His prophet Ezekiel: *Son of Man, prophesy and say, Thus saith the Lord; Say, a sword, a sword is sharpened, and also furbished: it is sharpened to make a sore slaughter . . . Slay utterly old and young, both maids, and little children, and women . . .* It was a scheme so wild and daring that it could only have been the product of the most wretched desperation and frustrate misery of soul; and of course it was doomed to catastrophe not only for whites but for Negroes—and for black men in ways which from the vantage point of history now seem almost unthinkable.

They did their job rapidly and with merciless and methodical determination. Beginning at the home of Travis—where five people, including a six-month-old infant, were slain in their beds—they marched from house to house on an eastward route, pillaging, murdering, sparing no one. Lacking guns—at least to begin with—they employed axes, hatchets and swords as their tools of destruction, and swift decapitation was their usual method of dispatch. (It is interesting that the Negroes did not resort to torture, nor were they ever accused of rape. Nat's attitude toward sex was Christian and high-minded, and he had said: "We will not do to their women what they have done to ours.")

On through the first day they marched, across the hot August fields, gaining guns and ammunition, horses and a number of willing recruits. That the insurrection was not purely racial but perhaps obscurely pre-Marxist may be seen in the fact that a number of dwellings belonging to poor white people were pointedly passed by. At midday on Monday their force had more than tripled, to the number of nineteen, and nearly thirty white people lay dead. By this time the alarm had been sounded throughout the county, and while the momentum of the insurgent band was considerable, many of the whites had fled in panic to the woods, and some of the farmers had begun to resist, setting up barricades from which they could fire back at Nat's forces. Furthermore, quite a few of the rebels had broken into the brandy cellars of the houses they had attacked and had gotten roaring drunk—an eventuality Nat had feared and had warned against. Nevertheless, the Negroes—augmented now by forty more volunteers—pressed on toward Jerusalem, continuing the attack into the next night and all through the following day, when at last obstinate resistance by the aroused whites and the appearance of a mounted force of militia troops (also, it must be suspected, continued attrition by the apple brandy) caused the rebels to be dispersed, only a mile or so from Jerusalem.

Almost every one of the Negroes was rounded up and brought to trial—a legalistic nicety characteristic of a time in which it was necessary for one to determine whether *his* slave, property, after all, worth eight or nine hundred dollars, was really guilty and deserving of the gallows. Nat disappeared immediately after the insurrection and hid in the woods for over two months, when near-starvation and the onset of autumnal cold drove him from his cave and forced him to surrender to a lone farmer with a shotgun. Then he, too, was brought to trial in Jerusalem—early in November 1831—for fomenting a rebellion in which sixty white people had perished.

The immediate consequences of the insurrection were exceedingly grim. The killing of so many white people was in itself an act of futility. It has never been determined with any accuracy how many black people, not connected with the rebellion, were slain at the hands of rampaging bands of white men who swarmed all over Southampton in the week following the uprising, seeking reprisal and vengeance. A contemporary estimate by a Richmond news-paper, which deplored this retaliation, put the number at close to two hundred Negroes, many of them free, and many of them tortured in ways unimaginably horrible. But even more important was the effect that Nat Turner's insurrection had upon the institution of slavery at large. News of the revolt spread among Southern whites with great speed: the impossible, the unspeakable had at last taken place after two hundred years of the ministrations of sweet old mammies and softly murmured "Yassuh's" and docile compliance—and a shock wave of anguish and terror ran through the entire South. If such a nightmarish calamity happened there, would it not happen *here*—here in Tennessee, in Augusta, in Vicksburg, in these bayous of Louisiana? Had Nat lived to see the consequences of his rebellion, surely it would have been for him the cruelest irony that his bold and desperate bid for liberty had caused only the most tyrannical new controls to be imposed upon Negroes everywhere—the establishment of patrols, further restrictions upon movement, education, assembly, and the beginning of other severe and crippling restraints which persisted throughout the slave-holding states until the Civil War. Virginia had been edging close to emancipation, and it seems reasonable to believe that the example of Nat's rebellion, stampeding many moderates in the legislature into a conviction that the Negroes could not be safely freed, was a decisive factor in the ultimate victory of the pro-slavery forces. Had Virginia, with its enormous prestige among the states, emancipated its slaves, the effect upon our history would be awesome to contemplate.

Nat brought cold, paralyzing fear to the South, a fear that never departed. If white men had sown the wind with chattel slavery, in Nat Turner they had reaped the whirlwind for white and black alike.

Nat was executed, along with sixteen other Negroes who had figured large in the insurrection. Most of the others were transported south, to the steaming fields of rice and cotton. On November 11, 1831, Nat was hanged from a live-oak tree in the town square of Jerusalem. He went to his death with great dignity and courage. "The bodies of those executed," wrote Drewry, "with one exception, were buried in a decent and becoming manner. That of Nat Turner was delivered to the doctors, who skinned it and made grease of the flesh."

III

Not long ago, in the spring of the year, when I was visiting my family in Virginia, I decided to go down for the day to Southampton County, which is a drive of an hour or so by car from the town where I was born and raised. Nat Turner was of course the reason for this trip, although I had nothing particular or urgent in mind. What research it was possible to do on the event I had long since done. The Southampton court records, I had already been reliably informed, would prove unrewarding. It was not a question, then, of digging out more facts, but simply a matter of wanting to savor the mood and atmosphere of a landscape I had not seen for quite a few years, since the times when as a boy I used to pass through Southampton on the way to my father's family home in North Carolina. I thought also that there might be a chance of visiting some of the historic sites connected with the insurrection, and even of retracing part of the route of the uprising through the help of one of those handsomely produced guidebooks for which the Association for the Preservation of Virginia Antiquities is famous—guides indispensable for a trip to such Old Dominion shrines as Jamestown and Appomattox and Monticello. I became even more eager to go when one of my in-laws put me in touch by telephone with a cousin of his. This man, whom I shall call Dan Seward, lived near Franklin, the main town of Southampton, and he assured me in those broad cheery Southern tones which are like a warm embrace—and which, after long years in the chill North, are to me always so familiar, reminiscent, and therefore so unsettling, sweet and curiously painful—that he would like nothing better than to aid me in my exploration in whatever way he could.

Dan Seward is a farmer and prosperous grower of peanuts in a prosperous agricultural region where the peanut is the unquestioned monarch. A combination of sandy loam soil and a long growing season has made Southampton ideal for the cultivation of peanuts; over 30,000 acres are planted annually, and the crop is processed and marketed in Franklin—a thriving little town of 7,000 people—or in Suffolk and Portsmouth, where it is rendered into Planters cooking oil and stock feed and Skippy peanut butter. There are other moneymaking crops—corn and soybeans and cotton. The county is at the northernmost edge of the Cotton Belt, and thirty years ago cotton was a major source of income. Cotton has declined in importance but the average yield per acre is still among the highest in the South, and the single gin left in the country in the little village of Drewryville processes each year several thousand bales, which are trucked to market down in North Carolina. Lumbering is also very profitable, owing mainly to an abundance of the loblolly pines valuable in the production of kraft wood pulp; and the Union Bag–Camp Paper Company's plant on the Blackwater River in Franklin is a huge enterprise employing over 1,600 people. But it is peanuts—the harvested vines in autumn piled up mile after mile in dumpy brown stacks like hay—that have brought money to Southampton, and a sheen of prosperity that can be seen in the freshly painted farmhouses along the monotonously flat state highway which leads into Franklin, and the new-model Dodges and Buicks parked slantwise against the curb of some crossroads hamlet, and the gaudy, eye-catching signs that advise the wisdom of a bank savings account for all those surplus funds.

The county has very much the look of the New South about it, with its airport and its shiny new motels, its insistent billboards advertising space for industrial sites, the sprinkling of housing developments with television antennas gleaming from every rooftop, its supermarkets and shopping centers and its flavor of go-getting commercialism. This is the New South, where agriculture still prevails but has joined in a vigorous union with industry, so that even the peanut when it goes to market is ground up in some rumbling engine of commerce and becomes metamorphosed into wood stain or soap or cattle feed. The Negroes, too, have partaken of this abundance—some of it, at least—for they own television sets also, and if not new-model Buicks (the Southern white man's strictures against Negro ostentation remain intimidating), then decent late-model used Fords; while in the streets of Franklin the Negro women shopping seemed on the day of my visit very proud and well-dressed compared to the shabby, stooped figures I recalled from the Depression years when I was a boy. It would certainly appear that Negroes deserve some of this abundance, if only because they make up so large a part of the work force. Since Nat Turner's day the balance of population in Southampton—almost 60 percent Negro—has hardly altered by a hair.

"I don't know anywhere that a Negro is treated better than around here," Mr. Seward was saying to the three of us, on the spring morning I visited him with my wife and my father. "You take your average person from up North, he just doesn't *know* the Negro like we do. Now, for instance, I have a Negro who's worked for me for years, name of Ernest. He knows if he breaks his arm—like he did a while ago, fell off a tractor—he knows he can come to me and I'll see that he's taken care of, hospital expenses and all, and I'll take care of him and his family while he's unable to work, right on down the line. I don't ask him to pay back a cent, either, that's for sure. We have a wonderful relationship, that Negro and myself. By God, I'd die for that Negro and he knows it, and he'd do the same for me. But Ernest doesn't want to sit down at my table, here in this house, and have supper with me—and he wouldn't want me in *his* house. And Ernest's got kids like I do, and he doesn't want them to go to school with my Bobby, any more than Bobby wants to go to school with *his* kids. It works both ways. People up North don't seem to be able to understand a simple fact like that."

Mr. Seward was a solidly fleshed, somewhat rangy, big-shouldered man in his early forties with an open, cheerful manner which surely did nothing to betray the friendliness with which he had spoken on the telephone. He had greeted us—total strangers, really—with an animation and uncomplicated good will that would have shamed an Eskimo; and for a moment I realized that after years amid the granite outcroppings of New England, I had forgotten that this *was* the passionate, generous, outgoing nature of the South, no artificial display but a social gesture as natural as breathing.

Mr. Seward had just finished rebuilding his farmhouse on the outskirts of town, and he had shown us around with a pride I found understandable: there was a sparkling electric kitchen worthy of an advertisement in *Life* magazine, some handsome modern furniture and several downstairs rooms paneled beautifully in the prodigal and lustrous hardwood of the region. It was altogether a fine, tasteful house, resembling more one of the prettier medium-priced homes in the Long Island suburbs than the house one might contemplate for a Tidewater farmer. Upstairs, we had inspected his son Bobby's room, a kid's room with books like *Pinocchio* and *The Black Arrow* and *The Swiss Family Robinson*, and here there was a huge paper banner spread across one entire wall with the crayon inscription: "*Two . . . four . . . six . . . eight! We Don't Want to Integrate!*" It was a sign which so overwhelmingly dominated the room that it could not help provoking comment, and it was this that eventually had led to Mr. Seward's reflections about *knowing* Negroes.

There might have been something vaguely defensive in his remarks but not a trace of hostility. His tone was matter-of-fact and good-natured, and he pronounced the word Negro as "*nigra*," which most Southerners do with utter naturalness while intending no disrespect whatsoever, in fact quite the opposite—the mean epithet, of course, is "*nigger*." I had the feeling that Mr. Seward had begun amiably to regard us as sympathetic but ill-informed outsiders, non-Southern, despite his knowledge of my Tidewater background and my father's own accent, which is thick as grits. Moreover, the fact that I had admitted to having lived in the North for fifteen years caused me, I fear, to appear alien in his eyes, *déraciné*, especially when my acculturation to Northern ways has made me adopt the long "e" and say "Negro." The racial misery, at any rate, is within inches of driving us mad: how can I explain that with all my silent disagreement with Mr. Seward's paternalism, I knew that when he said, "By God, I'd die for that Negro," he meant it?

Perhaps I should not have been surprised that Mr. Seward seemed to know very little about Nat Turner. When we got around to the subject, it developed that he had always thought that the insurrection occurred way back in the eighteenth century. Affably, he described seeing in his boyhood the "Hanging Tree," the live oak from which Nat had been hanged in Courtland (Jerusalem had undergone this change of name after the Civil War), and which had died and been cut down some thirty years ago; as for any other landmarks, he regretted that he did not know of a single one. No, so far as he knew, there just wasn't anything.

For me, it was the beginning of disappointments which grew with every hour. Had I *really* been so ingenuous as to believe that I would unearth some shrine, some home preserved after the manner of Colonial Williamsburg, a relic of the insurrection at whose portal I would discover a lady in billowing satin and crinoline who for fifty cents would shepherd me about the rooms with a gentle drawl indicating the spot where a good mistress fell at the hands of the murderous darky? The native Virginian, despite himself, is cursed with a suffocating sense of history, and I do not think it impossible that I actually suspected some such monument. Nevertheless, confident that there would be something to look at, I took heart when Mr. Seward suggested that after lunch we all drive over to Courtland, ten miles to the west. He had already spoken to a friend of his, the sheriff of the county, who knew all the obscure byways and odd corners of Southampton, mainly because of his endless search for illegal stills; if there was a solitary person alive who might be able to locate some landmark or could help retrace part of Nat Turner's march, it was the sheriff. This gave me hope. For I had brought along Drewry's book and its map, which showed the general route of the uprising, marking the houses by name. In the sixty years since Drewry, there would have been many changes in the landscape. But with this map oriented against the sheriff's detailed county map, I should easily be able to pick up the trail and thus experience, however briefly, a sense of the light and shadow that played over that scene of slaughter and retribution a hundred and thirty-four years ago.

Yet it was as if Nat Turner had never existed, and as the day lengthened and afternoon wore on, and as we searched Nat's part of the county—five of us now, riding in the sheriff's car with its huge star emblazoned on the doors, and its radio blatting out hoarse intermittent messages, and its riot gun protectively nuzzling the backs of our necks over the edge of the rear seat—I had the sensation from time to time that this Negro, who had so long occupied my thoughts, who indeed had so obsessed my imagination that he had acquired larger spirit and flesh than most of the living people I encountered day in and day out, had been merely a crazy figment of my mind, a phantom no more real than some half-recollected image from a fairy tale. For here in the back country, this horizontal land of woods and meadows where he had roamed, only a few people had heard of Nat Turner, and of those who had—among the people we stopped to make inquiries of, both white and black, along dusty country roads, at farms, at filling stations, at crossroad stores—most of them confused him, I think, with something spectral, mythic, a black Paul Bunyan who had perpetrated mysterious and nameless deeds in millennia past. They were neither facetious nor evasive, simply unaware. Others confounded him with the Civil War—a Negro general. One young Negro field hand, lounging at an Esso station, figured he was a white man. A white man, heavy-lidded, and paunchy, slow-witted, an idler at a rickety store, thought him an illustrious race horse of bygone days.

The sheriff, a smallish, soft-speaking ruminative man, with a whisper of a smile frozen on his face as if he were perpetually enjoying a good joke, knew full well who Nat Turner was, and I could tell he relished our frustrating charade. He was a shrewd person, quick and sharp with countrified wisdom, and he soon became quite as fascinated as I with the idea of tracking down some relic of the uprising (although he said that Drewry's map was hopelessly out of date, the roads of that time now abandoned to the fields and woods, the homes burned down or gone to ruin); the country people's ignorance he found irresistible and I think it tickled him to perplex their foolish heads, white or black, with the same old leading question: "You heard about old Nat Turner, ain't you?" But few of them had heard, even though I was sure that many had plowed the same fields that Nat had crossed, lived on land that he had passed by; and as for dwellings still standing which might have been connected with the rebellion, not one of these back-country people could offer the faintest hint or clue. As effectively as a monstrous and unbearable dream, Nat had been erased from memory.

It was late afternoon when, with a sense of deep fatigue and frustration, I suggested to Mr. Seward and the sheriff that maybe we had better go back to Courtland and call it a day. They were agreeable—relieved, I felt, to be freed of this tedious and fruitless search—and as we headed east down a straight unpaved road, the conversation became desultory, general. We spoke of the North. The sheriff was interested to learn that I often traveled to New York. He went there occasionally himself, he said; indeed, he had been there only the month before—"to pick up a nigger," a fugitive from custody who had been awaiting trial for killing his wife. New York was a fine place to spend the night, said the sheriff, but he wouldn't want to live there.

As he spoke I had been gazing out of the window, and now suddenly something caught my eye—something familiar, a brief flickering passage of a distant outline, a silhouette against the sun-splashed woods—and I asked the sheriff to stop the car. He did, and as we backed up slowly through a cloud of dust I recognized a house standing perhaps a quarter of a mile off the road, from this distance only a lopsided oblong sheltered by an enormous oak, but the whole tableau—the house and the glorious hovering tree and the stretch of woods beyond—so familiar to me that it might have been some home I passed every day. And of course now as recognition came flooding back I knew whose house it was. For in *The Southampton Insurrection*, the indefatigable Drewry had included many photographs—amateurish, doubtless taken by himself, and suffering from the fuzzy offset reproduction of 1900. But they were clear enough to provide an unmistakable guide to the dwellings in question, and now as I again consulted the book I could see that this house—the monumental oak above it grown scant inches, it seemed, in sixty years—was the one referred to by Drewry as having belonged to Mrs. Catherine Whitehead. From this distance, in the soft clear light of a spring afternoon, it seemed most tranquil, but few houses have come to know such a multitude of violent deaths. There in the late afternoon of Monday, August 22, Nat Turner and his band had appeared, and they set upon and killed "Mrs. Catherine Whitehead, son Richard, and four daughters, and grandchild."

The approach to the house was by a rutted lane long ago abandoned and overgrown with lush weeds, which made a soft, crushed, rasping sound as we rolled over them. Dogwood, white and pink, grew on either side of the lane, quite wild and wanton in lovely pastel splashes. Not far from the house a pole fence interrupted our way; the sheriff stopped the car and we got out and stood there for a moment, looking at the place. It was quiet and still—so quiet that the sudden chant of a mockingbird in the woods was almost frightening—and we realized then that no one lived in the house. Scoured by weather, paintless, worn down to the wintry gray of bone and with all the old mortar gone from between the timbers, it stood alone and desolate above its blasted, sagging front porch, the ancient door ajar like an open wound. Although never a manor house, it had once been a spacious and comfortable country home; now in near-ruin it sagged, finished, a shell, possessing only the most fragile profile of itself. As we drew closer still, we could see that the entire house, from its upper story to the cellar, was filled with thousands of shucked ears of corn—feed for the malevolent-looking razorback pigs which suddenly appeared in a tribe at the edge of the house, eying us, grunting. Mr. Seward sent them scampering with a shied stick and a farmer's sharp "Whoo!" I looked up at the house, trying to recollect its particular role in Nat's destiny, and then I remembered.

There was something baffling, secret, irrational about Nat's own participation in the uprising. He was unable to kill. Time and time again in his confession one discovers him saying (in an offhand tone; one must dig for the implications): "I could not give the death blow, the hatchet glanced from his head," or, "I struck her several blows over the head, but I was unable to kill her, as the sword was dull . . ." It is too much to believe, over and over again: the glancing hatchet, the dull sword. It smacks rather, as in *Hamlet*, of rationalization, ghastly fear, an access of guilt, a shrinking from violence, and fatal irresolution. Alone here at this house, turned now into a huge corncrib around which pigs rooted and snorted in the silence of a spring afternoon, here alone was Nat finally able—or was he forced?—to commit a murder, and this upon a girl of eighteen named Margaret Whitehead, described by Drewry in terms perhaps not so romantic or far-fetched, after all, as "the belle of the county." The scene is apocalyptic—afternoon bedlam in wild harsh sunlight and August heat.

> I returned to commence the work of death, but those whom I left had not been idle; all the family were already murdered but Mrs. Whitehead and her daughter Margaret. As I came around the door I saw Will pulling Mrs. Whitehead out of the house and at the step he nearly severed her head from her body with his axe. Miss Margaret, when I discovered her, had concealed herself in the corner formed by the projection of the cellar cap from the house; on my approach she fled into the field but was soon overtaken and after repeated blows with a sword, I killed her by a blow on the head with a fence rail.

It is Nat's only murder. Why, from this point on, does the momentum of the uprising diminish, the drive and tension sag? Why, from this moment in the "Confessions," does one sense in Nat something dispirited, listless, as if all life and juice had been drained from him, so that never again through the course of the rebellion is he even on the scene when a murder is committed? What happened to Nat in this place? Did he discover his humanity here, or did he lose it?

I lifted myself up into the house, clambering through a doorway without steps, pushing myself over the crumbling sill. The house had a faint yeasty fragrance, like flat beer. Dust from the mountains of corn lay everywhere in the deserted rooms, years and decades of dust, dust an inch thick in some places, lying in a fine gray powder like sooty fallen snow. Off in some room amid the piles of corn I could hear a delicate scrabbling and a plaintive squeaking of mice. Again it was very still, the shadow of the prodigious old oak casting a dark pattern of leaves, checkered with bright sunlight, aslant through the gaping door. As in those chilling lines of Emily Dickinson, even this lustrous and golden day seemed to find its only resonance in the memory, and perhaps a premonition, of death.

> This quiet Dust was Gentlemen and Ladies,
> And Lads and Girls;
> Was laughter and ability and sighing,
> And frocks and curls.

Outside, the sheriff was calling in on his car radio, his voice blurred and indistinct; then the return call from the county seat, loud, a dozen incomprehensible words in an uproar of static. Suddenly it was quiet again, the only sound my father's soft voice as he chatted with Mr. Seward.

I leaned against the rotting frame of the door, gazing out past the great tree and into that far meadow where Nat had brought down and slain Miss Margaret Whitehead. For an instant, in the silence, I thought I could hear a mad rustle of taffeta, and rushing feet, and a shrill girlish piping of terror; then that day and this day seemed to meet and melt together, becoming almost one, and for a long moment indistinguishable.

[*Harper's*, April 1965]

A Southern Conscience

"THERE IS A SAYING among the Negroes in Harlem," James Baldwin said recently, "to the effect that if you have a white Southerner for a friend, you've got a friend for life. But if you've got a white Northerner for a friend, watch out. Because he just might be the kind of friend who decides to move out when you move in." This is a sentiment which may be beguiling to a Southerner, yet the fact does remain that a Southern "liberal" and his Northern counterpart are two distinct species of cat. Certainly the Southerner of good will who lives in the North, as I do, is often confronted with some taxing circumstances. There was the phone call a number of years ago in the distant epoch before the present "Negro revolt," and the cautious interrogation from my dinner hostess of the evening: a Negro was going to be present—as a Southerner, did I mind? If I wished to stay away, she would surely understand. Or much later, when Prince Edward County in Virginia closed its schools, the deafening and indignant lady, a television luminary, who demanded that "we" drop bombs on "those crackers down there." (She got the state wrong, Virginians may be snobs but they are not crackers; nonetheless, she was proposing that "we" bomb my own kith and kin.) Or quite recently, a review in *The New Yorker* of Calder Willingham's *Eternal Fire*, a remarkably fine novel about the South which the reviewer, Whitney Balliett, praised extravagantly without knowing exactly why he was doing so, charging that the book was the definitive satire on Southern writing (though the book is funny, it is anything but satire, being too close to the bone of reality), and polishing off Faulkner, Welty, Warren, *et al.*, with the assertion that Southern fiction in general, in which the Negroes had served so faithfully as "a resident Greek chorus," had now terminated its usefulness. It is of course not important what this particular reviewer thinks, but the buried animus is characteristic and thus worth spelling out: white Southern writers, because they are white and Southern, cannot be expected to write about Negroes without condescension, or with understanding or fidelity or love. Unfortunately, this is a point of view which, by an extension of logic, tends to regard all white Southerners as bigots, and it is an attitude which one might find even more ugly than it is were it prompted by malice rather than ignorant self-righteousness, or a suffocating and provincial innocence. Nor is its corollary any less tiresome: to show that you really love Negroes, smoke pot and dig the right kind of jazz.

A tradition of liberalism has of course existed honorably in the South and is as much a part of its history as is its right-wing fanaticism and violence. The South in the nineteenth century had produced liberals of staunch fiber—the Louisiana novelist George W. Cable is a notable example—but less well known than the thread of liberalism woven into the fabric of Southern history is the fact that the South has also produced its flaming radicals. Lewis Harvie Blair was one of these. Born in Richmond in 1834, Blair came from a distinguished family which numbered among its antecedents a host of well-known theologians, college presidents, editors, generals and even a presidential aspirant or two. After serving as a cavalry officer in the Confederate army, Blair returned to Richmond, established a fortune through the manufacture of shoes and in real estate, and then in 1889, at the contemplative age of fifty-five, and while comfortably installed in his mansion on East Grace Street, wrote a flabbergasting book called *Prosperity in the South Dependent on the Elevation of the Negro*. It received almost no attention in its time, but now, bearing the title *A Southern Prophecy*, it has been resurrected by Professor C. Vann Woodward, who has also provided an introduction that is a model of clarity and insight. Certainly, in view of the time and place it was written, *A Southern Prophecy* is one of the most amazing and powerful exhortations ever written by an American.

The original title of the book is somewhat deceptive. As Woodward points out, it was perhaps inevitable that Blair should adopt a hard-boiled tone, appealing to Southerners to regard the plight of the Negro in terms of their own economic self-interest. Nevertheless, Blair was unable really to conceal his intense humanitarian concern and moral passion; the sense of an abiding indignation over injustice is on every page and helps give the work its continuing vitality. It was the Rotarian-style boosterism of the famous editor Henry Grady of Atlanta—whose gospel of the New South included white supremacy and the permanent degradation of the Negro masses—that provided the source of Blair's initial wrath. The New South propaganda, as Blair saw it—the vision of great and glittering cities springing from the wreckage of the Civil War —was the sheerest humbug. Look rather to the "real South," he insisted: this was a land of crushing poverty for "the six million Negroes who are in the depths of indigence . . . the hundreds of miles of poor country with its unpainted and dilapidated homesteads . . ." This was the reality behind the garish fantasy, and it would remain just that—a fantasy—until the entire South attained a single goal: total equality for the Negro, economic and social. Some of Blair's chapter headings may convey a sense of the scope of the work, and also a touch of Blair's own cranky intransigence:

If Highest Caste will not Elevate, Must Crush Lowest Caste to Powder—Race Prejudice must be Mollified and Obligated—Prejudice Mark of Inferiority—Courts of Justice must be Impartial to All Colors—Why Negroes do not Enjoy Such Impartiality

Negro not a Competent Voter; neither are Millions of White Voters; but Ballot Absolutely Essential to his Freedom—Ruin of the Commonwealth that Degrades its Citizens—Tyranny Destroys the State and Demoralizes the Citizens—Southerners cannot Escape the Demoralizing Effects of Tyranny

The Abandonment of Separate Schools—The Necessity Thereof and Why—It Doubles Basis for Schools—Separate Schools a Public Proclamation of Caste

Other Things we must Do—the Negroes should be Allowed Free Admission to All Hotels, Theatres, Churches, and Official Receptions—Why Negroes should not be restricted to Places for Negroes

"Let us put ourselves in the Negro's place," wrote Blair. "Let us feel when passing good hotels there is no admission here; we dare not go in lest we be kicked out; when entering a theater to be told to go up in the top gallery; when entering an imposing church to be told rudely: no place in God's house for you . . . would not we have our pride cut to the quick? Can we expect the ignorant, degraded, poverty-ridden Negro to rise with such burdens resting upon him, and if he sees no prospect of the burden's lifting?" Although it was the South that received the full force of Blair's implacable anger, the North was not spared, and in a stern, avuncular epilogue he said:

> For the North to clear its skirts of the charge of hypocrisy, it must change its own treatment of the Negro; for until it says, Follow my example instead of doing as I exhort, the seed it sows may be good, but it will fall upon hard and stony soil . . . Put your own Negroes in the way of supporting themselves with comfort, throw open all the avenues of life to them, encourage them to enter freely therein, relieve them of the dangers and the dread of being robbed, beaten, and imposed upon by ruthless white neighbors; in short, elevate them to the full stature of citizenship, and then you can appeal with hope of success to your white Southern brethren; but until you do these things, your purest, most unselfish efforts will be looked upon with suspicion . . .

The year 1889 was, of course, too late for anyone—North or South—to heed Blair's prophecy. Few people cared, anyway. All the momentum of history had gathered its bleak and gigantic power, and within the decade the horrid night of Jim Crowism had settled in. There is a sad sequel to the story of Lewis Blair. Some years before his death in 1916 he suffered the occupational disease of radicals—recantation—and in his private papers disavowed almost everything he had expressed with such conviction years before. But it hardly seems to matter now, for the force and urgency still throb through these pages, reminding us that such passion is not bound by geography or time but remains, quite simply, the passion that binds us together as men. And the final words of certainty seem even more apocalyptic now than at the moment when this splendid Confederate wrote them, seventy-five years ago: "The battle will be long and obstinate, with many difficulties, delays, and dangers . . . We older ones will not see that day, but our grandchildren will, for the light of coming day already irradiates the eastern sky."

[*New York Review of Books*, April 2, 1964]

Slave and Citizen

I CAN RECALL with clarity from childhood my North Carolina
grandmother's reminiscences of her slaves. To be sure, she was
an old lady well into her eighties at the time, and had been a young
girl growing up during the Civil War when she owned human
property. Nonetheless, that past is linked to our present by a space
of time which is startlingly brief. The violent happenings that occur
in Oxford, Mississippi, do not take place in a vacuum of the moment
but are attached historically to slavery itself. That in the Commonwealth of Virginia there is a county today in which no Negro child
has been allowed to attend school for over four years has far less
relevance to Senator Byrd than to the ante-bellum Black Laws of
Virginia, which even now read like the code of regulations from
an inconceivably vast and much longer enduring Nazi concentration camp.

As Professor Stanley Elkins has pointed out, the scholarly debate
over slavery has for nearly a century seesawed with a kind of top-
heavy, contentious, persistent rhythm, the rhythm of "right" and
"wrong." These points of view, shifting between the Georgia-
born historian Ulrich Phillips' vision of the plantation slave as an
essentially cheerful, childlike, submissive creature who was also in
general well treated (a viewpoint which, incidentally, dominated
historical scholarship for the decades between the two world wars),
and Kenneth Stampp's more recent interpretation of American
slavery (*The Peculiar Institution*) as a harsh and brutal system,
practically devoid of any charity at all, have each been so marred
by a kind of moral aggression and self-righteousness as to resemble,
in the end, a debate between William Lloyd Garrison and John C.
Calhoun—and we have had enough of such debates. Granted that

it seems inescapable that the plantation slave, at least, often displayed a cheerful, childlike and submissive countenance, and that plantation life had its sunny aspects; granted, too, that the system was at heart incredibly brutal and inhumane, the question remains: Why? Why was American slavery the unique institution that it was? What was the tragic essence of this system which still casts its shadow not only over our daily life but over our national destiny as well? Professor Frank Tannenbaum's brief work, *Slave and Citizen: The Negro in the Americas* (first published by Knopf in 1948 and now reprinted by Vintage), is a modest but important attempt to answer these questions.

Tannenbaum's technique is that of comparison—the comparison of slavery in the United States with that of coexisting slave systems in Latin America. Slavery was introduced by the Spanish and Portuguese into South America at the identical moment that it was brought to North America and the West Indies by the British, and its duration in time as an institution on both continents was roughly the same. But it is a striking fact that today there is no real racial "problem" in Brazil; a long history of miscegenation has blurred the color line, legal sanctions because of race do not exist, and any impediments toward social advancement for the Negro are insignificant. That this is true is due to an attitude toward slavery which had become crystallized in the Portuguese and Spanish ethic even before slaves were brought to the shores of the New World. For slavery (including the slavery of white people), as Tannenbaum points out, had existed on the Iberian peninsula throughout the fourteenth and fifteenth centuries. Oppressive an institution as it may have been, it contained large elements of humanity, even of equality, which had been the legacy of the Justinian Code. Thus Seneca: "A slave can be just, brave, magnanimous." Las Sieste Partidas, the body of law which evolved to govern all aspects of slavery, not only partook of the humanitarian traditions of the Justinian Code but was framed within that aspect of Christian doctrine which regarded the slave as the spiritual equal of his master, and perhaps his better. The law was protective of the slaves, and in conjunction with the church provided many incentives for freedom; and this attitude persisted when Negro slavery was established in South America. Despite its frequent brutality, the institution of slavery in Brazil, with its recognition of the slave as a moral human being and its bias in favor of manumission, had become in effect, as Tannenbaum says, "a contractual arrangement between the master and his bondsman"; and in such a relatively agreeable atmosphere it is not unnatural that full liberty was attained through a slow and genial mingling of the races, and by gradual change rather than through such a cataclysm as Civil War.

We are only beginning to realize the extent to which American slavery worked its psychic and moral devastation upon an entire race. Unlike the Spanish and the Portuguese, the British and their descendants who became American slave owners had no historical experience of slavery; and neither the Protestant church nor Anglo-American law was equipped to cope with the staggering problem of the status of the Negro: forced to choose between regarding him as a moral human being and as property, they chose the definition of property. The result was the utter degradation of a people. Manumission was totally discouraged. A slave became only a negotiable article of goods, without rights to property, to the products of his own work, to marriage, without rights even to the offspring of his own despairing, unsanctioned unions—all of these were violations of the spirit so shattering as to beg the question whether the white South was populated either by tolerant, amiable Marse Bobs or by sadistic Simon Legrees. Even the accounts of brutality (and it is difficult even now, when witnessing the moral squabble between those historians who are apologists and those who are neo-abolitionists, to tell whether brutality was insignificant or rampant) fade into inconsequence against a backdrop in which the total dehumanization of a race took place, and a systematic attempt, largely successful, was made to reduce an entire people to the status of children. It was an oppression unparalleled in human history. In the end only a Civil War could try to rectify this outrage, and the war came too late.

In Latin America the Negro achieved complete legal equality slowly through manumission, over centuries, and after he had acquired a moral personality. In the United States he was given his freedom suddenly, and before the white community credited him with moral status.

That is the problem we are faced with today: too many white Americans still deny the Negro his position as a moral human being.

Unfortunately, history does not give answers to the problems it leaves us. Professor Tannenbaum concludes his excellent study with the reasonable implication that the attainment by the Negro of a moral status may still take a very long time. It seems apparent that a very long time might be too long for our salvation.

[*New York Review of Books*, Inaugural Issue, February 1963]

In the Southern Camp

SOUTHERN WOMEN of all classes, probably more than women anywhere else, have for generations been valued for their physical beauty to the exclusion of any other quality. The ethos of the plantation, with its stress on male dominance, allowed, generally speaking, very little room for the development of women's intellectual capacities, except in a closeted way and then only with vast condescension on the part of the men. Generation after generation of this form of acculturation produced droves of famously beautiful women, but also—in combination with a diminished emphasis on education—a kind of endemic regional dumbness too well known and too persistently remarked upon to be dismissed.

That there are many exceptions to this state of things, especially nowadays, is another sign of the South's splendid resurgence as it joins the twentieth century; beauty and brains are not necessarily antipathetic in the same person. But until recent years the trials of a bright but plain woman in the South were more difficult than those of her sisters elsewhere who, though certainly fettered in many ways too, suffered less from the stigma of possessing actual intelligence. Difficult, perhaps, but in some ways more interesting. For even as recently as the 1940s, when I was growing up in the South, one could perceive the difference between the often stunning coed beauties who, like their counterparts in the past, fluttered effortlessly into poses of decorative blossoms, and those who were less favored physically but who were far more attractive because of their wit and charm. They created their own seductiveness.

. . .

Mary Boykin Chesnut was doubtless one of these: a not really good-looking woman (self-admittedly) whose very lack of beauty helped prevent her from becoming the stereotype of a plantation mistress—frail, dependent, vacuous—and whose compensating drive toward self-expression led her to writing one of the great chronicles of the Civil War. The likeness of Mary Chesnut that regards us from the dust jacket of the new edition of her book is rather plain—the nose too long, the jaw too broad, the eyes too large and dominating—but very winning nonetheless. The picture suggests intelligence and the whisper of mischief—clearly a woman one would have liked to know. That one does get to know her is the result both of her honesty and of the meticulous way in which she records her impressions of daily life in the South between the winter of 1861 and the summer of 1865.

Yet this is not really a "personal" narrative, and despite her candor and the piercing, almost ruthless way in which she dissects her own emotions, Mary Chesnut's journal has its greatest value for the modern reader in the extraordinary panorama it presents of a culture being rent asunder. Not for its autobiography, not for its "fortuitous self-revelations," says Professor C. Vann Woodward in his introduction to *Mary Chesnut's Civil War*, will the Chesnut chronicle be remembered, but "for the vivid picture she left of a society in the throes of its life-and-death struggle, its moment of high drama in world history."

Mrs. Chesnut was blissfully fortunate in having been near the center of the political affairs of the Confederacy throughout the Civil War. Born and reared in South Carolina and married to an ardent secessionist—a one-time United States senator who, after Fort Sumter, became an aide to Jefferson Davis—Mrs. Chesnut traveled forth from her native state to the early capital in Montgomery and thence to Richmond, where she abundantly records her impressions of the great and the near-great. A well-educated woman, fluent in French and an avowed Francophile, she seems in certain rudimentary ways a Southern Madame de Staël. Although by no means a philosophical or literary innovator like de Staël, she had nonetheless the same kind of intellectual energy and, like de Staël, possessed both a ferocious interest in powerful people and the magnetism to attract such people. Thus her observations of such figures as Jefferson Davis, Robert E. Lee, Wade Hampton and General Joseph Johnston are as fascinating in their intimacy as they are invaluable.

Here is a sketch of Jefferson Davis in June 1861:

> In Mrs. Davis's drawing room last night, the president took a seat beside me on the sofa where I sat. He talked for nearly an hour. He laughed at our faith in our own powers. We are like the British. We think every Southerner equal to three Yankees at least. We will have to be equivalent to a dozen now. . . . There was a sad refrain running through it all. For one thing, either way, he thinks it will be a long war. That floored me at once. It has been too long for me already. Then said: before the end came, we would have many a bitter experience. He said only fools doubted the courage of the Yankees or their willingness to fight when they saw fit. And now we have stung their pride—we have roused them till they will fight like devils.

And an insight into the domestic life of Robert E. ("Cousin Robert") Lee:

> General Lee told us what a good son Custis was. Last night their house was so crowded Custis gave up his own bed to General Lee and slept upon the floor. Otherwise General Lee would have had to sleep in Mrs. Lee's room. She is a martyr to rheumatism and rolls about in a chair. She can't walk.
>
> Constance Cary says, if it would please God to take poor Cousin Mary Lee—she suffers so—wouldn't these Richmond women *campaign* for Cousin Robert? In the meantime Cousin Robert holds all admiring females at arm's length.

A glimpse of Lee and Davis on the same day:

> Sunday Mars Kit walked to church with me. Coming out, General Lee was slowly making his way down the aisle, bowing royally right and left. I pointed this out to Christopher Hampton. When General Lee happened to look our way, he bowed low, giving me a charming smile of recognition. I was ashamed of being so pleased. I blushed like a schoolgirl.
>
> We went to the White House. They gave us tea. The president said he had been on the way to our house, coming with all the Davis family to see me. But the children became so troublesome they turned back.
>
> Just then little Joe rushed in and insisted on saying his prayer at his father's knee. . . . He was in his nightclothes.

But if Chesnut's journals were merely high-level gossip restricted to a circle of the celebrated men and women of the period, the book would have very limited appeal. The work is really an epic in which the accumulation of quotidian detail—the weather, parties, receptions, rumors, duels, love affairs, murders, promotions and demotions, intrigues, illnesses, celebrations—provides a sense of the rhythms of ordinary life during those chaotic four years in a way that no other book has done. We often tend to think of the Civil War in terms of its battles, all of which have been chronicled in such detail—in history and in fiction—that the savagery, say, of Chickamauga or the desperate anxiety of the ordinary soldier represented in *The Red Badge of Courage* becomes emblematic of the entire conflict. The romanticism of *Gone With the Wind* prevents that novel from furnishing us with a reliable picture of life away from the arenas of combat.

What gives Mrs. Chesnut's account such stunning verisimilitude is the way in which the war, despite its distance from the diarist and her friends in places like Richmond and Columbia, impinges on every facet of daily existence; scarcely a page of this extremely long journal does not have its allusion to the progress of the various campaigns, to the slow attrition being suffered by the Confederacy, to the hospital horrors, to privations, to lost battles and battles won, and—incessantly—to the dead, the mutilated, and men who have come home to die. Yet despite the appalling grimness of those years there is little of the morbid or despairing in Mary Chesnut's description of events. Underlying even the darkest passages is a cheerfulness of spirit, almost a buoyancy, that in effect aerates the narrative and provides much of its charm and readability.

The following passages, only a few pages apart, provide a characteristic juxtaposition of the somber and the lighthearted:

Yesterday we went to the capitol grounds to see our returned prisoners. . . . We walked slowly up and down until Jeff Davis was called upon to speak to the prisoners. Then I stood almost touching the bayonets, where he left me. Poor fellows! They cheered with all their might—and I wept for sympathy, enthusiasm, and all that moved me deeply. Oh! these men were so forlorn, so dried up, shrunken, such a strange look in some of their eyes. Others so restless and wild looking—others again, placidly vacant, as if they had been dead to this world for years. A poor woman was too much for me. She was hunting her son. He had been expected back with this batch of prisoners. She said he was taken prisoner at Gettysburg. She kept going in and out among them, with a basket of provisions she had brought for him to eat. It was too pitiful. She was utterly unconscious of the crowd. The anxious dread—expectation—hurry and hope which led her on showed in her face . . .

* * *

The church windows were closed that it might be a candlelight wedding. A woman in the gallery had a cataleptic fit, and they were forced to open a window. Mixed daylight and gas was ghastly and greatly marred the effect below. The poor woman made a bleating noise like a goat. Buckets of water were handed over the heads of the people, as if it was a fire to be put out, and they dashed water over her as fast as the buckets came in reach. We watched the poor woman from below in agony, fearing she might die before our eyes. But no—far from it. The water cure answered. She came to herself, shook her dress, straightened up her wet feathers, and put her bonnet on quite composedly. Then watched the wedding with unabashed interest—and I watched her. . . . For one thing, the poor woman could not have been gotten out of that jam, that crowd, unless, like the buckets of water, she had been handed out over the heads of the public.

Readability is perhaps an imprecise word to explain the fascination that this book exerts once one has become captured by its force and sweep, but it is there in a powerful way, and is quite simply a factor of the inherent literary nature of the work. Mrs. Chesnut clearly had the gifts of a novelist (she had written a couple of undistinguished though not unpromising works of fiction), and the novelistic talent is everywhere evident—in her dialogue, sharp observations, the felicitous use of language, the deft modulations in tone which are the novelist's stock in trade. In an essay on Mrs. Chesnut published in *Patriotic Gore* in 1962, Edmund Wilson remarked on her literary qualities: "The very rhythm of her opening pages at once puts us under the spell of a writer who is not merely jotting down her days but establishing, as a novelist does, an atmosphere, an emotional tone."

Wilson had been profoundly impressed by the journal, which he had read in an abridged form unfortunately entitled *A Diary from Dixie*. (Mrs. Chesnut herself disliked the word "Dixie," but the book was named by its editors, who brought out the work in 1905, nineteen years after her death.) He had also read and, with some reservations, admired a more recent and more extensive version of the diary put together by the novelist Ben Ames Williams. In the first version the editors had suppressed such matters as the gross injustice of slavery (thereby obscuring an extremely important aspect of Mrs. Chesnut, who was a vigorous opponent of the slave system), and Wilson's admiration for the Williams edition was due both to this enlargement of perspective and to the fact that it read like a good novel—something that appealed to the literary side of Wilson's critical sensibilities.

What Wilson could not have known was that considerably more of the novelistic imagination went into the making of Mrs. Chesnut's diary than one might think. For although she did keep an extensive journal during several of the Civil War years, it was not until 1881 —sixteen years after the war ended—that she sat down and began completely to rework her chronicle, fleshing out her story through a complex series of expansions and elaborations, adding new episodes and new material, condensing here, omitting there, shifting dates, telescoping entries, until the new version was no longer the actual record of the wartime days but what might be termed a reconstruction through memory. The liberties she took in this reworking of her own material were plainly great, but the final product was not the creation of one who has distorted or falsified history but of one who, through the prism of memory and in the calm of reflection, has perhaps cast a brighter and more revealing light upon past events than might have been shed in an actual journal, with its frequent myopia.

Confessing that he began the editing of this new, complete edition with a spirit of skepticism, Professor Woodward writes that "a growing respect for the author and the integrity of her work began to replace the original misgivings. Given the kind of liberties she took . . . Mary Chesnut can be said to have shown an unusual sense of responsibility toward the history she records and a reassuring faithfulness to perceptions of her experience of the period as revealed in her original journal."

Having read with considerable admiration Capote's *In Cold Blood* and Mailer's *The Executioner's Song*—and having been able to compare the two versions of Mrs. Chesnut's chronicle—I would say that Mrs. Chesnut played far less fast and loose with the facts and with "truth" than either of these writers, whose works we value precisely because of their fluid, interpretative nature, their refusal to be hamstrung by adhering to a mechanical account of events. (It may be that the most interesting aspect of the controversy that surrounds these books is not the blur they create between fact and fiction but the no man's land of terminology; as powerfully impressed as I was by *The Executioner's Song*, some stubborn intuition still tells me it is not a novel.)

In any case, we should not fault Mrs. Chesnut for her inconsistencies; she herself did not attempt to hide the fact that much of her final version was reworked and rewritten. Partly because of this, Professor Woodward has removed the word "diary" from the title, so that *Mary Chesnut's Civil War* really ends up being not a literal record but a history book *sui generis*, a new mixture of memoir and journalism to which only the most rigorously literal-minded reader could object on the grounds that it does not hew to the minutiae of chronology and fact.

If Professor Woodward had not, in the passage just quoted and elsewhere in his remarkably sensitive and careful introduction, taken such pains to explain the difference between the original diary and the later transformation, it would be somewhat easier to accept the charge made by Professor Kenneth S. Lynn, in the *New York Times Book Review*, that the Chesnut journal is a "hoax," and "one of the most audacious frauds in the history of American literature." It is offensive enough that Professor Lynn has called the book a hoax; what seems obtuse is his further insistence that Professor Woodward not only has exposed the hoax but has refused "to bestow the label upon it."

But if a hoax is something that is deliberately intended to trick or dupe, which I believe to be a scrupulous definition of the word, then nothing could be more wrong. As I said before, Mrs. Chesnut did nothing to hide the reworked nature of her journals. Further, even if such charges as Professor Lynn makes were true—for instance, that she cleansed the later version of her journal of anti-slavery sentiments to be more in tune with the mood of the post-war years—a criticism that does not hold up—it would hardly be of great significance, when one compares the haphazard and fragmentary nature of the early diary (containing, as Professor Woodward points out, "so many indiscretions, gaps, trivialities, and incoherencies") with the reflective finished work, radiating such vitality and truth. Professor Lynn wonders whether Edmund Wilson might not have wanted to retract all his praise for Mrs. Chesnut had he known the real nature of her achievement. I doubt that he would have wanted to do any such thing, any more than he would have preferred Proust's notebooks to *Swann's Way*.

. . .

Mary Chesnut's Civil War is important because, whatever one calls it—journal, memoir, chronicle, or an amalgam of these—the book remains a great epic drama of our greatest national tragedy. Even so, when the last page is finished and the panorama begins to fade, one is still haunted by the personality of the book's extraordinary author. How thoroughly—by force of her vivacity, her compassion and her wisdom—she helps rearrange in our consciousness certain shopworn images which might linger in regard to the emptiness of Southern women of her time is a measure of her great authority as a writer.

Doubtless there were many like her, but it was she who almost alone rose with such gallantry to the challenges of her era. For one thing, she was in certain matters decades ahead of her contemporaries of either sex. To be sure, she was not entirely alone among the women of her time and place in her detestation of slavery, but the voice she raised against the institution of slavery was among the loudest and most vehement. Reading her animadversions on the slave system, one wonders which she hated more: the plight of the slaves or that of her own female sex, doomed forever, it seemed, to the tyranny of male domination. Mary Chesnut was a passionate and outraged feminist; and one of the most fascinating aspects of her personality, and the tensions that energized her, was her constant awareness of the way in which the oppression of black slaves and the oppression of women were similar, indeed intertwined.

Have made the acquaintance of a clever woman, too—Mrs. McLean, née Sumner, daughter of the general. . . . They say *he* avoids matrimony.

"Slavery the sum of all evil," he says. So he will not reduce a woman to slavery. There is no slave, after all, like a wife.

* * *

So I have seen a negro woman sold—up on the block—at auction. The woman on the block overtopped the crowd. I felt faint —seasick. She was a bright mulatto with a pleasant face. She was magnificently gotten up in silks and satins. She seemed delighted with it all—sometimes ogling the bidders, sometimes looking quite coy and modest, but her mouth never relaxed from its expanded grin of excitement. I daresay the poor thing knew who would buy her.

I sat down on a stool in a shop. I disciplined my wild thoughts. . . .

You know how women sell themselves and are sold in marriage, from queens downward, eh?

You know what the Bible says about slavery—and marriage. Poor women. Poor slaves. . . .

Certainly one feels that she had earned the right to such awareness and to the consequent indignation; after all, these were the twin curses of the environment out of which she had sprung. Unlike Harriet Beecher Stowe—for whom she had considerable contempt—Mary Chesnut had been reared in a world where the horrors of slavery were a daily reality; just as real and just as grinding was the peculiarly Southern form of patriarchal domination—a nearly total exploitation of women by men. Her treatment of these themes, foreshadowing so much of that which has come to an upheaval in our own period, is in itself a splendid manifestation of moral courage, as well as prescience. It is such honest turmoil within the mind and heart of this questing woman that helps to bestow upon both the work and its creator an unshakable excellence.

[*New York Review of Books*, August 13, 1981]

The Oldest America

GEORGE WASHINGTON, never so versatile and wide-ranging in his interests as Thomas Jefferson, was nonetheless a man of many parts who knew well how to employ his leisure time. Firmly implanted in the American mythology is Washington the solemn, taciturn soldier and statesman, the Rembrandt Peale portrait of the postage stamps; less well known is the pre-Revolutionary Virginia planter who was devoted equally to horse racing and the theater and who regularly traveled the hundred and fifty miles south from Mount Vernon across the somnolent Tidewater to Williamsburg—then the capital of the colony—where he placed bets on the horses by day, and by night attended performances of Shakespeare by troupes imported from London. If today one should wonder how that Tidewater countryside appeared to Washington's eyes, the answer is: much as it does now. For to a degree largely unmatched in America, the region resembles in topography its ancient, earliest configuration.

It is the oldest part of our country, and suffered its upheaval and exploitation not in the nineteenth century like New England nor in the present century like California, but decades before we became a nation. Recklessly overcultivated in tobacco for more than a century, the once rich bottomlands and green fields became fallow and depleted, so that even by the time of Washington's later years the abandoned farms and pastures were becoming reclaimed by new growths of woodland—oak and ash and sycamore and scrub pine. Long before the invention of the steam locomotive, much of the region—especially in the northern reaches, in the area just south of the Potomac and bordering on Chesapeake Bay—had subsided into the lazy sleep of a depopulated backwater, lacking either industry or productive agriculture, and for this reason (somewhat rare in the pattern of American regional growth), the absence of factories and railroads and great superhighways left the landscape mercifully unmarked. For this reason, too, the Tidewater has retained, generally speaking, a unique, unspoiled loveliness. Of course, architectural styles have changed the face of the landscape; shopping centers and split-level houses, indistinguishable from those elsewhere in America, have set their imprint here and there upon the land, and one should not visit the Tidewater in the expectation that each small town will yield a glimpse of something resembling Colonial Williamsburg or a Christopher Wren church. Also, the sprawling industrial and military complex that has grown up around Norfolk and Hampton Roads does not represent the quality of the Tidewater of which I speak.

Nevertheless, the old mansions and the eighteenth-century courthouses and churches still exist, their weathered brick rising out of the countryside from behind a grove of oaks in the most pleasantly disarming way. Such great old manor houses as Westover and Brandon and Carter's Grove still reign in lordly and stunning elegance along the banks of the James (these are the homes that H. L. Mencken, in outrage over the encroachment of all that was hideous in American architecture, described as the most perfectly proportioned dwellings ever fashioned by man).

Yet beyond all these noble relics of the past, there is the landscape itself, sometimes unspectacular and ordinary (cornfields, pine woods, country stores) but more often possessing a sorrowing beauty—everywhere lovelier and more mellow and melancholy and fledged with green than the hard-clay country that dominates the higher elevations of the Upper South. All this has to do, of course, with the rivers, the noble waterways that indent the face of the Tidewater and give the region so much of its character, including, indeed, its very name. Rarely here is one more than a few miles from a great brackish tideland stream, like the Rappahannock or the York or the James (and these are monumental rivers, too, in breadth if not in length: the James at its mouth is nearly six miles across, one of the widest estuaries in America), so that what is specifically Southern becomes commingled with the waterborne, the maritime. Thus the vistas of the solitary stands of pinewoods and barren cornfields, the sawmill in a remote clearing, the sudden immaculate and simple beauty of a freshly painted clapboard Negro church in a sunny grove are combined with a sense of broad, flat reaches of tidal shallows, mighty river estuaries, fish stakes and oyster boats, inlets and coves and bays, wild sudden squalls blowing out of the Chesapeake, the serene magnificence of sunrise coming up over the mouth of the Rappahannock, blood-red through the milk of morning mists. This is a low, drowsing, placid topography, literally half drowned. From the exhausted land the people have turned to the water for sustenance—river and estuary and bay. There is an odd truth in the remark that every native of the Tidewater is a skilled boatman, even if he is a farmer.

I love the place names of the Virginia Tidewater—that juxta-position of the Indian and old England, which is more mellifluous and striking than any other place in America. The names of the counties alone are resonant with the past: Essex and Middlesex and York, Isle of Wight and Sussex, King William, Surry, Prince George, King and Queen. These are mingled with the ancestral names of the red men, who still exist in diminishing numbers, isolated on small reservations, where they make a modest living by fishing for the fat shad that still teem in the rivers bearing their tribal names: Pamunkey and Mattaponi, Chickahominy, Powhatan and Kecoughtan, Chuckatuck and Corotoman. Names like these have a lazy beauty, corresponding to the meandering pace of a bygone era.

Yet at the same time, no place of comparable area owns such an abundance of curiously or fancifully named hamlets and villages— Ark, Rescue, Ordinary, Naxera, Shadow, Zuni, Lively (the posted speed here is five miles an hour), Bumpass. These are often nothing more than a crossroads, a general store with a post office, and here one is most likely to hear the throaty, slurred Tidewater speech— beyond doubt the speech of the Father of His Country. Encapsu- lated in time and space, the natives of the remoter reaches of this part of Virginia still use the phonetic forms of a language spoken two and a half centuries ago by their ancestors, settlers from Devon and Dorset. Its quality cannot be fully savored unless heard, but it may be suggested by noting that in the Tidewater you never go out but "oot," and that "house" rhymes less directly with "mouse" than with "noose." Still occasionally heard is the "yar" sound, in which "garden" becomes "gyarden," "far" turns into "fyah," and that old family name of Carter, one of Virginia's most illustrious, is transmuted into "Cyatah." This locution was, in my childhood, largely the property of old ladies fragrant with lavender—usually Daughters of the Confederacy—and still hovers in my memory as the quintessential sound of Southern womanhood and good breeding. Alas, it is dying out and will soon be gone forever, absorbed into the flattened-out tonality of Basic American.

Neither the Tidewater nor the rest of Virginia is, of course, the Deep South, but the underlying quality of the region remains, ultimately, distinctly Southern, adumbrated by the memory of a tragic past. Some of the bloodiest battles of the Civil War were fought on this soil, the selfsame soil to which there was brought for the first time—at Jamestown, in 1619, in the form of a handful of African slaves—the institution that became, in large part, the basis for that awful conflict. The legacy still remains. A majority of the Tidewater counties is heavily populated by Negroes; in many counties Negroes outnumber whites in a ratio resembling parts of Alabama and Mississippi. Here, as elsewhere in the South (and the North), there are grievous inequities; it is not in order to minimize those inequities that I reflect on the fact that no part of the South where such a racial composition is found has been so free of friction or strife. The Ku Klux Klan has never found a welcome here; the reign of terror that swept the South in the 1920s and 1930s— the decades of blazing crosses and lynchings—would have been unthinkable in the Tidewater.

I suggest that over the reach of decades a certain way of life may produce attitudes—a sense of fair play, an abhorrence of violence, a respect for the dignity of men—that supersede all other considerations and come to dominate moral conduct. However strongly it may be argued that this is not enough, it remains a tradition to be reckoned with, and the Virginia Tidewater lays justifiable claim to such a heritage. The region possesses the shortcomings common to all places, but the land and its people have achieved a certain harmony. Perhaps more than in any other comparable part of America, men have learned to get along with one another. It would be a pleasant irony if the land where the American dilemma began—close by the shores of the tranquil and lovely James, with its memory of black chained cargoes—should by its way of life come to embody an answer to that same dilemma.

[*McCall's*, July 1968]

A Voice from the South

I'VE ALWAYS BEEN SURPRISED by my direct link to the Old South—the South of slavery and the Civil War. Many Southerners of my vintage, and even some of those who are considerably older, can claim an ancestral connection to that period only through a *great*-grandparent. "I have letters written during the war by my great-aunt," they will say, or "my great-grandfather was with Longstreet at Seven Pines." If they remember their grandparents, they usually remember elderly ladies and gentlemen whose own childhood memories are of the days of Reconstruction or afterwards. But it was from my own grandmother, who was in her late eighties when I was a boy of twelve or so, that I heard of her life as a little girl just before the war and of the sometimes remarkable events that took place in her life thereafter.

The Clark plantation, where she was born Marianna at midcentury, was a small fiefdom of several thousand acres on the lower reaches of the Pungo River in eastern North Carolina. Even now Hyde County is a remote region, low-lying, with the desolate marsh-and-pinewoods beauty of land bordering on the sea. In those days, before highways and cars, before telephones, the remoteness must have been a globe of near-perfect silence, with only the diurnal sounds of plantation business obtruding: cartwheels squeaking, a blacksmith's hammer, the fuss and grumble of livestock—at night an immense quiet. Whenever, in my fantasy of the place, I hear human voices, the voices are almost always those of black people, calling from the cabins or the fields, through an August haze. This was a mercantile enterprise after all, and the black people made up its vital force and were its essential personnel. My grandmother's father, Caleb Clark, was a major entrepreneur; he owned upwards of thirty-three slaves, a large number for the upper South. And it was they who labored to produce the plantation's crops—cotton and cotton meal, shingles and turpentine—much of which was transported by boat up through the inland waterway to Norfolk for shipment north and to Europe.

In the late nineteenth century, and well into the early decades of this century, there were many sentimental novels written by Southerners, still infatuated with life in antebellum times, in which the central figures are a child and an older person reminiscing about those bygone years; in these chronicles there was never a world so idyllic as that of the plantation, with its celebrations, its pleasant frivolities and domestic commotions, its possum hunts and horse races and sewing bees, its natural disasters that always resolved themselves benignly, the genteel collision of white people and their black servitors in encounters touching or droll but never menacing.

Curiously, I recall myself as a boy being a character in just such a novel, and the older person was none other than my grandmother, then living in the small town of Washington—popularly known as Little Washington—not many miles from that arcadian domain in Hyde County where her childhood was spent experiencing precisely those joys that the sentimental novelist described. Or at least that is the way she represented her early life to me, and of course she could be excused because of her extreme youth for having failed to be aware of the desperate and sorrowful undercurrents that lay beneath the genial surface of the Clark plantation. In the same way my own extreme youth allowed me to be beguiled by her description of the two little slave girls she owned. Approximately her own age, they had been legally deeded to her by her father, and they had the priceless names of Drusilla and Lucinda. Drusilla and Lucinda—they were names right out of one of those heartrending chronicles where the young heroine nurses her beloved charges through dire illnesses such as scarlet fever, and braids their hair, and knits woolen stockings to protect their skinny little black legs from the winter cold. But the fact is that my grandmother actually performed these good offices. They were no maudlin romantic invention. Much of what she told me had a quality of innocence, even beatitude, and she was telling the truth as she saw it, at least.

But suddenly—and why shrink from the obvious locution?—it was all gone with the wind. From the outset of the war Federal troops had occupied eastern North Carolina, and in 1862 a small force of General Burnside's men marched onto the Clark plantation and ransacked the place from end to end. They were efficient devastators and destroyed much of the property, but my grandmother recalled that the most terrible result of the Yankees' plunder was hunger. Their chief objective had been food and provisions and they stripped the premises of every edible ounce. The troops were surly, loud and uncouth; they were from Ohio, and that state for her forever had a special stigma among the generally hated Northern states, causing her to pronounce the name with a kind of aspirated loathing, O-high-O. One particularly vivid image she left me with was the maneuver whereby the scores of smoked and cured hams and bags of meal in the cellar were removed from the house: a chain of blue-jacketed soldiers, like a bucket brigade, passing hams and bags one after another out the window and into the wagons below. The monsters waved their flags and brandished their rifles, and they used dreadful cuss words, my grandmother said, language no Southerner would use. Then they departed and the Clark family began to starve; for weeks the family—and the black people, too—subsisted on what they could scrounge from the fields and woods, until finally some meager supplies began to arrive regularly from friends in Tarboro, smuggled through the Union lines. All of us are by now acquainted with human beings who have suffered pain of nearly every description, but aside from a few of the survivors of Auschwitz, my grandmother was the only person I've ever known—certainly the only American—who could describe the harrowing pain of continual starvation.

Meanwhile, over in Little Washington, which was in the hands of the Federals, my grandmother's husband-to-be—my grandfather Alpheus Whitehurst Styron—had sneaked his way out of town to join the Confederate army. He was a rambunctious kid of fifteen with enough inbred Southern chutzpah then to lie about his age in order to sign up with one of the units of General Robert Hoke, who for many months had laid siege to the town in a campaign to drive the Yankees out. He was assigned to a job as courier, and this provided him with many scary and hairbreadth adventures as he moved in and out of the town through the cordon of Union pickets. But his splendid career as boy warrior was brief, and terminated abruptly in 1864 when the Union troops were ordered to abandon their stronghold and leave Washington. Before departing, hundreds of soldiers went on a nasty spree through the streets, pillaging stores and warehouses and private homes; then they burned down the pretty little town. One responsible historian has written that, for its size, no Southern community was so completely devastated, including those in the path of Sherman's infamous march. The wars of the twentieth century, with their hideous massacres of civilians and reprisals against the innocent, have made such episodes appear like mere gross misbehavior; a spirit of gallantry, now virtually defunct, prevailed on both sides of the Civil War, and the atrocities to which most of us have become anesthetized were in those days almost never a part of the repertory of violence. There were no Babi Yars, no Lidices, no Oradours, no My Lais. But the invaders were experts in the science of destruction, and it requires no stretch of credulity to speculate that, had the fortunes of war and geography been different, the Confederate troops would have been capable of the same evil mischief. Whatever, as Vann Woodward observed in *The Burden of Southern History*, the South in its ruination—of which the destroyed town of Washington was a symbol—became the only region in America to experience the tragic exhaustion and trauma of defeat (along with the bitterness of the vanquished) that has been the common lot of so many millions of Europeans. So it is no wonder that many years later, living serenely in a Washington now restored, my grandmother should still have been affected by the brutality and privation she had suffered as a little girl, and her gentle yet animated face turned aggrieved, pale as ice at the recollection of the barbarians who had abused and starved her. It is not difficult for me, recomposing my own memories, to see in that face the same wintry hauntedness of a Russian woman I knew whose town was overrun by the Germans. Both had psychic wounds and both were unforgiving.

When I had these memorable encounters with my grandmother I was living not far north in the Virginia Tidewater, near the small city where I was born. Newport News was indisputably a Southern community, but it lacked many of the characteristics we commonly associate with a Southern environment. It was a rootless and synthetic town, created from the ground up in the 1890s by the Northern railroad tycoon Collis P. Huntington, who perceived in the lower James River a perfect setting for his shipbuilding enterprise, while obviously being enticed by the prospect of cheap, nonunion Southern labor, much of it black. My father, a graduate of North Carolina State College, was an engineer at the shipyard. Newport News also became a bustling ocean port and chief terminus for the Chesapeake and Ohio Railroad, which was a major transporter of coal from the Appalachian mines, tobacco from the Carolinas, Virginia, and Kentucky, and grain from the Midwest. Among its lesser but continuous exports were the elderly horses saved from the Kansas City dog-food factories but headed for a more dreadful fate by being consigned to Spain, where they became the terrorized and often gored-to-death mounts of picadors in bullfights. As a boy I remember seeing hundreds of these cadaverous old nags huddled in the rain, and only learned of their purpose years later when Hemingway mentioned Newport News in *Death in the Afternoon*. I would not go so far as to say that, metaphorically, these wretched beasts represented for me the dreariness of the city, yet it was a strangely soulless community and, despite what I still reckon to have been a relatively happy childhood spent in and around the place, I never discovered its center, its identity. Certainly I could argue with myself that in writing my first novel, *Lie Down in Darkness*, I made a stab at plumbing that identity, and even perceiving glints of natural beauty, usually those of river and estuary and bay; but it was difficult to establish a spiritual connection with such a city, basically callow and without a past to supply it with those necessities of Southern life—myth and tradition.

A connoisseur of the unaesthetic, H. L. Mencken, once rated the town second in ugliness only to Altoona, Pennsylvania. It is true that those who were the most favored economically might, as is customary, build houses commanding a gorgeous view—in this case the broad James or the wide and spectacular Hampton Roads—but essentially the city was raw, clamorous, industrial, and unsightly, with a big, drab white slum and an even drabber and bigger black slum, a part of which, even in those days before cocaine or crack had been heard of, was prey to such unceasing violence that it bore the lurid name Blood Fields. Aside from all this it was hard to love a place where much of the population was transient, shifting, faceless: swarms of country boys, black and white, seeking railroad or shipyard jobs, an endless invasion of seamen from merchant ships, and a horde of soldiers and sailors from every base in the swollen military encampment which the lower Tidewater was becoming in the years before World War II. As I've implied, the city inflicted on me little actual misery. I had happy times as a kid, and I loved the great murky expanse of the James River, in which, or on which, swimming or sailing, I dwelled with such comfortable abandon that I felt it to be as fundamentally my habitat as a gull or a shad's. But I remained an alien in my birthplace, uncharmed and unattached. Would I have so easily fled Richmond, or Mobile, or Jackson, Tennessee, or Cheraw, South Carolina? Numberless factors shape one's needs and longings, and I may have been forced to escape any native environment. At any rate, a line I wrote in the diary I kept as a fourteen-year-old became a prophecy: *I've got to get the hell away from here.*

But throughout my boyhood, whatever my dissatisfactions with the city, I felt an acute consciousness of myself as a Southerner. I also acquired, by that osmotic process that most Southerners experience, a hyperintense sense of place. Despite its instability and its grimy atmosphere, Newport News was in Dixie; you would never really confuse it with Sandusky or Duluth. At a time when most urban areas, both north and south, were still predominantly white, Newport News was nearly forty percent black—or Negro, as we were permitted to say in those days—largely owing to the vast numbers of immigrants from the Southeastern farms who found jobs in the shipyard. Jim Crow reigned and segregation was as omnipresent as it is today in Johannesburg, though in those years, unlike the restive black South Africans now, the victims of Virginia apartheid were frozen in the weird time warp that had held them captive since the Civil War; they fitted, seemingly uncomplaining and precisely where they belonged—or where white people wanted them to belong—within the matrix of community life, in which the timeless status quo had smothered protest and rendered revolt inconceivable. I didn't get the intimate connection with Negroes that I might have had in the country or a small town. To my bemused and attentive eye, as a boy, Negroes were participants in a bewildering magic trick, appearing and disappearing at the whim of some prestidigitator, who caused them to throng the stage of the city by the thousands—especially at four o'clock, the shipyard quitting time—but who then made them vanish in a puff, so that at night the same main street would be occupied only by Caucasians, not a single black soul in sight; they had all been whisked away into their baleful ghetto beyond the C&O tracks where they were occupied, according to legend, with cutting each other up in Blood Fields, and where the only white persons present would be the merchant sailors paying visits to the seedy whorehouses along Warwick Avenue.

This vanishing act did indeed baffle me, so much so that any awareness of Negroes was honed to an exquisite receptivity not by their presence so much as by their absence. I was still quite young when I began to wonder at this absence. Why weren't they in school with me? Why didn't they belong to the Presbyterian church, like I did? Why weren't they in the movie theaters, at the baseball games?

Why were Florence, the cook, whom I was so fond of, and old William, who mowed the lawn and told me funny stories, finally such strangers, disappearing at night into a world of utter mystery? Because they were absent, even though constantly visible and present, Negroes exacted a powerful and curiously exotic hold on my boyhood; their lives, their peculiarity, their difference, their frustrating untouchability all fascinated me, and finally comprised a kind of obsession. I wasn't dumb: I knew that they had lives beyond the sweat of hard ill-paid labor and Saturday night mayhem and being whores, and I struggled in my way to get to know them. For one thing, I knew they led—many of them at least—a religious life, a life of incandescent faith. The presence in the city of two messianic figures, Elder Solomon Lightfoot Michaux and his arch-rival Bishop Grace—known as Daddy Grace—was testimony to that, and their competitive mass baptisms in Hampton Roads, thousands of the faithful being immersed in the briny waters while shouting songs of salvation, were spectacles I was drawn to, agitated and wide-eyed. I had a deep hunger to divine the nature of this spirituality, so alien to my pallid Presbyterianism, with its numbing Sunday school sessions and querulous hymns, its purple sabbath melancholy. There was a wild and forthright gladness in the religion of black people. Its music—the gospel sound and those spirituals, that gave voice to such depths of anguish and highs of almost manic ecstasy—moved me to inexpressible feelings, feelings I'd never had before and wouldn't experience again until, on a different but equally genuine level of response, I began to listen to Mozart and Bach.

Somehow I must have been aware that the key to my preoccupation with Negroes and their religion was slavery. Even so, I couldn't quite shake off the ambivalence toward them that was a product of my upbringing. Bigotry, foolish and fangless but real nonetheless, was essentially a part of my character, as it was for nearly all my contemporaries, and what little understanding I had of Negro history must have been colored by the prevailing platitudes. But at least I was groping for enlightenment. One of my first attempts at literary composition was a high-school theme called "Drusilla and Lucinda, Two Little Slave Girls." I recall almost nothing about this work. I'm sure it was as mawkish and absurd as the official state history texts which the Commonwealth of Virginia had prepared for its youngest citizens and whose rubrics concerning the transcendental sweetness of slave times I innocently accepted. (Consider the historical objectivity of the set of two volumes, one of which, for freshmen, had portrayed on its cover Robert E. Lee, while the other, for sophomores, has a photograph of Lee's horse Traveller, fixed in taxidermy's timeless paralysis and on display at Washington and Lee.) I've often wondered how such prejudice and propaganda didn't desensitize me to the much closer approximations of truth I found in history books when I was later contemplating my own work on slavery.

I have not overlooked the fact that the suffering my grandmother endured as a child was the grim though perhaps not unnatural consequence of a war that was fought over the very existence of slavery. Within certain sound moral standards she may be regarded as having been the pitiable victim of a struggle in which right prevailed. This idea hadn't really penetrated my consciousness either, as a boy. I recall how in 1937, the year before she died, I looked forward to our trips down to Little Washington. She was now nearly eighty-seven years old and partially paralyzed from a stroke, but her mind was still quick; she was a tiny little lady, so frail and light that my father carried her in his arms like a child. For me the pleasure and the excitement of the trip began when our car—a 1930 Oldsmobile my father won in a raffle—left the sooty urban bloat of Newport News behind, and we passed over the James River bridge into southside Virginia. A short distance beyond the end of the bridge began the fields of peanuts and cotton; they were doubtless the northernmost cotton fields in America and were symbolic to me of the forlornly beautiful, funky rural South into which we were penetrating, the South of pine forests and unpainted farm shacks, Bull Durham signs and coffee-brown sluggish streams winding through swamps, mule teams off in the distance and shabby little Negro churches in a stand of ancient oak trees, rattletrap Fords and tumbledown graveyards and a sense of universal poorness and sadness—the eternal Southern countryside. In Washington, my grandmother, bedridden now, always greeted us with the look of startled then expanding joy of one who had waited a long and anxious time for our visit.

After the Civil War she had lived a good, satisfying, philoprogenitive (she'd had eight children) life, though one beset by many knocks and adversities. When she married my grandfather, some years after his dashing career as a boy courier, he was ambitious for good old American success and in due course built up a thriving little business manufacturing chewing tobacco and snuff. Good old American catastrophe struck one year in the 1880s, however, when those original Southern robber barons, the rapacious Dukes, *père et fils*, founders of the American Tobacco Company—my father always called them "those piratical devils" and was sorely injured when I became a student at the university bearing their name—ran my grandfather out of business through some wicked monopolistic maneuver, one which, though perfectly legal in those freebooting days, left the family nearly destitute. My grandfather somehow recovered and made a moderately decent living thereafter as the proprietor and captain of a small steamship first used for hauling farm cargo to Norfolk and later taking passenger tours through Pamlico Sound. But my grandmother had had to live a domestic life of considerable hardship and, now widowed for many years, she could not quite throw off that burden of hardship, which showed in her tired eyes and brittle-looking work-worn hands, though her spirits were unquelled and chipper.

On one of those visits my mother came along, and I recall how her presence complicated matters, for she was a Northerner, born in western Pennsylvania. It was not until that trip, perhaps because I was getting a little older and more perceptive, that I realized the strained relations that must have always existed between the two women. My grandmother was a lady of bountiful nature and kindness, and it is difficult to believe that she was intentionally rude to my mother, who herself was amiable and outgoing and possessed a desire to please and who, I'm sure, made a strenuous effort to reach out to my grandmother, as if to say, I am of a different generation. The war is long over, let us bind up the old wounds. But try as she might to avoid it, and I'm sure she had tried, the remoteness my grandmother displayed, the chilliness, the hostility she felt not toward my mother herself but toward her Northernness, had in some way made itself all too evident; on the trip back to Virginia I heard my mother say to my father in a hurt, strained voice: "She has never really liked me, has she?" And despite my father's pained explanations, his denials, I think it may have been *then* that I understood how truly lacerating to my grandmother's spirit the war had been and how unexceptional it was that she could not eradicate from memory that appalling visitation with its rampaging footfalls and deafening yells of the Ohio marauders who destroyed in a day nearly all that she knew existed. How perfectly normal and human it had been to hoard up the injustice of those weeks when her belly shriveled into a knot, and when, soon after, she saw the only community she had known burned to cinders. A few others might have had the magnanimity to forget and pardon, but my grandmother apparently did not; it was a failing I always found easy to disregard.

She once told me in those last days, squeezing my hands, "Billy, always remember you're a Southerner." She would have greatly disapproved, I fear, the choice I made to live in the North. But if I had been able, in recent years, to reach her through the void, I may have had to tell her some truths she would have found disappointing. I would have to tell her that the North is not so bad a place to make a home, certainly in the bucolic region in which I dwell, where the people are at least as good-natured and as easygoing as Southerners, just as often displaying the generosity Southerners are famous for, and where the gently rolling landscape has the harmonious contours of the uplands of north Georgia or Alabama. I would tell her that it is much too cold in the winter where I live, and that the bland native cuisine is such that I long for the sumptuous Tidewater meals I remember; but one can fly away for the winter, and as for the cuisine—you can import almost anything edible from the South now, overnight mail, and gorge on Florida oysters and Carolina quail at home. I would tell her that our back roads have noisy rednecks and the ether teems with country music.

Sometimes I miss the South, but often I don't, since, when I view the region from afar, or when I make my frequent visits, it seems to resemble the North at its most shopping mall–ridden and architecturally berserk. Walker Percy, a writer for whom my esteem is unsurpassed, once spoke in an interview of the Connecticutization of the South, or parts of it, but this seemed to me an unnecessary disparagement of my adopted state, for if anyone shrinks, as I do, from the high-tech and runaway urban glut of Georgia's capital city, the idea of the Atlantaization of the modestly proportioned cities of Connecticut creates dread. It would seem to me that the dynamism of American society in the past few decades has allowed the development of a homogeneity in which it is very hard to regard either the ills or the excellences of life as being the peculiar property of one region or another. Such are the excellences I've seen in the South recently—side by side with certain atrocities, to be sure—that I could live there with the greatest happiness, were my transplantation to the North not so long-lived and complete.

Essentially my grandmother was right, and I have heeded her counsel: I've never forgotten that I am a Southerner. A mere decade from now her descendants will celebrate her 150th anniversary—a span of time of such magnitude that I am touched with awe that I was once so intimately bound up with her being. To remember her now as she was, fading and frail, in the realization that those hands I embraced—the skin like tissue, the flesh warm with life yet invaded by a dying chill—were hands that once braided the hair of a little black girl who was her property, were hands that scratched for food in the harsh Carolina earth in a war that separated her and the little black girl forever: the remembrance of those hands is alone enough for me to forge a lasting bond with our unfathomable past, and to prevent me from being anything but a Southerner, wherever I live.

[*The Sewanee Review*, Fall 1989]

THE HABIT

The Habit

THE LAMENTABLE HISTORY of the cigarette is that of a mortally corrupting addiction having been embraced by millions of people in the spirit of childlike innocence. It is a history which is also strikingly brief. Cigarettes began to be manufactured extensively around the turn of the century, but it was not until as recently as 1921 that cigarettes overtook chewing tobacco, as well as pipes and cigars, in per capita consumption, and the 1930s were well along before cigarette smoking became the accepted thing for ladies.

The popularity of cigarettes was inevitable and overwhelming. They were not offensive in close quarters, nor messy like pipes and cigars. They were easily portable. They did not look gross and unseemly in a lady's mouth. They were cheap to manufacture, and they were inhalable. Unlike the great majority of pipe and cigar smokers, whose pleasure is predominantly oral and contemplative, most cigarette smokers inhale deep into their lungs with bladelike, rhythmic savagery, inflicting upon themselves in miniature a particularly abrasive form of air pollution. Further, the very fact of inhalation seems to enhance the cigarette's addictive power. Unhappily, few suspected the consequences in terms of health until long after cigarette smoking had gained its colossal momentum. That this type of auto-contamination is a major cause of lung cancer—that it is also a prime causative factor in deaths from coronary artery disease, bronchitis, asthma, emphysema, among other afflictions—was established, and for the first time well publicized, only a decade ago. The effect this knowledge has had upon the public consciousness may be suggested by the fact that sales this year reached the galactic sum of one-half trillion cigarettes—

one hundred billion more than in 1953. There is something historically intimidating in the idea that cigarette smoking as a mass diversion and a raging increase in lung cancer have both come about during the lifetime of those who are now no more than fifty years old. It is the very *recentness* of the phenomenon which helps make it so shocking. The hard truth is that human beings have never in such a brief space of time, and in so grand and guileless a multitude, embraced a habit whose unwholesome effects not only would totally outweigh the meager satisfactions but would hasten the deaths of a large proportion of the people who indulged in it. Certainly (and there seems little doubt that the Surgeon General's report will make this clear) only nuclear fallout exceeds cigarette smoking in gravity as a public health problem.

For its lucid presentation of the medical evidence alone, *The Consumers Union Report on Smoking* would be a valuable document. "The conclusion is inescapable," the *Report* begins, "and even spokesmen for the cigarette industry rarely seek to escape it: we are living in the midst of a major lung cancer epidemic. This epidemic hit men first and hardest, but has affected women as well. It cannot be explained away by such factors as improved diagnosis. And there is reason to believe that the worst is yet to come." Yet despite this minatory beginning the tone throughout is one of caution and reasonableness, and the authors—who manage an accomplished prose style rare in such collective undertakings—marshal their facts with such efficiency and persuasion that it is hard to imagine anyone but a fool or a tobacco lobbyist denying the close association between smoking and lung cancer. Yet, of course, not only lung cancer. The *Report* quotes, for instance, data based on an extensive study of smokers and non-smokers among English physicians, where the death rate *from all causes* was found to be doubled among heavy cigarette smokers in the group of men past 65, and quadrupled in the group 35 to 44. And the *Report* adds, with the modest and constructive irony that makes the book, if not exactly a joy, then agreeable to read: "These death rates among smokers are perhaps the least controversial of all the findings to date. For with respect to any particular disease there is always the possibility, however remote, that mistaken diagnosis and other conceivable errors may cast doubt on the statistics. But death is easily diagnosed."

In the end, however, what makes the *Report*'s message supportable to those distracted souls among the millions of American smokers who may wish to kick the habit—or who, having kicked the habit, may wonder if it is not too late—is a kind of muted optimism. For all present evidence seems to indicate that the common cocktail party rationalization ("I've smoked too long to stop now, the damage is done") has no real basis in fact. In research carried out by the American Cancer Society, microscopic studies of the lung tissues of ex-smokers have shown a process in which precancerous cells are dying out instead of flourishing and reproducing as in the tissues of continuing smokers. Here the *Report* states, in regard to a carefully matched group composed in equal numbers of nonsmokers, ex-smokers and smokers: "Metaplastic cells with altered nuclei [i.e., precancerous cells] were found in 1.2 percent of the slides from the lungs of nonsmokers, as compared with 6.0 for ex-smokers—and *93.2 percent* for current smokers."

Certainly such evidence, combined with the fact that ex-smokers have a lung cancer death rate which ranges down to one fifth of that of smokers who continue to smoke, should be of the greatest practical interest to anyone who ponders whether it may be worthwhile abandoning what is, after all, a cheerless, grubby, fumbling addiction. (Only the passion of a convert could provoke these last words. The *Report* was an aid to my stopping a two-pack-a-day habit which commenced in early infancy. Of course, stopping smoking may be in itself a major problem, one of psychological complexity. For myself, after two or three days of great flaccidity of spirit, an aimless oral yearning, aching moments of hunger at the pit of the stomach, and an awful intermittent urge to burst into tears, the problem resolved itself, and in less than a week all craving vanished. Curiously, for the first time in my life, I developed a racking cough, but this, too, disappeared. A sense of smugness, a kind of fatness of soul, is the reward for such a struggle. The intensity of the addiction varies, however, and some people find the ordeal fearfully difficult, if not next to impossible. I do have an urgent suspicion, though, that the greatest barrier to a termination of the habit is the dread of some Faustian upheaval, when in fact that deprivation, while momentarily oppressive, is apt to prove not really cruel at all.)

But if the *Report* is splendidly effective as a caveat, it may be read for its sociological insights as well. Certainly the history of commerce has few instances of such shameful abdication of responsibility as that displayed by the cigarette industry when in 1952 the "health scare," as it is so winsomely known in the trade, brought about the crisis which will reach a head in this month's report by the Surgeon General. It seems clear that the industry, instead of trying to forestall the inevitable with its lies and evasions, might have acquitted itself with some honor had it made what the *Report* calls the only feasible choices: to have urged caution on smokers, to have given money to independent research organizations, to have avoided propaganda and controversy in favor of unbiased inquiry. At the very least the industry might have softpedaled or, indeed, silenced its pitch to young people. But panic and greed dominated the reaction, and during the decade since the smoking–lung cancer link was made public, the official position of the industry has been that, in the matter of lung cancer, the villain is any and everything *but* the cigarette. Even the American Cancer Society is in on the evil plot and, in the words of one industry spokesman, "relies almost wholly upon health scare propaganda to raise millions of dollars from a gullible public."

Meanwhile, $200 million was spent last year on cigarette ballyhoo, and during these last crucial ten years the annual advertising expenditure has increased 134 percent—a vast amount of it, of course, going to entice the very young. One million of these young people, according to the American Public Health Association, will die of smoking-induced lung cancer before they reach the age of seventy years. "Between the time a kid is eighteen and twenty-one, he's going to make the basic decision to smoke or not to smoke," says L. W. Bruff, advertising director of Liggett & Myers. "If he does decide to smoke, we want to get him." I have never met Mr. Bruff, but in my mind's eye I see him, poised like a cormorant above those doomed minnows, and I am amused by the refinement, the weight of conscience, the delicate interplay of intellectual and moral alternatives which go into the making of such a prodigious thought. As the report demonstrates, however, Mr. Bruff is only typical of the leaders of an industry which last year received a bounty of $7 billion from 63 million American smokers. Perhaps the tragic reality is that neither this estimable report nor that of the Surgeon General can measurably affect, much less really change, such awesome figures.

[*New York Review of Books*, December 26, 1963]

This piece about smoking had a singular effect on a number of people of my acquaintance. Almost more than anything I have written, it demonstrated the immediate way in which an opinion, if strongly enough expressed, can have practical results. As soon as they had read the piece, a large group of my friends, plainly gripped by anxiety, quickly stopped smoking. This included—aside from my three-pack-a-day brother-in-law—Robert Brustein, John Hollander, Peter Matthiessen, Jason Epstein and Norman Podhoretz— representative members of the country's intellectual community who are still nonsmokers and, at this writing, alive and well.

FOREBEARS

"O Lost!" Etc.

T HE SHADE of Thomas Wolfe must be acutely disturbed to find that his earthly stock has sunk so low. All artists want fame, glory, immortality, yet few were so frankly bent on these things as Wolfe was, and no writer—despite his agonizing self-doubts— seemed so confident that they lay within his grasp. The unabashed desire for perpetuity moves in a rhythmic, reappearing theme through all of his works. In a typically boisterous apostrophe to the power of booze in *Of Time and the River* he chants:

> You came to us with music, poetry, and wild joy when we were twenty, when we reeled home at night through the old moon-whitened streets of Boston and heard our friend, our com- rade, and our dead companion, shout through the silence of the moonwhite square: "You are a poet and the world is yours." . . . We turned our eyes then to the moon-drunk skies of Boston, knowing only that we were young, and drunk, and twenty, and that the power of mighty poetry was within us, and the glory of the great earth lay before us—because we were young and drunk and twenty, and could never die!

But poor Tom Wolfe if not dead is currently moribund, and the matter of his resuscitation is certainly in doubt. The young, one is told, being gland- and eyeball-oriented, read very little of anything anymore, and if they do it is likely to be Burroughs or Beckett or Genet or a few of the bards of black humor or camp pornography. Of the older writers, Hemingway and Fitzgerald are still read, but Wolfe seldom. When the literary temper of a generation is occult, claustrophobic, doom-ridden, and the qualified snigger is its char- acteristic psychic response, no writer could be so queer as the shambling, celebratory hulk of Thomas Wolfe, with his square's tragic sense and his bedazzled young man's vision of the glory of the world. What a comedown! In Europe, with the possible exception of Germany, he is not very well known. No, the reputation of Wolfe is in very bad shape; I suppose it was inevitable that, a short time ago, when I asked a college English major what he thought of the work of Thomas (not Tom) Wolfe he actually *did* reply seriously, "You mean the Tangerine Streamlined Whatever-it's-called guy?"

Yet it would be hard to exaggerate the overwhelming effect that reading Wolfe had upon so many of us who were coming of age during or just after World War II. I think his influence may have been especially powerful upon those who, like myself, had been reared, as Wolfe had, in a small Southern town or city, and who in addition had suffered a rather mediocre secondary education, with scant reading of any kind. To a boy who had read only a bad translation of *Les Misérables* and *The Call of the Wild* and *Men Against the Sea* and *The Grapes of Wrath* (which one had read at fourteen for the racy dialogue and the "sensational" episodes), the sudden exposure to a book like *Look Homeward, Angel*, with its lyrical torrent and raw, ingenuous feeling, its precise and often exquisite rendition of place and mood, its buoyant humor and the vitality of its characters and, above all, the sense of youthful ache and promise and hunger and ecstasy which so corresponded to that of its eighteen-year-old reader—to experience such a book as this, at exactly the right moment in time and space, was for many young people like being born again into a world as fresh and wondrous as that seen through the eyes of Adam. Needless to say, youth itself was largely responsible for this feverish empathy, and there will be reservations in a moment in regard to the effect of a later rereading of Wolfe; nonetheless, a man who can elicit such reactions from a reader at whatever age is a force to be reckoned with, so I feel nothing but a kind of gratitude when I consider how I succumbed to the rough unchanneled force of Wolfe as one does to the ocean waves.

Among other things, he was the first prose writer to bring a sense of America as a glorious abstraction—a vast and brooding continent whose untold bounties were waiting every young man's discovery—and his endless catalogues and lyric invocations of the land's physical sights and sounds and splendors (a sumptuous description of the Boston waterfront, for instance, where "the delicate and subtle air of spring touches all these odors with a new and delicious vitality; it draws the tar out of the pavements also, and it draws slowly, subtly, from ancient warehouses, the compacted perfumes of eighty years: the sweet thin piney scents of packing boxes, the glutinous composts of half a century, that have thickly stained old warehouse plankings, the smells of twine, tar, turpentine and hemp, and of thick molasses, ginseng, pungent vines and roots and old piled sacking . . . and particularly the smell of meat, of frozen beeves, slick porks, and veals, of brains and livers and kidneys, of haunch, paunch and jowl . . .") seemed to me anything but prolix or tedious, far from it; rather it was as if for the first time my whole being had been thrown open to the sheer *tactile* and *sensory* vividness of the American scene through which, until then, I had been walking numb and blind, and it caused me a thrill of discovery that was quite unutterable. It mattered little to me that sometimes Wolfe went on for page after windy page about nothing, or with the most callow of emotions: I was callow myself, and was undaunted by even his most inane repetitions. It meant nothing to me that some astonishingly exact and poignant rendition of a mood or remembrance might be followed by a thick suet of nearly impenetrable digressions; I gobbled it all up, forsaking my classes, hurting my eyes, and digesting the entire large Wolfe *oeuvre*—the four massive novels, plus the short stories and novellas, *The Story of a Novel*, the many letters and scraps and fragments, and the several plays, even then practically unreadable—in something less than two weeks, emerging from the incredible encounter pounds lighter, and with a buoyant serenity of one whose life has been forever altered.

I think it must have been at approximately this moment that I resolved myself to become a writer. I was at college in North Carolina at the time; it was October, Wolfe's natal, favorite, most passionately remembered month, and the brisk autumnal air was now touched, for the first time in *my* life, with the very fragrance and the light that Wolfe's grand hymn to the season had evoked:

October has come again—has come again. . . . The ripe, the golden month has come again, and in Virginia the chinkapins are falling. Frost sharps the middle music of the seasons, and all things living on the earth turn home again . . . The bee bores to the belly of the yellowed grape, the fly gets old and fat and blue, he buzzes loud, crawls slow, creeps heavily to death, the sun goes down in blood and pollen across the bronzed and mown fields of old October . . . Come to us, Father, while the winds howl in the darkness, for October has come again bringing with it huge prophecies of death and life and the great cargo of the men who will return . . .

With words like this still vivid in my brain, I gazed at the transmuted tobacco-hazed streets of Durham, quite beside myself with wonder, and only the appearance of a sudden, unseasonable snowstorm frustrated my immediate departure—together with a friend, similarly smitten—for Asheville, over two hundred miles away, where we had intended to place flowers on the writer's grave.

Now thirty years after Wolfe's death, the appearance of Andrew Turnbull's biography marks an excellent occasion to try to put the man and his work in perspective. Turnbull's work is a first-rate study, and not the least of its many worthy qualities is its sense of proportion. Too many biographies—especially of literary figures— tend to be overly fleshed out and are cursed with logorrhea, so that the illustrious subject himself becomes obliterated behind a shower of menus, train tickets, opera programs, itineraries and dull mash notes from lovelorn girls. I could have done without so many f the last item in this present volume—from Wolfe's paramour Anne Bernstein who, though by no means a girl, often fell to gushing at inordinate length; but this is a small complaint, since throughout the book Turnbull generally maintains a congenial pace and supplies us with just the proper amount of detail. One of the surprises of the biography is the way in which it manages to be fresh and informative about a person who was probably the most narrowly autobiographical writer who ever lived. The very idea of a life of Thomas Wolfe is enough to invoke dismay if not gentle ridicule, since our first reaction is, "But why? Everything he did and saw is in his books." Yet Turnbull, clearly with some calculation, has expertly uncovered certain facts having to do with Wolfe's life which, if not really crucial, are fascinating just *because* we realize that we did not know them before. The actual financial situation of Wolfe's family in Asheville, for example, is interesting, since the impression one gets of the deafening tribe of Gants in *Look Homeward, Angel* is that of a down-at-the-heel, lower-middle-class clan which may not have been destitute but which always had a hard time of it making ends meet. The truth of the matter, as Turnbull points out, is that by Asheville standards the Wolfes were literally affluent, belonging to the "top two percent economically." Likewise it turns out that Wolfe had a touch of the sybarite in him; as an instructor at New York University he chose to live by himself in lodgings that for the time must have been very expensive, rather than share quarters with several others as practically all of the instructors did. Such details would be of little interest, of course, were they not at variance with the portraits of Eugene Gant–George Webber, whose careers in the novels are considerably more penurious, egalitarian and grubby.

Wolfe was an exasperating man, a warm companion with a rich sense of humor and touching generosity of spirit and, alternately, a bastard of truly monumental dimensions, and it is a tribute to the detachment with which Mr. Turnbull has fashioned his biography that the good Wolfe and the bad Wolfe, seen upon separate occasions, begin to blend together so that what emerges (as in the best of biographies) is a man—in this case a man more complex and driven even than is usual among those of his calling: obsessively solitary yet craving companionship, proud and aloof but at the same time almost childishly dependent, open-handed yet suspicious, arrogant, sweet-hearted, hypersensitive, swinishly callous, gentle—every writer, that is, but magnified. In his mid-twenties on board a ship returning from Europe, Wolfe met and fell in love with Aline Bernstein, a rich and well-known New York stage designer who was eighteen years older than he was. In the ensuing affair, which was bizarre and tumultuous to say the least, Mrs. Bernstein quite clearly represented a mother figure, an image of the Eliza Gant from whom, in his first two novels, Tom-Eugene is constantly fleeing as from a Fury, and, with cyclic regularity, returning home to in helpless and sullen devotion. (Julia Wolfe nursed her son until he was three and a half and cut off Tom's beautiful ringlets at nine only after he had picked up lice from a neighbor. How Wolfe escaped being a homosexual is a mystery, but no one has ever made that charge.) The same ambivalent feelings he had toward his mother he expressed in his relations with Aline, who, though extremely pretentious and rather silly, did not deserve the treatment she suffered at his hands, which was largely abominable. He was of course capable of great tenderness and it is obvious that they had many happy moments together, but one cannot help feeling anything but rue for the plight of the poor woman, who had to be subjected to interminable grillings by him about her former lovers and who, when circumstances forced them apart, still was made to endure a barrage of letters in which in the most irrational and cruel terms he accused her of betrayal and unfaithfulness. He also shouted at her that she smelled like goose grease, adding the attractive observation that "all Jews smell like goose grease." It was a hopeless situation, and although it makes for grim reading, the section on Wolfe's stormy time with Aline is one of the most illuminating in the book, revealing as it does so much of the man's puerile inability to form any real attachment to anyone, especially a woman—a shallowness of emotional response, on a certain level at least, which caused him to be in perpetual flight and which may be a key to both his failings and his strengths as a writer.

There was also, naturally, his editor Maxwell Perkins—still one more relationship filled with *Sturm und Drang* and, on the part of Wolfe, impositions and demands on another's time and energy so total as to be positively hair-raising. Obviously Perkins was a very fine gentleman, but that a broad streak of masochism ran through his nature there can also be no doubt; only a man born to enjoy terrible suffering could have absorbed the pure fact of daily, committed *involvement* which Wolfe's tyrannically dependent personality imposed. It was of course untrue, as had been hinted during Wolfe's years at Scribner's, that Perkins *wrote* any part of Wolfe's books but certainly he was instrumental in putting them together—maybe not quite as instrumental as Bernard De Voto implied in his famous review of *The Story of a Novel* but a thoroughly dominating force nonetheless. There is no other way that we can interpret the hilarious statement which Turnbull—perhaps with irony, perhaps not—makes in a section on the finishing of *Of Time and the River*: "Early in December Perkins summoned Wolfe to his office and told him the book was done. Wolfe was amazed." Yet if it is true that Wolfe wrote the words of the books and if it is also true, as someone said, that the trouble with Wolfe was that he put all of his gigantic struggle into his *work* and not his *art*—a nice distinction—it does look as if De Voto might not have been too far off the mark, after all, in asserting that Perkins caused much of the "art" that exists in the sprawling work of Thomas Wolfe. Which is to say a semblance, at least, of form. And it is the lack too often of an organic form—a form arising from the same drives and tensions that inspired the work in the beginning—which now appears to be one of Wolfe's largest failings and is the one that most seriously threatens to undermine his stature as a major writer. The awful contradiction in his books between this formlessness and those tremendous moments which still seem so touched with grandeur as to be imperishable is unsettling beyond words.

Rereading Wolfe is like visiting again a cherished landscape or town of bygone years where one is simultaneously moved that much could remain so appealingly the same, and wonderstruck that one could ever have thought that such-and-such a corner or this or that view had any charm at all. It is not really that Wolfe is dated (I mean the fact of being dated as having to do with basically insincere postures and attitudes: already a lot of Hemingway is dated in a way Wolfe could never be); it is rather that when we now begin to realize how unpulled-together Wolfe's work really is—that same shapelessness that mattered so little to us when we were younger—and how this shapelessness causes or at least allows for a lack of inner dramatic tension, without which no writer, not even Proust, can engage our mature attention for long, we see that he is simply telling us, often rather badly, things we no longer care about knowing or need to know. So much that once seemed grand and authoritative now comes off as merely obtrusive, strenuously willed, and superfluous. Which of course makes it all the more disturbing that in the midst of this chaotically verbose and sprawling world there stand out here and there truly remarkable edifices of imaginative cohesion.

Wolfe's first novel, *Look Homeward, Angel*, withstands the rigors of time most successfully and remains his best book, taken as a whole. Here the powers of mind and heart most smoothly find their confluence, while a sense of place (mainly Altamont, or Asheville) and time (a boy's life between infancy and the beginning of adulthood) lend to the book a genuine unity that Wolfe never recaptured in his later works. Flaws now appear, however. A recent rereading of the book caused me to wince from time to time in a way that I cannot recall having done during my first reading at eighteen. Wolfe at that point was deeply under the power of Joyce (whom Wolfe, incidentally, encountered years later on a tour of Belgium, Turnbull relates in an engaging episode, but who so awed him that he was afraid to speak to the great Irishman) and if the influence of *Ulysses* can be discerned in the book's many strengths it can also be seen in its gaucheries. An otherwise vivid passage like the following, for example (and there are many such in the book), is diminished rather than reinforced by the culminating Joyce-like allusion:

> Colonel Pettigrew was wrapped to his waist in a heavy rug, his shoulders were covered with a gray Confederate cape. He bent forward, leaning his old weight upon a heavy polished stick, which his freckled hands gripped upon the silver knob. Muttering, his proud powerful old head turned shakily from side to side, darting fierce splintered glances at the drifting crowd. He was a very parfit gentil knight.

But *Look Homeward, Angel* can be forgiven such lapses precisely because it is a youthful book, as impressive for its sheer lyricism and hymnal celebration of youth and life as is the Mendelssohn Violin Concerto, from which we do not expect profundities, either. In addition, the novel is quite extraordinary *alive*—alive in the vitality of its words (Wolfe wrote many bad sentences but *never* a dead one), in its splendid evocation of small-town sights and sounds and smells, and above all and most importantly, in the characters that spring out fully fleshed and breathing from the pages. The figures of W. O. and Eliza Gant are as infuriatingly garrulous and convincing now as when I first made their acquaintance, and the death of the tragic older brother Ben is fully as moving for the simple reason that Wolfe has made me believe in his existence. With all of its top-heaviness and the juvenile extravagances that occasionally mar the surface of the narrative, *Look Homeward, Angel* seems likely to stand as long as any novel will as a record of early-twentieth-century provincial American life.

It is when we run into *Of Time and the River* and its elephantine successors, *The Web and the Rock* and *You Can't Go Home Again*, that the real trouble begins. One of the crucial struggles that any writer of significance has had to endure is his involvement in the search for a meaningful theme, and Wolfe was no exception. The evidence is that Wolfe, though superbly gifted at imaginative projection, was practically incapable of extended dramatic invention, his creative process being akin to the settling into motion of some marvelous mnemonic tape recorder deep within his cerebrum, from which he unspooled reel after reel of the murmurous, living past. Such a technique served him beautifully in *Look Homeward, Angel*, unified as it was in time and space, and from both of which it derived its dramatic tension; but in the later works as Tom-Eugene-George moved into other environments—the ambience of Harvard and New York and, later, of Europe—the theme which at first had been so fresh and compelling lost its wings and the narrator became a solipsistic groundling. Certainly the last three books are still well worth reading; there is still the powerful, inexorable rush of language, a Niagara of words astonishing simply by virtue of its primal energy; many of the great set pieces hold up with their original force: old Gant's death, the *Oktoberfest* sequence in Munich, the apartment-house fire in New York, the portraits of Eugene's Uncle Bascom, Foxhall Edwards, the drunken Dr. McGuire—there are many more. These scenes and characterizations would alone guarantee Wolfe a kind of permanence, even if one must sift through a lot of detritus to find them. But there is so much now that palls and irritates. That furrow-browed, earnest sense of discovery in which the reader participates willingly in *Look Homeward, Angel* loses a great deal of its vivacity when the same protagonist has begun to pass into adulthood. In *Of Time and the River,* for example, when Eugene has become a student at Harvard, we are introduced to a young student named Francis Starwick:

> He spoke in a strange and rather disturbing tone, the pitch and timbre of which it would be almost impossible to define, but which would haunt one who had heard it forever after. His voice was neither very high nor low, it was a man's voice and yet one felt it might also have been a woman's; but there was nothing at all effeminate about it. It was simply a strange voice compared to most American voices, which are rasping, nasal, brutally coarse or metallic. Starwick's voice had a disturbing lurking resonance, an exotic, sensuous and almost voluptuous quality. Moreover, the peculiar mannered affectation of his speech was so studied that it hardly escaped extravagance. If it had not been for the dignity, grace and intelligence of his person, the affectation of his speech might have been ridiculous. As it was, the other youth felt the moment's swift resentment and hostility that is instinctive with the American when he thinks someone is speaking in an affected manner.

In the first place, his voice wouldn't "haunt one who had heard it forever after." This exaggerated sensibility, this clubfooted, gawky boy's style, becomes increasingly apparent throughout all of Wolfe's later work, in which the author-protagonist, now out in the world of Northern sophisticates, falls unconsciously into the role of the suspicious young hick from Buncombe County, North Carolina. In the passage just quoted the reader, Starwick—indeed, everyone but Eugene Gant—is aware that Starwick is a homosexual, but these labored and sophomoric observations have so begun to dominate Wolfe's point of view that much later on in the book, when Starwick's homosexuality *is* revealed, Eugene's chagrin over that belated knowledge fills the reader with murderous exasperation. The same passage illustrates another trait which crops up increasingly in the later books, and that is a tendency to generalize promiscuously about places and things which demand, if anything, narrow and delicate particularization—especially about a place as various and as chaotically complex as America. The part about voices, for instance. Most American voices, though sometimes unpleasant, are not generally "rasping, nasal, brutally coarse or metallic"; forty or fifty million soft Southern voices alone, including presumably Wolfe's, are—whatever else—the antithesis of all those careless adjectives. Nor is it at all accurate to proclaim either that "the American"—presumably meaning all Americans—feels resentment and hostility at affected speech or that the reaction is peculiarly American. Many Americans are simply tickled or amused by such speech, while at the same time it is surely true that if resentment and hostility are felt, they can be felt by the French over French affectations as well. Wolfe's writing is filled with such silly hyperbole. Similarly, a statement such as "we are so lost, so naked, and so lonely in America"—a refrain that reappears over and over again in Wolfe's work—seems to me the worst sort of empty rant, all the more so because Wolfe himself surely knew better, knew that lostness, nakedness, loneliness are not American but part of the whole human condition.

It is sad that so much disappoints on a rereading of Wolfe, sad that the "magic and the singing and the gold" which he celebrated so passionately seem now, within his multitudinous pages, to possess a lackluster quality to which the middle-aging heart can no longer respond. It is especially sad because we can now see (possibly because of the very contrast with all that is so prolix and adolescent and unfelt and labored) that at his best Wolfe was capable of those epiphanies that only writers of a very high order have ever achieved. I am thinking particularly of the death of W. O. Gant, in *Of Time and the River*, where the cancer-ridden old man lies in bed, falling in and out of a coma as he drowses over the landscape of his youth in Pennsylvania.

Towards one o'clock that night Gant fell asleep and dreamed that he was walking down the road that led to Spangler's Run. . . .

It was a fine morning in early May and everything was sweet and green and as familiar as it had always been. The graveyard was carpeted with thick green grass, and all around the graveyard and the church there was the incomparable green velvet of young wheat. And the thought came back to Gant, as it had come to him a thousand times, that the wheat around the graveyard looked greener and richer than any other wheat he had ever seen. And beside him on his right were the great fields of the Schaefer farm, some richly carpeted with young wheat, and some ploughed, showing great bronze-red strips of fertile nobly swelling earth. And behind him on the great swell of the land, and commanding that sweet and casual scene with the majesty of its incomparable day was Jacob Schaefer's great red barn and to the right the neat brick house with the white trimming of its windows, the white picket fence, the green yard with its rich tapestry of flowers and lilac bushes and the massed leafy spread of its big maple trees. And behind the house the hill rose, and all its woods were just greening into May, still smoky, tender and unfledged, gold-yellow with the magic of young green. And before the woods began there was the apple orchard halfway up the hill; the trees were heavy with the blossoms and stood there in all their dense still bloom incredible.

And from the greening trees the bird-song rose, the grass was thick with the dense gold glory of the dandelions, and all about him were a thousand magic things that came and went and never could be captured.

At this point Gant in his dream encounters one of the neighbors, a half-wit named Willy Spangler, and he stops and they chat together for a moment. Gant gives Willy a plug of chewing tobacco, then he turns to continue his walk when Willy says anxiously:

"Are ye comin' back, Oll? Will ye be comin' back real soon?"

And Gant, feeling a strange and nameless sorrow, answered:

"I don't know, Willy"—for suddenly he saw that he might never come this way again.

But Willy, still happy, foolish, and contented, had turned and galloped away toward the house, flinging his arms out and shouting as he went:

"I'll be waitin' fer ye. I'll be waitin' fer ye, Oll."

And Gant went on then, down the road, and there was a nameless sorrow in him that he could not understand, and some of the brightness had gone out of the day.

When he got to the mill, he turned left along the road that went down by Spangler's Run, crossed by the bridge below, and turned from the road into the woodpath on the other side. A child was standing in the path, and turned and went on ahead of him. In the wood the sunlight made swarming moths of light across the path, and through the leafy tangle of the trees: the sunlight kept shifting and swarming on the child's gold hair, and all around him were the sudden noises of the wood, the stir, the rustle, and the bullet thrum of wings, the cool broken sound of hidden water.

The wood got denser, darker as he went on and coming to a place where the path split away into two forks, Gant stopped, and turning to the child said, "Which one shall I take?" And the child did not answer him.

But someone was there in the wood before him. He heard footsteps on the path, and saw a footprint in the earth, and turning took the path where the footprint was, and where it seemed he could hear someone walking.

And then, with the bridgeless instancy of dreams it seemed to him that all of the bright green-gold around him in the wood grew dark and somber, the path grew darker, and suddenly he was walking in a strange and gloomy forest, haunted by the brown and tragic light of dreams. The forest shapes of great trees rose around him, he could hear no bird-song now, even his own feet on the path were soundless, but he always thought he heard the sound of someone walking in the wood before him. He stopped and listened: the steps were muffled, softly thunderous, they seemed so near that he thought that he must catch up with the one he followed in another second, and then they seemed immensely far away, receding in the dark mystery of that gloomy wood. And again he stopped and listened, the footsteps faded, vanished, he shouted, no one answered. And suddenly he knew that he had taken the wrong path, that he was lost. And in his heart there was an immense and quiet sadness, and the dark light of the enormous wood was all around him; no birds sang.

After this passage Gant awakes suddenly to find himself gazing into the eyes of his wife, Eliza, who is maintaining vigil at his bedside. There follows then a long colloquy between the dying man and the woman (who has never called him anything but "Mr. Gant")—a disconnected, faltering, fragmented murmuration of words, profoundly moving, in which they re-experience all the old sorrows and failures of the tormented, bitter, yet somehow triumphant life they have lived together for forty years. At last—

He was silent again, and presently, his breath coming some-what hoarse and labored, he cleared his throat, and put one hand up to his throat, as if to relieve himself of some impediment.

Eliza looked at him with troubled eyes and said:

"What's the matter, Mr. Gant? There's nothing hurtin' you?"

"No," he said. "Just something in my throat. Could I have some water?"

"Why, yes, sir! That's the very thing!" She got up hastily, and looking about in a somewhat confused manner, saw behind her a pitcher of water and a glass upon his old walnut bureau, and saying, "This very minute, sir!" started across the room.

And at the same moment, Gant was aware that someone had entered the house, was coming towards him through the hall, would soon be with him. Turning his head towards the door he was conscious of something approaching with the speed of light, the instancy of thought, and at that moment he was filled with a sense of inexpressible joy, a feeling of triumph and security he had never known. Something immensely bright and beautiful was converging in a flare of light, and at that instant, the whole room blurred around him, his sight was fixed upon that focal image in the door, and suddenly the child was standing there and looking towards him.

And even as he started from his pillows, and tried to call his wife he felt something thick and heavy in his throat that would not let him speak. He tried to call to her again but no sound came, then something wet and warm began to flow out of his mouth and nostrils, he lifted his hands up to his throat, the warm wet blood came pouring out across his fingers; he saw it and felt joy.

For now the child—or someone in the house—was speaking, calling to him; he heard great footsteps, soft but thunderous, imminent, yet immensely far, a voice well-known, never heard before. He called to it, and then it seemed to answer him; he called to it with faith and joy to give him rescue, strength and life, and it answered him and told him that all the error, old age, pain, and grief of life was nothing but an evil dream; that he who had been lost was found again, that his youth would be restored to him and that he would never die, and that he would find again the path he had not taken long ago in a dark wood.

And the child still smiled at him from the dark door; the great steps, soft and powerful, came ever closer, and as the instant imminent approach of the last meeting came intolerably near, he cried out through the lake of jetting blood, "Here, Father, here!" and a strong voice answered him, "My son!"

At that instant he was torn by a rending cough, something was wrenched loose in him, the death gasp rattled through his blood, and a mass of greenish matter foamed out through his lips. Then the world was blotted out, a blind black fog swam up and closed above his head, someone seized him, he was held, supported in two arms, he heard someone's voice saying in a low tone of terror and pity, "Mr. Gant! Mr. Gant! Oh, poor man, poor man! He's gone!" And his brain faded into night. Even before she lowered him back upon the pillows, she knew that he was dead.

Wolfe would have to be cherished if only for the power he exerted upon a whole generation. But even if this were not enough, the clear glimpses he had at certain moments of man as a strange, suffering animal alone beneath the blazing and indifferent stars would suffice to earn him honor, and a flawed but undeniable greatness.

[*Harper's*, April 1968]

An Elegy for
F. Scott Fitzgerald

IT IS PERHAPS INEVITABLE that nearly all very good writers seem to be able to inspire the most vehement personal reactions. They might be quite dead but their spirits remain somehow immortally fleshed, and we are capable of talking about them as we talk about devoted friends, or about a despised neighbor who has just passed out of earshot. In certain cases it amounts to a type of bewitchment. Thus I heard only a short time ago a conservative, poetasting lawyer say that as much as he admired the work of Dylan Thomas, he would never allow the philandering rascal in his house.

Of course, the passions such writers arouse are especially strong when the writer—unlike, say, William Faulkner, who sedulously cultivated the private life—is F. Scott Fitzgerald, whose life has fallen so under the dominion of the legend that this occasionally tends to obscure the fact that he possessed, at his best, an original and beautiful talent. Nonetheless, it is the mythic aspects of a writer's life that generate all the gossip, the ugly resentment along with the tender sentiments, and Fitzgerald has by now had a disproportionate share of both. Here, for instance, is Katherine Anne Porter, in a recent *Paris Review* interview: "Even now when I think of the twenties and the legend that has grown up about them, I think it was a horrible time: shallow and trivial . . . The remarkable thing is that anybody survived in such an atmosphere—in the place where they could call F. Scott Fitzgerald a great writer! . . . I couldn't read him then and I can't read him now . . . Not only didn't I like his writing, but I didn't like the people he wrote about. I thought they weren't worth thinking about." One senses a sort of gratuitous outrage here which has less to do with Fitzgerald's talent than with the Fitzgerald myth. It is hard to believe that Miss Porter, who is such an estimable writer herself, is really so down on Fitzgerald's "writing"; one feels rather that she simply doesn't want him in her house. But if the Fitzgerald myth can elicit calumny, it can also inspire quivering obeisance, such as this from Professor Arthur Mizener, a professional Fitzgeraldian, who is reduced to a kind of stammer: "Fitzgerald's greatest value for us is his almost eponymous character, the way his life and his work taken together represent what in the very depths of our nature we are—we Americans, anyhow, and—with some variations—perhaps most men of the western world." Spoken like a born undertaker.

Yet, since in Fitzgerald's case the myth and the work *are* indissolubly mingled, what is so fascinating about this large collection of letters, edited by Andrew Turnbull, is that in a sense it allows the writer to explicate his own legend. So revealing are these letters —to Zelda and his daughter, Scottie, to Edmund Wilson and Hemingway and Maxwell Perkins and his friends Gerald and Sara Murphy, among others—that one might feel that nothing further needs to be said about the writer's life. As for the book itself, one could question, as Malcolm Cowley has already done, Mr. Turnbull's arrangement—grouping the letters according to the person they are written to rather than running them chronologically and thus allowing them to tell their own story—but this is a small matter. The book remains a fascinating one.

From the very beginning there is a pervasive feeling of honesty in Fitzgerald's letters, and though some of the earliest correspondence contains a touch of collegiate fakery, of the innocuous kind, there is very little posturing. Unlike the letters of those writers who have written with a sense of posterity mooning at their elbow (Thomas Wolfe is a good example), Fitzgerald's were composed with a spontaneity that must have been one of the most fetching aspects of his charm as a person. In fact, a writer with less spontaneity and more guile would never have written words like these, in a letter of 1920, to his agent, Harold Ober: "Enclosed is a new version of 'Barbara,' called 'Bernice Bobs Her Hair,' to distinguish it from Mary Rinehart's 'Bab' stories in the *Post*. I think I've managed to inject a snappy climax into it." Such an utterance I think helps explain why these early letters are the least satisfying and least interesting of the collection. For though, to be sure, this was the decade of the matchless *Gatsby* and several of the finest stories —"Absolution," "The Rich Boy," "The Baby Party"—it was also the time of an astonishing amount of pure waste, when the hectic, frazzled and, above all, expensive life the Fitzgeralds were leading resulted in the production of a great deal of sloppy and hastily written fiction. As a result, these early letters, strewn with such complaints as "If I don't in some way get $650.00 in the bank by Wednesday morning I'll have to pawn the furniture" are often tedious; we are, after all, witnessing not the struggle of a desperate pauper, a Mozart or a Franz Schubert, but that of a spoiled young writer living far beyond his means, and much of Fitzgerald's belly-aching is cause for legitimate exasperation. Even so, even when Fitzgerald has put us out of sorts with his clamorous preoccupation with his "standard of living," when his silly conceit and his youthful pomposity about his not-very-good early work has begun to aggravate us the most, the artist in Fitzgerald, the conscientious and coolly disciplined craftsman suddenly comes through, and we find him writing to Perkins in 1924 about the nearly finished *Gatsby*: "In my new novel I'm thrown directly on purely creative work—not trashy imaginings as in my stories but the sustained imagination of a sincere yet radiant world. So I tread slowly and carefully and at times in considerable distress. This book will be a consciously artistic achievement." Oppressively superficial as he may have appeared during the twenties—and may have been in important respects—he never abandoned, even then, this stony, saving honesty and self-awareness.

In his biography of Fitzgerald, Turnbull quotes Rebecca West as saying: "I knew Zelda was very clever but from the first moment I saw her I knew she was mad." She was speaking of the year 1923, three years after Zelda married Fitzgerald. By 1930, when Zelda was a patient in a Swiss sanitarium, the "gay parade," as Fitzgerald called the decade, was over, and the *allegro vivace* which had dominated the mood of his life dwindled and died, replaced by something at first only elusively somber, then steeped in an unutterable melancholy: it was a tone which from then on never disappeared. By 1932, living in Baltimore and slipping slowly into alcoholism (though still toiling away at *Tender is the Night*), Fitzgerald is writing to Perkins: "Five years have rolled away from me and I can't decide exactly who I am, if anyone." Throughout these letters of the early and mid-thirties there are marvelous flashes of wit and warmth, his intense concern for books, for literature, never flags—he seems to have read everything; no writer ever had such appreciative and generous interest in his contemporaries, such an acute, unjealous response to excellence, along with a fine nose for a fraud—but the sense of melancholy, of encroaching danger, shadows over these pages like a bleak, wintry afternoon. (Again to Perkins, 1934: "The mood of terrible depression and despair is not going to become a characteristic and I am ashamed and felt very yellow about it afterward. But to deny that such moods come increasingly would be futile.") Since her apparent recovery in Switzerland, Zelda has had two breakdowns. *Tender is the Night* appears and is a critical and financial failure. Hemingway, whom he admires almost to the point of worship, turns on him, cruelly lampooning him in *The Snows of Kilimanjaro* with the famous episode about "the very rich," calling him "poor Scott Fitzgerald." ("Dear Ernest," he replies in a letter, "please lay off me in print." Then he adds: "It's a fine story—one of your best." Fitzgerald's magnanimity was truly incalculable. Although much later, to Perkins, he writes bitterly of this betrayal, saying: "Once I believed in friendship, believed I *could* make people happy and it was more fun than anything. Now even that seems like a vaudevillian's cheap dream of heaven, a vast minstrel show in which one is the perpetual Bones.") And as Fitzgerald fights against his drinking, and frets and broods, the sense of oncoming doom grows and grows. One is reminded of the harrowing lines from Job: *I was not in safety, neither had I rest, neither was I quiet; yet trouble came.*

And so it comes. In Turnbull's biography there is a terrible chapter describing those months that must have been the abyss of Fitzgerald's career. The time is 1936 and the place is Asheville, where Fitzgerald—now nearly broke and in debt, ill of tuberculosis, a frail alcoholic masochist smothering in the warm love of his own failure—has set up residence in order to be near the sanitarium to which Zelda has been committed. Zelda is at this point desperately off; she has taken to carrying a Bible, and occasionally, garbed in the superannuated flapper's clothing of the twenties, she kneels in public to pray. When the haggard couple arrives one evening to call on neighbors, Zelda is bearing with her a bunch of water lilies she has gathered on the way, and she reminds one guest of Ophelia; later, on the terrace, Fitzgerald leads her to a stone wall and proclaims, "You're the fairy princess and I'm the prince," and for several minutes they ring changes on this sentiment—Zelda wide-eyed, still lovely, and utterly mad, Fitzgerald gazing at her trans-figured with sorrow. The entire desolating passage—perhaps because of its semipublic nature (to the very end, the Fitzgeralds were always being *observed*)—reads like nothing so much as a travesty, a reverse image of one of those elaborate gay pranks of a decade or so before, when they would go to a party in a taxi, he on the roof, she on the hood, or when at the theater they would sit together silent during the funny parts and then laugh uproariously when the house was still. Yet sad as this vignette is, an incident soon occurs which drives Fitzgerald even further away from himself and reality—to the black edge of death and madness. Ever generous and trusting, he also possesses the true writer's immense vanity, and mistakenly grants an interview to the New York *Post*, whose editor sees in Fitzgerald's fortieth birthday an opportunity to make hay with the myth of the twenties and its most distinguished surviving symbol, and dispatches to Asheville an expertly ingratiating reporter named, rather aptly, Michael Mok. Taken off guard, Fitzgerald is polite and as garrulous as his combination of illnesses will allow, and Mok's front-page article—certainly as grimy a claim to immortality as ever fell to any newspaperman—begins as follows:

> The poet-prophet of the post-war neurotics observed his for-tieth birthday yesterday in his bedroom in the Grove Park Inn here. He spent the day as he spends all his days—trying to come back from the other side of Paradise, the hell of despondency in which he has writhed for the last couple of years. Physically he was suffering the aftermath of an accident eight weeks ago when he broke his right shoulder in a dive from a fifteen-foot spring-board. But whatever pain the fracture might still cause him, it did not account for his jittery jumping off and onto his bed, his restless pacing, his trembling hands, his twitching face with its pitiful expression of a cruelly beaten child. Nor could it be held responsible for his frequent trips to a highboy, in a drawer of which lay a bottle. Each time he poured a drink into the measur-ing glass behind his table, he would look appealingly at the nurse and ask, "Just one ounce?"

After reading this article, Turnbull tells us, Fitzgerald tried to kill himself, swallowing the contents of a vial of morphine, which was a sufficient overdose to make him vomit and save his life. But, "gradually anger and despair gave way to shame. He had touched bottom. The article rallied his self-respect and laid the foundation for a comeback of sorts." That "comeback" comprised the last four years of Fitzgerald's life, which were, of course, largely the Hollywood years, the time of feverish sickness and near-destitution, of eleven-dollar bank balances and seedy apartments, of humiliating hack work for the movies, and the excruciating effort to wrest from his talent ("a delicate thing—mine is so scarred and buffeted that I am amazed that at times it still runs clear") one last good book which might resurrect him from the oblivion into which he had been cast. Reading about these appalling, ugly and very courageous years, one is again struck by that sense of ironic transposition which dominates the Fitzgerald legend. It all seems like a romantic movie based on the Artist's Life yet run off at a frantic clip backwards: the glittering success, the money and the fame all coming at the beginning, until, finally, contrary to romantic conventions, we observe the hero terminating his career quite as bleakly as a hopeful yet unpublished poet begins his own—and in the chill and hideous garret of Hollywood. One somehow looks for self-pity: it would be expected in a man who had fallen so far and so hard. And to be sure, there is the natural lament of a writer who feels that both his work and his memory have been banished forever from the public mind. "My God, I am a forgotten man," he cries, and his concern for *Gatsby*, then out of print, is the well-founded anxiety of any writer over the mortality of an offspring. "To die, so completely and unjustly after having given so much!" he protests to Perkins, and adds in that wonderfully characteristic tone of Fitzgerald's, a tone of mingled modesty and pride: "Even now there is little published in American fiction that doesn't slightly bear my stamp—in a *small* way I was an original." But although the quality of these last letters is often elegiac, rueful and sometimes tinged with bitterness, there is very little self-pity. That this is so is part of their great dignity, and considering the mean and woeful circumstances, something of a marvel. Even the lousy films he worked on caused him anguish. A letter to Joseph Mankiewicz, for instance—wheedling, imploring, cajoling—attempting to persuade the producer to restore Fitzgerald's original touches to the script of a movie, is almost insupportable in its degradation. "Oh Joe, can't producers ever be wrong?" he demands, and the sense of futility is suddenly like a howl in a closet: "I'm a good writer—honest."

But throughout this bedraggled finale of his life, he was sustained by his intense concern for his daughter, Scottie, then at Vassar, and by his enduring devotion to Zelda; the letters included here to his wife and daughter are the best in the book, and those to Scottie, taken together, form a small masterpiece. It is hard to imagine that more winning letters from a father to a child have been written by an American. They are hortatory to a degree—Fitzgerald's solicitude for her welfare, doubtless because of Zelda's continuing illness and his doubled responsibility, can only be described as ferocious—but they are also tender, allusive, witty, stern, playful and, finally, informed by wisdom. One cannot read them without feeling a vast respect for this man who—sick and poor, feeling himself forgotten —could retain the splendid equanimity, the compassion and humor, the *love* that sounds through these pages like a heartbeat. Nor is it possible to scorn someone who in the midst of penury and raging sick fevers and neglect still had the boldness of spirit to try for "a big book." He survives what he believed to be his failure triumphantly, a loving and courageous man.

Fitzgerald was not above pettiness, and his most destructive fault was perhaps his lack of self-esteem. But a quality of abiding charity was at the root of his character, and if a collection of letters has the power to illuminate the myth by suffusing it with the sense of a dominant virtue, then this collection succeeds, for it is everywhere filled with Fitzgerald's charity. In 1937, Fitzgerald's close friends of the Riviera days, Gerald and Sara Murphy, had suffered the death within the space of two years of two of their three young children. The letter which Fitzgerald wrote them upon the death of their second child seems appropriate to quote in its entirety, if only for the reason that it may be one of the most beautiful letters of its kind that we have.

Dearest Gerald and Sara:
    The telegram came today and the whole afternoon was so sad with thoughts of you and the happy times we had once. Another link binding you to life is broken and with such insensate cruelty that it is hard to say which of the two blows was conceived with more malice. I can see the silence in which you hover now after this seven years of struggle and it would take words like Lincoln's in his letter to the mother who had lost four sons in the war to write you anything fitting at the moment. The sympathy you will get will be what you have had from each other already and for a long, long time you will be inconsolable.
    But I can see another generation growing up around Honoria and an eventual peace somewhere, an occasional port of call as we all sail deathward. Fate can't have any more arrows in its

quiver for you that will wound like these. Who was it said that it was astounding how deepest griefs can change in time to a sort of joy? The golden bowl is broken indeed but it *was* golden; nothing can ever take those boys away from you now.

Scott

[*New York Review of Books*, November 28, 1968]

A Second Flowering

F OR TOO LONG there has existed a misconception as to what comprises a literary generation. Most of the writers of the post–
World War II era, linked only by the common fact that their
work commenced sometime during the years after Hiroshima, have,
I'm sure, wondered at one time or another why the notion of belonging to a "generation" has seemed so ill-fitting or embarrassing.
Born in 1925, I have always considered Saul Bellow, born a decade
earlier, as much a part of "my" generation as Philip Roth, who is
eight years younger than I am. This comprises a time span of
eighteen years, and I have remained uneasy with the idea—pleased
enough to be associated with two writers I consider admirable but
rather put off by its palpable lack of logic. It should not have
bothered me (not that it has to any great degree), for as Malcolm
Cowley points out, we have all been merely victims of an error of
definition.

"A generation," he writes accurately, "is no more a matter of
dates than it is one of ideology. A new generation does not appear
every thirty years. . . . It appears when writers of the same age
join in a common revolt against the fathers and when, in the process
of adopting a new life style, they find their own models and
spokesmen."

In this case he is speaking of that gorgeously endowed group of
creative spirits, born in the charmed, abbreviated space of years
between 1894 and 1900, whose collective self-discovery as literary
artists was so dazzling that it remains an almost comic irony that
we know them as the Lost Generation. Specifically, the representa-
tives Cowley deals with are Hemingway, Fitzgerald, Dos Passos,
Cummings, Thornton Wilder, Faulkner, Wolfe and Hart Crane.

(Edmund Wilson should have been included, and Cowley laments his absence.) Together they made up "the second flowering" of the title of Malcolm Cowley's book, which is at once a memoir, a series of biographical essays, a literary re-examination, a tribute, and a memorial to that extraordinary company of writers, about whom he wrote earlier in *Exile's Return* and elsewhere.

It is possible to approach a work like this with just a touch of resentment. We have read about the Lost Generation until our heads are water-logged with its self-congratulation, its nostalgia. One broods over the gallons, the tuns, the tank cars of ink spilled out on the lives and work of these men—Hemingway's bibliography alone must be on its way to several volumes requiring sturdy book ends—and one thinks: Enough. Whatever the honesty, the wit, the grace, even the possible originality of the new offering, do we really want or need another account of Scott and Zelda's Riviera turn and the golden couple's tragic decline, or the way Hemingway's magnetic appeal was so often negated by his contemptible treatment of his friends, or Wolfe's hysterical self-concern and *Weltschmerz*?

These are not just thrice-told tales, they seem by now to be so numbingly familiar as to be almost personal—tedious old gossip having to do with some fondly regarded but too often outrageous kinfolk. And if the work also affects a critical stance, do we look forward to still more commentary on *The Bear* or Cummings' love lyrics? Or another desolating inventory of the metaphors in *Gatsby*? In *A Second Flowering* all of these matters are touched upon, yet it is testimony to Cowley's gifts as both a critic and a literary chronicler that the angle of vision seems new; that is, not only are his insights into these writers' works almost consistently arresting but so are his portraits of the men themselves.

Of course it helped to be present, and it was Cowley's great fortune to have often been very much on the scene; he was an exact contemporary. "I knew them all and some have been my friends over the years," he writes. A lesser commentator might have made a terrible botch of it just because of this propinquity and friendship, giving us one of those familiar works of strained observation, at once fawning and self-flattering, where the subject is really victimized as if by a distorting lens held scant inches from the nose.

Several of the writers under consideration—notably Hemingway and Fitzgerald—have already undergone such mistreatment. But

Cowley's affection for these writers, his honesty and devotion to what they stood for, are too deep and inward-dwelling—this feeling pervades every page of the book—for him to sentimentalize them or falsify their image. That he admires them all needs no saying—it is a sign of his critical integrity that one can search in vain to find him in a posture of adulation; even the magnificent achievement of Faulkner, whom Cowley regards as the greatest of the group, is an achievement that he feels (perhaps in a form of antiphonal response to Faulkner's own remark that his generation would be judged upon the "splendor of our failures") falls short of the very highest level and one that cannot properly be set beside the work of such giants as Dostoevsky and Dickens.

One of the finest parts of Cowley's book, incidentally, is the now famous pioneering essay on Faulkner, published in 1945 as the introduction to the Viking *Portable Faulkner*, which is a lucid jewel of exegesis. It opened up Faulkner's world for me when I was a very young man struggling to read a difficult writer who was then out of print, little known and less understood. Nearly a quarter of a century later, during which time Faulkner has been smothered in scholarship, the essay is still fresh and brilliant.

Cowley can be as rough and relentless as an old millwheel in his judgments, whether it be upon some odious personal quality, such as Hemingway's unregenerate and infantile competitiveness, or on a matter of literature. Either way, the critic cuts close to the bone. In college I read *U.S.A.* with the awe of a man discovering a new faith. Yet one passage in Cowley is the most succinctly stated I have ever read in explanation of the sad bankruptcy of Dos Passos' later fiction: "He broke another rule that seems to have been followed by great novelists. They can regard their characters with love or hate or anything between, but cannot regard them with tired aversion. They can treat events as tragic, comic, farcical, pathetic, or almost anything but consistently repulsive."

Cowley's criticism of *The Sun Also Rises*, while considerably more generous in its overall feeling, has the same kind of tough abrasiveness. But again, although he can be rueful about the failures and lapses of the writers—scolding Cummings for his frequent triviality, Wolfe about his "mania for bigness"—the prevailing tone is not that of a dismantler of reputations, a type often so prompt to scuttle into sight with his little toolkit at the end of an era, but one of generosity and preoccupying concern, as if Cowley knew he was an overseer—a kind of curator of some of the loveliest talents, however self-damaged and flawed, that America ever produced.

It is clear that Cowley still takes delight in having known them, and one can appreciate his delight. To recollect one's own modest familiarity with the ancestors is irresistible. Being of another time and place, I had no opportunity to know them—though on a couple of very brief occasions I saw two of the gentlemen plain. (I will not invade the privacy of Mr. Wilder, with whom I am acquainted, and who is a noble survivor.) By the time I came to the pleasure of reading, in the forties, Fitzgerald and Hart Crane and Wolfe—my earliest passion—had met untimely deaths.

Later, in New York in the early fifties, I met E. E. Cummings for a weird, bewitched hour or so. It was for tea at the tiny apartment of a pleasant old lady in Patchin Place, where Cummings also lived. Let Cowley describe him as he also appeared to me: "He had large, well-shaped features, carved rather than molded, eyes set wide apart, often with a glint of mischief in them. . . . In later years, when he had lost most of the hair and the rest was clipped off, he looked more like a bare-skulled Buddhist monk." Although the poet was considerably older than the Cummings of Cowley's reminiscence when I met him, and his tempo must have been slower, his manner more subdued, Cowley's further description corresponds nicely to my impression during that little encounter. What a talker!

"He was the most brilliant monologuist I have known," writes Cowley; "what he poured forth was a mixture of cynical remarks, puns, hyperboles, outrageous metaphors, inconsequence, and tough-guy talk spoken from the corner of his wide, expressive mouth: pure Cummings, as if he were rehearsing something that would afterward appear in print."

My only other contact with the Lost Generation was when I had lunch with Faulkner a single time, again in New York. Faulkner was then writing in an office at Random House. What I remember most vividly about this gentle, soft-speaking, somber-eyed little man with the drooping gray mustache is not his conversation, which was rambling and various (he talked lovingly and a lot about horses—one reason being that he was preparing to write an article on the Kentucky Derby for *Holiday*—and about Truman Capote, whose talent he genuinely admired but whose personality left him rather unnerved), but a beguiling item of literary marginalia. I had gotten up to go to the men's room, and when I returned Faulkner had vanished. "He said to tell you he'd see you again," said Robert Linscott, the Random House editor who had been dining with us. "Bill sometimes gets that strange look in his eye and that means he can't sit still another minute. He's just got to go back to the office and work."

What Linscott then told me supported an observation that Cowley makes—that is, how generally unremarked or indeed unknown is the influence that certain members of the Lost Generation had upon each other. Cowley singles out the effect of Hemingway's work on Faulkner—an unlikely connection until one rereads Faulkner's short masterpiece, "Red Leaves," that grim and marvelous tale set in the autumnal light of early-nineteenth-century Mississippi, when the Indians owned black slaves and practiced human sacrifice.

Linscott related how Faulkner had once told him about the great difficulty he had in getting down the feel and atmosphere of the story to his satisfaction. It was not the story itself; the painful part had to do with the dialogue, a grappling with Anglicized Choctaw which thoroughly buffaloed Faulkner, since he had no idea how to render imaginary Indian talk into English. Finally, according to Linscott, Faulkner solved the problem while rereading a book he admired very much, *Death in the Afternoon*. The stilted, formalized Castilian-into-English which Hemingway had contrived seemed to Faulkner's ear to have just the right eccentric intonation for his Indians, and so his dialogue became a grateful though individualized borrowing—as anyone who compares the two works will readily see.

But these blurred yet memorable impressions—notes of an old-time fan—are mere filigree compared to the actuality of the books themselves, which penetrated the consciousness of so many young men of my time with the weight and poignancy of birth or death, or first love, or any other sacred and terrible event. With Wolfe alone I felt I had been captured by a demon, made absolutely a prisoner by this irresistible torrent of language. It was a revelation, for at eighteen I had no idea that words themselves—this tumbling riot of dithyrambs and yawping apostrophes and bardic cries—had the power to throw open the portals of perception, so that one could actually begin to feel and taste and smell the very texture of existence.

I realize now the naïveté of so many of Wolfe's attitudes and insights, his intellectual virginity, his parochial and boyish heart, his inability to objectivize experience and thus create a believable ambience outside the narrow range of self—all of these drastically reduce his importance as a writer with a serious claim on an adult mind. However, some passages—including the majestic death of old Gant in *Of Time and the River*—are of such heartrending power and radiant beauty that for these alone he should be read, and for them he would certainly retain a place in American literature.

Cowley makes somewhat the same point in his section on Wolfe in *A Second Flowering*, which is the most clear-headed brief analysis of Wolfe and his work that I have seen in print. If others of such passages as I just mentioned "had each been published separately," Cowley writes, "Wolfe might have gained a different reputation, not as an epic poet in prose, but as the author of short novels and portraits, little masterpieces of sympathy and penetration." But then Cowley doubts that he would have cared for that kind of fame. Mania for bigness again.

His portrait of Wolfe, while unsparing in its details about all that made the man such a trial to himself and others—his paranoia, his nearly fatal lack of self-criticism, his selfishness and grandiosity, all the appurtenances of a six-foot-seven-inch child writing in his solipsistic hell—is nonetheless enormously sympathetic and filled with respect. "He had always dreamed of becoming a hero," Cowley writes, "and that is how he impresses us now: perhaps not as a hero of the literary art on a level with Faulkner and Hemingway and Fitzgerald, but as *Homo Scribens* and *Vir Scribentissimus*, a tragic hero of the act of writing."

And so the other fathers also quickly took possession. I was soon reading *Gatsby* and *In Our Time* and *The Sound and the Fury* with the same devouring pleasure that I had read Wolfe. Perhaps I sound too idolatrous. It would be misleading to give the impression that the Lost Generation had exclusive hold on our attention—we who were coming out of college in the forties and early fifties. Recalling my own licentious eclecticism, I realize I was reading everything, from Aeschylus to John Donne to Flaubert to Proust to Raymond Chandler. Yet I think it has to be conceded that rarely has such a group of literary figures had the impact that these writers have had upon their immediate descendants and successors.

This is not to say that at least a good handful of the writers and poets who followed them have failed to be artists in their own right—several of them masterly ones—and who if they genuflect before the fathers do so with pride as well as gratitude. It is only that the influence of the older men—themselves influenced by Eliot and Joyce and Whitman and Mark Twain—has been at once broad and profound to an exceptional degree, so that while we have thankfully moved out of their shadow we have not passed out of their presence.

It is impossible to conceive, for example, that anyone born during the twenties or afterward who was crazy enough to embrace literature as a vocation was not at one time or another under the spell of Hemingway or Faulkner or Fitzgerald, to mention only the most richly endowed members of the generation. The final question is: Aside from the sharply individuated gifts that each possessed, what did they share as writers that may at least partly explain their common genius and its continuing hold on us?

Cowley's speculations are worth our attention. He starts with such considerations—superficial at first glance until one perceives their appropriateness for that epoch—as the fact that all of the members of the group except for Fitzgerald were WASPs, that most were from the Midwest or the South and that all sprang from the middle class. "They all had a Protestant ethic drilled into them, even if they were Catholics like Fitzgerald." Cowley also notes, in a passage which is an oblique commentary on the squalor we have produced in our schools, that every one of these men was the recipient of a sound, old-fashioned early education which placed a premium on the classics, English literature, syntax and Latin grammar while ignoring social studies, civics, baton twirling and other depravities.

Except for Dos Passos and Hemingway, whose friendship was destroyed because of the Spanish Civil War, they were generally either unconcerned or sophomoric in regard to politics. They had all had the experience of World War I, a "nice war," in Gertrude Stein's phrase, which had left most of the men physically intact, restless and filled with reservoirs of unexpected energy. It was a war, however, that was foul and ugly enough to unite them all against "big words and noble sentiments."

Ultimately more important, it seems to me, is Cowley's somewhat paradoxical but compelling notion that although each of these writers was an individualist, committed heart and mind to solitary vision, they were all bound together subconsciously by a shared morality which viewed the husbanding of one's talent as the highest possible goal. Thus, he argues, the garish myth has been deceptive. Many of them indeed had a hunger for self-destruction and were spendthrift livers, but when it came to their talent they were passionate conservationists. Measured in terms of their refusal to allow their splendid gifts to become swallowed up in the vortex of their frenzied, foolish, alcoholic and often desperate lives, they were brave and moral men. In this sense, aside from the varied marvels of their best work, the writers of the Lost Generation provide us with a lesson in the art of self-realization.

"The good writers regarded themselves as an elite," Cowley writes. "They were an elite not by birth or money or education, not even by acclaim—though they would have it later—but rather by such inner qualities as energy, independence, rigor, an original way of combining words (a style, a 'voice') and utter commitment to a dream." Within the persuasive context of a book so free of idealization, so detached and balanced as *A Second Flowering*, such a statement seems enviable, exemplary and true. Only two things matter: talent and language. "Their dream," Cowley concludes, "was . . . of being the lords of language."

As for Malcolm Cowley himself, he is seventy-five this year and rightly considers himself one of the last members of a glorious team whose exploits and defeats it was his privilege to help explain. "Now most of the team is gone," he writes, "and the survivors are left with the sense of having plodded with others to the tip of a long sandspit where they stand exposed, surrounded by water, waiting for the tide to come in." It should be of consolation to him that it is unthinkable that this beautiful, honest book will not be read as an indispensable companion piece to the works of Hemingway, Fitzgerald, Faulkner, Wolfe and all the rest as long as they are read and have bearing upon men's common experience. *Ave atque vale!*

[*New York Times Book Review*, May 6, 1973]

HELL
RECONSIDERED

Hell Reconsidered

FEW BOOKS possess the power to leave the reader with that feeling of awareness which we call a sense of revelation. Richard L. Rubenstein's *The Cunning of History* seems to me to be one of these. It is a very brief work—a long essay—but it is so rich in perception and it contains so many startling—indeed, prophetic— insights that one can only remain baffled at the almost complete absence of attention it suffered when it was first published in 1975. When I first read Rubenstein's book about Auschwitz I felt very much the same effect of keen illumination that I did when, in the early stages of writing *The Confessions of Nat Turner*, I happened to read Stanley Elkins' *Slavery*—a work which shed fresh light on American Negro slavery in such a bold and arresting way that, despite the controversy it produced, it has become a classic study. It is perhaps a fitting coincidence that Rubenstein discusses Elkins at some length in this book; certainly both writers share a preoccupation with what to my mind is perhaps the most compelling theme in history, including the history of our own time—that of the catastrophic propensity on the part of human beings to attempt to dominate one another.

If slavery was the great historical nightmare of the eighteenth and nineteenth centuries in the Western world, slavery's continuation in the horror we have come to call Auschwitz is the nightmare of our own century. Auschwitz, like the core of hell, is the symbolic center of *The Cunning of History*, and while the theological and political ramifications radiating from this center provide many of the book's most illuminating insights, it is Auschwitz—simply

Auschwitz—that remains Rubenstein's primary concern. We are still very close to Auschwitz in time; its unspeakable monstrousness—one is tempted to say its unbelievability—continues to leave us weak with trauma, haunting us as with the knowledge of some lacerating bereavement. Even as it recedes slowly into the past it taxes our belief, making us wonder if it really happened. As a concept, as an image, we shrink from it as from damnation itself. "Christmas and Easter can be subjects for poetry," wrote W. H. Auden, "but Good Friday, like Auschwitz, cannot. The reality is so horrible."

To this he might have added the near-impossibility not just of poetry but of prose, even of an expository sort. That the subject is almost totally beyond the capacities of the mass media may be seen in the failure of the recent television series *Holocaust* to convey any sense of the complex nature of Auschwitz—a matter which I shall revert to later. The critic George Steiner has suggested the ultimate response: silence. But of course writers cannot be silent, least of all a searching writer like Rubenstein, who has set himself the admirable but painful task of anatomizing the reality within the nightmare while the dream is still fresh.

As near in time as Auschwitz is to us, it is nonetheless a historical event, and one of the excellences of Rubenstein's book is the audacious and original way in which the author has confronted the event, wringing from its seeming incomprehensibility the most subtle and resonant meanings. This is an unusual achievement when one considers how frequently analyses of the historical process become little more than tendentious exercises reflecting the writer's bias, which in turn corresponds to the pieties of the era in which he writes. So often the product is less history than wish-fulfillment, reinforcing the prejudices of his contemporaries and their hearts' desire.

A brief word about the dramatic shift in attitudes in the writing of the history of American Negro slavery may serve to illustrate this. During the roughly three quarters of a century between the Emancipation Proclamation and World War II, the historiography of slavery generally reflected the mood of a society which remained profoundly racist, committed to the notion of racial inferiority and to the unshakable virtues of segregation. Towering above all other historians of slavery in the decades before the war was the Georgia-born scholar Ulrich B. Phillips, whose work, despite certain undoubted merits of scholarship, was heavily weighted in favor of the portrayal of slave times as an almost Elysian period, in which contented slave and indulgent master were united in an atmosphere of unexacting, productive labor and domestic tranquillity.

By the 1940s, however, the social upheavals of the preceding decade had drastically affected the national consciousness, bringing with them a perception of the outrages and injustices still being perpetrated on the Negro. Also, a certain sophistication had evolved regarding the psychology of suffering. It would thus seem inevitable, in this new atmosphere of nagging guilt and self-searching, that the writing of the history of slavery would undergo drastic revisionism, and it was just as likely that the new portrait of antebellum times would be the very antithesis of Ulrich B. Phillips' softly tinted idyll; most of the new scholarship (epitomized by Kenneth M. Stampp's *The Peculiar Institution*) represented slavery as unremittingly harsh, cruel and degrading, with few if any redeeming aspects. It was one of the great virtues of Elkins' *Slavery*, coming a few years later, that it struck violently through the obfuscations and preconceptions that had dictated, often self-righteously, the views of the apologists for slavery on the one hand and its adversaries on the other, and, in effect, demanded that the institution be examined from any number of new and different angles objectively, in all of its difficult complexity.

Unlike slavery—which, after all, has had its quixotic defenders—Auschwitz can have no proponents whatever. Therefore I am not suggesting that in *The Cunning of History* Rubenstein is acting as an intermediary in a debate or is synthesizing opposing points of view. I am saying that, like Elkins, Rubenstein is forcing us to reinterpret Auschwitz—especially, although not exclusively, from the standpoint of its existence as part of a continuum of slavery which has been engrafted for centuries onto the very body of Western civilization. Therefore, in the process of destroying the myth and the preconception, he is making us see that that encampment of death and suffering may have been more horrible than we had ever imagined. It was slavery in its ultimate embodiment. He is making us understand that the etiology of Auschwitz—to some, a diabolical, perhaps freakish excrescence which vanished from the face of the earth with the destruction of the crematoriums in 1945—is actually embedded deeply in a cultural tradition which stretches back to the Middle Passage from the coast of Africa, and beyond, to the enforced servitude in ancient Greece and Rome. Rubenstein is saying that we ignore this linkage, and the existence of the sleeping virus in the bloodstream of civilization, at risk of our future.

If it took a hundred years for American slavery to become demythified, we can only wonder when we can create a clear understanding of Auschwitz, despite its proximity to us in time. For several years now I have been writing a work—part fiction, part factual—which deals to a great extent with Auschwitz, and I have been constantly surprised at the misconceptions I have encountered with enlightened people whenever the subject has come up in conversation. The most common view is that the camp was a place where Jews were exterminated by the millions in gas chambers—simply this and nothing more. Now, it is true that in their genocidal fury the Nazis had consecrated their energies to the slaughter of Jews en masse, not only at Auschwitz, where two and a half million Jews died in the gas chambers, but at such other Polish extermination centers as Belzec, Treblinka, Majdanek and Chelmno. And, of course, countless victims died at camps in Germany. A directive from the Reichsführer SS, Heinrich Himmler, in 1943 plainly stated that all European Jews would be murdered without exception, and we know how close to success the carrying out of that order came.

But at Auschwitz—the supreme example of that world of "total domination" which Rubenstein sees as the arch-creation of the Nazi genius—there was ultimately systematized not only mass murder on a scale never known before but mass slavery on a level of bestial cruelty. This was a form of bondage in which the victim was forced to work for a carefully calculated period (usually no more than three months) and then, through methods of deprivation calculated with equal care, allowed to die. Slaving at the nearby factory of I. G. Farben or at the Farben coal mines (or at whatever camp maintenance work the SS were able to contrive), the thousands of inmates initially spared the gas chambers were doomed to a sick and starving death-in-life perhaps more terrible than quick extinction, and luck was more often than not the chief factor involved in their survival.

As Rubenstein points out, only in a situation where human bodies were endlessly replaceable could such a form of slavery attempt to be efficient—but the Nazis, who aspired to be among this century's leading efficiency experts, had no cause for concern on this count, supplied as they were with all the Jews of Europe, besides thousands of Poles, Russian prisoners of war, and others. And although the concept was not entirely unique in the long chronicle of bondage (for a period in the West Indies the British, with a glut of manpower, had no qualms about working slaves to death), certainly no slaveholders had on such a scale and with such absolute ruthlessness made use of human life according to its simple *expendability*. It is this factor of expendability, Rubenstein explains in his persuasive first chapter—an expendability which in turn derives from modern attitudes toward the stateless, the uprooted and rootless, the disadvantaged and dispossessed—which provides still another essential key to unlocking the incomprehensible dungeon of Auschwitz. The matter of populations declared to be surplus (whether by Nazi Germany or other superstates, past and future), which Rubenstein touches upon again and again, haunts this book like the shadow of a thundercloud.

But slave labor is pointless without an end product, and what did slave labor produce at Auschwitz? Of course, on one level, slaves—Jews and non-Jews—slaved to kill Jews. On April 4, 1943, it was decreed that the Auschwitz gas chambers—previously employed to exterminate Jews and gentiles without differentiation—would be used to kill only Jews. Therefore much of the energies of those able-bodied prisoners selected to live for a while was either directly or peripherally expended in the business of getting on with the Nazis' main obsession: the murder of all the Jews in Europe.

But this was not all. One of the gaps in the knowledge of many people I have talked to is their ignorance of the fact that one of the chief functions of Auschwitz was to support a vast corporate enterprise involved in the manufacture of synthetic rubber. Anyone who has studied the Nazi period, especially that aspect of it having to do with the concentration camps, is usually both impressed and baffled by seemingly unresolvable contradictions, by the sheer caprice and irrationality of certain mandates and commands, by unexplainable cancellations of directives, by *Ordnung* in one area of operation and wild disorder in another. The SS, so celebrated for their discipline and methodicalness, seemed more often than not to have their collective heads in total disarray. Witness Himmler's order early in 1943 concerning the annihilation of the Jews; nothing would seem more unequivocal or more final. Yet this imperious command—surely one of the most awesome and terrible in history

—was completely countermanded soon after it was conceived and handed down, replaced by a directive which ordered all able-bodied Jewish adult arrivals at Auschwitz not to the crematoriums but to work.

We can only surmise the reason for this quick reversal, but it should not take too long to conclude that pressures from I. G. Farben–Auschwitz, operators of the rubber factory, were among the decisive factors in Himmler's decision, and that at the behest of the directors of the company (which only a few years before had been helping to supply peaceful European households with tires and doormats and cushions and ashtrays), thousands of Jews each day would rejoice in their "reprieve" from the ovens at Birkenau, only to realize that they had joined the legions of the walking dead.

It is ironic that the immolation of these doomed souls (and there were among them, I think it necessary to emphasize, hundreds of thousands of non-Jews) came to naught; we know now that for various reasons the nearby factories produced very little synthetic rubber to aid the struggles of the Wehrmacht, yet it was through no lack of effort on the part of either I. G. Farben or the SS that the enterprise was fruitless. There was a constant conflict, within the SS, between the lust for murder and the need for labor, and thus the Farben works were often supplied with sick or incapacitated prisoners temporarily saved from the crematoriums. But chiefly the failure to produce matériel was less the result of insufficient or inadequate manpower than of a technological mismanagement which, as it so often did, belied the Nazis' claims to being paragons of efficiency. What had really been demonstrated was the way in which the bureaucratization of power in the service of a new kind of soulless bondage could cause total domination of human beings that makes the oppression of traditional, old-fashioned Western slavery—with its residue of Christian decency and compassion—seem benevolent by comparison.

As Rubenstein says in an important passage:

> The death-camp system became a society of total domination only when healthy inmates were kept alive and forced to become slaves rather than killed outright. . . . As long as the camps served the single function of killing prisoners, one can speak of the camps as places of mass execution but not as a new type of human

society. Most of the literature on the camps has tended to stress the role of the camps as places of execution. Regrettably, few ethical theorists or religious thinkers have paid attention to the highly significant political fact that the camps were in reality a new form of human society.

And in another passage Rubenstein concludes with stunning, if grim, perception: "The camps were thus far more of a permanent threat to the human future than they would have been had they functioned solely as an exercise in mass killing. An extermination center can only manufacture corpses; a society of total domination creates a world of the living dead."

Sometime ago I watched a late-night discussion program on television, the moderator of which was the entertainer David Susskind. Assembled for the event that evening were perhaps half a dozen writers whose expertise was in the subject of the Nazis and their period, and also in the continued presence of a kind of *Lumpen* underground Nazism in America. I believe most of these men were not Jewish. I remember little about the program save for the remarkably foolish question posed by Susskind near the end. He asked in effect: "Why should you gentiles be interested in the Nazis? Why, not being Jewish, are you concerned about the Holocaust?"

There was a weak reply, *sotto voce*, from one of the participants to the effect that, well, there were others who suffered and died too, such as numerous Slavs; but the remark seemed to be ignored and I bit my tongue in embarrassment for all concerned, of course unable to utter what I was longing to say, namely, that if the question was unbelievably fatuous, the reply was shamefully feeble and off the mark. Most emphatically (I wished to say) Mr. Susskind *should* be enlightened about the vast numbers of gentiles who partook in the same perdition visited upon the Jews, those who were starved and tortured to death at Ravensbrück and Dachau, and the droves who perished as slaves at Auschwitz. Such ignorance seemed to me by now impermissible.

In this respect the fatal date April 4, 1943, which I referred to before, is instructive. For if that day demonstrates the way in which the dynamo of death was cranked up to ensure the Final Solution, it also plainly shows how the policy of extermination had never been limited to the Jews. Nor did the new policy indicate any preservative concern on the part of the Nazis for the Poles and other undesirables—only that their deaths as slaves would come about less methodically than the deaths of the Jews, who had been suddenly tendered unquestioned priority in the process of annihilation by gas.

The statistics are meager, and so we have no way of knowing the number of non-Jews who were murdered in the gas chambers prior to this cut-off date; not many, compared to the Jews, but certainly they numbered in the tens of thousands. Yet to escape the crematoriums was, of course, to gain only the most feeble hold on the possibility of survival. Statistics regarding the non-Jews who perished during the four years of the existence of Auschwitz as a result of starvation and disease are likewise inexact but somewhat more reliable. It would appear that out of the four million who died, perhaps three quarters of a million—or approximately a fifth of the total—fell into the category which the Nazis termed Aryan. This was at Auschwitz alone. Multitudes of innocent civilians were murdered elsewhere.

These vast numbers would possibly seem less meaningful if the victims had been part of the mere detritus of war, accidental casualties, helpless by-products of the Holocaust; but such was not the case, and there can no longer be any doubt about which other people were to fall within the scope of the Nazis' master scheme for genocide. Rubenstein quotes from a letter written in the fall of 1942 by Otto Thierack, the German minister of justice, who stated his intention of granting to Himmler "criminal jurisdiction" over Poles, Russians and Gypsies, as well as Jews, and whose use of the word "extermination" is blunt and unequivocal. There is, I think, something profoundly minatory and significant—telling much about the Nazis' eventual plan for these "subhuman" peoples of the East—in the little-known fact that the first victims of Zyklon B gas at Auschwitz were not Jews but nearly one thousand Russian prisoners of war.

In the face of the destruction of the European Jews, so nearly completely successful and so awesomely the product of a single-minded evil beyond comprehension, one hesitates before bringing up the suffering of these other people. Nonetheless, the unutterable degradation, horror and vile deaths which they so often shared with the Jews remain to trouble the mind—all the more so because of the continuing ignorance regarding their fate. Theirs is a history of anguish which still seems to dwell dimly if at all in the public consciousness. It also must be remembered that these human beings perished not randomly but often by systematic means and in prodigious numbers. A man who is possibly our most unimpeachable witness, Simon Wiesenthal, the head of the Jewish Center of Documentation in Vienna, expressed his feelings on the matter in a recent interview:

> I always insist that the victims must not be divided into Jews and non-Jews. I brought over eleven hundred Nazis before courts in different countries, Nazis who killed Jews and gentiles and Gypsies and Serbs and so on, and I've never thought about the religion of the victims. I've battled for years with Jewish organizations, warning them that we shouldn't always talk about the six million Jews who died in the Holocaust. I say let's talk about *eleven million* civilians, among them six million Jews, who were killed. It's our Jewish fault that in the eyes of the world this whole problem became reduced to the problem between the Nazis and the Jews; the problem obviously was much broader. The Jews need the help of others to prevent new holocausts.

But the point I struggled vainly to make, looking at David Susskind and murmuring to myself in the dark, was that even if all this were not true—even if the Jews had been without any exception the inheritors of Hitler's hatred and destruction—his question would have been very close to indecent. I could not help thinking whether there was something paradigmatically American (or certainly non-European) in that question, with its absence of any sense of history and its vacuous unawareness of evil.

By contrast, how pervasive is the sense of evil in Rubenstein's essay, how urgent is the feeling that an apprehension of the devil's handiwork and an understanding of the Holocaust are the concern of Jew and non-Jew alike. We are all still immersed in this deepest pit. In *The Cunning of History*, written by a Jewish theologian, the fact of the Holocaust as *the* cataclysmic tragedy of the Jewish people is assumed, *a priori*, as it should be, just as it is assumed that the annihilation of the Jews acquired a centrality in the Nazis' monstrous order of things. Rubenstein's analysis of the historical sources of anti-Semitism provides some of his most illuminating passages.

But among the qualities which I find so powerful about Rubenstein's book, as opposed to a great deal which has been written about Auschwitz, is how, despite the foregoing, he has acquired a perspective—a philosophical and historical spaciousness—that has allowed him to anatomize Auschwitz with a knowledge of the titanic and sinister forces at work in history and in modern life which threaten *all* men, not only Jews. I intend no disrespect to Jewish sensibility, and at the same time am perhaps only at last replying to Mr. Susskind, when I say how bracing it is to greet a writer who views totalitarianism as a menace to the entire human family. As an analyst of evil, Rubenstein, like Hannah Arendt, is serene and Olympian, which probably accounts for the unacceptability I have been told he has met with in some quarters.

Rubenstein's apprehension of the larger menace of Nazism, and Simon Wiesenthal's insistence that we must recognize the ecumenical nature of its evil—the "broader problem"—found little echo or corroboration in last April's television series *Holocaust*. It must be clear by now that even with good intentions the rendering of major historical events in their subtlety and complexity is quite beyond the power of American television. And *Holocaust* may have been, in its soft-headed vulgarity, one of television's more creditable dramatic efforts. Like *Roots*, the earlier TV extravaganza about American Negro slavery, the program was obviously "carefully researched," and its nine and a half hours of slick footage possessed, one felt, an underpinning of authenticity that seemed to permit little major violation of the basic historical record. In fact, as in the earlier sequences of *Roots*, which captured some of the aspects of the African slave trade with surprising verisimilitude, the initial parts of *Holocaust*, in episodes depicting the effects of the Nazi poison as it invaded the lives of Jews and incipient fascists alike, had moments of striking and cautionary power. It became all the more oppressive, then, that aside from its totally objectionable features in matters of taste—mainly the strident commercials which intruded at intervals like chanted obscenities—the series slid into rhythmically spaced troughs of sentimentality and melodrama.

When drama erodes into melodrama one of the warning signals is the appearance of token figures. In *Roots*, which soon vitiated its early promise by turning the history of slavery into an equation in which all black was good and all white was evil, tokenism came in the form of a single decent white man; in *Holocaust*, the brief glimpses of an anti-Nazi Christian prelate and a "good" Nazi official (and also one or two Jewish Kapos and finks) served as a kind of bogus leavening to what had degenerated into skillfully rigged but hollow theatrics. Least of all did the program deal satisfactorily with that appalling edifice which provided the culminating scenes and, presumably, lent to the series its metaphorical meaning—Auschwitz.

The scenes of naked Jews being consigned to the gas chambers, though embarrassingly staged, were presented with graphic emphasis. But despite an off-hand allusion to I. G. Farben, which seemed both strained and obvious, and a brief reference to the Poles, which, in the context in which it was made, gave the mistaken impression that theirs was an infinitely more pleasant lot than that of the Jews, there was conveyed no sense whatever of the magnitude and deadliness of the slave enterprise. There was no suggestion that in this inconceivably vast encampment of total domination (predominantly gentile at any given time) there were thousands of Poles and Russians and Czechs and Slovenes dying their predetermined and wretched deaths, that in droves Catholic priests and nuns were being subjected to excruciating and fatal medical experiments, that members of Polish and other European resistance groups (whose struggle and great courage were never once hinted at in the program) were being tortured and, in some cases, gassed like the Jews. In short, the suffering and martyrdom of these others were ignored, to the great loss of historical accuracy and, I am afraid, of moral responsibility. We shall perhaps never even begin to understand the Holocaust until we are able to discern the shadows of the enormity looming beyond the enormity we already know.

[*New York Review of Books,* June 29, 1978]

In his 1980 Nobel Prize acceptance speech, Czeslaw Milosz expressed alarm over the fact that the actual existence of the Holocaust was being questioned in books and pamphlets published throughout Europe and America. He then went on to say: "[The poet] feels anxiety, though, when the meaning of the word Holocaust undergoes gradual modification, so that the word begins to belong to the history of the Jews exclusively, as if among the victims there were not also millions of Poles, Russians, Ukrainians, and prisoners of other nationalities. He feels anxiety, for he senses in this foreboding of a not distant future when history will be reduced to what appears on television, while the truth, because it is too complicated, will be buried in the archives, if not totally annihilated."

VICTIMS

INTRODUCTION

In the spring of 1960, when I was living in Rome, I joined
with a group of American writers in sending to an Italian
newspaper a letter which supported the forthcoming execution
of the notorious California criminal Caryl Chessman. As I
recall, most of us—while being half-heartedly against capital
punishment—were annoyed at the extraordinary international
fuss being made over Chessman. This was an imbroglio in
which, we maintained, there was largely ignored the fact that
Chessman—a dyed-in-the-wool bastard if ever there was
one—had for twelve years been granted every consideration
within the most tolerant and flexible system of judicial appeals
anywhere in the world. To be sure, we conceded, he had
committed only rape—an important point. But why should
Governor Edmund G. Brown pardon him, we argued, when
other American criminals, including rapists, who had received
no publicity would go to their mean deaths unnoticed and
unmourned? The Chessman case had provoked a wave of
anti-Americanism unequaled in its special fierceness since the
execution of the Rosenbergs seven years before (when I had
also been in Italy, and had personally felt the mood of
reproach), and I think now that our letter may have been
in reaction to this more than anything else.

There was, it is true, a great deal of ignorance abroad in
Europe regarding the complexity of our criminal codes, which
still vary so oddly from state to state. Among other things, it
seemed impossible to be able to convince any European that
President Eisenhower, who was being deluged by telegrams
from all over the globe, could not possibly intervene in this
situation, since Chessman was not a federal offender. We also

pointed out—a little speciously, I imagine—that there were numerous American states which had no capital punishment and that one of them, Michigan, had abolished legalized murder longer than almost any jurisdiction in the world, including Italy. I suspect that the letter created a meager impression on Italian readers; certainly it may have made one or two narrowly legalistic points while evading the moral issue entirely. At any rate, Chessman went to the gas chamber, and his ashes were scattered over the Pacific. Thereafter I felt a little uneasy about the letter, but it soon faded from my mind. (One peripheral impression still lingers from that summer: of my housekeeper, a rather intelligent woman from Naples, wondering aloud how a nice person like me could come from America, where there was so much barbarity and violence. It could never happen here, she declared, and I despondently agreed with her—only a few years before the shadow of terrorism and vicious kidnapping swooped down upon Italy like a bat's wing.)

A year or so later I was still troubled about my attitude toward the death penalty—an attitude that remained (as in the Chessman letter) ambivalent. The death penalty is not, to my mind, the paramount issue society has to face, but its existence in America (especially now that practically all civilized nations have abolished it) remains a persistent and painful sore. Furthermore, it is one of the few moral issues about which it is almost impossible to harbor mixed feelings, at least after one has studied the matter carefully. Proponents and opponents might disagree violently with one another, but they have at least taken their stand; only people of slovenly intellectual habits can retain an ambivalence of feeling about anything so absolute, so final.

In my own case, I became firmly opposed to the death penalty soon after that year in Rome. I had been asked by *Esquire* to write an essay, or essays, on almost anything I might choose as a subject. It was an attractive notion, and— doubtless still pricked with guilt over the Chessman business —I resolved to settle my feelings first by a study of the issue and then by writing about it. My reading in the field of capital punishment, which was quite extensive, left me with no doubts as to where a rational and fair-minded human being should stand on the matter as we passed into the second half of this bloody century. Camus's great essay "Reflections on the Guillotine" was alone almost enough—in its persuasive logic and eloquence—to make me an enemy of capital punishment. As for the specific subject (the once doomed Benjamin Reid, whose story comprises the main essay of the section), I stumbled onto the case by the most fortunate of chances. While I was composing my final thoughts about the subject, I happened upon a small item on a back page of the *New York Times*. The article said only that a condemned killer, Benjamin Reid, awaiting execution in Connecticut, had been denied further appeal by a federal court and that his date with death had been rescheduled. The fact that I lived in Connecticut was a convenient reason for choosing Reid to write about, rather than some other condemned man or woman. Aside from the Connecticut aspect, there was nothing at all I knew about Reid—his age, race, background or even the exact nature of his crime. Going in blindly, so to speak, I became determined to deal with Benjamin Reid and his case as an unabashed advocate of abolition, regardless of what terrible things I might discover about the criminal and his crime. The following essay—and its companion piece, "Aftermath"—is the result of this somewhat precipitate foray into what might be termed advocacy journalism.

In a collection of essays like this volume, where the author has been required to reread prose which he has not seen for years, there is a mingled sense of unease and satisfaction. Some of the pieces seem to hold up very well, others disappoint. The two Benjamin Reid articles appear to me to fall in the at least slightly disappointing category, if only by defects of the quality of the writing, which in the main essay seems overwrought, and in "Aftermath" rather flat. I would like to think, though, that in the first case the *ad hominem* tone that now grates on my ear might be excused because of the shameless zeal I was determined to bring to my plea, which was also instrumental—I'm unashamed to say—in saving Benjamin Reid's life. The aftermath of "Aftermath," which I have appended in a special note, may, however, be instructive to those who have not learned that in the terrible cosmos of our prison system, and among the disadvantaged and the broken who are forced to dwell there, there are seldom any happy endings.

The Death-in-Life
of Benjamin Reid

THE CONNECTICUT STATE PRISON at Wethersfield is a huge, gloomy Victorian structure whose very appearance seems calculated to implant in the mind of the onlooker the idea of justice in its most retributive sense. It is one of the oldest prisons in America. Uncompromisingly somber, the penitentiary suggests not only that crime does not pay but that whosoever is a wrongdoer is quite conceivably beyond redemption. On death row, the condemned cells were built for an epoch when, after a man was told he must die, the supreme penalty was administered far more swiftly than in these present days of interminable legal postponements. Each cell still measures only seven by seven feet, implying momentary residence. A strong electric light shines in the face of the condemned all night and all day. The condemned are not allowed to communicate with one another, and until very recently, were denied even the solace of an earphone radio. To live on death row at Wethersfield is in effect to dwell in solitary confinement until the day of one's execution. As I write these words (mid-October 1961) the state of Connecticut is preparing to kill a twenty-four-year-old felon named Benjamin Reid. Reid is no Caryl Chessman; as a matter of fact, he is subliterate and possesses an intelligence which, if not so low as to be called defective, can only be described as marginal. The condemned at Wethersfield are allowed to read and to write letters, but it is doubtful that Ben Reid has availed himself much of these privileges; and this is a circumstance which must have made his confinement all the more forsaken, because Reid has lived in the presence of the electric chair for four years and three months.

On a bitterly cold night in Hartford in January of 1957, Ben Reid, who was nineteen at the time, waylaid a middle-aged woman in a parking lot and beat her to death with a hammer. His avowed and premeditated motive was profit (the woman was a friend of his mother's and had been known to carry large sums of money with her), but this aspect of his crime he so ruinously botched that he got nothing. Over $2,000 was discovered on the woman's frozen body, which Reid in his final panic had jammed into a car. It would appear that Reid scarcely bothered to conceal his tracks, fleeing to the home of a relative in New Haven, where he was found in short order by the police. He seemed rather relieved to be caught. He made several confessions, and in the summer of that same year, was brought to trial by jury in the Superior Court at Hartford. The trial was a fairly brief one, as murder trials go. On June 27, 1957, Reid was sentenced to die by electrocution. He was taken to Wethersfield (a suburb of Hartford, and except for the eyesore of its prison and several small factories, a lovely elm-lined New England town) and there in his tiny cell, brightly illuminated night and day, he has been for more than four years, awaiting what must be, for him, the ever present but always undiscoverable moment of his death.

There is, of course, no such thing as absolute justice, but even advocates of capital punishment will grant that when a human's life is at stake, there should be the closest approximation of absolute justice the law can attain. In terms of absolute justice, to make evident the reasonableness of Ben Reid's execution for murder it would have to be proved that his crime was morally more reprehensible than a similar crime for which some other murderer received a lesser sentence. There have been, and still are, murderers whose crimes repel us by their violence and brutality quite as strongly as does Ben Reid's. Some of these criminals have been put to death as creatures past salvation; more frequently sparing their lives, the state has sentenced them to serve a life term, with the possibility of parole, or a number of years, and by this relative leniency has granted, at least theoretically, the rather more lucid assumption that some men's crimes are not so depraved as to place them forever beyond redemption. But the logic of this random choice is as fearful as it is mysterious. The wickedness, the inherent immorality, of any crime is a quality which it is beyond the power of any of us to weigh or measure. Ben Reid's crime, however, has been weighed, and Reid himself has been found completely and irrevocably wanting. Neither absolute justice nor any kind of justice, so far as the eye can see, has been served. It might be interesting to learn something about this young man, and perhaps discover why the state has judged him irredeemable, past hope of recovery.

Warden Lewis E. Lawes of Sing Sing, an expert foe of the death penalty, once said that in order to be executed in America a person had to be three things: poor, a man and black. He was speaking of the North as well as the South. He was also admittedly generalizing, if not being somewhat facetious, for a great many white men and a few women of both races have, of course, been executed, and on exquisitely rare occasions the state has taken the life of a criminal of wealth. But the implication of his remark, it is safe to say, is borne out by the statistics—North and South—and Ben Reid fills the bill: he is a poor black man. To read of his background and career is to read not only of poverty and neglect and a mire of futile, petty crime and despair, but, in the end, of a kind of wretched archetype: the Totally Damned American. If one wished to make a composite portrait of the representative criminal upon whom the state enacts its legal vengeance, one's result would be a man who looked very much like Ben Reid. Like his victim, who was also a Negro, he was born in a dilapidated slum area on the north side of Hartford. When he was two his father died, leaving his mother virtually destitute and with several children to support besides Ben. These years toward the end of the Depression were bleak enough for a large number of Americans; for people in the situation of Ben Reid and his family the times were catastrophic and left ineradicable scars. When Reid was almost eight his mother got into a shooting scrape and was grievously wounded; she was left crippled for life and partially paralyzed. At this point Reid was forced to enter the Hartford County Home, and there he remained for eight years. He was not alone among his family to become a ward of the People; during the time he was at the county home his twin brother was committed to the state hospital for the insane at Norwich, while an older sister, adjudged to be mentally deficient, was sent to the Mansfield State Training School. Most children are released from the county home at the age of fifteen, but since no one wanted Reid, he received the dispensation granted, in special cases, to the totally unwanted and was privileged to stay an extra year. One pauses to speculate, hesitates, goes on, feeling presumptuous (there is no other word) as one tries to imagine Ben Reid's thoughts during this weary, bedraggled era. He was never too bright, so probably—unlike other adolescents somewhat more richly endowed in mind as well as circumstance—he entertained no Deep Thoughts about life at all. To Reid, coming out of oblivion into this existence which, so far as one can tell, had seemed to guarantee the unfulfillment and frustration of every ordinary childish yearning, life must have begun to appear simply and demonstrably lacking in significance. Lacking in significance, it must necessarily have lacked any values whatever, and it is not at all surprising that Reid, soon after he was sent away from the county home, began feloniously and empty-headedly to trifle with those values in life which society so highly regards.

When the county home finally discharged him, the nation was experiencing a time of prosperity such as no country has ever seen, but very little of this abundance rubbed off on Ben Reid. For a year or so he was shunted from one foster home to another; he went hungry again from time to time, and there were occasions when he was reduced to foraging from garbage cans on the back streets of Hartford. It was during this period that Reid had his first brush with the law, in an involvement which has come to seem numbingly typical of his age and background: he was caught acting as a runner for a narcotics peddler, and for his offense was placed on probation. A few months later he tried to rob a store, hopelessly bungled the endeavor and was sentenced to serve a term in the state reformatory at Cheshire. It is apparent that he was in no way reformed. However, it may be said that after his release from the reformatory, an episode occurred in Reid's life which tends in some small way to alleviate the harshness and ugliness of his career until then. He met a girl. She was a few years older than he, but they began seeing each other and presumably fell in love, and they were married in 1956. It might have been an answer to Reid's trouble, but it wasn't. He was unable to get a job. Not long after their marriage Ben began to brood about money and commenced hitting the wine bottle. His wife apparently did her best to straighten him out, but these efforts led to nothing. She was pregnant and had just left him when Reid, thinking about money, went out into the snow that night and committed the crime for which he is now scheduled to die.

Often, it seems, what appears to be justice is merely a shadow image of justice, determined by queer circumstances which can only be discerned in retrospect. This sinister element in the law might alone be enough to cast final doubts upon the infliction of the death penalty; for only under conditions of absolute justice—

a kind of aseptic legal vacuum completely invulnerable to fleeting social panic, hysteria, shifts in public temper—could we presume to condemn a man utterly, and absolute justice nowhere exists. It of course cannot strictly be proven, but it seems at least probable that had Ben Reid not come to trial at the particular time he did, he would not have been condemned to die. The reason for this conjecture is the existence in Hartford at that same time of two particularly vicious criminals: a huge, lantern-jawed ex-con and ex-resident of death row named Joseph ("The Chin") Taborsky and his moronic accomplice, Arthur Culombe. Taborsky, who was a psychopath of fearfully sadistic dimensions, and Culombe, a kind of torpid, blinky-eyed caricature of the dim-witted henchman, had finally been apprehended after a series of holdup-murders which had terrorized central Connecticut and, quite literally, sent many of the people of Hartford in off the streets. A notable feature of their *modus operandi* was to make their victims kneel down at their feet before shooting them. Taborsky and Culombe had been dubbed by the newspapers, with scant originality though in luminous headlines, "The Mad Dog Killers," and when they came to be tried there can be no doubt that the public, which attended the trial in droves, was in something less than a mood of composure. Ben Reid was tried at the same time and in the same building. His mother, crippled and woefully concerned, was the only spectator on the first day of the trial, when the jurors were sworn in, and except for Reid's wife and one or two interested onlookers, remained the only spectator until the trial's end. The People's interest was in the Mad Dogs, not in Ben Reid. There seems little doubt that the Taborsky-Culombe affair next door, with its public hubbub and its reverberant atmosphere of mass outrage, did nothing to help Ben Reid's case, and in fact subtly contaminated his own courtroom with the odor of vengeance.

The trial, as I have said, lasted only a few days. Reid's defense was almost nonexistent; he had, after all, killed someone with what in the legal sense is surely malice and premeditation. His defense counsel (since Reid had no money, this job fell to the public defender) made strenuous efforts in his client's behalf, outlining his squalid background and the nature of his upbringing. But the jury (Respectability in its pure, concentrated essence, disarmingly mild-eyed and benign, like a Norman Rockwell tableau: five Christian housewives and among the rest, as might be anticipated in Hartford, a clutch of insurance adjusters) was not terribly moved.

Testifying in his own behalf, Reid seemed confused. Once when asked why, after his first blow, he continued to strike the woman, he replied that she had seemed to be suffering so that he wanted to put her out of her pain. Now, asked the same question by the prosecutor, he could only mumble hopelessly, "I don't know. I started to shake. I lost control of myself. I didn't want her to die." In his final summation, the prosecuting attorney expressed a few personal regrets but went on to add that we must not be swayed by the fact of a person's sordid environment; after all, some of our most valued citizens have struggled up to eminence from the lower depths, fighting their way to fame and fortune, ladies and gentlemen, while people like this criminal sitting here, etc. It had the echo of a thousand courtrooms: Look at Al Jolson and Eddie Cantor. Look at Joe Louis! It was the old American death-cry, and there is no reply to it, save the negative one, to be spoken in a whisper, that when life is an issue we have no God-given right to measure the gallant strength of a few men against the imponderable weakness of a foundling like Ben Reid. The jury was asked if it would like to retire and deliberate right away, or if it would like to have lunch first. It replied that it would like to have lunch. After it fed itself it retired and came back with the verdict in a little over an hour. As happens with rather enigmatic frequency in capital trials, the judge flubbed the reading of the death sentence. In setting the date of execution, he said, "the year 1958," instead of "the year 1957," and the entire pronouncement, for the record, had to be read over again. Up until this time Reid had showed very little emotion during the trial, except for the moment when the prosecutor began to describe his crime in its bloody detail, at which point, in a gesture which can only be described as childlike, he furiously clapped his hands over his ears. Now perhaps he felt that the judge was damning him twice. At any rate, he broke down and wept.

One curious fact which tends to underline the basic senselessness of capital punishment is the way in which we are regularly brought into touch with an evil apart from the nagging, chronic, yet somehow endurable distress which the death penalty itself causes us: this is the almost unendurable incongruity it manifests in its choice of victims. If in Caryl Chessman, for instance, we were confronted with a plucky, dogged, intelligent man (so intelligent, in fact, as to have blurred in the minds of many people the nature of his morality, which was that of a cynical, self-justifying hoodlum; he verged as close to an embodiment of the perfect son of a bitch as the mind can conceive) who possessed the right at least to the possibility of redemption, in Ben Reid we are faced with a man so egregiously lacking in gifts, so totally desolate in circumstance, in quality of mind and spirit, that though he bears an almost antipodean relationship to Chessman as a man, we find ourselves questioning by this very contradistinction his implacable abandonment by society. Of course, the facts of heredity and environment cannot be allowed completely to eliminate responsibility and guilt. Reid's crime was an appalling one—one of such blind ruthlessness that it should have been apparent at the outset that he must be removed from the community until that time when it might reasonably be made certain that he could take his place again among his fellow men. Failing this approximate certainty, it would have to be made sure that he was incarcerated for good. But here we are not speaking of correction. We are not even speaking of that reasonable punishment which might carry with it vitalizing connotations of remorse and contrition. We are speaking of total abandonment. Perhaps not so wise but no less unfortunate than Chessman, Reid too had been judged beyond salvation. It is this abrupt, irrevocable banishment, this pre-emption by the state of the single final judgment which is in the providence of God alone—and the subtle but disastrous effect this act has upon the whole philosophy of crime and punishment—that wrecks the possibility of any lasting, noble concept of justice and causes the issue of the death penalty to become not peripheral, but central to an understanding of a moral direction in our time.

Against an awesome contemporary backdrop of domestic trouble and crisis, and the lingering image of concentration camps, and the threat of mass annihilation, the case of Ben Reid might seem an event of such small moment that there is hardly any wonder that it has commanded no one's attention. It is a case little enough known in Hartford, much less in the state of Connecticut or the broad, busy world. If it is true that crime in general, save in its most garish, tabloid aspects, fails to gain our serious regard, it may also be said that the question of capital punishment commands even less interest on the part of thinking people, especially in America. It becomes one of those lofty moral issues relegated to high school debates. To most thinking people, crime is something we read about at breakfast. The infliction of the death penalty, even further removed from our purview, is a ceremony which takes place in the dead of night, enacted, like some unnamable perversion, in shame and secrecy, and reported the next morning, on a back page, with self-conscious and embarrassed brevity. Our feelings are usually mixed; conditioned by two decades of James Cagney movies, and the memory of the jaunty wisecrack when the warden comes and the last mile commences, few of us can escape a shiver of horrid fascination which the account of a man's judicial execution affords us. But the truth is that few of us, at the same time, are left without a sense of queasiness and discomfiture, and indeed there are some—not simply the quixotic or the "bleeding hearts," as Mr. J. Edgar Hoover describes those who abhor the death penalty—who are rendered quite inescapably bereft. "For certain men, more numerous than is supposed," wrote Albert Camus, "knowing what the death penalty really is and being unable to prevent its application is physically insupportable. In their own way, they suffer this penalty, too, and without any justification. If at least we lighten the weight of the hideous images that burden these men, society will lose nothing by our actions." This is not alone an interior, personal viewpoint which would subvert a general evil in the name of delicate feelings; Camus's other arguments against capital punishment are too fierce and telling for that. The fact remains that all of us, to some degree, are spiritually and physically diminished by the doctrine of legal vengeance, even though it manifests itself as nothing more than a chronic, insidious infection beneath the public skin. We need only the occurrence of a sudden Chessman, flaunting his anguish like a maddened carbuncle, to make evident the ultimate concern we have with our own debilitating and corrupting sickness. That we do not discuss this problem until a Chessman appears is only an indication of one of our most ruinous human feelings—our inability to think about any great issue except in the light of the unique, the glamorous, the celebrity. Chessman was indisputably unique as a criminal and as one condemned; it is not to demean that uniqueness to declare that we shall never resolve the issue of capital punishment until we ponder it in terms not alone of Chessman, but of Ben Reid.

It is more than likely that apathy about the question is generated by the knowledge that capital punishment is on the decrease. With great pride the commonwealth acknowledges that, on the average, it now exterminates only about fifty people a year—like stars on a flag, one for each sovereign state. A common attitude might be articulated in the words of *Time* magazine, which said during the

Chessman affair: "If opponents of capital punishment were patient enough, they could just sit back and wait for it to fade away—in practice, if not on the statute books. But abolitionists try to hasten that fade-away by argument." Aside from the fact that very few evils have been hastened into extinction without the benefit of incessant argument, such a statement represents a blindness to the profounder truths which seems to seize *Time* at intervals. There is very little patience among men who are waiting to die. "To sit back and wait for it to fade away" is of small consolation to the "160 or so" people (including Ben Reid) who *Time* in the same article stated were awaiting execution on death rows all over America at the time of the Chessman affair. I do not know how *Time*'s writer visualized the number 160—if indeed he tried to visualize it at all: larger than fifty maybe? less than a thousand? As for myself, the more I ponder 160 condemned faces, the more the number acquires a queerly disproportionate hugeness, and to use any phrase which implies such a gradual, far-off diminution seems to me, quite simply, a triumph of indifference.* Moreover, I am not at all sure that capital punishment will in fact fade away, as long as Mr. J. Edgar Hoover, the guardian of our public morals, has any say in the matter.

Mr. Hoover, according to a news item last June in the New York *Herald Tribune*, for the first time in his long career as our premier law-enforcement officer, has allowed himself, in what I suppose must be called a policeman's trade journal, to proclaim his belief in the efficacy of the death penalty. The article went on to describe the particular malfeasance which had impelled Mr. Hoover to take this position. It was a singularly hideous crime. A California woman, who happened, incidentally, to be pregnant, enticed a little girl of six into a car. There in the woman's presence her thirty-year-old husband raped the "screaming" child, who thereupon was bludgeoned to death by the wife with a tire jack. Apprehended and tried swiftly, the man was sentenced to die in the gas chamber, while his wife received life imprisonment. Past any doubt this was a deed so horrible as to tempt one to view it

* In 1982, there were nearly 1,000 American prisoners on death row. Although actual executions have decreased, the number of condemned has vastly increased, and the United States remains the single major Western nation in which the death penalty not only exists but is on the march. —W. S. (1982)

almost metaphysically, as if it were enacted in a realm beyond even abnormal behavior. All of our emotions are unhinged, displaced, at the contemplation of such a monstrous crime. As Anthony Storr, writing in a recent issue of the *New Statesman*, remarks: "To rape and murder a little girl is the most revolting of crimes. It is easy to sympathize with those who feel that a man who could do such a thing should be flogged or executed. . . . We think of our own young daughters and we shudder. The child rapist has alienated himself from our society, and we want to eliminate him, to suppress him, to forget that he ever existed."

Yet as one thinks about the *Herald Tribune* article and the crime and, more particularly, Mr. Hoover's attitude toward it, it seems evident that in lending his great prestige to the furtherance of capital punishment and, moreover, in using this particular case as an example of its presumed "efficacy," Mr. Hoover (who, after all, is not a law-giver, but a law-enforcement officer) is committing a two-fold error. Because where one might say, *purely for the sake of argument*, that the death penalty was effective in preventing such crafty and meticulously deliberate crimes as kidnapping for ransom, or treason, or even the hijacking of airplanes, one would be almost obliged to admit, if he had any understanding of criminal behavior, that its value in a crime of this type was nil. For the two wretched people who perpetrated this outrage were not, in any sense of the word, rational, and clearly not susceptible to rational controls. To believe that by taking away the life of even one of these sickening perverts we shall deter others from similarly mad acts is demonstrably a false belief: only one conceivable end is served, and that is vengeance, an emotion which—instinctive as it may be—society can no longer afford. As Anthony Storr goes on to say: "It is also important that we should not simply recoil in horror, but that when we catch the child rapist we should study him and the conditions which produced him. In that way only may we be able to . . . offer help to those who are driven by similar desires. . . . You and I may imagine that we could never rape a child and then murder it: but, if we are honest with ourselves, we have to admit that even this potentiality exists within us. We do not know what internal pressures drive the rapist, nor what conditions determine his dreadful acts. But he cannot be regarded as a different kind of animal with different instincts; for he is also human, and subject to the same laws and the same forces which determine the desires of every one of us. It is tempting to treat him as something utterly foreign from ourselves and so avoid looking into our own depths. . . . To condemn him as inhuman is to fall into the trap of treating him as he treated his victims: as a thing, not a person, a thing on whom we can let loose our own sadistic impulses, not a fellow creature who might, even yet, be redeemed."

At this juncture, whether we are viewing a child rapist or Ben Reid, we are admittedly faced with problems that do not lend themselves to ready solutions. For one thing, there is the familiar question: "Wouldn't Ben Reid, when all is said and done, be better off dead if he had to serve a life sentence in prison?" This, or something like it, is a commonly heard sentiment, often uttered by people who are compassionate and well-meaning. But in the end it only emphasizes a corollary evil of capital punishment—the equally vengeful notion that there is no alternative to the death penalty save a sentence of perpetual incarceration. Significantly, if it is true that a life term with no hope of parole is worse than death (and one cannot help but agree that it may be worse), it becomes necessary to ask why we do not sentence our most villainous offenders to life, reserving the death penalty for lesser criminals. But more importantly, to assume that short of killing a man, we must doom him to a lifetime behind prison walls is to succumb to the doctrine of retaliation in its most hateful sense; and it is the practice of capital punishment more than any other single factor that tends to blight our administration of justice and to cast over our prisons the shadow of interminable revenge and retribution. Now, it would appear that some criminals are hopelessly incorrigible. Taborsky would seem to be mad or half mad, or, though sane within the legal sense of the word, seemingly devoid of any kind of understanding of right or wrong; from these people it would certainly be clear that we must protect ourselves by keeping them behind high walls forever. At the very least, as Anthony Storr points out, we can study them and learn why they and their kind behave as they do. A majority of criminals, however—including those whose deeds have been quite as ugly as Ben Reid's—are amenable to correction, and many of them can be, and have been, returned to society. As for Ben Reid, in arbitrarily inflicting upon him the sentence of death, in denying him even the chance of rehabilitation that we have just as arbitrarily granted others, we have committed a manifest injustice; and the death penalty, once again, reveals its ignoble logic.

It has been argued that opponents of capital punishment are swayed by emotion, that they are sentimental. To the degree that sentimentality may be considered a state of mind relying more upon emotion than reason, it would seem plain that it is the defenders of the death penalty who are the sentimentalists. If, for example, it could be proved that capital punishment was an effective deterrent to crime, even the most emotionally vulnerable, diehard humanitarian would be forced to capitulate in favor of it. But, unable to fend off the statistical proof that it is no deterrent at all, proponents of capital punishment find themselves backed into a corner, espousing emotional, last-ditch arguments. In the present instance, its lack of deterrent effect may be shown in the fact that it did not deter Ben Reid. Even more strikingly it is true in the case of the terrible Taborsky, finally executed, who had barely escaped electrocution for murder once (he was released from death row on a judicial error and freed from prison), whereupon he committed the series of brutal slayings I have mentioned. If it is evident that Taborsky should never have been released into society, it seems almost as clear that he is a case in point of that theory, proposed by a number of serious observers, that the death penalty in significant and not too rare instances actually exerts a fatal lure, impelling certain unbalanced people to crimes which ordinarily they would not commit. (In a recent English case one Frederick Cross of Stockport, near Manchester, said in testimony: "When I saw the man in his car I got the idea that if I was to kill him I would be hanged. . . . I don't wish to be defended at all. I killed him so that I would be hanged." The victim was a complete stranger. Cross achieved his desire: he was hanged.) Finally, in order to make reasonable the argument that capital punishment is a deterrent, why is it that the public is not incessantly exposed to its horrible finality, forced to witness the barbarous rite itself, and thereby made to reflect on the gruesome fate awaiting malefactors? But it remains a secret, shameful ceremony and except for the most celebrated cases, it is even indifferently reported in the press. Until by legislative mandate all executions are carried on the television networks of the states involved (they could be sponsored by the gas and electric companies), in a dramatic fashion which will enable the entire population—men, women and all children over the age of five—to watch the final agonies of those condemned, even the suggestion that we inflict the death penalty to deter people from crime is a farcical one.

Shorn of all rational, practical arguments, those who favor the death penalty must confront those who would eliminate it upon the solitary grounds of vengeance, and it is here, upon these grounds and these grounds alone, that the issue will have to be resolved. There is no doubt that the urge for revenge is a strong human emotion. But whether this is an emotion to be encouraged by the state is a different matter. As for Ben Reid, how much actual vengeance society still harbors toward him can only be a matter of conjecture. It would be a disgrace to all of us to say that it could be much. Having dwelt in his seven-by-seven cell on death row, as I have said, for over four years, he would seem to have endured such a torture of bewilderment, anxiety and terror as to make the question of vengeance academic. Since that day in June 1957 when he entered his cell on death row, there have been numberless writs, reprieves, reversals, stays of execution, all carried out in that admirable spirit of Fair Play which marks American justice but which, like a pseudosmile masking implacable fury, must seem to a condemned man pitiless and sadistic beyond any death sentence. A year and a half ago, indeed, it appeared that Ben Reid would have his opportunity for redemption; the judge of the U.S. District Court vacated his conviction on the grounds that his trial had been "fundamentally unfair" because the police had exacted his confessions without informing him of his rights to counsel or, for that matter, of any of his rights. At this point Reid's attorney told him the good news: it looked as if he was going to live. This past September, however, the U.S. Circuit Court of Appeals in New York took a different view: since counsel had not brought up the point of illegal confessions at the trial, Ben had in effect "waived his rights." Thus the lower court was overruled—not without, however, a vigorous dissenting opinion by one of the justices, Judge Charles E. Clark, one-time dean of the Yale Law School, who said that the view that Reid waived his rights "borders on the fantastic in any human or practical or, indeed, legal sense." Reid has just recently been granted a reprieve, until April 30, 1962, in order that his case may be argued before the U.S. Supreme Court. Especially in the light of Judge Clark's angry dissent, it seems likely that Reid's case will at least be accepted for review. Whether by these nine old metaphysicians, as Mencken called them, the legal point will be resolved in Reid's favor remains, as usual, a mystery. In any event, for Reid it has been a splendid ordeal. His present lawyer (who, incidentally, is also a Negro) has protested to the state, asking his removal from the tiny cell. After four years there, he contends, Ben's mind has badly deteriorated. Nowhere else on earth is a man dragged by such demoralizing extremes to the very edge of the abyss.

"The little man, despite the pratings of Democracy," Judge Curtis Bok has written of the death penalty, "is still the scapegoat." And he added this observation: "Someday we will look back upon our criminal and penal processes with the same horrified wonder as we now look back upon the Spanish Inquisition." Should the U.S. Supreme Court turn down his appeal, I am told that there is an outside chance at least that Ben Reid—due to those considerations of environment and mentality which his lawyer initially argued for in vain—may have his sentence commuted by the State Board of Pardons. This is highly unlikely: the Board of Pardons has never yet commuted a death sentence of a man convicted under the same Connecticut law. But there is a chance. If this comes to pass and Reid is allowed to live, he will gain, aside from the fragments of his life, an ironic kind of victory: nothing could demonstrate more cruelly the travesty of justice which is capital punishment than this shabby and belated mercy, predicated upon the identical arguments which were advanced in his favor in a court of law nearly five years before. On the other hand, should the fact if not the spirit of justice be served, and Ben Reid goes to the electric chair one night this spring, it may be said that the soul which is taken will already have been so diminished by our own inhumanity that what shall be lost is hardly a soul at all, and that the death penalty—having divested a man not alone of his life but of that dignity with which even the humblest of men must be allowed to face death itself—has achieved its ultimate corruption. *Or when saw we thee sick, or in prison, and came unto thee!* It is perhaps a late date in history to summon up the Gospel in behalf of a derelict Negro boy; having abandoned him, it does not become a Christian society to waste a shred of its jealously guarded piety upon him whom it has cast out into darkness. Only the condemned can truly know the heaviness of guilt; it settles upon their spirits like the weight of all the universe, and the quality of their bereavement is solitary and unique among humankind. To attempt to soothe this bereavement through Christian homilies would seem to be, like that final promenade with the chaplain whispering from Holy Writ, an act of outrageous hypocrisy. Yet somehow, try as we might to evade the verdict, we find ourselves being measured:

Inasmuch as ye have done it unto one of the least of these my brethren, ye have done it unto me. Until, searching our hearts, we can reconcile these words with the murder we inflict, in the name of justice, upon Ben Reid, and his fellows likewise outcast and condemned, we stand ourselves utterly condemned.

[*Esquire*, February 1962]

Benjamin Reid: Aftermath

THE ADMINISTRATION of criminal justice in Connecticut is unique in really spectacular ways. Although in many practical respects, of course, the state is among the most advanced in the union, there are aspects of its criminal code which echo that of Sicily in the fifteenth century. Connecticut is one of the few states in the United States which vest pardoning power in a board. Its Board of Pardons, established in 1883, consists of five responsible citizens appointed by the governor with the advice and consent of the state Senate. Fundamentally, the concept of a separate board was well-intentioned, in that it removed the awful responsibility of the pardoning power from a single man (and also from the political arena), while at the same time it placed that power in the hands of a body of people better equipped in terms of both time and experience to judge each individual plea. Yet insofar as a condemned man is concerned, the existence of a board of pardons constitutes an unprecedented and, it might be said, almost intolerably cruel paradox. For where in other states the governor could be expected to exercise his power of commutation by granting clemency without ceremony on any day far in advance of the date of execution, the Connecticut Board of Pardons sits as a sort of second, final tribunal, and it convenes on the morning of the day that the condemned man is scheduled to die. Thus, as the minutes tick away toward the fatal evening the condemned man, who is likely to be present at the proceedings, is forced to endure what amounts to the simulacrum of another trial, sweating out this ultimate, ghastly ritual whose climax is the proclamation, quite irreversible, either of mercy totally belated (else why not mercy in the beginning?) or of immediate death. Society has perhaps conceived of nothing quite so subtly undermining to the soul since the Inquisition.

But this is not all Ben Reid would have to endure at the hearing. He would have to endure the knowledge that in over ten years the Board of Pardons had not once commuted the sentence of a man convicted under the 1951 law. This was not due necessarily to a failure of mercy; it was due rather, once again, to failure of the Connecticut law, which in criminal matters is so freakish and capricious as to stun the reason, and at best is permeated by the kind of stubborn, ominous reverse logic that haunts *Alice in Wonderland*. It doubtless begins with the fact that Connecticut, unique in so many ways, is the only state in the United States (and indeed probably the only jurisdiction in the civilized world) that does not consider its first-degree life prisoners to be eligible for parole. This in turn results from a state of mind which assumes all murderers (who are in reality overwhelmingly better parole risks than forgers and thieves) to be a species of uncontrollable brute likely to run amok in the streets. (Even second-degree murderers get a tougher break in Connecticut than anywhere else in the United States. The average time served for second-degree murderers before parole in Connecticut over a recent eleven-year period was the highest in the nation: eighteen years, vs. ten years in California and eight years in New Jersey.) Further, in 1951, in a well-meaning effort to rid the state of an archaic law calling for mandatory execution in all convictions for first-degree murder, the legislature passed an act (mentioned above), now in effect, which states: "Any person who commits murder in the first degree . . . *shall* suffer death *unless the jury* . . . recommends imprisonment in the State Prison for life, in which case the sentence of the court *shall* be imprisonment for life without benefit of release . . ." (Italics mine.) In actuality, this statute was an enormous step backward, and its consequences need to be explained. One of the results of the act—without precedent in any state in the union—is loony and nightmarish in the extreme: what it means is that a first-degree murderer *must* be sentenced to a sort of living death without any possibility whatever of release, or that he *must* be sentenced to actual death, like Reid, whereby he stands at least a chance to live through intercession of the Board of Pardons, and in such a case is likely to be eventually paroled. Here the dilemma and anguish of our contemporary attitudes toward punishment reach their mad climax. Under such circumstances, what convicted felon would not opt for the sentence of death? Even so, his chances to live are only theoretical, since the Board of Pardons—which under the mandatory-death-penalty statute felt free to commute death sentences to life imprisonment when they thought that the nature of the case demanded it—has been understandably reluctant to overrule a jury which, representing the will of the people, had had two sentences from which to choose. Therefore, no person condemned after the 1951 act in Connecticut has ever had his sentence commuted by the board. It was mainly because of this complex and wholly irrational situation that thoughtful observers were not giving Ben Reid much of a chance.

The hearing took place last June 25. It was public, and it began promptly at ten o'clock in an airy, spacious, newly painted conference room on the second floor of the administration building of the state prison at Wethersfield. It was a beautiful, sunny day, hot but tolerably so because of a pleasant breeze, and through the windows one could see the great elms and neat lawns of the town of Wethersfield, and watch children bicycling along the streets, so that the effect—save for the presence of two or three guards— was hardly that of a prison at all, but of a meeting room in some New England school or college. The irony was almost too explicit: it did not seem either the day or the place to ponder death. At the far end of the room, at a table perhaps twenty feet long, sat the five members of the board—two lawyers, a judge of the state Supreme Court, a professor emeritus of political science at Wesleyan University, and a physician. All men in their fifties and sixties, they were gray-haired, solemn and distinguished-looking; indeed, several of them so combined steely-gray handsomeness and juridical gravity that they seemed ready to be cast as judges in a movie. They were also, as I say, extremely solemn, almost forbidding in manner, Connecticut Yankees to a man, and I had the distinct feeling that mercy might be wrung from their hearts, but only under mighty compulsion. The spectators—sixty or so in all—sat on hard chairs at the other end of the room. Between spectators and the board there was another table, and on opposite sides of this table sat members of Reid's counsel, who would argue for clemency, and the state's attorney and his aides, who, presumably, would present reasons why Reid should be executed.

Shortly after ten, Reid was brought in by a guard. Dressed in freshly pressed prison khaki, shirt open at the throat, he was a tall muscular young Negro, and his face seemed to me curiously impassive and expressionless as he slumped down into a wooden armchair. I realized with a start that he was the first person I had ever seen whose death seemed almost inevitable and only twelve hours away.

Now, it should be said here that no longer was Reid completely friendless and alone, as he had been during the five years he had spent in his condemned cell. Since the previous winter, after a young Trinity College student named George Will had learned of Reid's predicament and imminent execution, an extraordinary amount of activity had been organized in his behalf. Will had written an impassioned letter which was published in the college newspaper. This had resulted in a committee, composed of three Trinity faculty members, three members of the Trinity administration and six students, which had set about energetically during the ensuing months to try to save Reid's life. The committee was headed by George Will and Albert E. Holland, the latter the vice president of Trinity College and a man who might be expected to have rather severe strictures about capital punishment. Holland had spent several years in a Japanese prison camp during World War II and had endured more than one bad moment when his custodians began promiscuously lopping off heads. Like such vocal opponents of capital punishment as Arthur Koestler and Jean-Paul Sartre—who suffered similar experiences in Spain during the Civil War and for whom the issue of the death penalty has grim personal relevance—Holland was no quixotic adventurer, and his efforts to save Reid had consumed a large part of his time for over four months. With other members of the committee, Holland had dug deep into Reid's past. It had been a past of nearly monumental poverty and neglect, and much information about his squalid upbringing, it is important to note, had not been admissible as evidence at Reid's trial. The committee had pored over dozens of the melancholy records and documents scattered back through almost all the years of his wretched career—welfare records of the Reid family; juvenile-court reports; records of the Hartford County Temporary Home, where Reid had spent eight of his youthful years, and those of the state reformatory where he had also been lodged for a time; psychiatric reports and trial transcripts and records of Reid's unsuccessful appeals to higher courts. They had also interviewed a score of people who had been associated with

Reid at one time or another—parole officers, social workers, officials of various welfare and correctional institutions where he had spent the greater part of his life. In addition, the committee had engaged itself in a great deal of legal research: even on the surface of Reid's case it had been shockingly apparent that, in terms of equality of justice, his death sentence had caused him to be a singular victim in more than one respect, and the exhaustive, meticulous investigation which the Trinity group made of capital cases in the state over a period of forty years brought forth some remarkable conclusions, best expressed in a single statement made in the bulky mimeographed dossier which the committee presented to the board that morning: "Our study shows that prior to 1957 [the year of Reid's conviction] the State of Connecticut had not even tried on a first-degree murder charge, let alone sentenced to death, a person like Benjamin Reid who at the time of his crime was an adolescent, with a mental capacity of an eleven-year-old child, with a most unfortunate family heritage and background, and with no previous record of violence."

Now as we sat in the hot, still meeting room, it was Holland's task to present these facts to the board. One of the first persons he called to testify also made one of the most dramatic pleas of the day. This was Robert Satter, a prominent Hartford lawyer who had followed Reid's post-trial career with an abiding interest. It had for a long time been Satter's belief—shared by others—that of the multitude of injustices surrounding Reid's conviction one of the worst was that involving the sinister connection between Reid and the notorious mass-murderer Joseph Taborsky. It was Satter's contention that it had been the public furor and vengeful outcry attending Taborsky's trial that had infected Reid's own nearby courtroom and similarly sealed Reid's fate. A mild, scholarly-looking, sandy-haired man, Satter asked the board to consider a literary allusion. "You may recall the conclusion of *Moby Dick*," he said, "how, as the ship *Pequod* sinks beneath the waves, the arm of a sailor appears from the depths to hammer a pennant against the mast. Just as the nail is being driven home, a gull flies by, and its wing, interposing itself between hammer and mast, is nailed fast to the spar, so that the final glimpse of the doomed ship is this bit of fluttering life being dragged with it into the deep." There was nothing histrionic about Satter and his manner; his words were splendidly afire. Pausing, he gestured toward Reid. If Benjamin Reid should die this night, he continued, his life, like that of Melville's gull, would have been sacrificed just as surely as if the arm of Joseph Taborsky had reached from the grave to drag him down into oblivion. It was a marvelously delivered speech, all in very low key, and when Satter had finished there was a long, rather uneasy silence in the room.

The first hour or so of the general plea, including Satter's statement, was based on the question of equality of justice, and Holland had plenty of statistics at hand to show that the state of Connecticut had granted clemency or given lesser sentences to many criminals whose background and mental capacity were infinitely superior to Reid's, and whose crimes had often been far more cold-blooded and ruthless. But this was only the first part of the plea. Now, as the morning lengthened, Holland began to call witnesses to testify to Reid's fearful and blighted upbringing. There were a dozen or so in all, and they included a Negro policewoman who had been assigned to the slum area where Reid had been reared (she described the section as a "jungle"), various welfare workers and parole officers who had known and worked with Reid, and finally, a gentle-spoken middle-aged white woman named Mrs. Neva Jones, who had been the nurse at the Hartford County Home during the eight years Reid was there, and who had flown up from North Carolina to be present at the hearing. Partly due to the fact that he was at first barely literate, Reid had corresponded with no one during his long and lonely stay on death row, but late in 1961, as his execution approached, he and Mrs. Jones began to exchange letters. Excerpts from his letters were read at the hearing. They were remarkable, in style often resembling nothing so much as that of a man who in a general sense was quite lost but on the verge of a miraculous verbal discovery (actually, as he told Mrs. Jones, his main reading matter had been the Bible and a dictionary): "In your most recent letter you made mention of my vocabulary as being increase, well the reason is due to the fact that I do read quite a bit, and by doing this, I feel that I can express myself more clearly logically speaking, by studying neologistical expressions excerpted from the different literature I study." But there was no doubt, as Holland pointed out to the board, that the letters were those of a man profoundly conscious of his wrongdoing ("I do not want sympathy, I just merely want a chance to show everyone that I have reformed and repented of my wrong that was done thoughtlessly senselessly") and, even more important, were the expression of one struggling toward some kind of enlightenment.

There was an unconscious irony in one questioning statement, which might sum up the thoughts of condemned, miserable, desolate, guilty men everywhere: "I know that I have done wrong but have I done worse than the worse or am I the worse period."

As the hearing began to draw to a close between noon and one o'clock, and with Reid's moment of execution only hours away, I became uneasily aware that all through the proceedings one member of the board had been in the habit of gazing abstractedly for long periods out the window. But there was no diminution of attention among the audience when the final witness appeared: Reid's mother, badly crippled with an arm adrift from her side like a helpless wing, who said, almost inaudibly, "I ask you, would you grant him life, please"; and Reid himself, who stood stiffly in his khaki uniform in a strained, awkward half-bow and, his voice almost a whisper, made a brief plea for mercy.

The next-to-the-last presentation was made by Louis Pollak, professor of law at Yale, who capped even this morning's mountainous evidence of injustice with a brilliant analysis of the possibility of constitutional infirmities in Reid's case. He pointed out that although it was true that the United States Supreme Court had declined to hear Reid's appeal, there had been, in the long history of the case as it proceeded from court to higher court, enough dissent and doubt (as to whether Reid's rights had been violated) on the part of a few distinguished jurists to make it incumbent upon the board to consider this grave aspect of the case before consigning Reid to oblivion. It was a masterly plea, and it seemed difficult to surmount in terms of force and effect, but it was at least equaled by the presence of the final person to speak. This was a tall, athletically built, trimly tailored man, very grim, who approached the board and formally identified himself as Judge Douglass Wright. He had been the prosecutor in the original Reid trial and has since become a judge. The hearing room was utterly still, for this was a spectacle almost unique in American jurisprudence: a prosecutor interceding in behalf of the prisoner only hours before his doom. Wright was brief and to the point: there was no doubt of Reid's guilt; the trial had been conducted with strict fairness. But such factors as Reid's youth at the time of his crime, his slum background, his marginal mentality, had caused Wright, in the years since the sentence of death, to feel that execution would be an injustice. He joined therefore with the others in making a plea for clemency.

After this, the case for the state seemed almost anticlimactic. The state's attorney, John D. LaBelle, an owlish, methodical man who kept shuffling through his notes, was quick to indicate in the strongest terms that Reid had been guilty, that in this "classic case of first-degree murder," justice, insofar as the state was concerned, had been done. But, like Judge Wright, he conceded that the board, constituted to dispense mercy, might grant such mercy in this case, and he added, "Whatever you do, it isn't going to upset our office one bit." The proceedings were ended. The board would announce its decision at three o'clock that afternoon.

Downstairs in the prison reception lobby a large group of God's underground, the Quakers, had assembled. They numbered a score or so. Some of them had attended the hearing, and all of them were now prepared to participate that night in a vigil at the prison should the appeal for clemency fail. I spoke to one Quaker, a Hartford businessman. "We will pray for Reid," he said, "which is all we can do." He began to speak with a kind of fury for a Quaker. "It is a fearful thing, isn't it? What right has the state to coop up a man—a boy—in a tiny cell for five years, and then exterminate him like a dog?"

Outside, the day was still blooming with summer and sunlight, and along the streets of Wethersfield, one of the supremely lovely New England towns, the children were still pedaling their bicycles. I met Louis Pollak; he was chatting with the Reverend William Coffin, Jr., the chaplain of Yale University, who had taken a personal interest in the Reid case. We were joined by Mrs. Jones, and the four of us decided to have lunch in a coffee shop on one of Wethersfield's elm-lined streets.

At lunch, Mrs. Jones, seeming only a little nervous about the outcome of the appeal, said, "Oh, I knew Ben real well. He was a sort of lonely little boy. And a bit lazy, I guess. But there was nothing mean about him. He was really so proud of himself whenever he accomplished anything good. You know, he was a trombone player and assistant leader of the band. He was a good trombone player, too. I'll never forget how proud he was, dressed up in that band uniform."

"How long did you know him, Mrs. Jones?" Coffin inquired.

"Oh, the whole time he was there. It must have been eight years. Imagine, eight years in the County Home! I guess he was sixteen when they let him go. But, you know, he wasn't *ready* to go back—back to that terrible slum. It's society's fault, really. I mean, all of us. People should know more about this situation, where these poor abandoned children are taken in for a while, and then sent back just at the wrong age to that awful environment. It's just a shame, really, and people should know about it."

At around two o'clock, as Coffin and I drove back to the prison, we saw Reid's mother. Quite alone, she was hobbling laboriously down the deserted, elm-shaded sidewalk in front of the prison toward a small sheltered enclosure that serves as a bus stop. There she sat down and began to fan herself. Coffin went up and greeted her. It was rather difficult to make conversation but I couldn't help asking where she was going.

"Well, I expect I'll just go on home," she said. "The Lord done answered my prayers, so I expect I'll just go right on home."

"Then you think the hearing went well?" I said.

"Well, I figures if they was going to do anything they would say so at the end of it. But they ain't said nothing, so I figures they going let Benjamin off, praise God. I knew Ben has repented, so the mercy's coming to him. The Lord sure done answered my prayers."

Of course, she hadn't gotten this quite straight, and no one seemed to have advised her of the board's operations, but neither Coffin nor I, exchanging glances, could figure out a way to correct her. In the end it didn't seem to matter, for as she left us with these words and the bus came lumbering up, I had the feeling for the first time that day that all was going to be well.

The decision, which came to the gathering in the reception room of the prison at 4:05, was that Reid's sentence had been commuted to life imprisonment, with the possibility of parole. There would be no necessity for the Quakers to keep their vigil. And a rent had appeared in the veil of immutable law.

It is of course important that Reid's life was saved. It is more important that he will not be left to rot. Whether the five years spent in the shadow of the electric chair have worked irreparable damage upon his spirit is something no one can say for sure, but judging from his letters alone, there is a sense of something struggling and questing, and therefore salvageable. At some time in the future he will be eligible for parole, and in the meantime the Trinity group has pledged itself to help him in his search for an identity. It may be said perhaps that in prison a man's identity cannot be much, but we who are on the outside looking in—we who are so prone to forget that all men must be given at least the possibility of redemption—are in no position to judge. Not only capital punishment, but all punishment in general, is one of our most crucial dilemmas; the death penalty is the wretched symbol of our inability to grapple with that dark part of our humanity which is crime. Equally as important as Reid's own salvation is the fact that his case and the struggle to save his life, which attracted so much attention, will have caused people to rearrange entirely their ideas about some of our penal and criminal processes. Certainly the law in Connecticut in regard to capital offenders is archaic and monstrous; and already, largely as a result of the Reid case, there is talk in some circles about pressing in the legislature for a "triple verdict" law, now in effect in California and Pennsylvania (1, to determine guilt; 2, to determine sanity; 3, to determine sentence), which will permit evidence to be introduced at trial that was generally denied to Reid, this denial contributing greatly to the fact that he was initially sentenced to death. If just this act is accomplished, Reid's anguish will not have been in vain, and the simple victory won that afternoon in Wethersfield—the victory of life over death—will have been transformed into something even larger in our unending search for justice.

[*Esquire*, November 1962]

AFTERMATH OF
"AFTERMATH"

This may be a good place to examine briefly certain aspects of the power of the written word. I have never wanted to claim credit for having saved a man's life, but as I was reminded years later by George F. Will (the "young Trinity College student," mentioned in "Aftermath," who has become a celebrated national columnist), the original essay did have the effect of causing the Trinity people and others to spring into action. So I suppose it may be inferred that had I not written the original essay, Ben Reid would most likely have gone to his doom. On a somewhat less dramatic note, I was pleased to learn that the second piece I wrote on Reid had the effect of changing the Connecticut law regarding capital punishment along the lines I detailed in the concluding passage. Robert Satter, now a judge, whose wonderful speech about *Moby Dick* still lingers in my memory among the bright moments of that day, later became a state legislator. It was he who, taking a cue from my article, introduced legislation that eventually brought about a more equitable procedure regarding capital offenders. So I felt that my initial ventures into journalism had hardly been wasted time.

But what about Benjamin Reid? Rereading the two pieces I wrote on his case, I became aware of how important to my argument against the death penalty was the Christian doctrine of redemption. This interests me now, because I thought that by the time I was past thirty-five—at the very least agnostic and surely swept by the bleak winds of existentialism—I had abandoned the Presbyterian precepts of my childhood. But I can see that the Gospels were as much a mediating force in my attempt to save Reid's life as were Camus and

Heidegger. And how sweet it was to see this candidate for
redemption come alive from his benighted dungeon in a way
that would quicken the heart of any Christian salvationist.
How beautiful it was to witness this outcast victim flower and
grow, once rescued and given that chance for which those
honest Quakers had prayed on their knees. For the simple fact
is that Ben Reid—now that he was snatched from the electric
chair and released into the general prison population—
demonstrated qualities of character, of will, and above all, of
intelligence that defied everyone's imagination. All of the
people connected with Reid's case had been deluded about his
mental capacity, which was as much a victim of having been
underestimated as Reid himself was a victim of foster homes
and deprivation. Far from being the borderline defective he
had been described as by many observers (including myself),
Reid, it turned out, was quite bright, in certain ways even
brilliant, and the metamorphosis he underwent in prison was
something to marvel at. He became a star baseball player, a
leader among the inmates; he secured his high school
equivalency diploma, began to take college work. A model
prisoner he was—in every sense of that worn and risky
description. A triumph of faith over adversity. Maybe
someday a winner.

Reid spent eight more years in prison before his time came
up for parole. In the middle of March 1970 I received a
telephone call from some of the people at Trinity College
who had taken an interest in Reid and had followed his career
through prison. It was highly probable that Reid would be
paroled in April, they said. What they proposed to do was
enroll Reid as a special student at Trinity, where he would
begin courses at summer school. Would I be willing, they
wondered, to let Reid stay in my house in Roxbury for a few
weeks while they put things in order at Trinity and began to
ready a permanent place for him there? My willingness
would be a not inconsiderable factor in obtaining the parole.
I immediately replied that I would indeed take Ben in.
Although I had never visited Reid in prison, we had
corresponded quite a few times over the years since his
commutation. His letters were well-reasoned, grammatically
correct, persuasive—so impressive, really, and showing such
signs of growth and blossoming that I could not stop

reproaching myself for having helped cast him as mentally deficient. A week or so before he was to be released into my custody, I visited him in the new state prison at Somers, near the Massachusetts border. I was impressed by his poise, his verbal agility, his warmth, his intelligence. The idea of my studio in Roxbury becoming Ben Reid's halfway house filled me with pleasure, and I understood the blessings of redemption.

Early in April, only a few days before the magical date, Reid walked off into the woods from a work detail just outside the gates of the prison. An alarm was sounded, and Reid was pursued by state police with dogs, but his trail was lost. After a night in the woods, during which time Reid had strayed into Massachusetts, he lingered through the early daylight hours outside a house in Longmeadow, a well-to-do, semirural suburb of Springfield. Reid found an automobile antenna and sharpened it into a weapon. He then entered the house where a thirty-seven-year-old woman was preparing breakfast for her two young children and the child of a friend. Forcing the woman and the children into her car, he made her cruise up and down the Connecticut River Valley for a large part of the day. At one point during the abduction, Reid told the woman to drive into the parking area of a deserted state park. There, he raped her. (In subsequent testimony some conflict developed as to whether there was an element of consent on the part of the woman, but this would seem to be an almost frivolous point.) Later on in the day, after the woman had driven him to Holyoke, he boarded a bus for New York but was spotted by a prison official and was quickly arrested. Tried that summer in Springfield for an assortment of crimes—including rape, kidnapping, forcible entry and assault with a deadly weapon—Reid was sentenced to ten to fifteen years in state prison. These horrible, bizarre and seemingly improbable events took place twelve years ago. At this writing—in the spring of 1982—Reid is approaching the end of his sentence at the Bridgewater facility in southeastern Massachusetts. This is a medium-security prison where, as before, he has been a model inmate. At the age of forty-four, he has spent all the years since the age of nineteen behind bars. Could it be—as I suspect—that Reid's frantic flight from freedom was a way to ensure staying incarcerated?

In the summer of 1981, when Jack Henry Abbott—
Norman Mailer's protégé—knifed to death a young aspiring
playwright on a Lower Manhattan sidewalk, a tempest of
public rage roared around Mailer's head. Had it not been for
Mailer's misguided zeal—it was said—had it not been for
the sentimental ardor which impelled him to espouse the
freedom of a murderous convict simply because he displayed
a literary gift, this terrible crime would not have taken place.
Well, yes and no. There was no doubt that the tragedy
happened, that it would not have happened had Abbott
remained in prison, and that Mailer was a critical factor in
Abbott's release. But as I replayed over and over again those
ugly events, I could find no possible way—with the memory
of Ben Reid's own near-release into my custody so immovably
fixed in my mind—to condemn Mailer for his role in the
awful story. There were significant differences, of course.
For one thing, Reid had escaped before his parole took effect,
although this is an academic point. Unlike Abbott, Reid had
displayed no artistic talent worth nurturing; he had seemed to
be merely an attractive and salvageable human being who
had behaved well in prison (unlike Abbott, who, whatever
the motivation, had killed a fellow inmate). Then, too, their
last crimes on the outside had been of different magnitudes—
manslaughter even in this day being an atrocity greater than
rape.

Nonetheless, the similarities of background were wickedly
familiar: broken homes, poverty, neglect, abuse, foster
parents, and the loathsome taste of incarceration at an early
age. And years and years of the inhumanity of prison life.
It is hardly possible to feel anything but revulsion for both
Reid's and Abbott's ultimate crimes, but it is plain that each
crime in its way was the result of perceptions wrenched and
warped by the monstrous abnormality of long imprisonment.
An almost unbearable fact here signals for attention: both
Reid and Abbott were in prison as *children*. Much was made
during the Abbott case about the alleged romanticism of
writers in their conjunction with prisoners; some of us have
been called, with a certain appropriateness, "jail groupies,"
and certainly there are writers who have had to answer for
their silly love affairs with criminals. But I am quite sure that
romance alone does not explain the fascination or the

constant devotion that many writers pay to those that live half-lives behind bars. Remembering one's own Elysian childhood in juxtaposition with that of Reid and of Abbott, I think it is fair to say that a concern for either of those wretched felons has to do less with romanticism than with a sense of justice, and the need for seeking restitution for other men's lost childhoods.

It could be argued that the power of the written word, effective in helping to save Ben Reid from death, had the unanticipated and certainly pernicious result of causing a suburban housewife terror and suffering. So there we are. Do we abandon our efforts to salvage prisoners because of the savage acts of Reid and Abbott? Almost as important is the question: Do we indeed now abandon Reid and Abbott themselves? As for the first question, neither Mailer nor I would have acted as big brothers—or as surrogate fathers, or role models, or simple sponsors—to these men had we known what they might perpetrate on two innocent people. But daily throughout this country prisoners whose records are every bit as flawed with violence as Abbott's and Reid's are released into freedom, and maintain clean records thereafter. Such a statistical consideration was not in my mind when I vouched for Reid (nor do I imagine it was in Mailer's), but our mistakes were committed within limits already well established by precedent. Therefore—speaking for myself alone—I can feel (and at times have felt) aching regret, but no guilt. We are neither the first nor the last to be shattered by this dilemma. And others will make fearful errors in helping their disadvantaged brothers seek redemption.

But, finally, do we abandon Jack Abbott and Ben Reid? Since Abbott was sentenced to fifteen years to life for his New York crime, he would now seem to be placed beyond any such consideration, at least for the time being. Reid's case is considerably more simple, since in only a few more years he will have paid his debt and will go free. When I asked Robert Satter—who had invested almost as much time as anyone in working selflessly in Reid's behalf—what he felt when he first heard of the escape and the rape, he replied that he experienced a sense of utter betrayal. So, I must confess, did I, and I have often wondered what might have been the consequences for me and my family had Reid—

suffering the emotional upheaval that caused him to erupt so violently—actually taken up residence with me as planned. In my grimmest imaginings I could not help thinking that he might have raped my daughter instead of the Longmeadow housewife. Yet—and I can only try to dream of the stoicism it required—Satter immediately went to Reid's aid again during the Springfield trial, offering legal and moral support to a man whom most people might have written off for good.

My own sense of betrayal has been strong, but not so complete that I have been able to turn my back on Reid's destiny. His conduct in the Massachusetts prison system has been once more, as I say, exemplary, and even if he has to serve a year or two more in Connecticut for his escape (he is hoping to be pardoned from this), it will not be long before he is free, after more than twenty-five years. It will doubtless become a difficult matter for Reid to adjust to freedom, and his return to society will have to be monitored with delicacy and care. But hope persists. I have talked to Ben Reid several times; he speaks of his remorse and his repentance, and of his conviction that he will make good on the outside, and I cannot explain why I believe him.

The Joint

TWENTY YEARS AGO, when he was thirty, a talented white college-educated jazz pianist named James Blake found himself serving a two-year sentence in the Duval County jail in Jacksonville, Florida, charged with petit larceny and breaking and entering. It was his first experience at doing time, and although Blake was absurdly out of character as a criminal type and, by his own admission, the world's most inept burglar, he discovered that confinement offered such sovereign satisfactions and fulfillments that he caused himself to be incarcerated at the Jacksonville jail or, even more happily, at "The Joint," the Florida State Penitentiary at Raiford, for thirteen of the next twenty years.

Blake's work—a collection of letters written to various friends, including two writers he had come to know and who had befriended him, Nelson Algren and James Purdy—comprises a vivid and illuminating chronicle. It is one of the most wickedly entertaining of its kind, a thief's journal that reflects the mordant, droll, nervously sensitive consciousness of a man for whom prison was far less a purgatory than a retreat, a kind of timeless, walled Yaddo for the gifted misfit.

Since the Marquis de Sade there has been a paucity of significant prison literature and there have been too few articulate recorders of prison life. In our own time, save for the work of Jean Genet, writings by and about prisoners have not often surpassed in quality the level of the Sunday supplements. Our legacy of inside accounts has tended to be characterized by garishly colored tall tales about escapes from Devil's Island, pedestrian reminiscences by celebrity cons, death-row sensationalism on the order of *The Last Mile*, and characteristically American examples of uplift and redemption, such as *The Birdman of Alcatraz.*

Many of these are well-meaning and even informative but often grossly lurid and, in any case, lacking the perceptions and insights necessary to render the prison environment and the lives of its victims with the complexity they deserve. There has been much earnest sociology, some of it readable, useful polemics by knowledgeable observers like John Bartlow Martin, and sympathetic accounts by such humane officials as Warden Lewis E. Lawes and Warden Clinton T. Duffy, who despite their sincerity and compassion retain the point of view of the overlord, the Establishment.

To some extent, this situation resembles that of the historiography of American Negro slavery. Of those "many thousand gone," only a few such eloquent witnesses as Frederick Douglass, William Wells Brown and Josiah Henson (all ex-slaves) survived to tell us what it was truly like to live under that unspeakable oppression. In particular Douglass, a superb psychologist who would be horrified to observe the foolishness being purveyed about Negro history by many present-day black militant intellectuals, knew that slavery (which to an important degree resembles prison in that both are closed, totalitarian systems) could foster rebelliousness and the wildest desire for freedom in the breasts of many men while at the same time the very ruthless and monolithic nature of its despotism might, in certain circumstances, wreck the personalities of other men, making them supinely content with bondage, eager and happy to genuflect before authority.

Like slavery, prison life is an abominable but nonetheless human situation in which men will respond to their predicament in diverse ways that still reflect their individuality and humanity. It is a measure of the excellence of James Blake's work and the grace of his survival that he has given us a record that is both an enormously revealing chronicle of life behind walls and a fascinating self-portrait by a man who continues to be steadfastly an individualist, telling his own truths.

Like Genet, Blake is both a prose stylist of distinction and a homosexual; the incandescent homosexual activity of prison life is of course the preoccupying concern—the obsession—of Genet and the entire jailhouse mystique of carnal love is a large element in Genet's recidivism, as, at least implicitly, it is for Blake. But here the resemblance ends. Genet is a visionary and a mystical genius, and Blake's gift, however beguiling, is a minor one. Then, too, his voice, unlike that of the Frenchman whose tone is passionately embroiled, remains detached, ironic, witty, lyrical.

If Genet is the rhapsodist of criminals and their greatest metaphysician, Blake is an artificer in light verse, the criminal's best satirist, a sardonic voice that is often surprisingly poignant—one is somehow reminded of Chaplin. An epistolary collection runs the risk of monotony, however; the reader begins to detect that solitary, self-concerned, droning sound. One of the strengths of Blake's letters is their consistent readability, the secret of which is a lilting, rueful, bittersweet awareness of the sheer monstrousness of things, and a gift for hilarity in the midst of a depiction of grim events that blows like a fresh wind through the pages and keeps them mercifully cleansed of self-pity.

Blake is especially brilliant in his descriptions of his fellow convicts—both the "straight" ones and those with whom he is having homosexual relationships—and often writes with a fine novelist's canny eye for detail, incorporating so much in a brief passage that its resonance, physical and moral, haunts one bleakly long afterwards:

> So now I am back on the J-Range where I feel more comfortable, and my cell partner is a check artist from Maryland who has been ostensibly rehabilitated to the extent that he is leaving on parole next week. Glib, devious, sadly shallow and incredibly beautiful, the Narcissine mirror that goes everywhere with him has prevented him from absorbing anything. (He was locked up with David Siqueiros in Mexico City and could only shrug when I asked him about it.) He claims he is the way he is because his mother held his hand in the fire when she caught him stealing. She should have put his head in the fire. No no no, that is quite wrong. He has been amiable, pleasant and almost completely absent, it has been like coming together with a Popsicle. Put the blame on the cosmos, put the blame on Mame. His prognosis, murky, and what is not?

Or, describing another relationship, Blake indulges his flair for extravaganza:

> I'm sharing a cell now with a young cat sentenced to the chair for gangbang. He's a beautiful child, a little solemn sometimes, which I guess is allowable under the circumstances. He asked me what I thought Eternity was like, and all I could offer was a guess—an Olivia de Havilland movie on television. . . . In a laudable attempt to dodge the thunderbolt (his case is on appeal) he

has been improving each shining hour by hitting the Glory Road
with the travelling bands of flagellants that haunt the jail—Holy
Rollers, Mormons, Baptists, Anabaptists—and he has become an
Eleventh Hour postulant in the Seventh Day Opportunists. These
pious acts swing a lot of weight, such is the Kingdom of Heaven.
Bless the boy, he's far too beautiful to go down for such a flimsy
transgression, and I hope he makes it. The Holy Ones have a
lobby in Tallahassee that don't quit.

Yet I should not want to give the impression that the tone of
these letters is one of unalloyed facetiousness in the face of adversity, for Blake is a profoundly serious writer, and the jocular tone
often is merely a decorative gloss upon insights that are original and
startling: "I remember a black lover I had. . . . Our arrangement
was an eminently workable one. We were aware that the powerful attraction we felt was because we were bizarre to one another,
and we were also aware that hate was just as much present as love
in our relationship. That was a really swinging affair, no nonsense
at all. Not a hell of a lot of conversation, but then there wasn't
much time for it, either."

But why is it that so many felons return to The Joint, abandon
freedom in favor of prison's seductive lure? We know through
their own confessions that many men—more than is comfortable
to think about—have murdered for the very reason that they were
aware that the consequence of their act would be the noose or the
electric chair. If this alone is almost sufficient justification for the
abolition of the death penalty, it would likewise seem that the hunger, the visceral longing, the truly quivering nostalgia that Blake,
representing so many other men, felt for The Joint when away
from it would be sound enough reason to abolish the institution of
the prison itself. More than once Blake committed crimes—chiefly
burglary as a result of the need for drugs—through a barely sub-
liminal impulse to achieve his reincarceration; it is this mighty urge
to return to the smooth, amniotic surroundings of The Joint—
where all things are provided and the tensions of a too-often-terrify-
ing and monstrous outer world are erased—that Blake anatomizes
better than any convict before him and, together with the theme
of homosexuality with which that urge is so closely connected,
helps give the book the quality of revelation.

If some of the true horrors of prison life are absent from *The
Joint* and if one does not obtain a sense of the dark midnight of
the soul that one gets from such prison sojourners as Wilde and

Dostoevsky, it is simply that for a man for whom prison is a shelter and a haven—a spiritual home—the horrors cannot seem so oppressive after all. Also, Blake is a self-confessed masochist; such a predilection for suffering, needless to say, takes care of a lot of things when one's associates, as Blake describes them once with a kind of half-hearted antipathy, are "dull and brutal and often more square than the squares outside."

In a remarkable passage written from freedom, Blake describes what it is about prison that he finds so irresistibly appealing; how many legions of men have felt the same way can only be a matter of conjecture, though it must assuredly be vast.

You know what's in my mind? The Joint. I thought I was getting off free from that experience. I thought they hadn't managed to touch me, but it colors every moment and every action of my life. I think always of the peace that I had there—this working to survive and surviving to work seems increasingly like an arrangement I would not have chosen were it up to me. Those gates, man, they're inviting. So much lovely time stretches out before you, time to read, to write, to play, to practice, to speculate, contemplate—and without the idiot necessity to Hold Up Your End. It is so well understood, the lines are so definitely drawn: I am Society and you are Not, and there is such a weary patience with nonconforming, it is infinitely restful.

Elsewhere:

[I feel] the inexplicable pull of The Joint, trying to fathom the Why of this incredible homesickness, trying to name for myself the kinship of the doomed I felt for the other cons when I was in.

Nearing the time of one of his paroles, Blake wrote to a friend:

There's a steady and joyful surge of anticipation when I think about the Outside. I think of the freedom to walk in the night under the stars in the blessed dark, after these endless months of living my life in the shrillness of daylight—savoring again the poignancy of twilight. When I think of how shining new things will seem to me, I am filled with excitement.

This of course is fustian (though truly meant at the time) and, significantly, the tribute it pays to liberty strikes perhaps the only false note in a unique, honest, moving book which, telling us much about the paradoxes of one man's mind, enhancing our knowledge about the nature of freedom (if only because it demonstrates that we are still unable to define it), also tells us much about ourselves and our most fallible institution, The Joint.

[*New York Times Book Review*, April 25, 1971]

A Death in Canaan

TOWARD THE END of Joan Barthel's excellent book about Peter Reilly, Judge John Speziale—the jurist who presided over the trial and who later granted Peter a new trial— is quoted as saying: "The law is imperfect." As portrayed in this book, Judge Speziale appears an exemplary man of the law, as fair and compassionate a mediator as we have any right to expect in a system where all too many of his colleagues are mediocre or self-serving or simply crooked. Certainly his decision in favor of a retrial—an action in itself so extraordinary as to be nearly historic—was the product of a humane and civilized intellect. Judge Speziale is one of the truly attractive figures in this book, which, although it has many winning people among its dramatis personae, contains more than one deplorable actor. And the judge is of course right: the law *is* imperfect. His apprehension of this fact is a triumph over the ordinary and the expected (in how many prisons now languish other Peter Reillys, victims of the law's "imperfections" but lacking Peter's many salvaging angels?), and is woven into his most honorable decision to grant Peter a new trial. But though he doubtless spoke from the heart as well as the mind and with the best intentions, the judge has to be found guilty of an enormous understatement.

The law (and one must assume that a definition of the law includes the totality of its many arms, including the one known as law enforcement) is not merely imperfect, it is all too often a catastrophe. To the weak and the underprivileged the law in all of its manifestations is usually a punitive nightmare. Even in the abstract the law is an institution of chaotic inequity, administered so many times with such arrogant disdain for the most basic principles of justice and human decency as to make mild admissions of "imperfection" sound presumptuous. If it is true that the law is the best institution human beings have devised to mediate their own eternal discord, this must not obscure the fact that the law's power is too often invested in the hands of mortal men who are corrupt, or if not corrupt, stupid, or if not stupid, then devious or lazy, and all of them capable of the most grievous mischief. The case of Peter Reilly, and Joan Barthel's book, powerfully demonstrate this ever-present danger and the sleepless vigilance ordinary citizens must steadfastly keep if the mechanism we have devised for our own protection does not from time to time try to destroy even the least of our children.

Naturally the foregoing implies, accurately, that I am convinced of Peter Reilly's innocence. I had begun to be convinced of at least the very strong possibility of his innocence when I first read Mrs. Barthel's article in the magazine *New Times* early in 1974. I happened on the article by sheerest chance, perhaps lured into reading it with more interest than I otherwise might have by the fact that the murder it described took place in Canaan, hardly an hour's drive away from my home in west-central Connecticut. (Is there not something reverberantly sinister about it, and indicative of the commonplaceness of atrocity in our time, that I should not until then have known about this vicious crime so close at hand and taking place only a few months before?) The Barthel article was a stark, forceful, searing piece, which in essence demonstrated how an eighteen-year-old boy, suspected by the police of murdering his mother, could be crudely yet subtly (and there is no contradiction in those terms) manipulated by law-enforcement officers so as to cause him to make an incriminating, albeit fuzzy and ambiguous, statement of responsibility for the crime. What I read was shocking, although I did not find it a novel experience. I am not by nature a taker-up of causes but in the preceding twelve years I had enlisted myself in aiding two people whom I felt to be victims of the law. Unlike Peter, both of these persons were young black men.

In the earlier of these cases the issue was not guilt but rather the punishment. Ben Reid, convicted of murdering a woman in the black ghetto of Hartford, had been sentenced to die in Connecticut's electric chair. His was the classic case of the woebegone survivor of poverty and abandonment who, largely because of his disadvantaged or minority status, was the recipient of the state's most terrible revenge. I wrote an article about Ben Reid in a national magazine and was enormously gratified when I saw that the piece helped significantly in the successful movement by a lot of other indignant people to have Ben's life spared. The other case involved Tony Maynard, whom I had known through James Baldwin and who had been convicted and sentenced to a long term for allegedly killing a marine in Greenwich Village. I worked to help extricate Tony, believing that he was innocent, which he was—as indeed the law finally admitted by freeing him, but after seven years of Tony's incarceration (among other unspeakable adversities he was badly injured as an innocent bystander in the cataclysm at Attica) and a series of retrials in which his devoted lawyers finally demonstrated the wretched police collusion, false and perjured evidence, shady deals on the part of the district attorney's office, and other maggoty odds and ends of the law's "imperfection," which had caused his unjust imprisonment in the first place.

These experiments, then, led me to absorb the Barthel article in *New Times* with something akin to a shock of recognition; horrifying in what it revealed, the piece recapitulated much of the essence of the law's malfeasance that had created Tony Maynard's seven-year martyrdom. It should be noted at this moment, incidentally, that Mrs. Barthel's article was of absolutely crucial significance in the Reilly case, not only because it was the catalytic agent whereby the bulk of Peter's bail was raised, but because it so masterfully crystallized and made clear the sinister issues of the use of the lie detector and the extraction of a confession by the police, thereby making Peter's guilt at least problematical to all but the most obtuse reader. Precise and objective yet governed throughout, one felt, by a rigorous moral conscience, the article was a superb example of journalism at its most effective and powerful. (It was nearly inexcusable that this piece and its author received no mention in the otherwise praiseworthy report on the Reilly case published by the *New York Times* in 1975.) Given the power of the essay, then, I have wondered later why I so readily let Peter Reilly and his plight pass from my mind and my concern. I think it may have been because of the fact that since Peter was not black or even of any shade of tan he would somehow be exempt from that ultimate dungeon-bound ordeal that is overwhelmingly the lot of those who spring from minorities in America. But one need not even be a good Marxist to flinch at this misapprehension. The truth is simpler. Bad enough that Peter lived in a shacklike house with his "disreputable" mother; the critical part is this: *he was poor*. Fancy

Peter, if you will, as an affluent day-student at Hotchkiss School only a few miles away, the mother murdered but in an ambience of coffee tables and wall-to-wall carpeting. It takes small imagination to envision the phalanx of horn-rimmed and button-down lawyers interposed immediately between Peter and Sergeant Kelly with his insufferable lie detector.

This detestable machine, the polygraph (the etymology of which shows that the word means "to write much," which is about all that can be said for it), is to my mind this book's chief villain, and the one from which Peter Reilly's most miserable griefs subsequently flowed. It is such an American device, such a perfect example of our blind belief in "scientism" and the efficacy of gadgets; and its performance in the hands of its operator—friendly, fatherly Sergeant Timothy Kelly, the mild collector of seashells—is also so American in the way it produces its benign but ruthless coercion. Like nearly all the law-enforcement officers in this drama, Sergeant Kelly is "nice"; it is as hard to conceive of him with a truncheon or a blackjack as with a volume of Proust. Plainly, neither Kelly nor his colleague Lieutenant Shay, who was actively responsible for Peter's confession, are vicious men; they are merely undiscerningly obedient, totally devoid of that flexibility of mind we call imagination, and they both have a passionate faith in the machine. Kelly especially is an unquestioning votary. "We go strictly by the charts," he tells an exhausted boy. "And the charts say you hurt your mother last night."

In a society where everything sooner or later breaks down or goes haywire, where cars fall apart and ovens explode and vacuum cleaners expire through planned obsolescence (surely Kelly must have been victim, like us all, of the Toastmaster), there is something manic, even awesome, about the sergeant's pious belief in the infallibility of his polygraph. And so at a point in his ordeal Peter, tired, confused, only hours removed from the trauma of witnessing his mother's mutilated body, asks, "Have you ever been proven totally wrong? A person, just from nervousness, responds that way?" Kelly replies, "No, the polygraph can never be wrong, because it's only a recording instrument, reacting to you. It's the person interpreting it who could be wrong. But I haven't made that many mistakes in twelve years, in the thousands of people who sat here, Pete." Such mighty faith and assurances would have alone been enough to decisively wipe out a young man at the end of his tether. Add to this faith the presumed assumption of

Peter's guilt on the part of the sergeant, and to this the outrageously tendentious nature of his questioning, and it is no wonder that a numb and bedraggled Peter was a setup for Lieutenant Shay, whose manner of extracting a confession from this troubled boy must be deemed a triumph of benevolent intimidation. Together the transcripts of the polygraph testimony and Peter's confession—much of which is recorded in this book—have to comprise another one of those depressing but instructive scandals that litter the annals of American justice.

Yet there is much more in the case of Peter Reilly, set down on these pages in rich detail, which makes it such a memorable and unique affair. What could be more harmoniously "American," in the best sense of that mangled word, than the spectacle of a New England village rising practically en masse to come to the support of one of their own young whom they felt to be betrayed and abandoned? Mrs. Barthel, who lived with this case month in and month out during the past few years, and who got to know well so many of Peter's friends and his surrogate "family," tells this part of the story with color, humor and affection; and her feeling for the community life of a small town like Canaan—with its family ties and hostilities, its warmth and crankiness and crooked edges—gives both a depth and vivacity to her narrative; never is she lured into the purely sensational. As in every story of crime and justice, the major thrust of the drama derives from its central figures, and they are all here: not only the law's automata—the two "nice" cops whose dismal stratagems thrust Peter into his nightmare at the outset—but the judge, prosecutor and counsel for the defense. Regarding these personages, Mrs. Barthel's art most often and tellingly lies in her subtle selectivity—and her onlooker's silence. What she allows the State's Attorney, Mr. Bianchi, simply to utter with his own lips, for instance, says more about Mr. Bianchi and the savagery of a certain genus of prosecutorial mind than any amount of editorializing or speculative gloss. As for the fascinating aftermath of the trial—Arthur Miller's stubborn and deservedly celebrated detective work in company with the redoubtable Mr. Conway, the brilliantly executed labors of the new defense counsel, the discovery of fresh evidence that led to the order of another trial, and other matters—all of these bring to a climax an eccentric, tangled, significant and cautionary chronicle of the wrongdoing of the law and its belated redemption.

Joan Barthel's book would deserve our attention if for no other reason than that it focuses a bright light on the unconscionable methods which the law, acting through its enforcement agencies and because of its lust for punishment, uses to victimize the most helpless members of our society. And thus it once again shows the law's tragic and perdurable imperfection. It also reminds us that while judicial oppression undoubtedly falls the heaviest on those from minority groups, it will almost as surely hasten to afflict the poor and the "unrespectable," no matter what their color. But rather triumphantly, and perhaps most importantly, *A Death in Canaan* demonstrates the will of ordinary people, in their ever astonishing energy and determination, to see true justice prevail over the law's dereliction.

[Introduction to *A Death in Canaan*, by Joan Barthel; Dutton, 1976]

Death Row

IN OCTOBER 1983, four days before he was scheduled to be executed in the electric chair at the Florida state prison at Starke, something took place that enraged Shabaka Sundiata Waglini more than any single event during his nearly ten years on death row. They came into his cell and measured him for his burial suit. The bloodlessly finicky, mechanical tailoring procedure upset him violently.

I recently met him, and he said, call me Shabaka. Shabaka—thirty-four years old when he faced death, born Joseph Green Brown in Charleston, South Carolina—had been convicted for the 1973 murder, along with the robbery and rape, of a Tampa white woman. "Shabaka," a name he took before going to prison, means "uncompromising" in Swahili.

Shortly after the suit was measured, Shabaka was asked to order his last meal—he could have virtually anything he wanted—but he rejected the offer as gratuitously insulting.

One shrinks from thinking how a man prepares himself to face this form of extinction. While little can be said in favor of any type of execution, death by electric current is truly primitive, a method that has not really been improved—if improvements are imaginable—since a convicted murderer received the inaugural 2,000 volts at New York's Auburn prison in 1890. It is a broiling process at intensely high temperature. The doctors who ascertain death must wait six or seven minutes for the body to cool down so they can touch it. Pigs and cattle go more expeditiously into that good night. Shabaka thought about the manner of his dying more than once.

He had good reason to believe that because he was black he had been dealt cards from a stacked deck.

As it happened, a juror at his trial had sent an affidavit to Shabaka's minister, the Rev. Joe Ingle of the Nashville-based Southern Coalition of Jails and Prisons, asserting that a jury member had advocated the chair for Shabaka, a former Black Panther, because "that nigger's been nothing but trouble since he came down here, and he'll be trouble until we get him off the streets."

One's mouth goes dry at such an utterance, especially in light of the recent United States Supreme Court decision that racial prejudice, as a decisive factor in the administration of the death penalty, is theoretical and therefore of no importance.

In truth, racial discrimination, far from being of no importance, has an omnipresence that the remarks of that Florida juror utterly confirm. After trials like Shabaka's, how can the Court's ruling appear anything but a cruel and monumental deceit?

In the United States, blacks and Hispanics suffer the death penalty in grave disproportion. They also tend, like Shabaka, to be poor, and therefore they receive legal counsel that more often than not is slipshod and deficient. Shabaka possessed a couple of sorry impediments when he went into his trial: He was black and penniless. These conditions represent one of several arguments amid a constellation of many arguments against the death penalty.

But what would be the case in favor of killing Shabaka? (A previous armed robbery hardly gained him sympathy.) There is no doubt that the crime of which he had been convicted was terrible. Those who felt no qualms about placing him in the electric chair, including many of clear and subtle intelligence, might have wished to justify his execution on one or the other, or both, of two grounds. There really aren't any more. The most obvious of these is deterrence: By putting Shabaka and all other brutal killers to death, we think we dissuade the like-minded from committing similar crimes.

But it never has been proved that the death penalty prevents murder. Indeed, there is convincing evidence—displayed among other damning exhibits in Amnesty International's recent report on the death penalty in America—that executions frequently cause an increase in violent crimes.

In some countries—Canada, for example—the murder rate has fallen after abolition of the death penalty. Sincere foes of that penalty rarely are sentimentalists. There are those who would have opposed Shabaka's execution for any reason—feeling it was cruel and barbaric, or merely because it violated the sanctity of life. The resolve of many pragmatic opponents would be undermined were there hard proof that the death penalty prevents murders—but proof does not exist.

The crime that sealed Shabaka's fate was one that would bring out retributive fury in most people. Simple vengeance would have been the other rationale for seeking his death. The impulse toward vengeance is understandably relentless; many people, not necessarily bloodthirsty, would without shame declare a wish to have Shabaka killed just as a way to get even. And why shouldn't we acknowledge this? For, paradoxically, it is in the realm of vengeance that the feelings of many death penalty supporters and some opponents converge, though they do not coincide.

Any harsh sentence imposed for a particularly brutal crime contains an element of retaliation, satisfying a need on the part of the victim's ghost, the close survivors, and perhaps even society.

At the time of Shabaka's trial, there were quite a few onlookers who, though they rejected the death penalty, admitted they wanted to see Shabaka suffer a very hard time. But they also rejected a vengeance that extended to the electric chair, with its irremediable finality.

By the time Shabaka's date with the executioner neared in 1983, he had made as good use of his time as a man can under the circumstances. He worked on his case, wrote letters, and, like many inmates, became a devoted reader. He greatly fancied modern American novels and developed a love for classical music. As he sweated it out, there were scores of convicts throughout America's prison system who were doing time for crimes that were almost identical to the one for which Shabaka had been condemned.

Those who were truly dangerous among these criminals would, or should, never be released. Others, after serving long terms—an average of twenty years or more—would be released on parole, and scarcely a soul among them would be returned to prison for a subsequent crime.

Why hadn't Shabaka been permitted to join this favored majority? Why had he and a small fraction of other felons been singled out to die while vastly larger numbers of criminals paying penance for misdeeds virtually the same as his were allowed to work out their destinies?

The absence of answers—which emphasizes the blind inequity of the death penalty—is another major reason why its use is immoral and unacceptable. But in Shabaka's case, the questions were really academic—because he was innocent.

The legalized killing of innocent people is the final indictment of capital punishment. For years, Shabaka had insisted on his innocence of the rape, robbery, and murder. All along, he had admitted to a robbery—but this at a time and place different from those of the murder.

Only fifteen hours before Shabaka's appointment with death, a three-judge panel of the Federal circuit court of appeals in Atlanta stayed the execution on grounds that the case merited further examination. Shabaka returned to his cell and began to petition for a new trial.

In the years that followed, ugly details came to light: During the first trial, the prosecutor had concealed Federal Bureau of Investigation evidence showing that the fatal bullet could not have been fired from Shabaka's gun. Shabaka based his new claim on this fact and on his assertion that the prosecutor had allowed a crucial witness to lie, while also misleading the jury in his closing argument.

Last year, the circuit court ordered a new trial. Before it could begin, the original witness admitted he had lied. Florida, sensing it had no case, abandoned its prosecution, and early last March Shabaka left jail a free man, his only possessions being the clothes on his back and his legal papers. Between the ages of twenty-three and twenty-seven, he had spent the rich marrow of his youth on death row.

The Shabaka story illuminates the most sordid defects of capital punishment. His blackness and poverty helped doom him. He was ruthlessly cheated; it was never his privilege to be granted—even for a phantom crime—the incarceration that it meted out to others and that carries the possibility of redemption.

He would have died not a criminal but a victim whose innocence would have been as surely entombed as his body in its burial suit.

Today, Shabaka makes his home in Florida. There "decompressing," as he puts it, from his years in a cell, he reads and listens to tapes of classical symphonies. May he live in peace.

[*New York Times* Op-Ed Page, May 10, 1987]

Why Primo Levi
Need Not Have Died

WHY DID THE EMINENT ITALIAN WRITER Primo Levi die in the shocking way he did?

In the depths of a clinical depression, Mr. Levi, an Auschwitz survivor who had written eloquently of his ordeal under the Nazis, jumped down a stairwell in Turin in 1987.

The question appeared to haunt—indeed, nearly dominate—a recent symposium held at New York University and dedicated to Mr. Levi and his work, according to an article in *The New York Times*. Some participants reacted with simple incredulity.

Alfred Kazin, a distinguished literary critic, was quoted as saying: "It is difficult for me to credit a will to blackness and self-destruction in a writer so happy and full of new projects."

A friend, rejecting the idea that the writer had planned to kill himself, saw the death as the result of a "sudden uncontrollable impulse"—as if rational deliberation might have somehow colored the act with wrongdoing. In this and other statements, there was at least a tinge of disapproval, an unspoken feeling that through some puzzling failure of moral strength Mr. Levi had failed his staunchest admirers.

Apparently not expressed at the symposium, though quoted in the article, was the harshest example of such a viewpoint: a suggestion in *The New Yorker* that "the efficacy of all his words had somehow been cancelled by his death." This idea leaves the implication that the force and fervor of a writer's work is rendered invalid if, instead of expiring of natural causes, he takes his life.

What remains most deeply troubling about the account is the apparent inability of the symposium participants to come to terms with a reality that seems glaringly obvious. It is that Mr. Levi's death could not be dissociated from the major depression with which he was afflicted, and that indeed his suicide proceeded directly from that illness.

To those of us who have suffered severe depression—myself included—this general unawareness of how relentlessly the disease can generate an urge to self-destruction seems widespread; the problem badly needs illumination.

Suicide remains a tragic and dreadful act, but its prevention will continue to be hindered, and the age-old stigma against it will remain, unless we can begin to understand that the vast majority of those who do away with themselves—and of those who attempt to do so— do not do it because of any frailty, and rarely out of impulse, but because they are in the grip of an illness that causes almost unimaginable pain. It is important to try to grasp the nature of this pain.

In the winter of 1985–86, I committed myself to a mental hospital because the pain of the depression from which I had suffered for more than five months had become intolerable. I never attempted suicide, but the possibility had become more real and the desire more greedy as each wintry day passed and the illness became more smotheringly intense.

What had begun that summer as an off-and-on malaise and a vague, spooky restlessness had gained gradual momentum until my nights were without sleep and my days were pervaded by a gray drizzle of unrelenting horror. This horror is virtually indescribable, since it bears no relation to normal experience.

In depression, a kind of biochemical meltdown, it is the brain as well as the mind that becomes ill—as ill as any other besieged organ. The sick brain plays evil tricks on its inhabiting spirit. Slowly overwhelmed by the struggle, the intellect blurs into stupidity. All capacity for pleasure disappears, and despair maintains a merciless daily drumming. The smallest commonplace of domestic life, so amiable to the healthy mind, lacerates like a blade.

Thus, mysteriously, in ways difficult to accept by those who have never suffered it, depression comes to resemble physical anguish. Such anguish can become every bit as excruciating as the pain of a fractured limb, migraine, or heart attack.

Most physical distress yields to some analgesia—not so depression. Psychotherapy is of little use to the profoundly depressed, and antidepressants are, to put it generously, unreliable. Even the soothing balm of sleep usually disappears. And so, because there is no respite at all, it is entirely natural that the victim begins to think ceaselessly of oblivion.

In the popular mind, suicide is usually the work of a coward or sometimes, paradoxically, a deed of great courage, but it is neither; the torment that precipitates the act makes it often one of blind necessity.

The origins of depression remain a puzzle, despite significant advances in research. Many factors seem to be involved. Aside from the basic chemical disturbance in the brain and behavioral and genetic influences, psychological reasons must be added to the equation. Mr. Levi may have been bedeviled by buried conflicts unrelated to Auschwitz.

Or, indeed, his ordeal at Auschwitz may have imposed on his soul an insupportable burden; other writers wounded by the Holocaust (Paul Celan and Tadeusz Borowski come to mind) decided upon suicide as a way out of the blackness of memory. But the overwhelming majority of camp survivors have chosen to live, and what is of ultimate importance to the victim of depression is not the cause but the treatment and the cure.

What is saddening about Primo Levi's death is the suspicion that his way of dying was not inevitable and that with proper care he might have been rescued from the abyss.

Depression's saving grace (perhaps its only one) is that the illness seems to be self-limiting: Time is the real healer and with or without treatment the sufferer usually gets well.

Even so, presumptuous as it may be to speculate from such a distance, I find it difficult not to believe that if Mr. Levi had been under capable hospital attention, sequestered from the unbearable daily world in a setting where he would have been safe from his self-destructive urge, and where time would have permitted the storm raging in his brain to calm itself and die away, he would be among us now.

But, in any event, one thing appears certain: He succumbed to a disease that proved to be malignant, and not a shred of moral blame should be attached to the manner of his passing.

[*New York Times* Op-Ed page, December 19, 1988]

After the essay on Primo Levi was published in *The New York Times* I received an enormous number of letters, almost all of them from people who had experienced depression, directly or as a result of being associated with victims of depression, and who felt I had given voice to a subject too-long buried. The essay prompted an invitation from the department of psychiatry of the Johns Hopkins School of Medicine for me to speak at a symposium on mood disorders; this speech was eventually expanded into a long article in *Vanity Fair*, and eventually into a book, *Darkness Visible*.

DOWN
THE NILE

Down the Nile

In the autumn of 1849, Gustave Flaubert and a friend, Maxime Du Camp, made a wonderful trip to Egypt. At twenty-eight, Flaubert was a handsome, tall, high-spirited, neurotic young man with an ardent yearning for the exotic enchantments of the Orient. It may have been flight from his adored but incredibly dominating mother that in part impelled this journey, or perhaps it was disappointment over his first serious literary effort, *The Temptation of Saint Anthony*. More understandably, he had a serious and informed taste for antiquity and an irrepressible love of prostitutes, and in Egypt he knew he would find both in abundance. In any case, Flaubert, who was unknown as a writer (*Madame Bovary* would not appear until seven years later and bring him instantaneous fame), was even then indefatigably recording his impressions of the world, and his travel notes and letters from that nine-month odyssey along the Nile remarkably foreshadow the powers of observation and the acute sensibility that brought his masterpiece into being. By turns beautiful, rapturous, bawdy, hideous and brutal, his record is also from time to time quite funny. Not only because of the contrasts it presents between the Egypt of now and then but because of the similarities, it comprises a fascinating and instructive document, delicious reading in itself but required reading—let me assign it as a text: *Flaubert in Egypt*, translated and edited by Francis Steegmuller, Academy Chicago Limited Edition, 1979—for all present-day voyagers along the Nile.

It can accurately be said that there is almost no place on earth that any longer is safe from tourism. When cruises to the Galápagos Islands are within reach of middle-class vacationers, and jumbo jets from New Zealand fly past the ice mountains of Antarctica for panoramic sightseeing trips (and tragically crash, as one plane did not long ago), we have truly begun to inhabit the "global village." Not only is the Nile no exception, it was beginning to be overrun by tourists even in Flaubert's time, when the exigencies of transportation were complicated to a degree that people accustomed to modern luxury travel can only reflect upon with discomfort. In the Egypt of the mid-nineteenth century, the invaders were already on the scene, inflicting their characteristic wounds. Their ubiquitous spoor—the inescapable graffiti—caused Flaubert some of his deepest moments of depression. "In the temples we read travelers' names; they strike us as petty and futile. We never write ours; there are some that must have taken three days to carve, so deeply are they cut in the stone. There are some that you keep meeting everywhere—sublime persistence of stupidity." At the Pyramid of Khepren his despair deepens. Under the name of Belzoni, the great archaeologist, he discovers "no less large, that of M. Just de Chasseloup-Laubat. One is irritated by the number of imbeciles' names written everywhere: on the top of the Great Pyramid there is a certain Buffard, 79 rue Saint-Martin, wallpaper-manufacturer, in black letters; an English fan of Jenny Lind's has written her name; there is also a pear, representing Louis-Philippe."

Tourism is, in general, a human activity that is neither desirable nor undesirable, merely existing in relationship with some landscape or other because people in their incessant curiosity will travel and observe and explore. Under certain circumstances, however, and usually after the passing of a long period of time, tourism becomes absolutely essential to the life of a place, becomes symbiotic, indeed so organically linked as to resemble the teeming bacterial flora that inhabits the human alimentary tract and that contributes to the body's very survival. Over the past one hundred and fifty years or so, Egypt has developed just such a relationship with its legions of visitors. The tourists who pour in season after season, year after year, comprise a critical factor in Egypt's economy; remove tourism, and the country would suffer a catastrophic blow. What makes the present situation so ironic, and so gloomy to contemplate, is that the very tourism that supplies Egypt with an essential part of its sustenance is threatening to destroy the body of the host. Aggravating as they were to Flaubert, and are to the modern visitor, the composers of graffiti are a minor annoyance compared to the larger menace. Both the proliferation of people—in multinational droves becoming more uncontrollable each year—

and the sheer physical damage caused by so many millions of shoes stirring up so many tons of abrasive dust, by countless lungs exhaling huge volumes of corrosive carbon dioxide into the fragile environment of the tombs, have brought on a situation of real crisis. Expert observers believe that only immediate and drastic measures will enable Egypt to save the Nile and its treasures for future generations.

As if this were not enough, there is the matter of the dam—the High Dam at Aswan. Built in the 1960s by the Russians at the behest of Gamal Abdel Nasser, then Egypt's president, this vast edifice—now the second-largest rock-filled dam in the world—was intended to usher in the nation's new economic millennium; by the trapping of billions of tons of Nile water in a prodigious reservoir named Lake Nasser, the river would be subjugated, while judicious control and manipulation of the water would bring cheap electrical energy to the entire Nile Valley, along with the potential for millions of newly irrigated acres of fertile land. That much of this has already been accomplished seems indisputable, but, it is becoming increasingly clear, the cost may eventually cancel out the benefits. Many observers believe that the negative effects wrought upon the river by the dam will prove in the long run to be, quite simply, disastrous. I was to learn in detail about these consequences and to view at first hand some of the harbingers of the Nile's change for the worse (I had been on the river once before, in 1967) during a recent February trip down the waterway from Aswan to Cairo, when I was from time to time made uneasily aware that I, too, along with my companions on the voyage, had become yet another manifestation of the tourist pestilence. But even so, it was possible to take some comfort from the fact that the auspices under which we traveled were both dignified and felicitous. Our host on the trip, and a good friend of each of the dozen or so Americans and Europeans whom he had invited aboard the M.S. *Abu Simbel*, was Prince Sadruddin Aga Khan, son of the late Aga Khan and until recently the High Commissioner for Refugees of the United Nations. Married to an Egyptian and profoundly involved in Egypt, its culture and its history, the prince has a house in Cairo; even more significantly, it was in large measure due to his efforts through UNESCO that the majestic colossi and temples of Abu Simbel and Philae were rescued from the encroaching waters created by the High Dam. Thus, plainly, although we were traveling in privacy and style (the comfort of a boat of one's own is something one need not apologize for), the prince's intimate connection with the Nile and his concern for its heritage and its future allowed his guests a unique perspective—without overly solemnizing what still remains, despite the foregoing auguries, one of the most mysteriously ravishing and moving journeys it is possible to make on the face of the earth.

"Handsome heads, ugly feet" is Flaubert's comment upon the Colossi of Abu Simbel, those gargantuan figures that stand guard on the shores of the Upper Nile, six hundred miles from Cairo; in 1850 the four statues were still partially buried under the sand. Flaubert's companion, Du Camp, made the first known photographs of these sandstone figures of Rameses II, after a boat trip from Cairo that lasted nearly two months. Our own trip from Cairo to Abu Simbel (which we visit before boarding our vessel in Aswan) takes a bare two hours by Egypt Air Boeing 737. In these upper reaches of the waterway, the Nile itself, of course, has become obliterated below the vast and murky expanse of Lake Nasser, which spills out across the desert in a desolate pool nearly the size of Delaware. Interspersed with jagged rock promontories and devoid of vegetation at its edges save for a rare patch of the palest green, like lichen, the lake from the air has an evil, unearthly look, resembling the kind of lake astronauts might encounter beneath the mantle of Saturn or Venus. We land on the recently built airstrip, step out into desert air, which at noon is briskly chill, and are thankful that it is winter. In the depths of summer it has sometimes become so hot that planes have been unable to land; the tarmac melts, turned to the consistency of black glue. A brief overland trip by bus brings us to the site.

Rescued from the flood and, by a marvel of engineering, hoisted above it nearly two hundred feet, the Abu Simbel colossi are appallingly big, exceeding all preconceived notions (derived from photographs, even Du Camp's flat, primitive ones) of their bigness; they are simply *immense*. And awe-inspiring, without a doubt. That these great effigies might have been allowed to sink without trace beneath the waters of Nasser's lake is unthinkable. But despite the sense of awe that they elicit—monuments to human ingenuity, human toil—they do not, for me at least, inspire that ineffable thrill of pleasure that one experiences in the presence of great heroic art. This could be partly due to that "pitiless rigidity" of which Flaubert complained in regard to Egyptian sculpture; or it might be because the colossi, with their enigmatic smiles that so often seem to possess the faintest shadow of a smirk, are simply intimidating, vainglorious, invoking the idea not of true grandeur but of pelf, influence, power. Also, to reproduce one's self four times in figures sixty-six feet high would seem to be a redundancy. The playwright Arthur Miller, one of the *Abu Simbel*'s voyagers, sits in the chill afternoon light regarding these grandiose duplications (a cast on a recently fractured ankle renders Miller less mobile than the rest of us). "Think of the poor people in those days," he muses, "who dared to come down the river to invade Egypt from the south. One look at this display and they'd be ready to run back home." One agrees. They are paradigms of a universal motif: human domination. They would not look out of place adorning the façade of the Chase Manhattan Bank. Even so, they may be more perishable than one might imagine. Farida Galassi, the eloquent French-born Egyptologist who is our guide and who has lived in Egypt for most of her seventy-four years, speaks dispiritedly of the future of the colossi, remarking that she and some of her colleagues feel that the elevation of the statues to higher ground is not only a mere reprieve but a move that in itself contains the seeds of doom. The reason for this is that the old site offered shelter to these vulnerable sandstone figures, while the new location provides exposure to frequent sandstorms, which could prove to be completely destructive in no more than an eyewink in Egyptian time— seventy-five to a hundred years. Thus the High Dam, in a perverse and unpredicted way, may claim Abu Simbel as a victim after all.

Our eponymous vessel awaits at dockside in Aswan. The son of a shipbuilder, I look over the M.S. *Abu Simbel* with thoughtful attention and am utterly pleased. Relatively small by Nile standards—one hundred and twenty feet long—she and her sister vessel, the *Aswan*, were built in 1979, the first metal boats to be constructed in Egypt. With a catamaran bottom, she is able to negotiate the shallows. She has nice clean lines, with no furbelows or waste space; yet there are ample cabins with efficient plumbing and abundant hot water (essential after each day's desert dust), a comfortable dining saloon with bar and, perhaps most attractive of all, an open upper deck of fine proportions, allowing visual access to what for many travelers is a Nile voyage's greatest glory: the incomparable river itself and the timeless tableaux of its shores. Flaubert and Du Camp navigated the Nile by *cange*, a small sailboat also supplied with oarsmen. "Our two sails, their angles intersecting," Flaubert wrote, "swelled to their entire width, and the *cange* skimmed along, heeling, its keel cutting the water. . . . Standing on the poop that forms the roof of our cabin, the mate held the tiller, smoking his black wood *chibouk*." Flaubert and his friend traveled with a crew of twelve, a fairly high ratio for two passengers; our baker's dozen requires twenty in the crew, likewise a high ratio when one considers that none are oarsmen. A passage by sail and oar would surely have its own enchantments, and such a trip can still be managed for one or two adventurers; but this form of cruising has virtually disappeared from the river. We are enfolded, rather, in soothing decadence. The food is excellent, often superb. Fully air-conditioned, our vessel travels downstream at an almost vibrationless eight knots, powered by twin one-hundred-and-fifty-horsepower Caterpillar engines. But if our motors are modern, our helm is nearly as ancient as the river itself. There is not a single navigational aid on the Nile—not a buoy, not a marker or a beacon—and our helmsmen steer by sight, most often discerning the bars and shoals in this generally shallow river by the characteristic rippling effect on the surface (sometimes completely undetectable to the casual eye) and proceeding boldly at night as long as moonlight permits. They are incredibly gifted navigators but, alas, not perfect; once in a great while, the boat scrapes bottom.

We remain in Aswan for a day or two. The city, situated above the rapids of the river and its clumps of vivid green islands, is a beautiful one, even though its runaway growth (from fifty thousand to almost a million in twenty years) is a measure in itself of Egypt's huge population explosion. Just as the city dominates the river, the city is dominated by the High Dam. Dams, with their attendant benefits and mischief, are not new to Aswan. Around the turn of the century, the British built a dam that, though lower than the new Russian model, was considered a prodigy among dams in its day, allowing the cultivation of vast tracts of land in middle Egypt. It also caused the submergence, for most of the year, of the nearby Temple of Philae, a grand edifice of the Ptolemaic period dedicated to the goddess Isis. Sixty years later the High Dam threatened inundation of Philae forever. But thanks to the similar, almost super-human efforts that saved Abu Simbel, Philae was rescued, lifted up stone by stone with astonishing precision and deposited in perfect rebirth of itself on a nearby island. Thus was effected over the High Dam a major cultural triumph. It is a pity that such triumphs are few, for it is becoming clear that the harm inflicted by the new dam is enormous. Just one unforeseen case in point may be demonstrated by a crucial difference between the old dam and the new. Whatever its drawbacks, the British structure, with its elaborate chain of sluiceways, did permit an unquestionably major function: it allowed most of the huge tonnage of silt to pass through. By contrast, the High Dam is badly flawed in this respect: so much silt has backed up in Lake Nasser that it has become an obstruction, making necessary a diversionary channel to deposit this life-giving soil in, of all places, the desert.

That the Americans, largely because of the politics of John Foster Dulles in the 1950s, were prevented from being the builders of the High Dam is perhaps just as well. Certainly, among other things, Americans are now spared the blame for that appalling monument to Egyptian-Russian friendship, which stands two hundred and fifty feet high at the dam site. Dazzlingly white and constructed in the shape of what may crudely be described as four symmetrically arranged winglike pylons rising toward heaven, the monument achieves an effect just the opposite of upward aspiration, resembling nothing so much as the exposed fins of a colossal concrete artillery shell that has embedded itself in the earth. As we ascend to the top in an elevator, Prince Nicholas Romanoff, a collateral descendant of the czar who can at other times speak with deep affection of things Russian, comments glumly on the traditional failure of Russian architecture, interestingly theorizing that as architects, Russians have been so uninspired because the country has always lacked in quantity that requisite material: stone. In any case, although the view from the top of the structure is spectacular —offering a bright blue vista of the waters of Lake Nasser; the surrounding desert; and also the dam itself, stretching an amazing two miles across the crest of the site—one is scarcely heartened by what one hears now about the dam's further pernicious effects on the river, to which it was supposed to bring an unmixed shower of blessings.

The greater part of the water of the Nile comes from heavy rainfall in Ethiopia. Because of seasonal vagaries, the volume of Nile water is produced with irregularity, but for thousands of years, life along the river has been governed by the annual flooding, whether little or great or just enough. Too much water in this flood and there is risk of a destructive inundation; too little water and the fields grow dry for want of irrigation. This is an oversimplified description of the hydrology of the Nile, about which there have been written many scientific volumes and about which, too, much remains a mystery. The High Dam, aside from its hydro-electric capabilities, was built to put an end to the unpredictable nature of the annual flood and, in effect, to stabilize the flow of water from Aswan to the sea. Probably the most serious conse-quence of such stabilization is this: while, indeed, the damage that comes from uncontrolled flooding has been eliminated, there has resulted a situation in which the great deposits of silt, so necessary to agriculture, have also been eliminated. Thus the land has sud-denly and for the first time become seriously dependent on artificial fertilizer, which is extremely expensive and something few Egyp-tian farmers can afford. Also, at the mouth of the Nile, fish in the Mediterranean used to feed on organisms conveyed by the silt, but now that the silt is gone, fish and fisheries have been decimated. It is an ecological nightmare. The long-range effects are incalcu-lable—and cannot be good.

Another unforeseen result of the dam is one that demonstrates in a rather weird way man's ability to alter the very normality of certain natural phenomena. It of course almost never rains in the desert, and the green richness of Egypt comes about entirely be-cause of the Nile. But through the formation of Lake Nasser's mammoth reservoir, one of the largest of its kind anywhere, there has been created around it a microclimate in which large-scale condensation and precipitation occur from time to time, and rain falls, reportedly often in torrents. Many villages in the Upper Nile region, made of mud brick and totally unprepared for such freak-ish downpours, have suffered severe damage because of the High Dam. In other times, people were at least forewarned about occa-sional inundations.

A few miles north of the dam, at the Temple of Philae, I remem-ber Flaubert's reflection: "The Egyptian temples bore me pro-foundly." This is not entirely true, for it is belied by his vigorous descriptions at other moments in his journal; often his reactions to these antique glories are deeply appreciative and recorded with excitement. Yet there is something genuine in his boredom, and his friend Du Camp wrote: "The temples seemed to him always alike. . . . At Philae he settled himself comfortably in the cool shade of one of the halls of the great Temple of Isis to read *Gerfaut*, by Charles de Bernard." Visiting Philae myself and recalling this passage, I do not quite feel disposed to sit down and read, but I can begin somehow to partake in Flaubert's dissatisfaction (or is it merely impatience?) with these places, wondrous as they are and as essential as one feels it is that they be seen and visited and strenuously preserved. There are moments of melting and exquisite beauty in Egyptian art—the friezes, the statuary, the gods and goddesses—but for me the glory lies less in the art itself than in a resonance of time and history. This is felt (or, paradoxically, almost heard) in the architecture; for, as Flaubert wrote, "everything in Egypt seems made for architecture—the planes of the fields, the vegetation, the human anatomy, the horizon lines." And here Flaubert begins to reveal what it is about the Nile that most deeply moves him and engages his passionate attention: the people and the landscape of unparalleled enchantment. I am afraid that it is a feeling that I share. Witness, for instance, his dutiful description of the Temple of Esna: "This temple is 33m. 70 long and 16m. 89 wide, the circumference of the columns is 5m. 37. There are 24 columns. . . . An Arab climbed onto the capital of a column to drop the metric tape. A yellow cow, on the left, poked her head inside." Plainly, it is the cow that interests Flaubert, not the temple. It is much the same with me.

I wish to board the *Abu Simbel* and leave Aswan on an upbeat note, wanting to feel at ease with this majestic river, but it is very hard. I think of the "sociological" concerns I would like to touch upon but cannot. By Egyptian standards Aswan is as clean as, say, Toronto, yet its back streets smell of filth, of urine and corruption. Much of Egypt smells like this. I cannot hesitate even a second to ponder the squalor and poverty of Egypt; it would require the passion, the commitment, of an entire book. Meanwhile, my concern is with the dam and its twin goblin, tourism. Realizing the possible absurdity of my obsession with the latter when I am but a particle of the tourist mass, I find that what I see still bothers me sorely. Above Cairo, Flaubert's Nile was virtually empty, its mode of navigation primitive; certainly the river did not lack a few travelers, but when Flaubert writes about them they take on the quality of being unannounced, rare, a little strange. ("A *cange* carrying a party of Englishmen comes sailing furiously down the river, spinning in the wind.") Berthed near us at quayside are two enormous boats of the Sheraton hotel chain. Ungainly, totally utilitarian, they are painted in garish blue, white and gold colors and are capable of accommodating one hundred and seventy-five persons.

These barges, together with their two sister vessels, are typical of the bloated floating hotels that have replaced the much smaller, humanly scaled paddle-wheelers that cruised the river as recently as 1975; those were stylish old boats, really, with the charm of Mark Twain's Mississippi. They carried a reasonable number of passengers. Unsurprisingly, the Sheraton monsters have been made possible by the High Dam, since the fluctuating depth of the water in the old days prevented vessels of such bulk and displacement. At temple sites they disgorge tourists in nearly unmanageable hordes. Also, besides carrying far too many people, these boats are of such size and power that their wake has begun to contribute to the erosion of riverbanks already eroded badly enough. In the gentle dusk they possess a truly wounding unsightliness. And I cannot decide who has produced the greatest eyesore here in lovely Aswan—Sheraton or, once again, the Russians, who during the building of the High Dam erected a hotel that unpardonably interrupts the serene, low skyline like some grandiose airport control tower. (There have been, since the departure of the Russians, serious thoughts about blowing up this structure, but like the dam, it is built for such permanence as to make the cost of demolition prohibitive.)

But during the days that follow on the *Abu Simbel*, almost all anxieties concerning the Nile's future are absorbed in contemplation of the river itself. When one is removed from the population centers like Aswan—and there are few of these—it seems impossible that anything could seriously encroach upon this timelessness. In benign hypnosis I sit on deck for hour after hour, quite simply smitten with love for this watercourse, which presents itself to the gaze in many of its aspects exactly as it did five thousand years ago. "Like the ocean," Flaubert wrote, "this river sends our thoughts back almost incalculable distances." Beyond the fertile green, unspooling endlessly on either bank, is the desert, at times glimpsed indistinctly, at other times heaving itself up in harsh incandescent cliffs and escarpments, yet always present, dramatizing the fragility but also the nearly miraculous continuousness of the river and its cycles of death and resurrection. Sometimes life teems, as at the edge of a village where men and women, children, dogs, donkeys, goats, camels, all seem arrested for an instant in a hundred different attitudes; a donkey brays, children shout and whistle at us, and the recorded voice of a muezzin from a spindly minaret follows us in a receding monotone.

At other times life is sparse, intermittent: a solitary buffalo grazing at the end of an interminable grassy promontory, seemingly stranded light-years from anything, as in outer space. A human figure on a camel, likewise appearing far from any habitation, robes flapping in the wind, staring at us until we pass out of sight. Undulant expanses of sugar cane, furiously green; groves of date palms; more cane in endless luxuriant growth; then suddenly: a desolate and vast sandbar, taking us many minutes to pass, that could be an unmarked strand at the uttermost ends of the earth—one could rot or starve there and one's bones never be found. Now in an instant, a fabulous green peninsula with dense undergrowth, feathery Mosaic bulrushes, a flock of ducks scooting along the shore. We pass by a felucca, drifting, its sail down. One robed figure kneels in prayer; the other figure, with an oar, keeps the bow pointed toward Mecca. Then soon, as we move around a gentle bend, history evaporates before the eye, and there is an appalling apparition: a sugar refinery belching smoke. But *infernal* smoke! Black smoke such as I cannot recall having seen since childhood in the 1930s, during a trip past the terrible mills and coke ovens of western Pennsylvania. There are no smoke pollution controls along the valley—another bad sign for the beleaguered Nile.

Furthermore, lest I become too beguiled by the river's charms, I am sobered by evidence of still another kind of havoc wrought by that hulking barrage at Aswan. This threatens the very existence of the monuments themselves and can be viewed graphically at the Temple of Esna, thirty miles south of Luxor, on the west bank of the river. The harm being done is the result of the titanic volume of water behind the High Dam, the pressure of which has altered and, together with overirrigation, slowly raised the subterranean water table along the valley. In places the water contains a heavy saturation of salts, which, rising to the surface, have begun to attack not only the land but the foundations of many of the temples. Quite corrosive white streaks of this ominous residue can be plainly seen everywhere; but at the ancient Temple of Abydos (which we visit a few days later), the wonderful and mysterious underground structure known as the Oserion (aptly called "an idea in stone") has become sacrificed not to the salt but, even worse, to the water itself, and much of the great architecture is flooded forever. Thus, like an unshakable and troubling presence, the High Dam adumbrates the future of man, his heritage, and nature up and down the valley. In the gorgeous lush green fields beyond Esna, I glimpse a stunning juxtaposition that tells much about the confusion—the triumph and error, gain and miscalculation—that ensues when man attempts to modify any natural force as prodigious as the Nile: adrift in the air, a web of high-tension wires, humming, gleaming, the very emblem of newly harnessed energy; directly beneath the wires, a sickly and ravaged field not long ago cultivated in thriving vegetables, now overlaid with huge dirty-white oblongs of deadly salt.

But what is the future of the Nile? Do these alarming portents mean that the outlook for the river is inescapably somber? At the moment, one can only speculate. If it is remarkable that human beings in their recklessness and folly have, in the past hundred years or so, nearly destroyed some of their greatest and most beautiful rivers and lakes, it is equally remarkable that those very waterways have proved to be capable of survival, even health, given enough time and given the human determination to reverse the death process. The Thames, the beautiful Willamette in Oregon, and to some extent the Hudson—still in the midst of resuscitation—are just a few examples of this provisional deliverance; and it may be that even the awful felony committed upon the James in Virginia—the wanton dumping of tons of a lethal insecticide into the stream, causing a contamination of marine life that destroyed fishing and the fishing industry for years—will be alleviated by time, with the poisons eventually washed away and the natural equilibrium once again achieved. Pollution along the Nile (including much sewage and trash pollution from tourist boats) is a potential problem; more subtle and dangerous is a form of pollution by disease—and once again the culprit is the High Dam, the sins of which begin to bemuse one by the sheer monotony of their enumeration. This has to do with bilharzia (also known as schistosomiasis), the gravely debilitating, often fatal parasitic disease that is endemic in lower Egypt. Many experts in environmental medicine believe that the disease—caused by microscopic blood flukes that breed in the bodies of snails, then float about in shallow water and penetrate into the bloodstream of mammals, including human beings—was minimized in its extent by the annual flushing action of the great Nile flood, which swept up countless quantities of the snails and their larval guests and removed them from the shallows, where people were most likely to become infected. But the dam changed all this. Now the general stillness of the water means a more prolific generation of snails and parasites, more frequent infestation in the backwaters and possibly more disease, despite strenuous public-health campaigns.

The Nile is the ancient mother-river of the Western world, and it is impossible to conceive of her failure to survive these present vicissitudes. Although what man has done in the past twenty years may appear inexplicably thoughtless, and vainglorious, too—interrupting that immemorial ebb and flow, shattering a rhythm that existed eons before man himself appeared on these seductive banks —one feels that it does not really spell the end, although much cruel injury has been done. Human beings are both resilient and ingenious in crisis—never more so than when guiltily surveying the harm that they have inflicted themselves—and one can conceive of the unhurried pace of Egyptian time allowing men to forestall more ruin and even perhaps to rectify some (though certainly not all) of the damage that may now seem beyond repair. Finally, there might be controlled here on the Nile one of the worst of the pollutions of man: the aimless proliferation of his own peripatetic self.

Toward the end of our trip, stopping to view the Colossi of Memnon at Thebes, I recall a typical Flaubertian animadversion. "The colossi," he wrote, "are very big, but as far as being impressive is concerned, no. . . . Think of the number of bourgeois stares they have received! Each person has made his little remark and gone his way." This sour putdown inevitably causes me to think of the hordes of tourists who stream past the colossi on their way to or from the Valley of the Kings. As a fragment of one of these hordes, but momentarily detached, I stand at midday on top of the towering cliff overlooking the enormous Temple of Deir el Bahari, certainly the dominating man-made presence in this valley of temples and tombs. Far below on the desert floor, dozens of buses and vans are disgorging their human cargo. The visitors represent nearly every nationality in the world, and as they proceed up and down the terraces ascending to the colonnade at the temple's upper level, they seem an orderly but overwhelming mass, almost numberless; they remind me of the throngs of Disneyland or, even more claustrophobically, as I go down and move among them, of the mob of which I was a gawking young member at the New York World's Fair in 1939. It is fortunate that they—or I should say, we—have been barred permanently from many of the tombs, for it has been demonstrated that the acid exhalations of our breath combined with our million-footed shuffling in the dust has caused irreparable damage already. But people keep coming in ever increasing legions, and it may be that these very numbers, uncontrolled, will soon prove to be more injurious to Egypt than the High Dam.

This is not an alarmist view—it is based on solid evidence—but even so, the situation might change for the better through a strict and systematic program of regulation. Prince Aga Khan, who has made a study of the tourist crisis, believes that a rigorous policy on the part of the Egyptian government would, in not too long a time, finally restrain this runaway influx of travelers, lessening the attrition at the historic sites and making a trip to the Nile a happier event for everyone, including the Egyptians. The policy would commence not only with the limiting of permits for the building of hotels and boats but with supervision—through expert architectural advice—of the construction of these boats and hotels, so as to avoid such atrocities as the hostelry the Russians put up at Aswan or the oversize Sheraton barges. Hotels and tourist villages would be developed in conformity with local traditions and landscape and, just as importantly, be decentralized. They would be moved away from the already preposterously engorged centers of Luxor and Aswan. Such measures would benefit both the tourist and the less economically prosperous population of the backward areas. The sites themselves would undergo drastic changes and management: rotation of tourist groups according to seasonal timetables in order to avoid overlapping and overcrowding; modernization of access roads; installation of advanced systems of dust and humidity control in the tombs, along with better superintendence and better lighting. These are strenuous measures, but in the opinion of the prince, neither impossible to implement nor economically unfeasible; the vast sums of money that tourists bring to Egypt (and which now seem to benefit Egyptian antiquities in only the most marginal way) should be sufficient to pay for such a program, with much left over. But the need is immediate.

. . .

How many trips in the world does one really want to make again? For me, not many. But I could go back to the Nile over and over, as if in mysterious return homeward, or in quest for some ancestral memory that has been only partially and tantalizingly revealed to me—as at that interval when one passes from sleep to waking. On the last evening aboard the *Abu Simbel* there comes to me a moment when I know the reason why I shall always want to come back to this river. Moored to the riverbank at the edge of a small village, the boat is peaceful, all energies unwound; at dusk, alone, I go up on deck and feel in my bones the chill of the coming night. In the village I see a nondescript street, children, a camel, a minaret. Far back on the river two feluccas rest as if foundered immovably upon a sandbar; the light around them is pearl-gray, aqueous, and they seem to hover so delicately on the river that it is as if they were suspended in some nearly incorporeal substance, like gauze or mist. With their furled sails, they are utterly motionless; they are like the boats on an antique china plate of my childhood. As the light fades from the sky and the stars appear, the village is silhouetted against the faintest pink of the setting sun. I am aware of only two sounds: the clinking of a bell, perhaps on some cow or donkey, and now the voice of a muezzin from the minaret, intoning the Koran's summons in dark and monotonous gutturals. It is then, in a quick flood of recognition, that I feel certain that *I have been here before*, in some other century. But as the sensation disappears, almost as swiftly as it comes, I ponder whether this instant of déjà vu means anything at all; after all, I am a skeptic about mystical experiences. Nonetheless, the feeling persists, I cannot quite shake it off—nor do I want to. And so I remain there in the dusk, listening to the soft muttering of the muezzin and gazing at the distant feluccas miraculously afloat in the air. And then I wonder how many others—hypnotized like me by this river and the burden of its history, and by the drama of the death along its shores and waters, and eternal rebirth in all—might have known the same epiphany.

[*GEO*, September 1981]

LOLLIPOPS

The Big Love

It usually requires a certain arrogance to say of a new book that it is a masterpiece. For one thing, the risks are large; in his runaway enthusiasms, the person who is rash enough to proclaim a new book "great," "a staggering achievement," "a work of art of the highest order" (these are the phrases most commonly employed) is likely to be proved wrong, even long before time and posterity have had a chance to assay his judgment. Recall, for example, *By Love Possessed*. A masterpiece? The reviewers seemed to think so, yet now it seems apparent that it wasn't that at all—at least not proven; opposed to what was originally claimed for it, too many people have considered it an unfair struggle and a thick-headed bore. At certain rare moments, however, there will appear a work of such unusual and revealing luminosity of vision, of such striking originality, that its stature is almost indisputable; one feels that one may declare it a masterpiece without hesitation, or fear that the passing of time might in any way alter one's conviction. Such a book is *The Big Love*, a biography of Beverly Aadland by her mother, Mrs. Florence Aadland. To Mrs. Aadland and her collaborator, Tedd Thomey, we owe a debt of gratitude; both of them must feel a sense of pride and relief at having delivered themselves, after God alone knows how much labor, of a work of such wild comic genius.

I would like to make it plain, however, that—as in most high comic art—there is a sense of moral urgency in *The Big Love* which quite removes it from the specious and, more often than not, sensational claptrap we have become accustomed to in popular biography. Witness the first line of the book—a first line that is as direct and in its own way as reverberant as any first line since "Call me Ishmael."

> There's one thing I want to make clear right off [Mrs. Aadland begins], my baby was a virgin the day she met Errol Flynn.
> [Continuing, she says:] Nothing makes me sicker than those dried-up old biddies who don't know the facts and spend all their time making snide remarks about my daughter Beverly, saying she was a bad girl before she met Errol. . . . I'm her mother and she told me everything. She never lied to me. Never.

Already it is obvious that we are in contact with a moral tone entirely different from, let us say, the lubricity of Errol Flynn's own biography, *My Wicked, Wicked Ways*, or the self-exploitation and narcissism so prevalent in those boring memoirs, which appear almost monthly, of yet another international lollipop. In striking this note of rectitude, Mrs. Aadland makes it clear that furthest from her desires is a wish to titillate, or in any way to make sensational an affair which, after all, ended in such tragedy and heartbreak for all concerned. Indeed, if it were not for the sense of decency and high principles which informs every page of *The Big Love*, we would be in the presence not of a comic masterwork at all, but only one more piece of topical trash, hardly distinguishable from the life of a Gabor sister.

The stunning blonde who was to become "Bev" to her mother and, at the age of fifteen, "Woodsie" (because of her resemblance to a wood nymph) to Errol Flynn, was conceived, so Flo Aadland tells us, in an apartment on Mariposa Avenue in Hollywood on December 7, 1941. The date, of course, was ominous, contributing much to further Flo's lasting suspicion that her own life, and now Bev's, was "preordained." Tragedy had dogged much of Flo's life. She possessed, for one thing, an artificial foot, the result of a traffic accident, and this misfortune—usually referred to as "the tragedy of my leg"—coupled with a previous miscarriage, had made it seem to her that life had hardly been worth living until Bev came along. Bev—who was a precocious child, walking at ten months, singing "all the radio commercials" at a year—altered the complexion of Flo's life entirely. "She was such a different baby, different in intelligence as well as beauty. I wondered . . . if she had

been given to me . . . to make up for the tragedy of my leg."
Shortly after this her speculation was confirmed when, riding with
little Bev on a Hermosa Beach bus, she met a female Rosicrucian
"who had made a deep study of the inner ways of life."

Discussing Bev, the Rosicrucian told Flo: " 'This baby has an old
soul. . . . She is very mature. . . . Were the babies you lost before
both girls?'

" 'Yes,' I said.

"The Rosicrucian lady nodded and then held both of Beverly's
hands tightly in her own. 'Twice before, this baby tried to be
born. . . . She has always known she was to fill the emptiness that
entered your life when you lost your leg. . . . And you must realize
this also. . . . This child has been born for untold fame and fortune.' "

Bev's early life was the normal one for a Hollywood youngster.
So gifted that she was able to sing, in immaculate pitch, a popular
song called *Symphony* at seventeen months, she was also almost
overwhelmingly beautiful, and at the age of three, impersonating
Bette Davis, won the costume beauty contest at the Episcopal Sunday School (an Episcopal activity peculiarly Californian in flavor).
Later she was chosen mascot for the Hermosa Beach Aquaplane
Race Association, cut the ceremonial tape for a $200,000 aquarium,
and, not yet six, played in her first movie, a Technicolor epic called
The Story of Nylon. As young as Bev was, she already exerted
upon men a stupefying enchantment. A Hollywood doctor—"a
very learned man, an authority on Eastern religions who had lec-
tured all over the world and written many books"—was the first
to pronounce the somber warning. "He held her hands the way
that Rosicrucian lady had done. . . . 'Mrs. Aadland,' he said seriously, 'wherever did you get this little girl?' . . . Then he sat down
in his chair and did a very strange thing. He closed his eyes and
passed his hand back and forth just above Beverly's bright blonde
curls. 'I think I see sort of a halo on this girl,' he said." Shortly Flo
hears the gloomy, admonitory words: " 'I think men will be terribly
affected by this girl. . . . Be very careful with your daughter. . . .
I think men are going to kill over this girl. I have the feeling in my
heart that she has the scent of musk on her.' " Her religious training
enables Flo to comprehend: "I knew what he meant [about musk].

It wasn't the first time I had run into that phrase. I had read it in the Bible."

When Flynn began seeing Bev—then aged fifteen, and dancing in the movie version of *Marjorie Morningstar*—Flo sensed no impropriety. Thrilled that her daughter should be dating such a famous man, "overwhelmed by the fact that my baby called this man Errol," she confesses that she nearly fainted dead away when first led into his presence. To be sure, she says, "I'd read about his trials for the statutory rape of those two teen-agers in 1942. And I'd seen the headlines in 1951 when he was charged with the rape of a fifteen-year-old French girl." As for Bev, however, "I still didn't believe he would take advantage of her." Against this gullibility may be measured Flo's near-insane outrage, some months later, when, during the course of a plane ride to join Errol in New York, Bev reveals not only that she was no longer chaste, but that Errol—on their very first night together—had done what the cynical reader knew he had done all along: he had, indeed, ravished her, tearing her seventy-five-dollar bolero dress, muttering "Woodsie, Woodsie" over and over, and "growling in his throat." Flo's indignation, however, is short-lived; despite this traumatic event, Bev seems deeply in love with Errol and Errol with Bev. On sober second thought, in fact, the future looks pretty rosy for Flo.

> While [Bev] talked, the love bloom was all over her—in her eyes, making her cheeks pink. "Mama," she said, "can't you imagine what it's going to be like with Errol from now on? Can't you imagine the lovely clothes, the spending, the famous people we'll meet? . . . Mama . . . he's told me how good I am for him. He's told me that we're going to write the Arabian Nights all over again."

And so the incredible joy ride commences, and the sedulous Florence is rarely absent from the scene, or at least its periphery. There are drinking bouts, yachting trips, dances, and other social events, including a well-publicized nude swimming party at a country estate near New York which Flo, with characteristic delicacy, assures us was *not* an orgy. "Beverly later told me all about it. [The people] *weren't* riotously drunk or mad with passion. It was an unconventional but casual swim. Afterwards they got out, dressed, and enjoyed some pork chops and apple sauce together. Beverly helped serve the food and was complimented by the others on her clothes and manners." The East Coast holds Flo —L.A. born and bred—in its thrall; her description of the Connecticut countryside, "the homes with their unusual gabled roofs," has a quality both eerie and exotic, as if it were the Norwegian troll country. At one club function, a handsomely swank place, also in Connecticut, Bev has her first encounter with snow. "We sat down at a table . . ." Flo says, and describes a boring situation.

> I looked around for a movie magazine or something interesting to read, but could find only copies of *Time* and *Fortune*. . . . Pretty soon we noticed it was snowing outside. Without saying a word to me or anyone else, Beverly got up and went outside. It was the first time Bev had ever seen snow falling and, being a native Californian, she was thrilled. I watched her through the large picture window. . . . She held up her arms gracefully and whirled them through the air, touching the falling snowflakes. She never looked lovelier. Her cheeks were flushed to a healthy pink and she wore one of her nicest outfits, a gorgeous peach-colored cashmere sweater and matching skirt. . . . As the big white snowflakes came down thicker and thicker, she did a very crazy thing. She took off her shoes and began dancing and skipping around on the golf greens. . . . She looked like an absolutely mad fairy princess, whirling and cavorting, holding her arms out so beautifully. . . . When she came in, she said: "Oh, Mother, it was so beautiful!" Her nose was red as a raspberry and when I touched it with my finger tip it felt like a cold puppy's nose.

The note of pathos here, fugitive but intensely real, as it is in all comic art of a high order, is the mysterious ingredient which pervades every page of *The Big Love* and compels the book, in a grotesque fashion that surpasses all aesthetic laws, to become a kind of authentic literary creation in spite of itself. It was along about the passage just quoted that I was persuaded that Tedd Thomey, Mrs. Aadland's ghost, was in reality Evelyn Waugh, come back after a long silence to have another crack at the bizarre creatures who inhabit the littoral of Southern California. In truth, however, from this point on the book more reasonably brings to mind Nathanael West's *The Day of the Locust*, if for no other reason than the fact that, as in that fine and funny book, in which horror and laughter are commingled like the beginning of a scream, the climax of *The Big Love* swiftly plunges toward nightmare and hallucination in a fashion that all but overwhelms the comedy. Errol Flynn dies of a heart attack in Vancouver, and Beverly goes to pieces. She becomes the unwilling object of the attentions of a young madman who, one night in Hollywood, rapes her at pistol point, and then in her presence blows out his brains—a tragedy which, Flo concludes, like the multiple tragedy of Errol Flynn and Beverly and Florence Aadland, must have been "preordained." Flo is charged with five counts of contributing to the delinquency of a minor; Beverly, in turn, is remanded into the custody of a movie-colony divine, the Reverend Leonard Eilers, whose wife, Frances, in an admirable spirit of Christian guardianship, is now chaperoning Bev during her appearances on the Midwest night-club circuit.

But at last the true comic spark returns, jewel-bright, in the ultimate scene of this terrifying, flabbergastingly vulgar and, at times, inexplicably touching book. It takes place, appropriately enough, in the celebrated Forest Lawn Memorial Park, whither Flo, out on bail, and Bev and a friend have gone one morning at dawn to deposit flowers on Errol's grave, near a spot called the Garden of Everlasting Peace.

> "My God," I said to Bev. "Can you imagine an unpeaceful man like the Swashbuckler in here?"
> We took the flowers from the car and placed them on the grave. . . . Then, although Errol's grave now had more flowers than any of the others, Beverly and our friend decided he deserved even more.
> So they went to the other graves and took only a few of the fresh flowers that had been left the day before. They took a bit of larkspur from one, a daisy from one and a lily from another. Then, frisking around like wood nymphs, the two of them leaped gracefully over Errol's grave, dropping the flowers at his head and feet.
> I watched them dance . . . for a few more moments and then I said to Beverly: "You didn't kiss him yet, did you?"
> "No, Mama," she said.
> Then she knelt down very carefully and touched her lips to the grass near Errol's headstone.
> "Mama!" she said suddenly.
> "What's the matter?" I said.

"Mama!" she said. "I just heard a big belly laugh down there!"
After that we left. . . . As we drove away, we waved and called
out gaily: "Good-by, Errol!"

It had been, Flo muses, "a tremendously swanky graveyard."

[*Esquire*, November 1961]

The article on Flo and Beverly Aadland was primarily
responsible for converting *The Big Love* into something of
a cult book, with a large and loyal following. One of the
chronicle's greatest admirers was W. H. Auden, who told me
he had given numerous copies to friends, and who quoted
Flo Aadland in his incomparable miscellany *A Certain World*.
(Auden had a great feeling for the bizarre; he also quoted
at length from the autobiography of Rudolf Höss,
Commandant of Auschwitz.) It is an immeasurable loss to
American literature that *The Big Love* is out of print.

Candy

Assuming that we are to use the word in a derogatory sense, any honest definition of pornography must be subjective. For me it reduces itself to that which causes me disgust. (There is also a good kind of pornography, like *Fanny Hill*, which may give pleasure.) In order to appreciate the satire on "bad" pornography in Terry Southern and Mason Hoffenberg's *Candy*, it is helpful to dip into some of the aids to erotic enjoyment which are currently filling the bookstores. One of the most notable of these works is *Sex and the Single Man* by Dr. Albert Ellis, author of an impressive number of studies, including the well-known *Sex Without Guilt*, *The American Sexual Tragedy* and *A Guide to Rational Living*. Dr. Ellis' most recent work is an elaborate, detailed training manual which pits the bachelor trainee ("you") against a hypothetical foe known as "your girlfriend." Most of the tactics in seduction are elementary, and the physiological terrain described by Dr. Ellis is old and trampled ground. The book's real distinction lies in its style; and since the style, among sexologists as among poets and novelists, is the measure of the man, let Dr. Ellis speak for himself: "Coitus itself can in some instances be unusually exciting and arousing. If your girlfriend is not too excitable at a certain time, but is willing to engage in intercourse, she may become aroused through doing so, and may wind up by becoming intensely involved sexually, even though she was relatively passive when you first started to copulate."

It is this kind of mechanical how-to-ism, with its clubfooted prose and its desolating veterinary odor, that constitute the really prurient writing of our time. It is pornographic and disgusting, and it is one of the major targets of *Candy* in its satirical foray against sickbed sex, both scientific and literary. *Candy* was first published in 1957 in Paris by the Olympia Press, which concealed the authors' names under the swank *nom de plume* "Maxwell Kenton." Although *Candy* is by no stretch of the imagination an obscene novel, a bizarre feature of the book's history is that it became—along with a number of others of the Olympia list—one of the few works in English ever to be banned by the French government on the grounds of indecency. This is a circumstance which might make the book appear positively satanic were it not for the fact that *Candy* is really a droll little sugarplum of a tale and a spoof on pornography itself. Actually, considering its reputation, it may be surprising to discover that much of the book is not about sex at all. At any rate, there was no official reaction in France when, in an evasive maneuver, *Candy*'s publisher continued to issue it under the name *Lollipop*. Now it comes to us in the United States from Putnam, unexpurgated, and with the real names of the authors revealed. Let us hope that Candy, the adorable college-girl heroine of the book, is not hounded into court after the fashion of Lady Chatterley—and this for a couple of reasons. First, since this book, too, is not a supreme masterpiece, we shall be spared the spectacle of eminent critics arguing from the witness stand that it is. But more importantly, *Candy* in its best scenes is wickedly funny to read and morally bracing as only good satire can be. The impure alone could object to it, and we should not risk letting ourselves be deprived of such excellent fun even when a certain wobbly and haphazard quality, which may be due to the problems created by collaboration, causes the book to creak and sag more often than it should.

Candy Christian—for such is her beautiful name—is a delectable, neo-Victorian American sophomore on the verge of emancipation: that is to say, she is a girl who has been freed of all unreasonable puritanical restraints, yet who dwells in a limbo where up-to-date young females are expected to give sexual pleasure without, however, experiencing pleasure themselves. To this extent, she vaguely resembles Dr. Ellis' endlessly besieged "girlfriend"—a nightmare in the mind of a *Playboy* reader—trembling maddeningly at the brink of desire. Yet Candy is not just neo-Victorian but post-1950; for where her college counterpart of half a generation ago was a furtive virgin who did something with boys called (the phrase is almost unprintable) "petting to climax," Candy is not much improvement, having replaced her virginity with a greedy narcissism based on fantasies of "need." Such fantasies compel a kind of idiot generosity, and the phrase "*Oh you do need me so!*" is Candy's constant secret thought about men.

The need-principle, we learn early in the story, has been engendered in Candy, through the influence of her Ethical Philosophy teacher, Professor Mephesto. This ass, full of devious altruism ("To give of one's self fully . . . is a beautiful and thrilling privilege," he mutters to Candy, a fat hand on her knee), is a wonderful caricature of the academic seducer, with his cozy little office and his afternoon sherry, his snuffling importunities (" 'It's an 'A' paper . . . Absolutely top-drawer . . . Comfort those whose needs are greatest, my dear,' he implored her"); and although Candy evades the gross fellow she is not without immediate remorse:

> Selfish! Selfish! she was thinking of herself. To be needed by this great man! And to be only concerned with my material self! She was horribly ashamed. How he needs me! And I deny him! I deny *him*! Oh how did I *dare*!

Thus simultaneously chastened and enlightened, Candy resolves to leave college, and it is her wide-eyed, warm-hearted journey through the great world which occupies the rest of the book. Part fantasy, part picaresque extravaganza (the resemblance between the names Candy and Candide is anything but coincidental), the story often suffers from the fact that its larger design is formless and episodic; a number of the sequences, unfortunately, seem to be dreamed-up, spur-of-the-moment notions in which the comic impact is vitiated by obvious haste and a sense of something forced. But in many of its single scenes the book is extremely funny: it is surely the first novel in which frenzied sexual congress between an exquisite young American girl and an insane, sadistic hunchback can elicit nothing but helpless laughter. And at its very best—as with Professor Mephesto—when we perceive that the comic irony is a result of the juxtaposition of Candy's innocent sexual generosity with duplicitous sexual greed, the book produces its triumphs. For none of Candy's seducers seems to realize that he needs only to ask in the most direct and human way in order bountifully to receive. Like Dr. Ellis, they are technocrats and experts, possessing a lust to bury this most fundamental of human impulses beneath the rockpile of scientific paraphernalia and doctrine and professional jabber. Swindlers by nature, they end up only by swindling themselves. It is part of our heroine's unflagging charm and goodness that she confronts each of these monsters with blessed equanimity. They include Dr. Irving Krankeit (*né* Irving Semite), a messianic psychotherapist crazed with the belief that a cure for the world's ills lies in masturbation; another medical wretch named Dunlap; Dr. Johns, an unorthodox gynecologist who submits Candy to an examination in the ladies' room of a Greenwich Village bar; and finally a really superb creation in the form of a character named Great Grindle. Grindle, an egg-bald guru with a luxuriant black mustache and a thick accent, is the spiritual leader of a group of male and female youths who call themselves Crackers —a sort of demented Peace Corps which labors in the national interest deep in the bowels of a Minnesota mine. In Grindle is the gathering together of a number of miscellaneous practices and faiths—Zen and yoga and Reichian orgone theory—and while his interest in Candy is ostensibly spiritual, it is clear from the outset that Grindle, no less than the other quacks she has encountered, is conceiving labyrinthine designs upon "the daring girl's precious little honeypot." And so, deep within a grotto the preposterous ogre sets his trap:

"Good!" said Grindle. "Now then, lace your fingers together, in the yoga manner, and place them behind your head. Yes, just so. Now then, lie back on the mossy bed."

"Oh gosh," said Candy, feeling apprehensive, and as she obediently lay back, she raised one of her handsome thighs, slightly turning it inward, pressed against the other, in a charming coy effort to conceal her marvelous little spice-box.

"No, no," said Grindle, coming forward to make adjustments, "legs well apart."

At his touch, the darling girl started to fright, but Grindle was quick to reassure her. "I am a doctor of the soul," he said coldly: "I am certainly not interested in that silly little body of yours . . ."

"Now this is a so-called 'erogenous zone,'" explained Grindle, gingerly taking one of the perfect little nipples which did so seem to be begging for attention . . .

"*I'll* say," the girl agreed, squirming despite her efforts to be serious . . .

"*This is* another of these so-called 'erogenous zones,'" announced Grindle contemptuously, addressing the perfect thing with his finger . . . "Tell me, how does it feel now?"

The lovely girl's great eyelids were fluttering.

"Oh, it's all tingling and everything," she admitted despairingly . . .

This is not pornography, but the stuff of heartbreak. It is hard to conceive that even Orville Prescott will not somehow be touched by such a portrait of beleaguered goodness.

[*New York Review of Books*, May 14, 1964]

THE
SERVICE

INTRODUCTION

I have never regarded the military profession as a villainous
calling. Military life was so much a part of my background
and my environment that I have sometimes marveled at the
fact that I am by now what I am, instead of a senior
major general in the Marine Corps with three "good" wars
under my belt, dreaming nightly of becoming Commandant.
Growing up, I was aware constantly of the military tradition
in my family, on both sides of the tree. I still possess a
magnificent silver-handled sword which was to be presented
to my great-great-uncle, who had served valiantly in the war
against the detested Mexicans. On his way back to North
Carolina in 1847, having begun to travel from New Orleans
to Memphis, he disappeared from a Mississippi river boat. It
was rumored that he was dumped overboard after a gambling
dispute. The sword is a venerable, scintillating remembrance
of that ill-starred and gallant forebear. His nephew, my
paternal grandfather, served in the Civil War as a sixteen-
year-old courier in a North Carolina regiment and was badly
wounded in one of the northern Virginia battles. On the
maternal side, the family were Yankees from western
Pennsylvania, but from that branch I claim circuitous kinship
with Stonewall Jackson. My mother's soldier brother was a
boyhood chum of George C. Marshall in the coal-and-coke
community of Uniontown (where, incidentally, my
grandfather became Henry Clay Frick's first mine
superintendent and a terrifying reactionary). This admired
uncle, who attended West Point at the same time that
Marshall was at the Virginia Military Institute, maintained
close ties with Marshall all through their military careers—
although my uncle, who never rose higher than colonel, cared

a bit too much for the bottle to emulate Marshall's single-minded and illustrious vocation. I adored my uncle, boozy as he was, and the high-water mark of my life's first twelve years was the pair of fifty-yard-line tickets he sent my father and me for the Army-Navy game of 1938.

The gray of West Point and the blue of Annapolis both stung my imagination during my high school years. To be a naval ensign or an Army lieutenant—it did not matter, so long as I might taste the glory of military life. I was as romantically war-struck as Cherubino, thrilled that the days to come might be one ecstatic *concerto di tromboni, di bombarde, di cannone* . . . Young as I was then, I am still surprised that as those years drew in toward Pearl Harbor I was not more conscious of the way in which these war fantasies were rapidly approaching reality, there in that thriving, energetic sprawl at the edge of Hampton Roads, where everything was being primed for the coming conflict. Certainly no landscape in the United States was more imbued with the sense of bristling martial affairs than this part of Tidewater Virginia.

We woke up daily to the lumbering drone of the new Flying Fortresses from Langley Field. Hampton Roads itself was ceaselessly dotted with blue silhouettes of monster warships. Navy fighter planes from the Norfolk air station joined the racket, shoals of sailors and masses of soldiers from Fort Eustis and Fortress Monroe jammed the streets of Newport News; and there seemed to be always an intermittent faraway cannonade from artillery practice and bombing runs, grumbling and flashing from all points of the compass. In my native Newport News itself all life was dominated by the biggest shipyard in America—where my father worked—and by the outlines of such naval behemoths as *Ranger* and *Yorktown* and *Enterprise*, each of which as a boy I witnessed slithering majestically down ways larded with tons of sheep tallow into the muddy James, which parted at the prodigious impact like the Red Sea making way for Moses. It was an incredibly busy, deafening, dynamic world I grew up in—all technology and energy revving up for the greatest clash of arms in history. In this environment, and with my deeply belligerent heritage, there is little wonder that the Service came to figure prominently in my disposition. There were of course patches of New South urban serenity amid all this discord (to be found here and there in *Lie Down in Darkness*), but in many ways the onrushing war made me what I became.

A strain of suicidal bravado—which I scarcely knew I possessed—caused me to join the Marine Corps when I was seventeen. Altogether, in World War II and in the Korean War, I served more than three years. I was both an enlisted man and an officer, and for a while at least, I felt more pride in being a Marine private than any pride I might have felt as a graduate of Annapolis or West Point. To be sure, there was a certain cooling off. My infatuation with military life dwindled fairly rapidly as I underwent the rigors of combat training; the lack of a few innate but essential physical skills (like those needed for swiftly dismantling a machine gun) and a deficiency in that ferocious quality known as "command presence" made me aware that I would doubtless not succeed in making a career of the Service. Nonetheless, though threat of the direst alternatives could not force me back into the Marine Corps (even if I were wanted), it was an experience that I would not have cared to miss, if only because of the way it tested my endurance and my capacity for sheer misery, physical and of the spirit. If the ordeal caused me to loathe war utterly, it also has allowed me to take quick offense at any easily expressed contempt for men who dedicate themselves to fighting our battles.

MacArthur

THE *Reminiscences* by General of the Army Douglas Mac-Arthur would be remarkable if for no other reason than that they may very well comprise the only autobiography by a great man which is almost totally free of self-doubt. There is no soul-searching here, none of the moments of despair, inquietude, fits of gloom that are recorded in the lives of even the most self-possessed of heroic men. MacArthur's solitary attack of desperation—so far as one can tell—occurred when he was nineteen, while still a plebe at West Point. The occasion was the investigation of a hazing incident in which young Douglas had been one of the victims. Called upon to divulge the names of the upperclassmen involved, he was naturally thrown into a state of anguish—all the more wrenching because of the presence at The Point of his mother, who had taught him stern rules about lying and tattling. This same lady (she was of an old Virginia family, and made her home for long periods with the General until he was past fifty) sent him the following poem during a recess of the court:

> Do you know that your soul is of my soul such a part
> That you seem to be fiber and core of my heart?
> None other can pain me as you, son, can do;
> None other can please me or praise me as you.
> Remember the world will be quick with its blame
> If shadow or shame ever darken your name.
> Like mother, like son, is saying so true
> The world will judge largely of mother by you.
> Be this then your task, if task it shall be,
> To force this proud world to do homage to me.
> Be sure it will say, when its verdict you've won,
> She reaps as she sowed: "This man is her son!"

"I knew then what to do," MacArthur adds. "Come what may, I would be no tattletale."

The last remark is characteristic. For if a serene confidence untouched by that daily incertitude which afflicts most humans is one of the most immediate and striking features of this book, so too is the style, which, it should be said at the outset, is disappointingly juvenile. When one recalls those august periods which had rallied so many Americans during World War II, it comes as a surprise that here the tone is distinctly flat and insipid, the laborious prose having been set down with that gauche, manly earnestness that one recollects as a prominent characteristic of the adventures of Tom Swift. One wonders whatever happened to the grandiloquent MacArthur, the MacArthur who endeavored through rhetoric to transform the drab reality of American military life into something as rich and as mythic as medieval knighthood—an ideal typified in the address in 1935 to the veterans of his own World War I Rainbow Division:

> Those days of old have vanished tone and tint: they have gone glimmering through the dreams of things that were. Their memory is a land where flowers of wondrous beauty and varied colors spring, watered by tears and coaxed and caressed into fuller bloom by the smiles of yesterday . . . We listen vainly but with thirsty ear for the witching melodies of days that are gone . . . Youth . . . strength . . . aspirations . . . wide winds sweeping . . . beacons flashing across uncharted depths . . . movements . . . vividness . . . faint bugles sounding reveille . . . far drums beating the long roll call . . . the rattle of musketry . . . the still white crosses.

This is terrible junk, but it has at least a certain impassioned rhythm, while the greater part of the autobiography, when it is not simply boyish in tone, is set down in that lusterless Eisenhowerese which is so favored by corporation executives and which may be the result of MacArthur's later years at Remington Rand.* At any rate, the book is often something of a struggle to get through.

The quotation above, incidentally, is taken from Richard H. Rovere and Arthur M. Schlesinger, Jr.,'s less than admiring but very fair *The General and the President*, published in 1951. A

---

* Or perhaps it is the influence of MacArthur's biographer, Major General Courtney Whitney. Although MacArthur claims to have "penned this book by my own hand," lines have been blandly plagiarized from Whitney's sycophantic *MacArthur: His Rendezvous with History* (1956).

course of supplementary reading is as essential to the *Reminiscences* as it is to Parson Weems's life of Washington; and the Rovere-Schlesinger work, although it is primarily concerned with the last, or Korean, phase of MacArthur's career, is the most informative of an abundant selection. Noting the seventeen years MacArthur spent out of the United States before his recall from Korea in 1951, Rovere and Schlesinger make the observation that "MacArthur is our greatest military expatriate; he was as much in rebellion against our civilization as ever Henry James or Henry Miller was, and he probably symbolized the non-homesick American better than they ever did." The key phrase here is "non-homesick," and certainly Rovere and Schlesinger's contention is more than supported by MacArthur's autobiography. For in trying to understand MacArthur it is important to remember how completely his life was dominated by the Army, by the concept of the professional soldier, and how from the moment of his birth the Army became his home and his only home.

Born in 1880, MacArthur was the son of an ambitious and extremely gifted young officer from Wisconsin, a Union veteran who married a Southern woman whose brothers had fought under Robert E. Lee; the family atmosphere seems to have been one of an exhilarating preoccupation with the military tradition and its achievements, past and present. MacArthur's father, Arthur MacArthur, eventually became the highest ranking officer in the Army. Douglas MacArthur's boyhood was spent almost entirely on Army posts, mainly in the Southwest, and after an Army education at West Point (his career there was illustrious; MacArthur does not dwell upon the exact nature of his education, but it must have been, at that time, parochial in the extreme), he rose with amazing speed to become, at thirty-eight, a brigadier general and the youngest divisional commander in the American Expeditionary Force. His military record in France was truly spectacular, and his personal courage has never been in doubt; he returned from World War I loaded down with decorations and glory.

For a man of such—let it be cautiously called—egocentricity, there is little wonder that the following fifteen years and more, dutiful and dedicated as they were, lacked savor, and therefore make dull reading in the *Reminiscences*: a colorless tour of duty as Superintendent at West Point, a brigade command in the peaceful Philippines, a corps command in Baltimore, directorship of the

Olympic Games committee. Even his five years as Army Chief of Staff (MacArthur writes with perfect aplomb that he accepted this high post solely at the demand of his mother, which must be the most awesome example we have of the influence of motherhood upon the national destiny) were singularly devoid of glamour, their only bright moment being his celebrated skirmish with the bedraggled Bonus Army on Anacostia Flats. This wasn't much of a war. It is understandable that at the age of fifty-five, having risen as high as one can rise in the Army, burdened with too much rank and heading for premature retirement, MacArthur was rent by such a keen nostalgia for the wartime days that it was like a gaping wound, and that in the midst of the early Roosevelt era—when military men were *déclassé*, anyway—he felt the need to give his Rainbow Division speech with its desperate and frustrated longing, its "thirsty ear" for "far drums beating the long roll call, the rattle of musketry, the still white crosses." He resigned to become chief military adviser to the Philippines, six years before the cataclysm at Pearl Harbor.

If it is impossible to share MacArthur's nostalgia for war, to share his passionate identity with the world of soldiering, it is at the same time easy to understand that nostalgia in the light of these fifty-five years. Anyone who has lived as a stranger for any length of time among professional military men, especially officers, is made gradually aware of something that runs counter to everything one has been taught to believe—and that is that most of these men, far from corresponding to the liberal cliché of the superpatriot, are in fact totally lacking in patriotism. They are not unpatriotic; they simply do not understand or care what patriotism is. Most of them, having been molded within the microcosm of Service—Army, Marine Corps, Navy, whatever—are spiritually bound to a Service, not a country, and the homage they pay to Old Glory they could pay to anyone's flag. A true military man is a mercenary (the calling is not necessarily ignoble, but certainly MacArthur's role in the Philippines was for all intents and purposes that of a mercenary soldier), and it is within the world of soldiering that he finds his only home. This is why MacArthur, owing no spiritual allegiance to his native land, was able to become the very archetype of an expatriate, hostile to America and understanding almost nothing of it. This is also one of the reasons why, during World War II and to a nearly disastrous degree in Korea, he found it so easy to defy civilian authority: what did these Secretaries of the Army and fussy Presidents—who, after all, were only Americans—know about the Service, which transcends all?

Nevertheless, if one understands the nostalgia for war which marked these years of his break with America, it still remains a nostalgia that is empyreal and histrionic. Only once in his career did MacArthur lead as small a body of men as a company—one somehow feels that the idea of MacArthur, even as a boy, in command of anything less than a division verges on the ludicrous—and this helps explain why his attitude toward the drab brown, smeary side of military life seems so rosy, and why the rare notice he pays to enlisted troops, whether singly or as a lacerated front-line unit, is always so condescending. MacArthur was a genuine militarist, but like all of this breed he was a hopeless romantic and almost totally without humor; it was his misfortune to collide head-on many times with that strain in the American character which is obdurate, wry, realistic and comical. Americans have in many ways been a bloodthirsty people, but except in odd spasms they have never been militaristic, and it is this important distinction that one must take into account when one contemplates MacArthur's amazing career. For MacArthur, military life may be symbolized by "beacons flashing across uncharted depths . . . faint bugles sounding reveille," but for many if not most of his countrymen it is something else: it *is* reveille. It is training manuals and twenty-mile hikes, stupefying lectures on platoon tactics and terrain and the use of the Lister bag, mountains of administrative paperwork, compulsive neatness and hideous barracks in Missouri and Texas, sexual deprivation, hot asphalt drill fields and deafening rifle ranges, daily tedium unparalleled in its ferocity, awful food, bad pay, ignorant people and a ritualistic demand for ass-kissing almost unique in the quality of its humiliation. The world that MacArthur thrills to makes most of his fellow Americans choke with horror.

Early in his narrative, describing how careful preparation allowed him to win the highest marks in high school, MacArthur says: "It was a lesson I never forgot. Preparedness is the key to success and victory." In 1939, in a statement not quoted in this book, he was saying complacently of the Philippines: "It has been assumed, in my opinion erroneously, that Japan covets these Islands. Proponents of such a theory fail fully to credit the logic of the Japanese mind." But the evidence is now that inadequate preparedness on MacArthur's part was a central factor in the catastrophe that engulfed the Philippines immediately after Pearl Harbor, and that the General's failure to implement properly certain crucial plans involving supply led directly to the eventual defeat on Bataan. MacArthur naturally does not linger on these matters, querulously placing the blame on the Navy, on something he calls "Washington," or an even more nebulous something called "my detractors" —a group that crops up with increasing frequency as the book drags on. There is one bracing passage from the Bataan-Corregidor section of the book, however: it is MacArthur's description of his departure by PT boat from the dock of the island, in the midst of incredible devastation:

> The desperate scene showed only a black mass of destruction. Through the shattered ruins, my eyes sought "Topside," where the deep roar of the heavy guns still growled defiance. Up there, in command, was my classmate, Paul Bunker. Forty years had passed since Bunker had been twice selected by Walter Camp for the All-American team. I could shut my eyes and see again that blond head racing, tearing, plunging—210 pounds of irresistible power. I could almost hear Quarterback Charley Daly's shrill voice barking, "Bunker back." . . .

It is at this point that MacArthur begins increasingly to yammer against censorship. He had been incensed when "Washington" forbade the release of information about the Death March on Bataan, and he writes of this incident: "Here was the sinister beginning of the 'managed news' concept by those in power." This statement was made by a man who could not have been unaware that it was public knowledge that he himself ran the most tightly controlled news agency of the war—an organization dedicated to glorifying MacArthur and so firmly under the General's thumb that one correspondent who was there called it "the most rigid and dangerous censorship in American history." ("If you capture Buna," MacArthur once said to General Eichelberger during the New Guinea campaign, "I'll give you a Distinguished Service Cross and recommend you for a high British decoration." Then he added: "Also, I'll release your name for newspaper publication.") Nevertheless, most of the field generals and even some of the admirals had enormous respect for MacArthur's strategical sense, and his fight back to the Philippines from Australia by way of New Guinea remains a brilliant achievement. Maybe it is unfair to complain that the General's account of these operations—which rank high among his genuine triumphs—seems to be abstract, distant, skimpy in its total effect. While it would be wrong to expect a commander of MacArthur's position to have spent much time on the front lines (although often during the war, communiqués from "MacArthur's Headquarters" misled many newspaper readers into believing that he had done just that), and therefore his account cannot be filled with the smoke of battle and the feel of troops and movement, it is precisely this lack that makes for dull reading when a General has reached that stage of command which is both Olympian and "global." Thus MacArthur writes: "On January 2, 1943, Buna Mission fell; Sanananda followed, and the Papua campaign . . . ended." This is the General's single allusion to Sanananda, a bitter and horrible struggle—unknown by name to most Americans—which resulted in as many deaths as the bloody and far more famous battle by the Marines for Tarawa. Another reason comes to mind for such a cavalier reference, and it is less pleasant. It is that in this book no less than in his wartime dispatches, MacArthur is concerned with minimizing his own loss of men.

MacArthur's habit of self-congratulation, beating its rhythmic way through these pages in a rattle of medals, decorations, flattery from underlings, and adulatory messages from chiefs of state, reaches a crescendo as the Philippines are retaken and it becomes clear that the war is going to be won. Certainly the work of no modern military leader is filled with so many utterances of admiration, love received and bestowed, and pure vanity; by comparison, the autobiography of Fleet Admiral Halsey, no mean hand himself at the immodest appraisal, seems a work of anemic self-abasement. Indeed, by the time MacArthur has reached Manila, the need to describe the charisma of his own physical presence has become so obsessive, and the narcissism is so unremitting, that the effect is somehow vaguely sexual, as if the General had begun to lure the unwilling reader into some act of collaborative onanism. He describes, for example, his first visit to the infamous Santo Tomás prison camp.

When I arrived, the pitiful, half-starved inmates broke out in excited yells. I entered the building and was immediately pressed back against the wall by thousands of emotionally charged people. In their ragged, filthy clothes, with tears streaming down their faces, they seemed to be using their last strength to fight their way close enough to grasp my hand. One man threw his arms around me, and put his head on my chest, and cried unashamedly. A once-beautiful woman in tatters laboriously lifted her son over the heads of the crowd and asked me to touch him . . . I was kissed. I was hugged. . . .

It is callous and offensive enough—even more so since it was written from the vantage point of mellow reflection—that this passage has for its dominant image not that wretched suffering itself but a man confusing himself with Christ. It becomes unspeakable when it seems very likely that MacArthur was employing characteristic fantasy in order to obscure the pathetic truth. Protesting Mac-Arthur's similar description of the "liberation" of another Manila prison camp, Bilibid, a survivor recently wrote a letter to *Life* magazine—where part of this book was first published—and claimed bluntly that the General's account was a lie. The prisoners were freed and taken elsewhere, he said, then "unaccountably" brought back to the prison, where MacArthur shortly joined them with his entourage of newspapermen. There was no grateful outburst of welcome, only "wobbly ranks of thin, terribly tired men standing in stony silence."

MacArthur's Southwest Pacific command was one prong of a two-pronged assault on Japan, the other being Admiral Nimitz's Central Pacific force composed primarily of the Navy and Marine Corps. At the beginning of the war MacArthur bitterly opposed this division of the power, and he hated the Navy with a passion; it comes as a pleasant surprise, therefore, that he nowhere makes the claim of having won the war in the Pacific single-handedly; and the General earns points by offering praise where praise is due, paying tribute to Halsey and Kinkaid and such Air Force men as Kennedy and even Major Bong, who contributed so much to the success of his own operations. MacArthur's unselfish respect for the achievements of other military men is very Prussian. Also it cannot be denied that his own great sweep up through New Guinea and its island outriders to the Philippines was a brilliant feat of aggressive warfare.

A kind of exultant momentum seems to take hold of MacArthur as the war concludes, and it carries him through to his undoubtedly fine achievements as the absolute dictator of a conquered Japan. Free of "Washington" at last, MacArthur seems to have undergone in Tokyo a kind of benign metamorphosis. Sternly aloof, authoritarian, he was able nonetheless to display enormous understanding, tact and even a heretofore concealed strain of magnanimity—as when he firmly resisted the yowls from America and its allies that Emperor Hirohito be tried as a war criminal. No less able a witness than Ambassador Edwin O. Reischauer has paid his earnest compliments to MacArthur's job of democratization, and similarly Roger Baldwin of the American Civil Liberties Union returned from Japan impressed by his reforms in such areas as constitutional rights, labor and the enfranchisement of women. Yet both Reischauer and Baldwin think that he outwore his stay, and Baldwin has felt that with such central issues as the unionization of government workers the General sided with reaction.

Typically, MacArthur's long account of his visitation to Japan is Promethean and lacking in any flaw; it is one of the General's failings that often as soon as he has begun to win the reader over with a sort of hulking charm, he doses him by a sudden convulsion of self-righteousness. Thus, despite his magnanimous treatment of the emperor, he was ruthless in his disposal of the case of General Homma, "the Beast of Bataan," who had reputedly engineered the Death March. In his excellent book *But Not in Shame*, John Toland has offered convincing evidence that MacArthur was simply out to get his old enemy of the Philippines and that he rigged a trial that did not faintly resemble a display of justice. Homma, aside from being a man of great personal dignity and humanity, had no inkling of the atrocities taking place at that distant edge of his command. Our hero must have known this, yet in reviewing the trial he ordered Homma peremptorily executed with a statement priggish and insufferable even for MacArthur:

> The proceedings show the defendant lacked the basic firmness of character and moral fortitude essential to officers charged with the high command of military forces in the field. No nation can safely trust its martial honor to leaders who do not maintain the universal code which distinguishes between those things that are right and those things that are wrong. . . .

In 1951, recalled from his command in Korea by President Truman, MacArthur received the grandest welcome ever accorded by the American people. The General notes this fact with pride in his *Reminiscences*, though perhaps at last it is some aberrant modesty that prevents him from recording what had already been spoken and written of him: "the greatest living master of English" (this from Dr. Norman Vincent Peale), "the greatest man alive," "the greatest man since Christ," "the greatest man who ever lived." To these must be added the highest encomium ever received by an American—certainly in the halls of Congress—when after MacArthur's famous speech to that body, Representative Dewey Short of Missouri, a man educated at Harvard and Oxford, said, "We heard God speak here today, God in the flesh." (In the *Congressional Record* he later revised this statement to read: "A great hunk of God in the flesh.") MacArthur had made a tragic blunder in Korea—failing, as he had with the Japanese in the Philippines, to prepare adequately for Chinese aggression—yet his terrifying plan to extend the war onto the Chinese mainland had been cheered on, in one of those rare militaristic spasms, by vast numbers of Americans. Why they had done so may have best been explained by the British scholar Geoffrey Barraclough:

> Whatever view one may otherwise take of his actions, he took his stand on American interests. It is perhaps understandable, in the tense international situation of 1950, that Truman and his advisers found it difficult to acknowledge in the face of the world that the United States had an imperial role in Asia, shaped by long history, which it was going to defend. MacArthur made no bones about it. He cleared the air of cant.

That "Washington," this time in the form of Harry Truman and the Joint Chiefs of Staff, foresaw that he would "involve us in the wrong war, at the wrong place, with the wrong enemy, at the wrong time," provided the margin of our salvation.

In spite of his noble protestations, MacArthur had a simple lust for war. Though he was an alien to our civilization, perhaps in the end he was really not so remote from it that it is possible for us to rest easy with his sentiments, his yearning, and with those men who share his yearning. Toward the last days of his career he claimed over and over to be a lover of peace, a man who hated more than anything the idea of war. Yet he gave a final, supposedly extemporaneous speech at West Point. And the lines of farewell from that speech recorded on the last page of the book—for a peace-lover they seem inappropriate but they do not surprise us; we have seen those very words before—are filled with the same old nostalgia:

The shadows are lengthening for me. The twilight is here. My days of old have vanished tone and tint; they have gone glimmering through the dreams of things that were. Their memory is one of wondrous beauty, watered by tears, and coaxed and caressed by the smiles of yesterday. I listen vainly, but with thirsty ear, for the witching melody of faint bugles blowing reveille, of far drums beating the long roll. . . . the crash of guns . . .

[*New York Review of Books*, October 8, 1964]

The Red Badge
of Literature

WHY IS IT that the war in Vietnam has inspired tons of journalism, most of it ordinary, yet such a small amount of imaginative literature? Could this be merely the continuation of a negative trend which began during the Korean War—a conflict which also produced little that was notable in the way of fiction, drama or poetry? For up until the past two decades the wars America engaged in proved to be the catalyst for memorable work from some of our finest writers. In the best of these works—those of Whitman and Melville, Hemingway, Dos Passos, E. E. Cummings, Mailer, James Jones—the writers seemed possessed by an almost Euripidean need to demonstrate the eternal tragedy and folly of warfare, its persistence as a mysterious and destructive force dwelling in the very matrix of our nature, its stupidity, its boredom and anguish, and the glorious heroism it sometimes calls forth in spite of itself. In retrospect, it may be that both the appeal and the vitality of these novels and poems—and of lesser yet beautifully crafted works like John Horne Burns's novel of World War II, *The Gallery*—had to do with a kind of residual unconscious romanticism. After all, the Civil War and the two world wars of this century, whatever their horrors and whatever the historical blunders and idiocies that propelled them into being, possessed moral aspects which could make an individual's participation in the conflict not entirely ignoble. Both Stephen Crane and Hemingway were conscious of the insanity, the brutalization of war, but there were still a few idealistic principles embedded in the Civil War and World War I, thus lending to *The Red Badge of Courage* and *A Farewell to Arms* certain ironies and contradictions which helped give to each, finally, a romantic and tragic resonance.

It is possible, then, that the further we remove ourselves from wars in which a vestige of idealism exists or—to put it the other way around—the more we engage in waging wars that approach being totally depraved, the less likely we are to produce imaginative writing that contains many plausible outlines of humanity. It is a long leap, both historically and aesthetically, from the clear, frightened, distinctive identity of the hero of Stephen Crane to the blurred, undifferentiated, curiously one-dimensional twentieth-century victims wandering or staggering through the Vietnamese landscape of Ronald J. Glasser's *365 Days;* yet it is a tribute to Glasser's great skill as a writer that from this most morally loathsome of wars, which has in some way degraded each person who has been touched by it, he has fashioned a moving account about tremendous courage and often immeasurable suffering. It is therefore a valuable and redemptive work, providing as it does a view of the war from the vantage point of a man who has not only been there but has himself, obviously, seen and suffered much.

Glasser is a physician, a former Army major who found himself assigned in 1968 to the U.S. Army hospital at Zama, in Japan. It was here that he first encountered the evacuated wounded from Vietnam, "the blind 17-year-olds stumbling down the hallway, the shattered high-school football player being wheeled to physical therapy." Trained as a pediatrician, Glasser relates how he began to feel a special empathy for these blown-apart, uncomplaining, sometimes hideously mangled casualties of war. "I soon realized," he writes, "that the troopers they were pulling off those med evac choppers were only children themselves. . . . At first, when it was all new, I was glad I didn't know them; I was relieved they were your children, not mine. After a while, I changed." In the act of changing, in the process of becoming involved with these boys, Glasser listened to many stories about the horrors of combat in Vietnam. They were grim stories mostly, touched with the cold hand of mortality and having to do with slow or sudden death and unspeakable wounds, yet some of the tales were wildly improbable and overlaid by the graveyard hilarity that inevitably accompanies any chronicle of warfare.

Recounted in a dry, dispassionate, superbly controlled and ironic voice, these anecdotes mingle at random with Glasser's own vividly observed, first-hand sketches of hospital life in Japan. The effect is disorganized, laconic, rather unsettlingly fragmentary, until one realizes that such a disjointed technique is perfectly suited to the outlines of the lunatic war itself: its greedy purposelessness, its manic and self-devouring intensity, its unending tableaux of helicopters crashing on missions to nowhere, futile patrols ending in bloody slaughter, instantaneous death in some remote mess area miles behind the action. Glasser's yeoman soldiers, aided by modern technology, are as miserably up to their necks in war as were those of Shakespeare. They trip over mines and are reduced to vegetables; after a night of grisly hand-to-hand murder they are enraged when the cook runs out of cornflakes; they nervously conspire to kill their swinish senior officers, and then chicken out. These awful vignettes are rendered with splendid understatement. It is a banal and senseless war, lacking either heroes or a chorus. Perhaps only an ear exquisitely attuned to the banal and senseless, like Glasser's, could do justice to such a nightmare: certainly many of these pages of callow, dyspeptic dialogue—uttered out of young souls quite trampled down with despair and fatigue—are as authentic and as moving a transcription of the soldier's true voice as any written in recent memory.

But if the war has been a war made up of victims and has been denied its true heroes, it has nonetheless had its moments of great sacrifice and courage in the face of incredible suffering. It is through Glasser's calm, unsentimental revelation of such moments that we are able to shake off some of the horror with which these pages are so often steeped and to see *365 Days* as the cleansing and redemptive document it is. Nearly all of Glasser's stories of combat, although admittedly secondhand (as was *The Red Badge of Courage*), are remarkable miniature portraits of men at war. It is in the hospital episodes, however, where the force of Glasser's professional concern melts with the compassion and sensibility of a gifted storyteller, that we are given scenes of wrenching power. In the last story in the book, Major Edwards, a doctor in the hospital burn unit, is faced with the hopeless task of saving a young soldier cruelly burned across 80 percent of his body. The tale is simple, the situation uncomplicated: a dedicated physician, through no other motive than that resulting from the mighty urge to hold back death, trying against all odds to salvage someone who himself is suffering, without complaint, ecstasies of pain. Two human beings, then, locked in the immemorial struggle against inexplicable fate. This is a familiar story and one that could have been both clinical and cloying, but Glasser's hand is so sure, his eye so clear, that the moment of the boy's imminent death and his last cry to the doctor —"I don't want to go home alone"—seem to rise to form a kind of unbearable epiphany to the inhuman waste and folly of war.

It is this quality, reverent at its best, enormously touching in its concern for the simple worth and decency of life, that gives *365 Days* its great distinction and may cause it—one hopes—to become one of those rare chronicles we can use to help alleviate the killing pain of this war, and its festering disgrace. For it shows that in the midst of their most brutish activity there is a nobility in men that war itself cannot extinguish. As Glasser says, in one of the most poignant of his passages, about the "medics":

> In a world of suffering and death, Vietnam is like a Walt Disney True-Life Adventure, where the young are suddenly left alone to take care of the young. . . . A tour of Nam is 12 months; it is like a law of nature. The medics, though, stay on line only seven months. It is not due to the good will of the Army, but to their discovery that seven months is about all these kids can take. After that, they start getting freaky, cutting down on their own water and food so they can carry more medical supplies; stealing plasma bottles and walking around on patrol with five or six pounds of glass in their rucksacks; writing parents and friends so they can buy their own endotracheal tubes; or quite simply refusing to leave their units when their time in Nam is over.
>
> And so it goes, and the gooks know it. They will drop the point, trying not to kill him but to wound him, to get him screaming so they can get the medic too. He'll come. They know he will.

[*Washington Monthly*, March 1972]

There was a rather grotesque aftermath to *365 Days*. In 1981, long after its publication, the book became a *cause célèbre* in the state of Maine, where it went on trial for the obscenity of its language. Glasser and his book were acquitted, but the case remains a remarkable example of the perennial confusion in the United States over the difference between the relatively benign obscenity of certain words and the total obscenity of war.

A Farewell to Arms

A SHORT TIME AGO, while talking to a group of students at a college in Virginia, I was seized by a dismal insight. The subject of war literature had come up and I said that it occurred to me suddenly that at the age of fifty-one—perhaps a mellow age but one I refused to regard as being advanced or venerable—I had lived through three wars, in two of which, both as an officer and as an enlisted man in the Marine Corps, I had been an active participant. I reviewed the wars in reverse order. Although I had been spared the war in Vietnam, except as an outraged and frustrated onlooker, I had been involved in the war against the Chinese and the North Koreans as well as the Japanese in World War II (the Marines have in recent years specialized in Oriental foes); as a matter of curiosity I threw in the fact that World War I—that pointless and heartrending conflict—ended only seven years before my birth.

The Virginia springtime was peaceful and bright as I brooded in this fashion, but I wondered aloud on the illusory nature of this peace. Was it going to last? Was it really peace? The students appeared to be perplexed, maybe a little bored. I reflected that given the almost cyclical nature of these terrible conflicts in our century—the seemingly inexorable pattern of their recurrence—no one could imagine an experienced odds-maker like Jimmy the Greek or, let us say, a sound actuarial mind regarding as anything but an outside chance the notion that war of serious magnitude involving American forces would not happen again. Perhaps soon, certainly within your own lifetime, I concluded somberly to the students—but since on those fresh young faces I saw nothing but incomprehension, we talked of other matters. I had the feeling that the battles of Vietnam for them were as remote as Shiloh or Belleau Wood.

It was with the memory of this episode that I turned to Philip Caputo's remarkable personal account of the war in Vietnam, *A Rumor of War*, and experienced from the very first page a chilling sense of déjà vu. Caputo and I are separated in age by approximately twenty years, and although there were significant differences in his Marine Corps experience and mine, I was struck immediately by the similarities. Born like me into a middle-class family, Caputo joined the Marines in 1960 (as I did during World War II) for the glory and the adventure, for the need to "prove something—my courage, my toughness, my manhood." In my own case, the Japanese were already our sworn enemy and it may be that patriotism inspired by war against a proven aggressor helped to motivate my choice; to wait and be drafted into the *Army* was unthinkable.

Caputo, enlisting in a time of nominal peace, concedes that "the patriotic tide of the Kennedy years" was an element for him in choosing the Marines (early in the book he bitterly, and correctly, speaks of John Kennedy as being "that most articulate and elegant mythmaker," who was as responsible as anyone for the Vietnam enterprise and for his own final disillusionment), but Caputo and I shared, quite unequivocally, I think, the quest for war's heroic experience: "war, the ultimate adventure, the ordinary man's most convenient means of escaping from the ordinary."

In the opening passages of his book, Caputo describes how directly from his classes in English literature he entered Marine Corps training at Quantico, where as an officer candidate he learned to slaughter people with rifles and knives and explosives or to blast them to pieces with rocket launchers. These passages could serve almost perfectly (excepting one or two trivial technological details) as the introduction to my own youthful military reminiscences. We went through virtually the same training ordeal, which in the Marine Corps remains unchanged to the present moment: the remorseless close-order drill hour after hour in the burning sun, the mental and physical abuse, the humiliations, the frequent sadism at the hands of drill sergeants, all the claustrophobic and terrifying insults to the spirit that can make an outpost like Quantico or Parris Island one of the closest things in the free world to a concentration camp. (I have learned that revolutionary changes have taken place, but only in recent months.) Yet this preparation, a form of meat processing which I do not think it hyperbolic to call infernal (it has on too many occasions actually maimed or killed), is intended to create an *esprit de corps*, a sense of discipline and teamwork, above all a feeling of group invincibility which sets the Marine Corps apart from the other branches of the service. And that the training has been generally successful can be demonstrated by the fierce pride with which it stamps its survivors.

It is for me a touchstone of the Marine Corps' fatal glamour—that training nightmare—that there is no ex-Marine of my acquaintance, regardless of what direction he may have taken spiritually or politically after those callow gung-ho days, who does not view the training as a crucible out of which he emerged in some way more resilient, simply *braver* and better for the wear. Another measure of the success of that training is that it could transform Philip Caputo of Westchester, Illinois, from an ordinary, bright suburban lad with amorphous ambitions into a highly trained technician in the science of killing, who in March of 1965, during those palmy "defensive" or "expeditionary" days of the war, landed at Danang eager for the fight, for the excitement, for medals, anxious to prove himself as a Marine officer, above all drawn to war with "an unholy attraction" he could not repress. One of the indispensable features of Caputo's narrative is that he is never less than honest, sometimes relentlessly so, about his feelings concerning the thrill of warfare and the intoxication of combat. At least in the beginning, before the madness. After sixteen months of bloody skirmishes and the ravages of disease and a hostile environment, after the psychological and emotional attrition, Caputo—who had begun "this splendid little war" in the jaunty high spirits of Prince Hal—was very close to emotional and physical collapse, a "moral casualty," convinced—and in 1966!—that the war was unwinnable and a disgrace to the flag under which he had fought to such a pitch of exhaustion.

There is a persuasive legitimacy in this hatred of a war when it is evoked by a man who has suffered its most horrible debauchments. But perhaps that is why we are equally persuaded by Caputo's insistence on a recognition that for many men, himself included, war and the confrontation with death can produce an emotion—a commingled exultation and anguish—that verges on rapture. It is like a mighty drug, certainly it approaches the transcendental. After becoming a civilian, Caputo was engaged for a long time in the antiwar movement. But, he says, "I would never be able to hate the war with anything like the undiluted passion of my friends in the movement." These friends, he implies, could never understand how for him the war "had been an experience as fascinating as it was repulsive, as exhilarating as it was sad, as tender as it was cruel." Some of Caputo's troubled, searching meditations on the love and hate of war, on fear, and the ambivalent discord that warfare can create in the hearts of decent men, are among the most eloquent I have read in modern literature. And when in a blunter spirit he states, "Anyone who fought in Vietnam, if he is honest about himself, will have to admit he enjoyed the compelling attractiveness of combat," he is saying something worthy of our concern, explaining as it does—at least in part—the existence of preparatory hellholes like Quantico and Parris Island, and perhaps of war itself.

Of course no war can be reckoned as good. Yet aside from the fact that for the Marines in the Pacific, World War II was at least a struggle against aggression, while the war in Vietnam was a vicious and self-serving intrusion, what finally differentiated the two conflicts from the point of view of the dirty foot soldier? Caputo's war and mine? As the earlier war recedes, and the Pacific battlefields become merely palm-shaded monuments in the remote ocean, there is a tendency to romanticize or to distort and forget. Bloody as we all know that conflict was, it becomes in memory cleaner and tidier—a John Wayne movie with most of the gore hosed away for the benefit of a PG-rated audience. The Marines in that war seem a little like Boy Scouts, impossibly decent. Could it be that the propinquity of the unspeakable horrors of Vietnam forces us to this more tasteful view? Yet it should be noted that World War II produced its own barbarities. As a young Marine lieutenant I knew a regular gunnery sergeant, a mortar specialist, who carried in his dungaree pocket two small shriveled dark objects about the size of peach pits. When I asked him what they were he told me they were "Jap's nuts." I was struck nearly dumb with a queasy horror, but managed to ask him how he had obtained such a pair of souvenirs. Simple, he explained; he had removed them with a bayonet from an enemy corpse on Tarawa—that most hellish of battles—and had set them out at the end of a dock under the blazing sun where they quickly became dried like prunes. The sergeant was highly regarded in the company and I soon got used to seeing him fondle his keepsakes whenever he got nervous or pissed off, stroking them like worry beads.

I have been prompted to set down this vignette because of its resemblance to Caputo's Vietnam, where in a trance of comparable horror the young officer, still innocent and untried in battle, watches one of his Australian allies display a couple of mementos taken from the Vietcong—"two dried and bloodstained human ears." With his tough fair-mindedness Caputo is quick to point out in a somewhat different context how ready the Vietcong and ARVN were to commit similar desecrations; and the cruelty of the French in the earlier Indochinese war is too well documented to dispute. Nonetheless, there is a continuity of events, a linkage of atrocity from war to war, that forces the conclusion that we are capable of demonstrating toward our Asian adversaries a ruthless inhumanity we would doubtless withhold from those less incomprehensibly different from us, less likened to animals, or simply less brown or yellow.

Racism was as important, ideologically, to the conduct of the Pacific war as racism was to the war in Vietnam. As a matter of fact, racism may have been more important to the Marines in the Pacific, since there was no such propagandistic cause as anti-Communism to impel those peach-cheeked youngsters to wage a war against an enemy caught up in the thrall of a fanatical, even suicidal nationalism. Pearl Harbor was a powerful incentive—as were the Japanese cruelties on Bataan—but still, these were not enough. Racism in warfare had already been initiated by the Germans, who, imputing to them a subhuman status, had begun to exterminate hundreds of thousands of Russian prisoners of war (many gassed at Auschwitz) while in general treating their Anglo-Saxon foes with acceptable decency. As for the Japanese, it was enough for us to establish an anthropoid identity and thus, having classified them as apes, we found it easy to employ the flamethrower—that ghastly portable precursor of the napalm bomb used in Vietnam—and fry them in their bunkers and blockhouses. ("They sizzle like a bunch of roaches," I remember being told by a flamethrowing corporal, who was delighted with the weapon.) There was also a normal amount of casual murder, torture of prisoners, and other crimes. (A friend of mine admitted to having slit the throats of two prisoners while he was a sergeant leading a patrol on Guam, though he later expressed honest remorse for the deed. A retired colonel now, he lives in La Jolla, where he grows prize dahlias.)

Psychologically, however, the Pacific war differed from Vietnam in that the Marines had not only a clearly defined commitment, a sense of purpose, but a decisive, freewheeling (albeit at times badly flawed) strategy which almost never allowed them to feel that they had settled into a pointless morass. The Marines were too busily on the go, too happy at their lethal task, to dabble in atrocity. After Guadalcanal the Marine Corps was constantly on the offensive (a state most conducive, for the infantryman, to that sense of qualified bliss Caputo dwells on), in battle not against a guerrilla enemy maddeningly lurking in the jungles of a huge land mass but against soldiers immured for the most part within plainly visible fortifications on plainly visible islands where there were few or no civilians.

Behind the fighting men, too, was a perpetual surge of national pride. It was a madly popular war. It was a war which accomplished successfully what history demanded of the Marine Corps: the almost total annihilation of the enemy—more bliss. That is what fighting men are for, to kill, but to kill purposefully and with a reasonably precise goal in view—not as in Vietnam to produce mere bodies for General Westmoreland's computer. And certainly not to get fouled up with civilians.

Thus the Pacific war may be viewed in retrospect as a discussible moral enterprise. It was an awful war, one of the worst: in it one could experience battle fatigue, unconscionable misery and pain, insane fear, deprivation, loathsome disease, stupefying boredom, death and mutilation in places with names like Tarawa, Peleliu, Iwo Jima—arguably the most satanic engagements in which men have been pitted against one another since the birth of warfare. But those who fought in the Pacific war, whatever the nature of their wounds or their diminishment, could emerge undefiled. What Philip Caputo demonstrates by contrast in his ruthless testament is how the war in Vietnam defiled even its most harmless and well-meaning participants. His is the chronicle of men fighting with great bravery but forever losing ground in a kind of perplexed, insidious lassitude—learning too late that they were suffocating in a moral swamp.

I have said that one of the most remarkable features of *A Rumor of War* is the fact that Caputo's bitter disaffection with the Vietnamese war and all it represented came when the war was in its infancy, 1966. Not that the war was anything but corrupt to begin with; still, there is something almost phenomenal in Caputo's micro-cosmic sixteen-month odyssey, as if compressed within its brief framework was the whole foul and shameful drama of the conflict which was to drag on for many more years.

Of course, as I have also said, the war began for Caputo in a spirit that was anything but shameful. Gung ho, a knife in his teeth, he was pining for the glamour, the action, and he got it. After a stagnant period of waiting and chafing at the bit on the perimeter around Danang, Caputo and his men went on the offensive in perhaps the very first engagement by American forces in Vietnam. It was not a big engagement, only a skirmish with the Vietcong, but it was filled with noise and excitement and a certain amount of danger, and this baptism under fire made Caputo "happy . . . happier than I have ever been." Reading this early episode from the vantage point of hindsight, knowing what the outcome had to be in the ensuing dreadful years, one feels a chill at all that youthful machismo and reckless bloodlust: it evokes all that is unripe and heedless and egregiously romantic in the American spirit.

Already the United States—bursting with unspent power and unused armaments, slowly and inexorably being maneuvered from "defense" into aggression by the generals and the politicians—was beginning to move from its phase of "expedition" into the colossal entanglements of a full-scale war. How easy it would have been at that point, one thinks, for the Marine Corps to have packed up its sea bags and departed, leaving our Asian brothers to resolve their strife in whatever way destiny willed. But we had fatally inter-vened, and one of the critical instruments of our intervention was dauntless, hot-blooded Lieutenant Philip Caputo, who, it must be remembered, was hardly dragooned into the fray. He was also a man without whom (together with his tough, resolute brothers in arms) the war could not have proceeded a single inch into those treacherous and finally engulfing jungles.

Caputo writes brilliantly about these early days around Danang, that period of eager expectation before the horrors descended and the war began to taste like something incessantly loathsome on his tongue. Even then, in that time of cautious waiting—a stationary war of skirmishes and patrols and skittish engagements with the Vietcong—it was not pleasant duty, but after all, this is what

Caputo had bought and bargained for: the unspeakable heat and the mosquitoes, the incessant clouds of dust, the boredom, the chickenshit from upper echelons (often described with ferocious humor, in the spirit of *Catch-22*), the dreary nights on liberty in the ramshackle town, the impenetrably lush and sinister mountain range hovering over the flyblown domestic landscape, already smeared with American junk.

> The convoy slows to a crawl as it passes through Dogpatch. The filth and poverty of this village are medieval. Green pools of sewage lie in the culverts, the smell mingling with the stench of animal dung and nuoc-maum, a sauce made from rotten fish. . . . Water buffalo bellow from muddy pens shaded by banana trees whose leaves are white with dust. Most of the huts are made of thatch, but the American presence has added a new construction material: several houses are built entirely of flattened beer cans; red and white Budweiser, gold Miller, cream and brown Schlitz, blue and gold Hamm's from the land of sky-blue waters.

Boredom, inanition, a sitting war; drunken brawls in Danang, whores, more chickenshit, the seething lust for action. All this Caputo embroiders in fine detail—and then the action came in a powerful burst for Caputo and his comrades. Suddenly there were pitched engagements with the enemy. There were the first extended movements into enemy territory, the first helicopter assaults, the first real engagements under heavy fire, and, inevitably, the first shocking deaths. War became a reality for Caputo; it was no longer a film fantasy called *The Halls of Montezuma*, and there is great yet subtle power in Caputo's description of how—in this new kind of conflict, against a spectral enemy on a bizarre and jumbled terrain (so different from such textbook campaigns as Saipan or even Korea)—the underpinnings of his morale began to crumble, doubt bloomed and the first cynical mistrust was implanted in his brain. These misgivings—which later became revulsion and disillusionment—arrived not as the result of a single event but as an amalgam of various happenings, each one repellent, which Caputo (as well as the reader) begins to perceive as being embedded in the matrix of the war and its specifically evil nature.

It is an evil more often than not underscored by a certain loathsome pointlessness. A nineteen-year-old Marine is discovered cutting the ears off a dead VC. After a huge engagement in which the battalion expends thousands of rounds of ammunition there are only four Vietcong dead. (Later three thousand troops supported by naval gunfire kill twenty-four VC in three days.) In pursuit of the enemy and fearing an ambush, one of the platoons goes berserk and burns down a hamlet, devastating the place entirely. In this instance none of the villagers is seriously hurt, yet there is a peculiar primitive horror about the scene, and Caputo does not even bother to make the point all too ominously adumbrated by his powerful description: hovering in that smoke and the sound of wailing women is our common knowledge that My Lai is only a few years away.

There were many brave men who fought in Vietnam, and many performed brave deeds, but the war itself disgraced the name of bravery. That "uncommon valor" of which the Marines are so justifiably proud—which still stirs men when they hear names like Belleau Wood and Guadalcanal and Peleliu—was as much in evidence on the banks of the Mekong and on the green walls of the Annamese Cordillera, about which Caputo writes with such strength and grace, as in those early struggles. But what names blaze forth from Vietnam? Men's courage passes from generation to generation and is never really extinguished; but it is a terrible loss that, try as we might, we cannot truly honor courage employed in an ignoble cause.

In this book Philip Caputo writes so beautifully and honestly about both fear and courage, writes with such knowing certitude about death and men's confrontation with the abyss, that we cannot doubt for an instant that he is a brave man who fought well long after that "splendid little war" became an obscene nightmare in which he nearly drowned. But he was dragged downward, and indeed the most agonizing part of his chronicle is found not in the descriptions of carnage and battle—as harrowingly re-created as they are —but in his own savage denouement when, driven into a raging madness by the senseless devastation he has witnessed and participated in, he turns into a monster and commits that mythic Vietnam-stained crime: he allows the murder of civilians. Although he was ultimately exonerated, his deed became plainly a wound forever engrafted on his soul. It seems the inevitable climax to this powerful story of a decent man sunk into a dirty time, in a far place where he was never intended to be, in an evil war.

In a passage near the beginning of *A Rumor of War*, Caputo— happy, optimistic, thirsting for battle—sits in an observation post overlooking the sun-dappled rice paddies, the green hills, the majestic ageless mountains of the Annamese range. He cannot even dream of the horrors yet to come. He is reading Kipling and his eyes fall upon some lines which may be among the most lucid ever written about the mad, seemingly unceasing adventures which bring young boys from Illinois to such serene, improbable vistas:

> The end of the fight is a tombstone
>   white with the name of the
>   late deceased,
> And the epitaph drear: "A Fool lies
>   here who tried to hustle the
>   East."

[*New York Review of Books*, June 23, 1977]

Calley

W HOLE SEAS, one feels, could not contain the tears that humanity must shed at the knowledge of the horror at My Lai. As one goes over the event yet another time—as one rereads Seymour M. Hersh's brilliant, pitiless account *My Lai 4*, published last year—one has to try to insulate one's self from the details of the massacre, protectively conjuring up visions of other atrocities, saying to oneself: "Keep thinking of Bengal, of the murder of the Huguenots, the sack of Magdeburg, of Lidice, Malmédy. Isn't this only what men have always done to other men?"

> Near them [writes Hersh] was a young Vietnamese boy, crying, with a bullet wound in his stomach. . . . The radio operator then stepped within two feet of the boy and shot him in the neck with a pistol. Blood gushed from the child's neck. He then tried to walk off, but he could only take two or three steps. Then he fell onto the ground. He lay there and took four or five deep breaths and then he stopped breathing. The radio operator turned to Stanley and said, "Did you see how I shot that son of a bitch?"

. . .

> Nineteen-year-old Nguyen Thi Ngoc Tuyet watched a baby trying to open his slain mother's blouse to nurse. A soldier shot the infant while it was struggling with the blouse, and then slashed at it with his bayonet.

. . .

> Nguyen Khoa, a thirty-seven-year-old peasant, told of a thirteen-year-old girl who was raped before being killed. G.I.'s then attacked Khoa's wife, tearing off her clothes. Before they could rape her, however, Khoa said, their six-year-old son, riddled with bullets, fell and saturated her with blood.

Until recently America had by luck or through divine providence been saved from being a truly militaristic nation, but it has in the past been a bloodthirsty one. Such passages as those just quoted therefore do not so intolerably rend the heart merely because they describe atrocities at the hands of wholesome American boys—these clean-cut American boys, after all, butchered the Indians and inflicted tortures on the Filipinos—but because just as we grieve for its victims we grieve for an America which, twenty-six years after the end of a war to save the world for democracy, finds itself close to moral bankruptcy—the criminal nature of its war in Southeast Asia symbolized by the My Lai carnage and by its fly-blown principal executor, First Lieutenant William Laws Calley.

For this reason Calley commands our most intense interest. Banal, stunted in mind and body, colorless, lacking even a native acumen, with an airless, dreary brain devoid of wit—he is not the first nobody whose brush with a large moment in history has personified that moment and helped define it. One thinks of Eichmann. Almost all comparisons between America and Hitler's Germany are strident and inept, but here the analogy seems appropriate. Both of them, the Nazi functionary and the loutish American officer, attempted exculpation of their enormous crimes through insistence that they were merely cogs in a great machine, that they were only carrying out orders, that the true guilt lay with others. Both of them finally, in their rancid ordinariness, symbolized the historic moment more dramatically than the flamboyant leaders they served.

Thus, as the Nazi concentration camps recede into the past, Eichmann seems to embody their memory, and even that of the entire Nazi regime, more significantly than does a Goebbels or a Himmler. It would slander the young men who have been forced to fight and die in Vietnam to say that Calley is an archetype of the soldier in this war. He may in the perspective of time, however, become more archetypal of the war's total moral degeneracy than its actual perpetrators—miscreants of the White House and the Pentagon too well known, too numerous and enjoying at the moment too much exposure to need naming here.

This is not to assume that on lower levels of authority there are not those who share in Calley's guilt. It is spelled out in Hersh's book, and one's conviction that other officers were criminally involved is reinforced by Richard Hammer's *The Court-Martial of Lt. Calley*, an excellent, straightforward piece of reporting which pursues the theme of Calley's individual guilt with almost puritanical zeal but which cannot help leaving the impression of the culpability of others. It is difficult to believe, for instance, that Lieutenant Colonel Barker, the task force commander who was whirling over the area in his helicopter as Charlie Company went about its bloody work, was not aware of the true nature of what was happening and should not have stopped it; but this can probably never be proved, for Barker was killed in another action.

But to focus upon the guilt of others is largely begging the question when it comes to judging Calley, for, as Hammer points out, we do not exonerate a criminal merely because his accomplices in the crime had the good luck to escape justice. Military life may be a repugnant notion to most of us; but the idea commonly nurtured by those civilians who most detest, or misunderstand, or indeed admire the military as an institution—that because it is engaged in killing it is an amoral place, or a place in which ordinary considerations of morality are irrelevant—is tempting and romantic but false. Despite the paradoxes involved, the military may remain our most intransigently "moral" institution;* and it was an unawareness of this fact on the part of those millions of Americans who thought Calley was persecuted, or considered him a sacrificial lamb, that led to their confusion.

Much, for instance, has been made of Calley's "orders." Is it not the first duty of a military man to obey orders from a superior? The answer is yes, but a strictly qualified yes. Calley and other witnesses contended that at Captain Ernest Medina's briefing the night before the assault, the captain ordered the company to "kill everything." Medina and still other witnesses have disclaimed such an order, maintaining that by "kill" or "waste" or "destroy" he did not mean unarmed men, women and children. This issue, in detail, remains obscure.

Yet the point is that if Medina did indeed give an order specifying the wholesale murder of helpless civilians, it was an illegal order, which Calley—especially as a commissioned officer, whose very commission implies that he is supposed to know better—was obliged to refuse to execute. His own orders to his troops to kill and the alacrity with which he himself sprang to the slaughter, on

---

* The reduction of Calley's sentence from life to twenty years, probably influenced by President Nixon's sympathy for the lieutenant, and which occurred after this review was written, tends to undercut any such venerable premise about the military service, and may simply be an indication of how corruptible it has really become.

the other hand, in contrast to those of the men who declined to join the bloodletting, illustrate dramatically how there existed that morning at My Lai the element of choice; and this is another dimension by which Calley must be judged and condemned.

It is a lamentable fact—though one perhaps not too surprising—that some of the GI's under Calley's orders embarked on private orgies of murder that defy words. But others of those "grunts" so ably depicted in Hammer's book drew back in shock and shame. Those white and black dogfaces from places like Holyoke, Massachusetts, and Providence and New Orleans, the deprived or the semideprived with their comic books and their bubble gum and their grass, these melting-pot types bearing names out of a patriotic World War II movie, Dursi and Maples and Grzesik—they were benumbed by the horror and they refused to kill; and their presence at Fort Benning as they bore witness against Calley brought out perhaps more than anything else the lieutenant's fathomless dereliction.

If this were not sufficient, there was the testimony of a fellow officer, Lieutenant Jeffrey LaCross, the leader of the third platoon, who said that he neither heard Medina give the command to kill everyone in the hamlet nor did he himself assume that anything should be done to the civilians other than to employ the usual practice of gathering them together and submitting them to interrogation. Having done just this on that day, he too demonstrated by contrast the measure of his fellow platoon leader's irresponsibility; and his testimony was badly damaging to an already brutally damaged Calley, who, it seemed plain as the trial drew to an end, had got his name entered on the rolls of history's illustrious mass murderers.

But what of Calley himself? Hammer's book is an honest, penetrating account of a crucially significant military trial; but his loathing for Calley is manifest on every page. Surely, one thinks, there must be some extenuation, some key to this man's character which will allow us a measure of compassion or at least of understanding so that despite his crimes some beam of warmth or attractiveness will flow out—some tragic or, God knows, even comic dimension that could permit us to mourn a little over this good ole boy from Florida gone wrong. Hammer stalks Calley so relentlessly that, despite resistance, one begins to feel the sweat of Christian charity being coaxed from one's pores. We therefore turn with eagerness to *Lieutenant Calley: His Own Story*, as told to

John Sack, hoping for that ameliorative detail or insight that might help cast a gentler light on the transgressor.

Alas, it is a vain hope, for Calley's whole identity—as recorded, according to his Boswell, "on five hundred thousand inches of magnetic tapes and a fiftieth ton of transcripts"—impresses the reader as being one of such stupefying vacuity, of such dwarfishness of spirit that one is relieved that his account does not yield us the luxury of even a fleeting affection. Furthermore, the book is an underhanded, self-serving document, one of those soulless apologias that have emanated many times before from base men. Simulating honesty, it attempts a cheap vindication, and in so doing, more firmly ratifies the guilt.

In his preface, after anesthetizing us with more statistics ("I talked to Calley for a hundred days. I asked him somewhere near ten thousand questions, or one question for each three-fourths of a sentence here"), Sack tells us how impressed he became with Calley's sincerity and appeals to the reader not to lose sight of it. One reader lost sight of it after about the tenth and a half page, although in fairness to Calley this may in part be the fault of the style, or technique rather: those five hundred thousand inches of magnetic tape ending up on the page as indigestible splinters and strips—one feels choked on acetate.

That a tape recorder, in proper hands, can be an effective amanuensis and collector of thoughts and voices was proved by the late Oscar Lewis, whose guiding intelligence brought an almost Balzacian sweep to his works of social anthropology. But Sack's intelligence does not guide. This lapse, in conjunction with the boyish squalor of Calley's mind, gives the book a fragmented, groping, almost hysterical quality, as if spoken by a depraved Holden Caulfield. There is an irresistible temptation to believe, in fact, that Sack, perhaps without knowing it, is bent upon hanging Calley on the gallows of his own "sincerity." Otherwise, it is hard to make sense of such a remarkable passage as that which comes near the beginning of the book, in which Calley describes his reaction to the news that he is likely to be prosecuted for the murders:

> I thought, *Could it be I did something wrong?* I knew that war's wrong. Killing's wrong: I realized that. I had gone to a war, though. I had killed, but I knew. *So did a million others.* I sat there, and I couldn't find the key. I pictured the people of Mylai: the bodies, and they didn't bother me. I had found, I had closed with, I had destroyed the VC: the mission that day. I

thought, *It couldn't be wrong or I'd have remorse about it* [italics Sack's].

Here in these few lines, which are fairly typical of the book in both style and substance, Calley manages to reveal at least three appalling facts about himself: that he is still unaware, or pretends to be unaware, of the difference between a massacre and lawful killing in combat; that he is still unmoved by the effects of his butchery at My Lai, when others who were there had been gruesomely haunted by the sight for months, at least one of them driven to the brink of mental breakdown; and that he is a liar. He is a liar, we see, because it is impossible that so many months after the event he still thinks that the victims of his slaughter—old men, women and children—had been really his enemies, the Vietcong.

Or what is one to say about a truly flabbergasting passage in which, at the very height of the carnage at My Lai, Calley describes how he rushes to prevent a GI from forcing a girl to perform a sexual act, and then asks himself rhetorically why he had been so "saintly"?

Because—if a GI is getting sex, "he isn't doing his job. He isn't destroying communism." Calley's puzzlement over moral priorities and options seems typically in the American grain, for he then goes on to brood:

> Of course, if I had been ordered to Mylai to rape it, pillage, and plunder—well, I still don't know. I may be old-fashioned, but I can't really see it. Our mission in Mylai wasn't perverted though. It was simply "Go and destroy it."

Or this episode, a few pages later, describing his encounter at My Lai with a defenseless civilian (apparently a Buddhist priest), whom he was convicted of murdering:

> *You sonofabitch.* And bam: I butted him in his mouth with my M-16. Straight on: sideways could break the M-16. He had frustrated me!

Sack should have been advised that sometimes sincerity does not appear to be a winning virtue. Yet, if indeed sincerity were a truly consistent component of this book, we might be able to accept at least part of it. The story is, however, implausible when it is not being greasily devious, and it is dominated by two tendentious themes. One of these themes—Calley's fear that civilians, whether they be old men or women or children, are really the enemy in disguise—pervades, indeed saturates, the narrative. It is allied with another theme—his hatred of Communism, which he cheerfully admits as a "run-of-the-mill average guy" that he doesn't understand—and together they form a linked motivation which even a very unperceptive reader would begin to perceive he is going to use to rationalize his crimes at My Lai.

Page after page is filled with his animadversions, if such they may be called, on the Communist menace. These passages alternate with those which express his terror of the civilian populace, his frantic suspicion that each innocent-appearing Vietnamese may in truth be a Vietcong concealing a weapon or ready to throw a bomb.

Curiously, when describing his fear, Calley is sometimes rather effective. His fear is certainly real enough, and understandable; and in his reflections on this fear and on the omnipresence of death amid the Vietnamese landscape he achieves on one or two pages, almost as if by accident, a kind of slovenly eloquence. Surely no one acquainted with the demoralizing character of the war in Vietnam would deny the legitimacy of such a fear.

Yet long before the book's halfway point—where Calley in his inimitably charmless way has even begun to invoke General Sherman's tactics in Georgia to justify atrocities against civilians—his tone has become so hectoring, so shrill, that we simply know he is out to hoodwink us into believing that he honestly thought the Vietcong were his victims that day at My Lai. It is an ineffably shabby performance; and by the time we arrive at the end, cringing as we observe Calley try to discredit the witnesses who had appeared against him at Benning, we are able to see why he inspired in Richard Hammer such healthy revulsion.

Certainly the loathsome and festering nature of the war in Vietnam provided fertile ground for such a catastrophe as My Lai. It is a particularly iniquitous war, this criminal venture which has implanted in the hearts of our apple-cheeked young warriors such a detestation of "slopes" and "slants" and "gooks." That there have been other atrocities and other My Lais may be painful to accept but not difficult to believe. To those numerous letters he received from other servicemen confessing to their own atrocities, Calley points with distorted pride, failing to realize—just as millions of people have failed to realize—that one outrage does not expunge another. Neither does the obvious culpability of others in this horror absolve Calley, whose trial and conviction may be one of the most critically significant events of recent times, in that it has been able to show in vivid outline the extent of the degeneracy to which this war and its leaders have brought us.

Mankind is sick nearly unto death of warfare, but until that remote day when its abolition is achieved, the wars our folly leads us to will have to be fought within the framework of those sometimes inadequate but necessary laws we have shaped to govern their course. In abstract, at least, it is obedience to this principle which has so far prevented our reaping the whirlwind of nuclear destruction. It is the depth of moral stupor to assume that in the pursuit of war, barbarous as it may seem to be, we must not be bound by rigorous codes.

Few of us may be enamored of the military, but the military is both a fact of life and an institution; and like any institution— like law or business or government itself—it must stand guard against the venal, the felonious and the corrupt. Thus to ignore the lesson of Lieutenant Calley is to ignore a crucial reality: that war is still steadfastly a part of the human condition, and that our very survival as human beings continues to depend on accommodating ourselves to ancient rules of conduct.

[*New York Times Book Review,* September 12, 1971]

Arnheiter

NEIL SHEEHAN's *The Arnheiter Affair* is a lively and thoroughly fascinating account of one of the most important controversies in modern American military history. The central figure of this true story, Lieutenant Commander Marcus Aurelius Arnheiter, was a naval officer of questionable ability in all departments when he was somehow given command of the destroyer escort *Vance* in the latter part of 1965. An Annapolis graduate, a fatuous worshiper of Lord Nelson, an ambitious, overbearing, thick-skinned man, he appeared to have almost none of the lambent human qualities that even the most zealous military officer must possess if he is effectively to command men, and his behavior from the outset was something less than auspicious. He made it plain that he knew little and cared less about the mechanics of running a ship, and soon established aboard a regime that Sheehan aptly describes as one of "whimsical tyranny." This extended from his insistence on saluting and upon immaculately clean daily dress—items of routine usually dispensed with on a small ship at sea—to the humiliating impromptu lectures he required of his officers after dinner, on such recherché subjects as how to use a finger bowl. A Protestant himself, he enforced (against regulations) strict attendance at his Protestant-oriented religious lectures, to the chagrin and outrage of the many Catholics among the crew. Sedulous in regard to his own creature comforts, he smoked cigars bought with money paid to a "Boner Box" by officers guilty of small infractions of the rules, and enjoyed twenty-minute showers with preciously hoarded water while the rest of the crew, bathless, sweated in the dreadful heat of the Gulf of Siam.

Arnheiter's lack of sensitivity about the nuances, the proprieties inherent in rank and privilege was almost boundless, but his official behavior as commanding officer of the *Vance* while patrolling the Vietnamese coast was even more bizarre. In a zone of the sea relatively far removed from any important enemy activity Arnheiter was forced to resort to ever more quixotic maneuvers in order to satisfy his bellicose fantasies. He once nearly ran his ship aground as he invented targets and emplacements on shore which he claimed were "demolished" by his three-inch guns. He "annihilated" detachments of Vietcong guerrillas (they turned out to be a flock of chickens), and dangerously set out to stalk a Red Chinese submarine. Also, in a desperate spasm of *machismo*, he radioed a series of false position reports in order to give the impression of intrepid seamanship. Finally, to cap it all, the relentless skipper fabricated an engagement with the enemy in which he claimed to have performed personally with conspicuous gallantry, and dictated a totally spurious commendation, the intent of which was to award himself the Silver Star. At this point, mercifully, the *Vance* and its by now despairing and morally bedraggled crew were spared further misery. The cumulative effect of Arnheiter's conduct could not go disregarded for long even in a navy that tends to insist that its officers can do little wrong. Arnheiter was relieved of his command at Manila Bay, some four months after the excruciating, hair-raising, sometimes wrenchingly comic odyssey began.

On the level of a nautical adventure alone, Sheehan's book makes an engrossing tale. The parallels with Captain Queeg in *The Caine Mutiny* are, of course, obvious. Like Queeg—indeed, like all fanatics—Arnheiter seemed cursed with a fatal humorlessness. Whimsy, yes, but no humor. One feels that even a vestige of a real sense of humor might have allowed the bedeviled captain some insight into the more ludicrous consequences of his own monomania; and his dire self-obsession and its tragicomic effects are unfolded by Sheehan with the skill and subtlety of a first-rate novelist. But examined on another level, *The Arnheiter Affair* tells us some important and disturbing things about the American people and their relationship to the military establishment. The Arnheiter affair did not end with the captain's relief from his command in the Philippines: it only began there. For with the single-minded self-righteousness of his breed, Arnheiter disclaimed the accusations against him and mounted a vociferous campaign to exonerate himself, protesting that he had been victimized by his subordinate officers, who had slandered him with trumped-up charges. For a brief but agreeable period it must have seemed to Arnheiter that his efforts in his own behalf would bear fruit. Valiant support chugged up to his side from the left and right, from the middle, from every hand. Americans have never fully understood the role of the military in their own society, and perhaps it is their native egalitarianism that has caused the citizenry to harbor an inane and nearly indefatigable passion for whoever appears to be the under-dog—witness the example of Lieutenant William Laws Calley.

Initially, Arnheiter was made to look like a martyr by the press and the other media. (Sheehan covered the story for the *New York Times*, and one of his winning points is a gentlemanly admission of his own knee-jerk liberal reaction to what then seemed Arn-heiter's beleaguered plight.) Yet the captain also found some of his most ardent defenders among the high Navy brass, including an illustriously placed officer who risked and ultimately ruined his career by campaigning in Arnheiter's defense. As usual it was a case of feverish wish-fulfillment—the captain as symbol satisfying every immediate and shoddy fantasy while failing to instill in any-one the desire to inspect the hard moral and legal aspects of the issue at hand. "To the liberals," Sheehan writes, "he was a little man who was victimized by an impersonal military institution. To the conservatives, the mutinous behavior of Arnheiter's subordinates was a manifestation of the general disorder and mockery of au-thority that was polluting the qualities of national life." But an official review of Arnheiter's case and Sheehan's own careful in-vestigation amply demonstrated that neither of these situations was the case. To put it in the simplest terms, the captain was exposed as a fraud and a menace.

Unlike the actions of Lieutenant Calley, Arnheiter's conduct did not result in injury or the loss of any human lives (although it clearly contributed to the mental breakdown of a crewman and helped wreck the career of at least one of the ship's officers), and consequently the case lacked some of the sensational aspects of the more recent scandal. Yet just as one of the revelations of Calley's court-martial lay in the shocking fact that a man of the lieutenant's wretched caliber and qualifications should never have been made an officer in the first place, so the Arnheiter affair demonstrated that the Navy likewise had much to answer for in justifying the pro-motion of an Arnheiter to such a delicate position of command. Arnheiter often appeared to be a simple clown, and the story as Sheehan has put it down does contain much comic flavor of the

Mister Roberts variety—this is what helps make the book so consistently entertaining—but the narrative is also filled with somber and sobering overtones. The author is not being at all facetious when he speculates upon how Arnheiter's imbecilic game of hide-and-seek with the Chinese submarine might easily have helped precipitate another world war. On this plane, the Arnheiter affair no less than that of Valley demonstrates the potential for disaster that exists for us when at any level of authority there is a crucial abdication of personal responsibility, and shows the danger that is always present when even one small device in the grotesque, precariously balanced supermechanism of war we have fashioned for ourselves is handed over to cranks and fanatics.

[*American Scholar*, Summer 1972]

The Wreckage of
an American War

THE MARINES WHO FOUGHT in the Pacific during World War II had much to fear, for the fighting was often lethal and barbaric. Yet because they were marines, with an intense feeling of identity, and were caught up in that mysterious group trance known as esprit de corps, they really did assume that they were invincible. Some of this hubris came from their brutal and very efficient training, but a great deal of their deepest confidence flowed from their leaders. Their officers, both commissioned and noncommissioned, were arguably the best in the world, and of these leaders no marine commanded more admiration than a colonel with a beguilingly menacing countenance and a pouter-pigeon strut named Lewis Burwell Puller.

Puller—the father of the author of *Fortunate Son*, a dark and corrosive autobiography—was nicknamed Chesty for the aggressive thrust of his carriage; he was and still is a legend, an embodiment of the marines in the same way that Babe Ruth embodies baseball or that Yeats stands for Irish poetry.

A native of the Virginia Tidewater, Puller was born at the end of the last century, close enough to the Civil War to be haunted by it and to be mesmerized by its Confederate heroes and victims. Like many of the high-level marine officers, disproportionately Southern by origin, who helped defeat the Japanese, Puller learned his infantry tactics while chasing and being chased by the guerrilla forces of Augusto Sandino in the Nicaraguan jungles; his spectacular exploits there won him two Navy Crosses.

During World War II, the last truly just war fought by Americans, Puller was awarded the Navy Cross two more times for gallantry under fire, at Guadalcanal and at Cape Gloucester, and his legend blossomed. Stories about him abounded. Respected extravagantly, he was also greatly feared, especially by very junior officers. It was rumored that he literally devoured second lieutenants; after all, at the gruesome battle of Peleliu, a derelict shavetail was summoned into Chesty Puller's tent and never a shred of him was seen again—he plainly had been eaten.

Puller exhibited little tact, especially with the press. In the aftermath of the deadly Guadalcanal campaign, an asinine journalist inquired, "Colonel, could you tell the American people what it is you're fighting for?" Puller replied, "Six hundred and forty-nine dollars a month." His fairness and concern for his troops were celebrated and were never so evident as during the retreat from Chosin Reservoir, during the Korean War, when as a regimental commander he led a rear-guard action of such tactical mastery that it manifestly saved countless American lives; this feat won him a fifth Navy Cross and promotion to brigadier general.

As Burke Davis portrays him in his fine 1982 biography, *Marine!*, Chesty Puller, despite the glory he gained in the mechanized setting of modern warfare, was a God-fearing fighting man of the old school, cast in the mold of Lee and Jackson, both of whom he idolized. Amid the most foulmouthed body of men in Christendom he was, if not prudish, restrained in speech. Some of the letters he wrote to his wife from various exotic hellholes are poignant, old-fashioned utterances that touch on the horrors of war but speak of a longing for repose in tones of spiritual anguish reminiscent of Stonewall Jackson. After he retired to his Tidewater village, nearly two decades before his death in 1971, he was proud when his only son, born when he was nearing fifty, went off as a second lieutenant to combat duty in Vietnam. That twenty-year-old man, his namesake—the "fortunate son" of this bitter though redemptive narrative—became one of the most grievously mutilated combatants to survive the ordeal of Vietnam.

The catastrophe happened on a blazing October day in 1968, when Lewis Puller Jr. was leading his platoon on a routine patrol through an especially sinister area of the countryside nicknamed the Riviera, a strip of rice paddies and wooded hills bordering the South China Sea. Mr. Puller had served in the combat zone for less than three months, but his activity had been intensely concentrated and appallingly violent. He had seen marines wounded and killed, had engaged in fierce firefights, had been exposed to booby traps; during an attack on a local village one of his men had inadvertently blown off the arm of an eight-year-old girl.

Mr. Puller is a gripping writer when he describes the heat and exhaustion, the physical brutalization, the incessant anxiety and danger suffered by young men engaged in that demented strife nearly a quarter of a century ago. Not without good reason he may be at his most vivid when he tells what happened to him.

That October day he stepped on a booby-trapped howitzer round and was rocketed sky-high. He "had no idea that the pink mist that engulfed me had been caused by the vaporization of most of my right and left legs. As shock began to numb my body I could see through a haze of pain that my right thumb and little finger were missing, as was most of my left hand." In addition, the explosion destroyed massive parts of both buttocks, ruptured an eardrum, split his scrotum and sent slivers of shrapnel through most of the rest of his body.

Hovering near death for many days, Mr. Puller developed a stress ulcer that required the removal of two-thirds of his stomach, augmenting the already intolerable pain. Transported stateside, he remained for nearly two years at the Philadelphia Naval Hospital, where, through the early phases of his stay, he was utterly helpless and so dependent on morphine that when he was briefly taken off it he was, as he says, "quickly reduced to the level of a snarling animal." When his weight dropped to less than sixty pounds and his stomach resisted food, he was given nourishment through a nasal tube.

These pages exude the whiff of authentic hell and are, accordingly, sometimes difficult to read. But because Mr. Puller writes with simplicity and candor, with touches of spontaneous humor, his outcry of agony and isolation, while harrowing, leaves one primarily overwhelmed with wonder at the torture a human being can absorb this side of madness.

Slowly the worst of the torment receded and slowly the recuperative process began: skin grafts, reconstructive surgery, endless hours on the operating table, all enacted in a continuum of diabolical pain. He regained some extremely limited use of his mangled hands, but the efforts to restore mobility to his legs through prosthesis, while tireless, were in vain; he would have to spend the rest of his life in a wheelchair. There were compensations, however, for his sacrifice: his face was unscathed and his basic senses, including his eyesight, remained intact. So did his sexual functioning. His young wife, who was pregnant when he went off to Vietnam, presented him with a son. Escaped like Ishmael from the vortex of oblivion, he had a future and also, clearly, a tale to tell.

Fortunate Son is an amazing tale, but in many ways an artless one, with great cumulative power yet more compelling as a raw chronicle than a work offering literary surprises. If its prose does not resonate as does Philip Caputo's eloquent *Rumor of War*, if the book lacks the surreal wackiness and scathing insights that made Michael Herr's *Dispatches* such an original tour de force, its act of bearing such passionate witness to a desecrated moment in history has its own importance and gives it a place among the meaningful works on the Vietnam nightmare.

As for Mr. Puller's future, it seemed in certain respects almost as calamitous as the experience of war. He acquired a law degree and an ambition to run (as a Democrat) for a Congressional seat in Virginia. By this time he had undergone the same traumatic insult as numberless veterans whose brother and sister Americans detested them for an event they conceived to be the handiwork of the warriors themselves. Smarting at this mad response but in a rage at the war and its real instigators in Washington, he made his feelings public, proclaiming that if he were called up again he would refuse to go.

Such statements, coming especially from the son of Chesty Puller, did not go down well in a state as profoundly hidebound as Virginia, where Mr. Puller also was rash enough to choose to run in a district bordering Hampton Roads—the very marrow of the military-industrial complex and a busy hive of patriots ill disposed to contemplate any such paradigm of the monstrousness of war.

His image as a horribly maimed veteran, rather than inspiring compassion and patriotic rapport, aroused resentment and guilt among the voters and plainly contributed heavily to his defeat. Then he slid into perhaps his deepest peril yet. He had always been an enthusiastic drinker, but shortly after his political loss his dependency became overpowering; he subsided into the near-madness of alcoholism, becoming so deranged and incapacitated that he came close to killing himself. With the help of Alcoholics Anonymous he recovered, and his wretchedly difficult but successful climb out of still another abyss makes up the rest of *Fortunate Son*, the coda of which culminates in a revealing irony: apparently at peace with himself and the world, Mr. Puller is currently a senior attorney in the office of the general counsel of the Department of Defense.

Or the irony may not be so striking after all. Throughout the book one senses in Mr. Puller a hesitation, an ambivalence about the marines that he seems unable to resolve. About the Marine Corps, he wonders at one point how "I could love and despise it with such equal ardor." This tells much about the powerful hold that military life, at its most idealistic, can have upon thoroughly decent men, quite a few of whom are capable of complex quandaries and apprehensions about what they are called upon to do.

What Mr. Puller was called upon to do was to fight in a war that never should have begun, but once begun tainted the souls of all those connected with it. Yet the quality of devotion sometimes inexplicably and maddeningly remains. Just before the famous gathering of 1971, when protesting Vietnam veterans planned to discard their medals on the steps of the Capitol, the author debated agonizingly with himself before putting his medals back in the closet.

"They had cost me too dearly," he writes, "and though I now saw clearly that the war in which they had been earned was a wasted cause, the medals still represented the dignity and the caliber of my service and of those with whom I had served."

It would be wrong for flag-wavers to misinterpret these words and cheer Mr. Puller's nobility, and just as wrong for those who reflexively condemn all wars to read them as the sentiments of the enslaved military mind. Like his father, who served heroically in several just wars—or at least understandable ones—Mr. Puller was a professional engaged in what many men of good will still regard as an honorable calling, and one likely to remain so until wars are made extinct; yet he was too young and too unaware, at least at the beginning, to realize the nature of his involvement in a national dishonor.

His father, Mr. Puller notes, came home twice from the Far East in triumph, while his own reception was one of scorn and jeers. The old man, he writes, almost never gave vent to his deepest emotions. But no wonder Chesty Puller finally wept, looking down at his legless and handless son, wreckage of an American war in which random atrocities would serve as the compelling historical memory, instead of the suffering and sacrifice, and for which there would be no Guadalcanal or Iwo Jima, no Belleau Wood, no Shiloh or Chickamauga.

[*New York Times Book Review*, June 16, 1991]

CHICAGO:
1968

Chicago: 1968

IT WAS PERHAPS UNFORTUNATE that Richard J. Daley, the hoodlum suzerain of the city, became emblematic of all that the young people in their anguish cried out against, even though he plainly deserved it. No one should ever have been surprised that he set loose his battalions against the kids; it was the triumphant end product of his style, and what else might one expect from this squalid person, whose spirit suffused the great city as oppressively as that of some Central American field marshal? And it was no doubt inevitable, moreover, a component of the North American oligarchic manner—one could not imagine a Trujillo so mismanaging his public relations—that after the catastrophe had taken place he should remain so obscenely lodged in the public eye, howling "Kike!" at Abe Ribicoff, packing the galleries with his rabble, and muttering hoarse irrelevancies about conspiracy and assassination, about the *Republican* convention ("They had a fence in Miami, too, Walter, nobody ever talks about *that!*") to a discomfited Cronkite, who wobbled in that Oriental presence between deference and faint-hearted suggestions that Miami and Chicago just might not be the same sort of thing.

That is what many of us did along about Thursday night in Chicago—retreat to the center, the blissful black interior of some hotel room, and turn on the television set. For after four days and nights in the storm outside, after the sleepless, eventually hallucinated connection with so many of the appalling and implausible events of that week, it was a relief to get off the streets and away from the parks and the Amphitheater and the boorish, stinking hotel lobbies and to see it as most Americans had seen it—even if one's last sight was that of the unspeakable Daley, attempting to explain away a shame that most people who witnessed it will feel to their bones for a very long time.

Yet, again, maybe in the immediate aftermath of the convention it was too bad that Daley should have hogged a disproportionate share of the infamy that has fallen upon the Democratic party; for if it is getting him off the hook too easily to call him a scapegoat, nonetheless the execration he has received (even the New York *Daily News*, though partly, of course, out of civic rivalry, carried jeering stories about him) may obscure the fact that Daley is only the nastiest symbol of stupidity and desuetude in a political party that may die, or perhaps is already dead, because it harbors too many of his breed and mentality. Hubert Humphrey, the departed John Bailey, John Connally, Richard Hughes, Ed Muskie—all are merely eminent examples of a rigidity and blindness, a feebleness of thought, that have possessed the party at every level, reaching down to those Grant Wood delegates from North Dakota who spilled out from the elevators into my hotel lobby every morning, looking bright-eyed and war-hungry, or like Republicans, whom they emulated through becoming one of the few delegations that voted against the pacific minority Vietnam plank *en bloc*. It has been said that if various burdensome and antiquated procedural matters—the unit rule, for instance—had been eliminated prior to this convention, the McCarthy forces might have gained a much larger and more significant strength, and this is at least an arguable point of view; for a long while I myself believed it and worked rather hard to see such changes come about (some did), but now in retrospect it seems that the disaster was meant to be.

Recalling those young citizens for Humphrey who camped out downstairs in my hotel, that multitude of square, seersuckered fraternity boys and country-club jocks with butch haircuts, from the suburbs of Columbus and Atlanta, who passed out "Hubert" buttons and "Humphrey" mints, recalling them and their elders, mothers and fathers, some of them delegates and not all of them creeps or fanatics by any means, but an amalgam of everything— the simply well-heeled, most of them, entrenched, party hacks tied to the mob or with a pipeline to some state boss, a substantial number hating the war but hating it not enough to risk dumping Hubert in favor of a vague professorial freak who couldn't feel concern over Prague and hung out with Robert Lowell—I think now that the petrification of a party that allowed such apathy and lack of adventurousness and moral inanition to set in had long ago shaped its frozen logic, determined its fatal choice months before Eugene McCarthy or, for that matter, Bobby Kennedy had come along to rock, ever so slightly, the colossal dreamboat. And this can only reinforce what appears to me utterly plausible: that whatever the vigor and force of the dissent, whatever one might say about the surprising strength of support that the minority report received on the floor, a bare but crucial majority of Americans still is unwilling to repudiate the filthy war. This is really the worst thought of all.

Right now, only a day or so after the event, it is hard to be sure of anything. A residue of anguish mingles with an impulse toward cynicism, and it all seems more than ever a happening. One usually sympathetic journalist of my acquaintance has argued with some logic but a little too much levity that the violent confrontations, like the show of muscle among the black militants, were at least only a psychological necessity: after all, there were no killings, few serious injuries; had there been no violence the whole affair would have been tumescent, impossibly strained, like *coitus inter-ruptus,* and who would have had a bruise or a laceration to wear home as a hero's badge? As for myself, the image of one young girl no older than sixteen, sobbing bitterly as she was being led away down Balbo Avenue after being brutally cracked by a policeman's club, is not so much a memory as a scene imprinted on the retina—a metaphor of the garish and incomprehensible week—and it cannot be turned off like the Mr. Clean commercial that kept popping up between the scenes of carnage. I prefer to think that the events in Chicago were as momentous and as fateful as they seemed at the time, even amid the phantasmagorical play of smoke and flood-lights where they were enacted.

One factor has been generally overlooked: the weather. Chicago was at its bluest and balmiest, and that gorgeous sunshine—almost springlike—could not help but subtly buoy the nastiest spirit and moderate a few tempers. Had the heat been as intense and as suffo-cating as it was when I first arrived in the city the Tuesday before the convention began, I feel certain that the subsequent mayhem would have become slaughter. I came at that time to the Credentials Committee meeting in the Conrad Hilton as one of four "delegate challengers" from Connecticut, presenting the claim that the popular vote in the state primaries had indicated that 13 delegates out of 44 should be seated for Eugene McCarthy, rather than the 9 allowed the McCarthy forces by John Bailey. Although logic and an eloquent legal brief by Dean Louis Pollak of the Yale Law School were on our side, the megalithic party structure could not be budged, and it was on that stifling day—when I scrutinized from the floor the faces of the hundred-odd cozy fat cats of the committee, two from each state plus places like Guam, nearly all of whom were committed to the Politics of Joy and who indeed had so embraced the establishment mythopoeia that each countenance, male or female and including a Negro or two, seemed a burnished replica of Hubert Humphrey—that I became fully aware that McCarthy's cause was irrevocably lost. Nor was I encouraged to hedge on this conviction when, sweating like a pig, I made a brief *ad hominem* plea in summation of our case, finished and sat down to the voice of the committee chairman, Governor Richard Hughes of New Jersey, who said, "Thank you, Mr. Michener." Later, the governor's young aide came up to apologize, saying that the governor knew full well who I was, that in the heat and his fatigue he must have been woolgathering and thinking of James Michener, who was a good friend of Mr. Hughes—a baffling explanation, which left me with ominous feelings about life in general.

When I returned as an observer to Chicago the following Sunday, the lobby of the Conrad Hilton resembled a fantasy sequence in some Fellini movie, people in vertical ascent and horizontal drift, unimaginable shoals of walleyed human beings packed elbow to elbow, groin to rump, moving sluggishly as if in some paradigmatic tableau of the utter senselessness of existence. It took me fifteen minutes to cross from one side of the hotel to the other, and although I endured many low moments during the convention, I think it was at this early point, amid that indecent crush of ambitious flesh, that my detestation of politics attained an almost religious passion.

The Conrad Hilton is the archetypal convention hotel of the universe, crimson and gold, vast, nearly pure in its efficient service of the demands of power and pelf, hence somehow beyond vulgarity, certainly sexless, as if dollar hustling and politicking were the sole source of its dynamism; even the pseudo-Bunny waitresses in the Haymarket bar, dungeon-dark like most Chicago pubs, only peripherally distract from the atmosphere of computers and credit cards. Into the Hilton lobby later that week—as into the lobbies of several other hotels—the young insurgents threw stink bombs, which the management misguidedly attempted to neutralize with aerosol deodorants; the effect was calamitous—the fetor of methane mingled with hair spray, like a beauty parlor over an open sewer —and several of the adjoining restaurants seemed notably lacking in customers. Not that one needed any incentive to abandon the scene, one fled instinctively from such a maggot heap; besides, there was much to study, especially in downtown Chicago on the streets and in the park, where the real action was, not at the convention itself (I only went to the Amphitheater once, for the vote on the minority report), whose incredible atmosphere of chicanery and disdain for justice could best be observed through television's ceaselessly attentive eye.

Since I somehow felt that sooner or later the cops would make their presence felt upon me more directly (a hunch that turned out to be correct), it appeared to me that they deserved closer scrutiny. They were of course everywhere, not only in the streets but in the hotel lobbies and in the dark bars and restaurants, in their baby-blue shirts, so ubiquitous that one would really not be surprised to find one in one's bed; yet it was not their sheer numbers that truly startled, as impressive as this was, but their peculiar personae, characterized by a beery obesity that made them look half again as big as New York policemen (I never thought I might feel what amounted to nostalgia for New York cops, who by comparison suddenly seemed as civilized as London constables) and by a slovenly, brutish, intimidating manner I had never seen outside the guard room of a Marine Corps brig. They obviously had ample reason for this uptight façade, yet it was instantly apparent that in their sight not only the yippies but all civilians were potential miscreants, and as they eyed passers-by narrowly I noticed that Daley, or someone, had allowed them to smoke on duty. Constantly stamping out butts, their great beer guts drooping as they gunned their motorcycles, swatting their swollen thighs with their sticks, they gave me a chill, vulnerable feeling, and I winced at the way their necks went scarlet when the hippies yelled "Pigs!"

On Tuesday night I left a party on the Near North Side with a friend, whom I shall call Jason Epstein, in order to see what was going on in nearby Lincoln Park. There had been rumors of some sort of demonstration and when we arrived, a little before midnight, we saw that in fact a group of young people had gathered there—I estimated a thousand or so—most of them sitting peacefully on the grass in the dark, illuminated dimly by the light of a single portable floodlamp, and fanning out in a semicircle beneath a ten-foot-high wooden cross. The previous night, testing the 11 P.M. curfew, several thousands had assembled in the park and had been brutally routed by the police, who bloodied dozens of demonstrators. Tonight the gathering was a sort of coalition between the yippies and the followers of a group of Near North Side clergymen who had organized the sit-in in order to claim the right of the people of the neighborhood to use the park without police harassment. "This is our park!" one minister proclaimed over the loudspeaker. "We will not be moved!"

Someone was playing a guitar, and folk songs were sung; there was considerable restlessness and tension in the air, even though it was hard to believe that the police would actually attack this tranquil assembly, which so resembled a Presbyterian prayer meeting rather than any group threatening public decorum and order. Yet in the black sky a helicopter wheeled over us in a watchful ellipse, and word got back to us that the police had indeed formed ranks several hundred yards down the slope to the east, beyond our sight. A few people began to leave and the chant went up: "Sit down! Sit down!" Most of us remained seated and part of the crowd began singing "The Battle Hymn of the Republic." Meanwhile, instructions were being given out by the old campaigners: Don't panic; if forced to the street, stay away from the walls and blind alleys; if knocked to the ground, use your jacket as a cushion against clubs; above all—walk, don't run.

The time was now about twelve-thirty. Vaseline was offered as a protection against Mace, wet strips of cloth were handed out to muffle the tear gas. The tension was not very pleasant; while it is easy to overdramatize such a moment, it does contain its element of raw threat, a queasy, visceral suspense that can only be compared to certain remembered episodes during combat training. "They'll be here in two minutes!" the minister announced.

And suddenly they were here, coming over the brow of the slope fifty yards away, a truly stupefying sight—one hundred or more of the police in a phalanx abreast, clubs at the ready, in helmets and gas masks, just behind them a huge perambulating machine with nozzles, like the type used for spraying insecticide, disgorging clouds of yellowish gas, the whole advancing panoply illuminated by batteries of mobile floodlights. Because of the smoke, and the great cross outlined against it, yet also because of the helmeted and masked figures—resembling nothing so much as those rubberized wind-up automata from a child's playbox of horrors—I had a quick sense of the medieval in juxtaposition with the twenty-first century or, more exactly, a kind of science fiction fantasy, as if a band of primitive Christians on another planet had suddenly found themselves set upon by mechanized legions from Jupiter.

Certainly, whatever the exact metaphor it summoned up, the sight seemed to presage the shape of the world to come, but by now we were up, all of us, off and away—not running, *walking*, fast—toward Clark Street, bleeding tears from the gas. The streets next to the park became a madhouse. The police had not been content to run us out of the park, but charging from the opposite direction, had flanked us, and were harrying people down the streets and up alleys. On a traffic island in the middle of Clark Street a young man was knocked to his knees and beaten senseless. Unsuspecting motorists, caught up in the pandemonium, began to collide with one another up and down the street. The crowd wailed with alarm and split into fragments. I heard the sound of splintering glass as a stone went through the windshield of a police car. Then somehow we disengaged ourselves from the center of the crowd and made our way down Wells Street, relatively deserted where in the dingy night clubs go-go girls oblivious to the rout outside calmly wiggled their asses in silhouette against crimson windows.

It hardly needs mention that Daley might have dealt with these demonstrators without having to resort to such praetorian measures, but violence was the gut and sinew of Chicago during the week, and it was this sort of scene—not the antiseptic convention itself, with its tedium and tawdriness and its bought and paid-for delegates—that makes its claim on my memory. Amid the confusion, I recall certain serene little vignettes: in the lobby of the Pick-Congress Hotel, Senator Tom Dodd flushing beet-red, smiling a frozen smile while being pounded on the back by a burly delegate, steelworker type, with fists the size of cabbages, the man roaring, "I'm a Polack! We know how to ride that greased pig, too!" Or the visit I made—purportedly to win over delegates to McCarthy—to the Virginia delegation, where I was told by at least three members of the group that, while nominally for Humphrey, they would bolt for Teddy Kennedy in a shot (this helped to convince me that he could have won the nomination hands down had he come to Chicago).

But it is mainly that night scene out of Armageddon that I recollect or, the next day, the tremendous confrontation in front of the Hilton, at the intersection of Michigan and Balbo (named for Italo Balbo, the Italian aviator who first dumped bombs on the Ethiopians) where, half blinded from the gas I had just caught on the street, I watched the unbelievable melee not from the outside this time, but in the surreal shelter of the Haymarket bar, a hermetically sealed igloo whose sound-resistant plate-glass windows offered me the dumbshow of cops clubbing people to the concrete, swirling squadrons of people in Panavision blue and polystyrene visors hurling back the crowds, chopping skulls and noses while above me on the invincible TV screen a girl with a fantastic body enacted a comic commercial for Bic ballpoint pens, and the bartender impassively mooned over his daiquiris (once pausing to inquire of a girl whether she was over twenty-one), and the Muzak in the background whispered "Mood Indigo." Even the denouement seemed unreal—played out not in the flesh but as part of some animated cartoon where one watches all hell break loose in tolerant boredom—when an explosion of glass at the rear of the bar announced the arrival of half a dozen bystanders who, hurled inward by the crush outside, had shattered the huge window and now sprawled cut and bleeding all over the floor of the place while others, chased by a wedge of cops, fled screaming into the adjacent lobby.

I left Chicago in a hurry—like many others—pursued by an unshakable gloom and by an even profounder sense of irrelevance. If all this anguish, all this naked protest, had yielded nothing but such a primitive impasse—perhaps in the end best symbolized not even by the strife itself but by a "victorious" Hubert Humphrey promising us still another commission to investigate the violence he might have helped circumvent—then the country truly seemed locked, crystallized in its own politics of immobility. There were, to be sure, some significant changes—removal of the unit rule for one—at least partially brought about by those who worked outside the establishment, including many amateurs in politics; had they been effected in less hysterical circumstances, they might have been considered in themselves prodigious achievements.

And there were some bearable moments amid all the dreck: the going to bed unblanketed on the cold ground by the fires in Grant Park when I came back just before dawn after our encounter with the police in Lincoln Park, the crowds by the hundreds hemmed in by National Guard troops (themselves Illinois plow-boys or young miners from places like Carbondale, most of them abashed and ill at ease—quite a contrast to the brutal belly-swagger of the cops—but all of them just as ignorant about the clash of ideologies that brought them up here from the prairies); or the next night when again there was a vigil in the park and over a thousand people, including protesting delegates from the convention, came bearing candles and sat until dawn beneath the stirring leaves singing "Where Have All the Flowers Gone?" as the waved their candles, a forest of arms; or the moment in the daylight, totally unexpected, when a busload of children, no more than six or seven years old, rode up from somewhere on the South Side with a gift of sandwiches for the demonstrators and slowly passed by in front of the park, chanting from the windows in voices almost hurtfully young and sweet: "We want peace! We want peace!" But these moments were rare and intermittent and the emotional gloss they provided was unable to alleviate not just the sense of betrayal (which at least carries the idea of promise victimized) but the sorrow of a promise that never really existed.

[*New York Review of Books*, September 26, 1968]

PORTRAITS
AND
FAREWELLS

Robert Penn Warren

I HAVE BEEN LUCKY to have known Red Warren well for quite a few years and to have been privy to certain personal matters known only between good friends. I am therefore aware of an interesting fact about Red's early life that is not generally understood by less favored mortals. This is that as a boy in his teens Red's simple but very red-blooded American ambition was to become an officer in the United States Navy. This, ladies and gentlemen, is the truth, not an idle fiction. Indeed, it was *more* than an ambition; it was a goal very close of attainment, for Red had obtained his appointment and was all but packed up and ready to leave the bluegrass of Kentucky for Annapolis when he suffered an injury to his eye which made it impossible for him ever to become a midshipman. There is irony in this, for it always has seemed to me that Red at least *looks* like a sailor. If you will glance at him now, you will see it: that seamed and craggy face which has gazed, like Melville's, into the briny abyss, that weather-wise expression and salty presence which have made him physically the very model of a sea dog; and as a consequence I have often become thoroughly bemused when speculating on Red's career if he *had* gone off to the Naval Academy. I would like to consider this prospect for a moment.

First, let no one underestimate the military mind; at the highest levels of command great brilliance is required, and for this reason Red would have been what is known as a "rising star" from the very beginning. Thus I visualize the scenario—if I may use that awful word—like this. Number one in his class at Annapolis, Red becomes the first naval Rhodes scholar at Oxford, where his record is also spectacular. He takes his degree in Oriental history, writing a thesis which is a revisionist examination of Genghis Khan, largely laudatory in tone. Later in my fantasy I see Red at the end of World War II, much decorated, at the age of forty the youngest captain in the seagoing navy, attending the Naval War College at Newport, writing learned dissertations on the nuclear capabilities of the Soviet fleet. His recommendation is: Let's press the button, *very softly*, before the Russians do. During the Korean War, a rear admiral now, he wins his fourth Navy Cross, is made commander in chief of the Pacific fleet, is on the cover of *Time* magazine, has a tempestuous though necessarily discreet affair with Ava Gardner. Through the dull and arid years between Korea and Vietnam, Red Warren plays golf with Eisenhower, rereads Thucydides and Clausewitz, hobnobs with Henry Luce, Barry Goldwater and Mendel Rivers, and is appointed Chief of Naval Operations under Lyndon Johnson.

I don't know why my fantasy brightens and becomes happy at this point. Maybe it's because I see Red Warren miraculously turn a major corner in his life, undergoing—as it were—a sea change. He becomes a *dove*! After all, a great Marine general, ex-Commandant David Shoup, did this: why not Red in my fantasy? Now as he reverses himself, the same grand historical imagination which in his alter ego produced *All the King's Men*, *World Enough and Time* and *Brother to Dragons* is suddenly seized with the folly and tragedy of our involvement in Southeast Asia, so that on one dark night in 1966 there is a confrontation, many hours long, between the admiral from Kentucky—now Chairman of the Joint Chiefs of Staff—and the Texas President, two Southerners eyeball to eyeball; and in this passionate colloquy it is the *Kentuckian* who finally gains the upper hand with his forceful, humanitarian argument—founded upon the ineluctable lessons of history of which he is master—that this war can only lead to futility, disaster and national degradation. I even see the droplets of sweat on Lyndon Johnson's forehead as, after a grave long pause, he gives in, saying, "God damn yore soft-hearted hide, Admiral Warren, you've convinced me!" And immediately I see him getting on the telephone to McNamara: "Bob, git those advisers out of Vietnam! We're going to nip this here dirty little war in the bud!"

But this kind of wish-fulfillment becomes almost unendurable, and so in my mind's eye I bring Red's naval career to a merciful close, seeing him as grim and cruel reason dictates he most likely *would* be today—not basking in well-deserved homage at the

Lotos Club but retired to the Pacific seaside at Coronado, cultivating prize asparagus or roses, writing letters to the San Diego
Tribune about stray dogs, queers and the Commie menace, and
sending monthly donations to Rabbi Korff.

So by that fateful accident years ago America lost a master
mariner but gained a major novelist and poet, a superb essayist, a
literary critic of great breadth and subtle discrimination, a teacher
of eloquence, a sly and hilarious storyteller, and altogether one of
the best human beings to break bread with, or join with in *spirituous*
companionship, or just simply *be around* in this desperate or any
other time . . .

I would like to conclude with a couple of brief reminiscences
having to do with Red Warren which in each case are oddly connected with—of all things for two good ole Southern boys—winter
snow. The first of these events occurred a long time ago in New
York City during the famous blizzard of late December 1947
(which many of you here doubtless still remember), when I—a
young and aspiring and penniless writer up from the Virginia
Tidewater living in a basement on upper Lexington Avenue—
first read *All the King's Men.* I think it is absolute and unimpeachable testimony to a book's impact on us that we are able to associate it so keenly with the time and the surroundings and the
circumstances in which we read it. Only a very great work can
produce this memory; it is like love, or recollections of momentous loving. There is what psychologists call a *gestalt*, an unforget-
tability of interwoven emotions with which the work will ever in
recollection be connected with the environment. Somehow the
excitement of reading *All the King's Men* is always linked in my
mind with the howling blizzard outside and the snow piling up in
a solid white impacted mass outside my basement window. The
book itself was a revelation and gave me a shock to brain and
spine like a freshet of icy water. I had of course read many novels
before, including many of the greatest, but this powerful and complex story embedded in prose of such fire and masterful imagery—
this, I thought with growing wonder, this was what a novel was
all about, this was *it*, the bright book of life, what writing was
supposed to be. When finally the blizzard stopped and the snow
lay heaped on the city streets, silent as death, I finished *All the
King's Men* as in a trance, knowing once and for all that I, too,
however falteringly and incompletely, must try to work such
magic. I began my first novel before that snow had melted; it is a

book called *Lie Down in Darkness*, and in tone and style, as any fool can see, it is profoundly indebted to the work which so ravished my heart and mind during that long snowfall.

Many years and many snowfalls later I was walking with Red Warren one late afternoon on, of all absurd things, *snowshoes* through the white silence of a forest in Vermont—a rather clumsily comical trek which, had you told the young man on Lexington Avenue he would be making it in the future, would have caused him both awe and incredulity. Red and I were by this time fast and firm friends, bonded in a friendship long past the need of forced conversation, and as we puffed along in Indian file across the mountainous snowdrifts, each of us plunged in his own private meditation, it creepily occurred to me that we were far away from home, far away from the road, still miles away from anything or anybody—and that, worst of all, it was almost night. I had a moment of terrible panic as I thought that Red and I, having unwittingly strayed in our outlandish footgear off the beaten track, would find ourselves engulfed by darkness in this freezing wilderness, utterly lost, two nonsmokers with not a match between us, or a knife to cut shelter—only our foolhardy, vulnerable selves, floundering in the Yankee snows. After the initial panic slid away and I had succumbed to a stoic reckoning, a resignation in face of the inevitable, it occurred to me that if I had to die there was nobody on earth, aside from perhaps Raquel Welch, that I'd rather freeze to death with than Robert Penn Warren: this noble gentleman from Guthrie, Kentucky, whose humane good sense and lyric passion had so enriched us all through these many novels and poems and essays and plays, and whose celebration of the mystery and beauty and, yes, even the inexplicable anguish of life had been one of those priceless bulwarks against death in a time of too much dying. Just then I heard Red casually say, "Well, here's the road." And I was a little ashamed of my panic, but not of those thoughts, which also had included my heartfelt thanks to God that Red Warren never became an admiral.

[Speech delivered at the Lotos Club, New York City, April 1975]

Peter Matthiessen

WHEN I FIRST MET Peter Matthiessen I was in my mid-twenties, feeling rather nervous and unhappy and very much out of my element on my initial visit to Paris. I had published a first novel to considerable acclaim in New York, but small word of the book's existence, and nothing of its success, had reached France during that balmy and beautiful spring of 1952, and I suppose I was a little disappointed that Peter did not display the deference I thought fitting to the situation. Thus at first glance I thought Peter a trifle cold, when in reality his perfectly decent manners were really all one should have expected in view of the fact that I was merely another of the dozens of visiting American firemen who, at the behest of well-meaning friends back in the States, came knocking at the Matthiessen door that year. Peter and his wife, Patsy, lived in a modest but lovely apartment on a Utrillo-like back street in Montparnasse; spacious, airy, its one big room filled with light, the Matthiessen pad (the word was just coming into use about then) became the hangout for many of the mob of Americans who had hurried to Paris to partake of its perennial delights, to drink in the pleasures of a city beginning to surge with energy after the miseries of the recent war. "U.S. Go Home" was painted by the Communists on every wall—it was possibly the most ignored injunction in recent history. For the Americans happily established there, Paris *was* home, and no place was more homelike than the Matthiessen establishment on the Rue Perceval. To this day I recollect with awe the sense of an almost constant open house, in which it was possible at practically any time to obtain music and food and drink (Peter was unfailingly generous with what seemed to be a nearly inexhaustible supply of Scotch) or, if need be, a spot to sleep off a hangover and—of course always—conversation. George Plimpton and Harold Humes were among the many visitors, and much of the conversation had to do with a literary magazine which the three friends were then in the process of bringing into hesitant life and which now, seemingly deathless, is known as the *Paris Review*. I am rather proud of the fact that the interview with me, done by Peter and George Plimpton, was the first of the celebrated *Paris Review* series (although not the first published)—first undoubtedly because at the time I was the only published novelist any of us knew.

We also talked a great deal about books and writing. We were swept up in the very midst of a postwar literary fever. Peter had not yet written a book (his fledgling effort, the affecting story "Sadie," had been published in the *Atlantic*) but he was, after all, barely twenty-five; he had time to burn and I remember telling him so, from the senior and authoritative vantage point of a writer who was two years older. So it is not to belittle Peter's capacity for work—and he is one of the most industrious writers alive—to say that much of our time during that spring and summer was spent at play. My French was rudimentary, while both Peter and Patsy had an excellent command of the language, and this helped bring me in contact with French people I might not have met; my linguistic ability slowly improved. That same savoir-faire of Peter's enabled me (a gastronomic idiot) to become acquainted with the native cuisine, and one of the remembered joys of that long-ago season, when a solitary dollar could buy considerable French joy, is our single-minded cultivation of the restaurants of Montparnasse and Saint-Germain-des-Prés. We had become good friends and I saw a lot of Peter during the following year in Europe—in Saint-Jean-de-Luz, where Peter and Patsy rented a house for the summer; in Rome, where to my enormous and happy surprise Peter turned up with a group of *Paris Review* cronies at my wedding the next spring; and finally during a splendid sojourn at Ravello, on the Amalfi Drive, where for several weeks Peter and Patsy (along with their newborn son, Lucas) shared a house with Rose and me and played tennis and interminable word games, talked for long hours about writers and writing, and swam in the then pellucid and unpolluted Mediterranean.

In 1954, when we all moved back to America, Peter set up housekeeping on Long Island and began to write seriously (though spending much of his time in good weather plying a trade as commercial fisherman), while Rose and I began to plant domestic roots in the hills of western Connecticut. During this period we kept close contact, visiting back and forth with considerable regularity, and it was at that time that I read Peter's first novel, *Race Rock*, in manuscript, beginning a tradition that has lasted to this day; amiably critical of each other's output, Peter and I have read (I think it is safe to say) nearly every word of each other's work—at least of a major nature—and I like to think that the habit has been mutually beneficial. Later I read *Partisans* and *Raditzer* with the same careful eye that I had *Race Rock;* as talented and sensitive as each appeared to be, the statement of a writer at the outset of his career, they were, I felt, merely forerunners of something more ambitious, more complex and substantial—and I was right. When *At Play in the Fields of the Lord* was published in 1965 there was revealed in stunning outline the fully realized work of 'a novelist writing at white heat and at the peak of his powers; a dense, rich, musical book, filled with tragic and comic resonances, it is fiction of genuine stature, with a staying power that makes it as remarkable to read now as when it first appeared.

But before *At Play* was published Peter had to begin that wandering yet consecrated phase of his career which has taken him to every corner of the globe, and which, reflected in a remarkable series of chronicles, has placed him at the forefront of the naturalists of his time. I saw Peter off in 1959 on the first of these trips—bidding him a boozy bon voyage athwart the Brooklyn docks, on a freighter that was to carry him up to the remotest reaches of the Amazon. Seemingly unperturbed, his spectacles planted with scholarly precision on his long angular face, he might have been going no farther than Staten Island, so composed did he seem, rather than to uttermost jungle fastnesses where God knows what beasts and dark happenings would imperil his hide. Weeks later I received a jaunty postcard from a distant and unheard-of Peruvian outpost, and I marveled at the sang-froid and the self-sufficiency but also at the quiet excitement the few words conveyed; in later years I would receive other droll, understated communiqués from Alaska, New Guinea and the blackest part of Africa.

From what sprang this amazing obsession to plant one's feet upon the most exotic quarters of the earth, to traverse festering swamps and to scale the aching heights of implausible mountains? The wanderlust and feeling for adventure that is in many men, I suppose, but mercifully Peter has been more than a mere adventurer: he is a poet and a scientist, and the mingling of these two personae has given us such carefully observed, unsentimental, yet lyrically echoing works as *The Cloud Forest, Under the Mountain Wall, The Tree Where Man Was Born* and *The Snow Leopard*. In the books themselves the reader will find at least part of the answer to the reason for Peter's quest. In these books, with their infusion of the ecological and the anthropological, with their unshrinking vision of man in mysterious and uneasy interplay with nature—books at once descriptive and analytical, scrupulous and vivid in detail, sometimes amusing, often meditative and mystical—Peter Matthiessen has created a unique body of work. It is the work of a man in ecstatic contemplation of our beautiful and inexplicable planet. To this body of natural history, add a novel like *At Play in the Fields of the Lord* and that brooding, briny, stormswept tone poem, *Far Tortuga*, and we behold a writer of phenomenal scope and versatility.

[Introduction to *Peter Matthiessen, A Bibliography: 1951–1979*, compiled by D. Nichols (Canoga Park, Calif.: Orirana Press, 1979)]

William Blackburn

WILLIAM BLACKBURN cared about writing and had an almost holy concern for the language. I realized this the first time out, with a brief theme in which we were required to describe a place—anyplace. In my two-page essay I chose a Tidewater river scene, the mudflats at low tide; attempting to grapple with the drab beauty of the view, groping for detail, I wrote of the fishnet stakes standing in the gray water, "looking stark and mute." A pretty conceit, I had thought, until the theme came back from Blackburn covered with red corrections, including the scathing comment on my attempt at imagery: "*Mute?* Did those stakes *ever* say anything?" This was my first encounter with something known among grammarians as "the pathetic fallacy."

A certain precision, you see, was what the professor was after and I was lucky to be made to toe the line early. Also, it was not a permissive era. Blackburn graded his themes with rigid unsentimentality. That theme of mine, I recall, received a D-minus, and through discreet inquiry I discovered that it was the lowest grade in the class (I think the highest was a C). Chastened, I began to regard Professor Blackburn with apprehension and awe, and both of these feelings were heightened by his redoubtable appearance and demeanor. A large, bulky, rather rumpled man (at least in dress), he tended to slump at his desk and to sag while walking; all this gave the impression of a man harboring great unhappiness, if not despair. Nor did he smile effortlessly. There was something distinctly cranky and dour about him, after so many teachers I had known with their Ipana smiles and dauntless cheer. He was ill at ease with strangers, including students, and this is why my first impression of Blackburn was one of remoteness and bearish gloom. Only a remarkably gentle South Carolina voice softened my initial feeling that he was filled with bone-hard melancholy and quiet desperation. For several weeks it seemed to me impossible that one could ever draw close—or be drawn close—to such a despondent, distant man.

But before too long my work got much better, and as it did I found myself able to strike through the Blackburnian mask. Possibly because I was so eager to meet his demanding standards, I sweated like a coolie over my essays, themes and fledgling short stories until my splintered syntax and humpbacked prose achieved a measure of clarity and grace. Blackburn in turn warmed to my efforts—beginning to sprinkle the pages with such invigorating phrases as "Nice!" and "Fine touch!"—and before the term was half through I had begun to acquire a clutch of Bs and As. More importantly, I began to know Blackburn, the great-hearted, humane, tragicomical sufferer who dwelt behind the hulking and lugubrious façade. One day to my astonishment he invited me to lunch. We went to an East Durham restaurant. The beer was good, the food atrocious. He spoke to me very little of writing, or of my own efforts (which did not bother me, my As were enough praise and this terrible lunch sufficient accolade), but much about reading. He asked me what I had read in my lifetime and was patient and understanding when I confessed to having read next to nothing. Most gently he then informed me that one could not become a writer without a great deal of reading. Read Thomas Mann and Proust, he said, the Russians, Conrad, Shakespeare, the Elizabethans. Perhaps, he added, I would like to sign up, next semester, for his course in Elizabethan literature. We were a little embarrassed and uneasy with each other. Occasionally there were blank silences as we munched on our ghastly wartime hot dogs. In the silences Blackburn would give a heaving sigh. All his life he was an expressive sigher. Then he would begin to rail, with marvelously droll venom, at the Duke University administration bigwigs, most of whom he regarded as Pecksniffs and Philistines. They were out to smother the Humanities, to destroy him and his modest writing class; they were Yahoos. He got superbly rancorous and eloquent; he had an actor's sense of timing and I laughed until I ached. Then he grew more serious again. To write one must read, he repeated, *read* . . .

Blackburn readily admitted that there was a great deal of logic in the accusation, so often leveled at "creative writing" courses, that no one could actually be taught to write English narrative prose. Why, then, did he persist? I think it must have been because, deep within him, despite all doubts (and no man had so many self-doubts) he realized what an extraordinarily fine teacher he was. He must have known that he possessed that subtle, ineffable, magnetically appealing quality—a kind of invisible rapture—which caused students to respond with like rapture to the fresh and wondrous new world he was trying to reveal to them. Later, when I got to know him well, he accused himself of sloth, but in reality he was the most profoundly conscientious of teachers; his comments on students' themes and stories were often remarkable extended essays in themselves. This matter of caring, and caring deeply, was of course one of the secrets of his excellence. But the caring took other forms: it extended to his very presence in the classroom—his remarkable course in Elizabethan poetry and prose, for instance, when, reading aloud from Spenser's *Epithalamion* with its ravishing praise, or the sonorous meditation on death of Sir Thomas Browne, his voice would become so infused with feeling that we would sit transfixed, and not a breath could be heard in the room. It would be too facile a description to call him a spellbinder, though he had in him much of the actor *manqué;* this very rare ability to make his students *feel*, to fall in love with a poem or poet, came from his own real depth of feeling and, perhaps, from his own unrequited love, for I am sure he was an unfulfilled writer or poet too. Whatever—from what mysterious wellspring there derived Blackburn's powerful and uncanny gift to mediate between a work of art and the young people who stood ready to receive it—he was unquestionably a glorious teacher. Populate a whole country and its institutions of learning with but a handful of Blackburns, and you will certainly have great institutions of learning, and perhaps a great country.

I deeply miss him, because ultimately he became more than a teacher to me. He became the reason why, after the war was over, I returned to Duke and why, too—although at this point the University and I were on mutually amicable terms—Duke acquired a meaning to me beyond the good times I enjoyed there and its simple power to grant me a bachelor's degree. Bill Blackburn had become a close friend, a spiritual anchor, a man whose companionship was a joy and whose counsel was almost everything to one still floundering at the edge of a chancy and rather terrifying career. It helped immeasurably to have him tell me, at the age of twenty-one, that I could become a writer—although I am still unable to say whether this advice was more important than the fact that, without him, I should doubtless never have known the music of John Milton, or rare Ben Jonson, or been set afire by John Donne. In any case, he was for me the embodiment of those virtues by which I am still able to value the school he served (despite bearish grudges and droll upheavals) so long and so well. Surely over the years the ultimate and shining honor gained by a university is the one bestowed upon it by a man like William Blackburn and his love, requited and unrequited, and his rapturous teaching.

[From *Duke Encounters*. Durham: Duke University Office of Publications, 1977]

William Faulkner

H E DETESTED MORE THAN ANYTHING the invasion of his privacy. Though I am made to feel welcome in the house by Mrs. Faulkner and his daughter, Jill, and though I know that the welcome is sincere, I feel an intruder nonetheless. Grief, like few things else, is a private affair. Moreover, Faulkner hated those (and there were many) who would poke about in his private life—literary snoops and gossips yearning for the brief kick of propinquity with greatness and a mite of reflected fame. He had said himself more than once, quite rightly, that the only thing that should matter to other people about a writer is his books. Now that he is dead and helpless in the gray wooden coffin, I feel even more an interloper, prying around in a place I should not be.

But the first fact of the day, aside from that final fact of a death which has so diminished us, is the heat, and it is a heat which is like a small mean death itself, as if one were being smothered to extinction in a damp woolen overcoat. Even the newspapers in Memphis, sixty miles to the north, have commented on the ferocious weather. Oxford lies drowned in heat, and the feeling around the courthouse square on this Saturday forenoon is of a hot, sweaty languor bordering on desperation. Parked slantwise against the curb, Fords and Chevrolets and pickup trucks bake in merciless sunlight. People in Mississippi have learned to move gradually, almost timidly, in this climate. They walk with both caution and deliberation. Beneath the portico of the First National Bank and along the scantily shaded walks around the courthouse itself, the traffic of shirtsleeved farmers and dewy-browed housewives and marketing Negroes is listless and slow-moving. Painted high up against the side of a building to the west of the courthouse and surmounted by a painted Confederate flag is a huge sign at least twenty feet long reading "Rebel Cosmetology College." Sign, flag and wall, dominating one hot angle of the square, are caught in blazing light and seem to verge perilously close to combustion. It is a monumental heat, heat so desolating to the body and spirit as to have the quality of a half-remembered bad dream, until one realizes that it has, indeed, been encountered before, in all those novels and stories of Faulkner through which this unholy weather—and other weather more benign—moves with almost touchable reality.

In the ground-floor office of the Oxford *Eagle*, the editor and co-owner, Mrs. Nina Goolsby, bustles about under a groaning air conditioner. She is a large, cheerful, voluble woman and she reveals with great pride that the *Eagle* has recently won first place for general excellence among weekly newspapers in the annual awards of the Mississippi Press Association. She has just returned from distributing around town handbills which read:

IN MEMORY
OF
WILLIAM FAULKNER

This Business Will Be
CLOSED
From 2:00 to 2:15 PM
Today, July 7, 1962

It was her idea, she says, adding, "People say that Oxford didn't care anything about Bill Faulkner, and that's just not true. We're proud of him. Look here." She displays a file of back issues of the *Eagle*, and there is the front-page headline: "Nobel Award for Literature Comes to Oxonian." There is a page from another issue, a full page paid for by, among others, the Ole Miss Dry Cleaners, Gathright-Reed Drug Company, Miller's Cafe, the A. H. Avent Gin and Warehouse Company. The emblazoned message reads: "Welcome Home, Bill Faulkner. We want to tell people everywhere—Oxford, and all of us, are very proud of William Faulkner, one of us, the Nobel Prize winning author." The page is full of pictures of Faulkner in Stockholm: receiving the Nobel Prize from the king of Sweden, walking in the snow with his daughter, crouched beside a sled where he is seen chatting with "a little Swedish lad."

"So you can see how proud we are of him. We've always been

proud of him," Mrs. Goolsby says. "Why, I've known Bill Faulkner all my life. I live not two blocks away from him. We used to stop and talk all the time when he was taking his walks. Lord, dressed in that real elegant tweed jacket with those leather patches on the elbows, and that cane curved over his arm. I've always said that when they put Bill Faulkner in the ground it just won't be right unless he has that tweed jacket on."

Back at the Faulkner house, the shade of the old cedars which arch up over the walkway and the columned portico offers only scant relief from the noonday heat. It is shirtsleeve weather, and indeed many of the men have removed their coats, around the front door where already some of the family has gathered: John Faulkner, himself a writer and almost a replica, a ghost of his brother down to the quizzical lifted eyebrows and downward slanting mustache; John's grown sons; another brother, Murry, sad-eyed, gentle-spoken, an FBI agent in Mobile; Jill's husband, Paul Summers from Charlottesville, Virginia, a lawyer: like Jill, he refers to Faulkner as "Pappy." The conversation is general: the heat, the advantages of jet travel, the complexities of Mississippi's antediluvian liquor laws. The group steps aside to allow passage for a lady bearing an enormous cake with raspberry-colored icing; it is only one of many to arrive this day.

Inside, it is a little cooler, and here in the library to the left of the door—just opposite the cleared living room where the coffin rests —it seems easier to pass the time. It is a spacious, cluttered, comfortable room. A gold-framed portrait of Faulkner in hunting togs, looking very jaunty in his black topper, dominates one wall; next to it on a table is a wood sculpture of a gaunt Don Quixote. There are gentle, affectionate portraits of two Negro servants painted by "Miss Maud" Falkner (unlike her son, she spelled the name without the "u," as does most of the family). Around the other walls are books, books by the dozens and scores, in random juxtaposition, in jackets and without jackets, quite a few upside down: *The Golden Asse*, Vittorini's *In Sicily*, *The Brothers Karamazov*, Calder Willingham's *Geraldine Bradshaw*, the *Short Stories of Ernest Hemingway*, *From Here to Eternity*, Shakespeare's *Comedies*, *Act of Love* by Ira Wolfert, *Best of S. J. Perelman* and many more beyond accounting.

Here in the library I meet Shelby Foote, the novelist and Civil

War historian and one of Faulkner's very few literary friends. A pleasant, dark Mississippian in his mid-forties (he is dressed in seersucker and looks extremely cool), he observes that, naturally, a mere Virginian like myself cannot be expected to cope with such heat. "You've got to walk through it gently," he counsels; "don't make any superfluous moves." And he adds depressingly, "This is just beginning to build up pressure. You should be around here in August."

Foote is searching for a book, an anthology which contains one of Faulkner's early poems—a short poem written more than thirty years ago called "My Epitaph." I join in the search, which leads us to Faulkner's workroom at the rear of the house. There is more clutter here, more books: *40 Best Stories from Mademoiselle, Doctor Zhivago*, Dos Passos' *Midcentury, Judgment of Julius and Ethel Rosenberg*, H. K. Douglas' *I Rode With Stonewall* (one of the books Faulkner was reading just before his death), a hundred others jammed into a low bookcase, several shelves of which contain parcels of books sent to Faulkner for autographing: all of these remain dusty and unopened. The heavy antique typewriter which Faulkner worked on has been taken away and in its place on the table rests, somewhat inexplicably, a half-gallon bottle of Old Crow, one-fourth full. Behind this table on a mantelpiece littered with ashtrays, ornamental bottles, a leaking tobacco pouch, there stands a small comic painting of a mule, rump up high, teeth bared in manic laughter. "I think Faulkner loved mules almost as much as people," Foote reflects. "Maybe more." He has found the book and the poem.

Now several electric fans are whirring in the downstairs rooms and hallways, and a buffet lunch is being served. The food at a Southern funeral is usually good, but this food is splendid: turkey and country ham and stuffed tomatoes, loaves of delectable soft homemade bread and gallons of strong iced tea. We sit informally around the dining-room table. The hour of the service is approaching and outside through the window the afternoon light casts black shadows of trembling oak leaves and cedar branches against the rich hot grass.

From far off comes a mockingbird's rippling chant. Suddenly someone in the family recalls that just the night before, they had run across something which must have been one of the last things

Faulkner had written, but that it was in French and they couldn't read it. It is brought forth and as a couple of us begin to puzzle it out we see that it is written in pencil on an envelope—the draft of a reply, in Faulkner's tiny, vertical, cramped, nearly illegible calligraphy, to an invitation to visit from someone in France—a note courteous, witty and in easy French. He said he couldn't come.

Promptly at two o'clock a hush comes over the house as preparations for the service begin. We put our coats back on. There are several dozen of us—all but a handful (like his publishers, Bennett Cerf and Donald Klopfer) members of the family, gathered here from all over the South, Mississippi and Alabama and Louisiana and Virginia and Tennessee—and we stand in the two rooms, the dining room, from which the table has been removed now, and the living room, where the coffin rests. The Episcopal minister in white surplice, the Reverend Duncan Gray Jr., is bespectacled and balding, and his voice, though strong, is barely heard above the whine and chattering vibration of the electric fans:

"*The Lord is my light and my salvation; whom shall I fear? the Lord is the strength of my life; of whom shall I be afraid?*"

The mockingbird again sings outside, nearer now. Through the hum of the fans the minister reads Psalm 46:

"*God is our refuge and strength, a very present help in trouble.*
"*Therefore will not we fear, though the earth be removed, and though the mountains be carried into the midst of the sea . . .*"

We repeat the Lord's Prayer aloud, and soon it is all over. There is a kind of haste to leave the house. The procession to the cemetery is up South Lamar Avenue through the center of town. As the line of cars stretches out ahead behind the black hearse and as we near the courthouse, it becomes plain that Mrs. Goolsby's campaign to close the stores has had good effect. For though it is now past two-fifteen, the stores are still shut up and the sidewalks are thronged with people. White and Negro, they stand watching the procession in the blazing heat, in rows and groups and clusters, on all sides of the courthouse and along the sidewalks in front of Grundy's Cafe and Earl Fudge's Grocery and the Rebel Food Center. I am moved by this display and comment on it, but someone who is a native of the region is rather less impressed: "It's not that they don't respect Bill. I think most of them do, really. Even though none of them ever read a word of him. But funerals are a big thing around here. Let a Baptist deacon die and you'll *really* get a turnout."

Our car comes abreast of the courthouse, turns slowly to the right around the square. Here the statue of the Confederate soldier ("Erected 1907" is the legend beneath) stands brave and upright on his skinny calcimine-white pedestal, looking like a play soldier and seeming vaguely forlorn. Both courthouse and statue loom over so much of Faulkner's work, and now, for the first time this day, I am stricken by the realization that Faulkner is really gone. And I am deep in memory, as if summoned there by a trumpet blast. Dilsey and Benjy and Luster and all the Compsons, Hightower and Byron Bunch and Flem Snopes and the gentle Lena Grove—all of these people and a score of others come swarming back comically and villainously and tragically in my mind with a kind of mnemonic sense of utter reality, along with the tumultuous landscape and the fierce and tender weather, and the whole maddened, miraculous vision of life wrested, as all art is wrested, out of nothingness. Suddenly, as the watchful and brooding faces of the townspeople sweep across my gaze, I am filled with a bitter grief. We move past a young blue-shirted policeman, crescents of sweat beneath his arms, who stands at attention, bareheaded, his cap clapped to his breast. Up North Lamar the procession rolls, then east on Jefferson.

The old cemetery has been filled, therefore his grave lies in the "new" part, and he is one of the first occupants of this tract. There is nothing much to say about it, really. It is a rather raw field, it seems to me, overlooking a housing project; but he lies on a gentle slope between two oak trees, and they will grow larger as they shelter him. Thus he is laid to rest. The crowd disperses in the hot sunlight and is gone.

At the end of *The Wild Palms*, an early novel of Faulkner's, the condemned hero, speculating upon the possibility of a choice between nothing and grief, says that he will choose grief. And certainly even grief must be better than nothing. As for the sorrow and loss one feels today in this hot dry field, perhaps it needs only to be expressed in Faulkner's own words, in the young poem he called "My Epitaph":

> If there be grief, let it be the rain
> And this but silver grief, for grieving's sake,

And these green woods be dreaming here to wake
Within my heart, if I should rouse again.
But I shall sleep, for where is any death
While in these blue hills slumbrous overhead
I'm rooted like a tree? Though I be dead
This soil that holds me fast will find me breath.

[*Life*, July 20, 1962]

Philip Rahv

I FIRST MET PHILIP in the mid-1950s at a dinner party in rural Connecticut, only a few years after my first novel had been published. Mine was a book which, for a first novel, had received considerable acclaim in the popular press; although in terms of what I conceived to be the New York literary establishment— most notably *Partisan Review*—my Southern gothic tragedy may as well have been printed on water. That evening, therefore, I felt myself dining, if not precisely among the enemy, then with a species of intellectual so high-powered and demanding that I could not help but feel intimidated, and a little resentful. I had of course read much of Philip's admirable and brilliant criticism, which made it all the more painful to feel something of a nonentity in his presence. And what a presence it was! There Philip sat across the table, heavy-lidded, glowering, talking in nearly unfathomable polysyllables—not so unfathomable, however, that I might fail to understand that he was cutting some poor incompetent wretch of a writer to shreds. But how devastating and deserved was that demolition job, how pitiless was his judgment upon that star-crossed nincompoop so misguided as to ever have taken pen in hand! I think I shivered a little, and after dinner sidled away. Later, though, when goodbyes were being said, I was dumbstruck when Philip approached me and took my hand, saying in that voice which was such a strange amalgam of fog and frog, "Hope to see you again. I liked your book." And then, as if to endorse this stunning statement, he added with a negligent flap of his arm, "It was a good book." When he was gone, the enormous astonishment lingered, along with an unabashed and immodest satisfaction.

Even then, before I knew him, I was powerfully aware that you had passed a crucial muster if, in the eyes of Philip Rahv, you had written "a good book."

In retrospect, I can understand that my initial discomfort in Philip's presence had to do in part with a mistaken prejudice. At a time when the urban Jewish sensibility was coming to the forefront of American literature, and the writing of Southerners was no longer the dominant mode, I shared some of the resentment of my fellow WASPs over what we construed as the self-conscious chauvinism often displayed by the literary establishment. Thus, in an awful momentary lapse, I had confused Philip with somebody like Leslie Fiedler. Certainly, I should have known better—should have known that among the things that characterized Philip's approach to literature were his utter lack of parochialism, his refusal to be bamboozled by trends or fashionable currents and, most importantly, his ability to appreciate a work in terms of difficult and complex values which he had laid down for himself and which had nothing to do with anything so meretricious as race or region or competing vogues. If one knew this—as I had after college and postcollege years during which *Partisan Review* was required reading—then to have earned the respect of Philip Rahv was exhilarating. I shudder to think what it must have been to experience Philip's disfavor.

Some years later I got to know Philip very well. Strangers often found it hard to understand how one could become a good friend of this brusque, scowling, saturnine, sometimes impolite man with his crotchets and fixations, his occasional savage outbursts and all the other idiosyncrasies he shared with Dr. Johnson. But I found it easy to be Philip's friend. For one thing, I was able almost constantly to relish his rage, which was a well-earned rage inasmuch as he was an erudite person—learned in the broadest sense of the word, with a far-ranging knowledge that transcended the strictly literary—and thus was supremely competent to sniff out fools. I discovered it to be a cleansing rage, this low, guttural roar directed at the frauds and poseurs of literature. He had, besides, an unerring eye for the opportunists in his own critical profession, where he vented his contempt in equal measure on the "trendy"—a word he virtually coined—and those who were merely windy and inadequate, the pretentious academics who might have had a simple-minded taste for novels but lacked utterly the acquaintance with politics, philosophy and history which was essential to the critical faculty and a civilized perception of things. If any critic had the right to be magisterial, it was Philip Rahv.

But if Philip was angry much of the time, there was beneath it all an affecting and abiding gentleness, a real if biting sense of humor, and throughout, a strange vulnerability. One felt that his arduous grappling with the world of men and ideas had caused him anguish, and that a sense of the disparity between the scrupulous demands of his conscience and vision—whether reflected in literature or life—and the excesses and lunacies of modern society had laid actual hands on him, wrenching him with a discomfort that was nearly intolerable. At the same time, I delighted in his ease and pleasure in preparing good food, in being a host for the men and women he respected and chose to charm. He was often a difficult and prickly soul, at once outgoing yet so secretive as to be almost unknowable. I was proud to be a friend, if only because he was a man who, steadfast to the end, held to those principles and ideas that he felt to be liberating, humane and—Philip, I can almost see you flinch at the word—eternal.

[Speech delivered at Memorial Service, Brandeis University, January 1974]

James Jones

From Here to Eternity was published in 1951 at a time when I was in the process of completing my own first novel. I remember reading *Eternity* while I was living and writing in a country house in Rockland County, not far from New York City, and as has so often been the case with books that have made a large impression on me, I can recall the actual reading—the mood, the excitement, the surroundings. I remember the couch I lay on while reading, the room and the wallpaper, white curtains stirring and flowing in an indolent breeze, and cars that passed on the road outside. I think that perhaps I read portions of the book in other parts of the house but it is that couch I chiefly recollect, and myself sprawled on it, holding the hefty volume aloft in front of my eyes as I remained more or less transfixed through most of the waking hours of several days, in thrall to the story's power, its immediate narrative authority, its vigorously peopled barracks and barrooms, its gutsy humor, and its immense, harrowing sadness. The book was about the unknown world of the peacetime army. Even if I hadn't myself suffered some of the outrages of military life, I'm sure I would have recognized the book's stunning authenticity, its burly artistry, its sheer richness as life. A sense of permanence attached itself to the pages. This remarkable quality did not arise from Jones's language, for it was quickly apparent that the author was not a stylist, certainly not the stylist of refinement and nuance that we former students of creative writing classes had been led to emulate.

The genial rhythms and carefully wrought sentences that English majors had been encouraged to admire were not on display in *Eternity*, nor was the writing even vaguely experimental; it was so conventional as to be premodern. This was doubtless a blessing. For here was a writer whose urgent, blunt language with its off-key tonalities and hulking emphasis on adverbs wholly matched his subject matter. Jones's wretched outcasts and the narrative voice he had summoned to tell their tale had achieved a near-perfect synthesis. What also made the book a triumph was the characters Jones had fashioned—Prewitt, Warden, Maggio, the officers and their wives, the Honolulu whores, the brig rats, and all the rest. There were none of the wan, tentative effigies that had begun to populate the pages of postwar fiction during its brief span, but human beings of real size and arresting presence, believable and hard to forget. The language may have been coarse-grained but it had Dreiserian force, the people were as alive as those of Dostoevski. One other item, somewhat less significant but historic nonetheless, caught my attention, and this was how it had fallen to Jones to make the final breakthrough in terms of vernacular speech which writers—and readers—had been awaiting for hundreds of years. The dread ƒ-word, among several others, so sedulously proscribed by the guardians of decency that even Norman Mailer in his admirable *The Naked and the Dead*, only three years before, had had to fudge the issue with an absurd pseudospelling, was now inscribed on the printed page in the speech pattern of those who normally spoke it. This alone was cause to celebrate, totally aside from the book's incandescent strengths.

It has been said that writers are fiercely jealous of each other. Kurt Vonnegut has observed that most writers display toward one another the edgy mistrust of bears. This may be true, but I do recall that in those years directly following World War II there seemed to be a moratorium on envy, and most of the young writers who were heirs to the Lost Generation developed, for a time at least, a camaraderie, or a reasonable compatibility, as if there were glory enough to go around for all the novelists about to try to fit themselves into Apollonian niches alongside those of the earlier masters. Many of us felt lucky to have survived the war, and the end of the war itself was a convenient point of reckoning, a moment to attempt comparisons. If the Armistice of 1918 had permitted prodigies such as Hemingway, Faulkner, and Fitzgerald to create their collective myth, wouldn't our own war produce a constellation just as passionately committed, as gifted and illustrious? It was a dumb notion (though it often cropped up in book chat), since we had overlooked the inevitable duplicity of history, which would never allow reassembly of those sovereign talents; we would have to settle for the elegant goal of becoming ourselves. But there was tremendous excitement about being a young writer in those days, and of taking part in a shared destiny. When I finished reading *From Here to Eternity* I felt no jealousy at all, only a desire to meet this man, just four years older than myself, who had inflicted on me such emotional turmoil in the act of telling me authentic truths about an underside of American life I barely knew existed. I wanted to talk to the writer who had dealt so eloquently with those lumpen warriors, and who had created scenes that tore at the guts. And then there was that face on the dust jacket, the same face that had glowered at me from bookstore displays and magazine covers and newspaper articles. Was there ever such a face, with its Beethovenesque brow and lantern jaw and stepped-upon-looking nose—a forbidding face until one realized that it only *seemed* to glower, since the eyes really projected a skeptical humor that softened the initial impression of rage. Although, as I later discovered, Jim Jones contained plenty of good clean American rage.

When I first met Jim, during the fall of that year, *Lie Down in Darkness* had recently been published, and we were both subjected to a considerable amount of not unpleasant lionization. Jim was a superlion; his book, after these many months, was still riding high on the best-seller lists. He had achieved that Nirvana which, if I may tell a secret, all writers privately cherish—critical acclaim *and* popular success. My book, on a much more modest level, had also done well critically and commercially, and in fact there was a period of several months during 1951 when still another first novel destined for some durability shared the best-seller list with Jim's and mine—*The Catcher in the Rye*. But Jim's celebrity status was extraordinary, and the nimbus of stardom that attended his presence as we tripped together from party to party around Manhattan was testimony to the appeal of those unforgettable looks but also to something deeper: the work itself, the power of a novel to stir the imagination of countless people as few books had in years. Moving about at night with Jim was like keeping company with a Roman emperor. Indeed I may have been a little envious, but the man had such raw magnetism and took such uncomplicated pleasure in his role as the midwestern hick who was now the cynosure of Big Town attention that I couldn't help being tickled by the commotion he caused, and his glory; he'd certainly earned it. It was a period when whiskey—great quantities of it—was the substance of choice. We did a prodigious amount of drinking, and there were always flocks of girls around, but I soon noticed that the hedonistic whirl had a way of winding down, usually late at night, when Jim, who had seemingly depthless stamina, would head for a secluded corner of a bar and begin speaking about books, about writers and writing. And we'd often talk long after the booze had been shut off and the morning light seeped through the windows.

Jim was serious about fiction in a way that now seems a little old-fashioned and ingenuous, with the novel for him in magisterial reign. He saw it as sacred mission, as icon, as Grail. Like so many American writers of distinction, Jim had not been granted the benison of a formal education, but like these dropouts he had done a vast amount of impassioned and eclectic reading; thus while there were gaps in his literary background that college boys like me had filled (the whole long curriculum of English and American poetry, for instance), he had absorbed an impressive amount of writing for a man whose schoolhouse had been at home or in a barracks. He had been, and still was, a hungry reader, and it was fascinating in those dawn sessions to hear this fellow built like a welterweight boxer (which he had occasionally been) speak in his gravelly drill sergeant's voice about a few of his more recherché loves—Virginia Woolf was one, I recall, Edith Wharton another. I didn't agree with Jim much of the time but I usually found that his tastes and his judgments were, on their own terms, gracefully discriminating and astute. He had stubborn prejudices, though—a blind spot, I thought, about Hemingway. He grudgingly allowed that Hemingway had possessed lyric power in his early stories, but most of his later work he deemed phony to the core. It filled him with that rage I mentioned, and I would watch in wonder as his face darkened with a scowl as grim as Caliban's, and he'd denounce Papa for a despicable fraud and poseur.

It sounded like overkill. Was this some irrational competitive obsession, I wondered, the insecure epigone putting down the master? But I soon realized that in analyzing his judgments about Hemingway I had to set purely literary considerations aside and understand that a fierce and by no means aimless, or envy-inspired, indignation energized Jim's view. Basically, it had to do with men at war. For Jim had been to war, he had been wounded on Guadalcanal, had seen men die, had been sickened and traumatized by the experience. Hemingway had been to war too, and had been wounded, but despite the gloss of misery and disenchantment that overlaid his work, Jim maintained, he was at heart a war lover, a macho contriver of romantic effects, and to all but the gullible and wishful the lie showed glaringly through the fabric of his books and in his life. He therefore had committed the artist's chief sin by betraying the truth.

Jim's opinion of Hemingway, justifiable in its harshness or not, was less significant than what it revealed about his own view of existence, which at its most penetrating—as in *From Here to Eternity* and later in *The Pistol* and *The Thin Red Line*—was always seen through the soldier's eye, in a hallucination where the circumstances of military life cause men to behave mostly like beasts and where human dignity, while welcome and often redemptive, is not the general rule. Jones was among the best anatomists of warfare in our time, and in his bleak, extremely professional vision he continued to insist that war was a congenital and chronic illness from which we would never be fully delivered. War rarely ennobled men and usually degraded them; cowardice and heroism were both celluloid figments, generally interchangeable, and such grandeur as could be salvaged from the mess lay at best in pathos: in the haplessness of men's mental and physical suffering. Living or dying in war had nothing to do with valor, it had to do with luck. Jim had endured very nearly the worst; he had seen death face to face. At least partially as a result of this he was quite secure in his masculinity and better able than anyone else I've known to detect musclebound pretense, empty bravado. It's fortunate that he did not live to witness Rambo, or our high-level infatuation with military violence. It would have brought out the assassin in him.

I went to Europe soon after this and was married, and Jim and I were not in close contact for several years. When we got together again, in New York during the waning 1950s, he too was married, and it was his turn to shove off for Europe, where he settled in Paris, and where he and Gloria remained for the better part of the rest of his life. We saw each other on his frequent trips to the United States, but my visits to Paris were even more frequent during the next fifteen years or so, and it is Paris, nearly always Paris, where I locate Jim when I conjure him up in memory. Year in and year out—sometimes with my wife, Rose, sometimes alone—I came to roost in the Joneses' marvelous lodgings overlooking the Seine, often freeloading (*à l'anglaise*, observed Gloria, who took a dim view of the British) so long that I acquired the status of a semipermanent guest. My clearest and still most splendid image is that of the huge vaulted living room and the ceiling-high doors that gave out onto the river with its hypnotic, incessant flow of barge traffic moving eastward past the stately ecclesiastic rump of Notre Dame. The room was lined with books, and an entire wall was dominated by the nearly one hundred thickly hulking, drably bound volumes of the official

United States government history of the Civil War. The very thought of shipping that library across the Atlantic was numbing. What Jim sometimes called Our Great Fraternal Massacre was his enduring preoccupation, and he had an immense store of knowledge about its politics, strategies, and battles. Somehow in the lofty room the dour Victorian tomes didn't really obtrude, yet they were a vaguely spectral presence and always reminded me how exquisitely *American* Jim was destined to remain during years in Paris. War and its surreal lunacy would be his central obsession to the end, and would also be that aspect of human experience he wrote best about.

Into this beautiful room with its flood of pastel Parisian light, with its sound of Dave Brubeck or Brahms, there would come during the sixties and early seventies a throng of admirable and infamous characters, ordinary and glamorous and weird people—writers and painters and movie stars, starving Algerian poets, drug addicts, Ivy League scholars, junketing United States senators, thieves, jockeys, restaurateurs, big names from the American media (fidgety and morose in their sudden vacuum of anonymity), tycoons and paupers. It was said that even a couple of Japanese tourists made their confused way there, en route to the Louvre. No domicile ever attracted such a steady stream of visitors, no hosts ever extended uncomplainingly so much largess to the deserving and the worthless alike. It was not a rowdy place—Jim was too soldierly to fail to maintain reasonable decorum—but like the Abbey of Thélème of Rabelais, in which visitors were politely bidden to do what they liked, guests in the house at 10, Quai d'Orléans were phenomenally relaxed, sometimes to the extent of causing the Joneses to be victimized by the very waifs they had befriended. A great deal of antique silver disappeared over the years, and someone quite close to Jim once told me they reckoned he had lost tens of thousands of dollars in bad debts to smooth white-collar panhandlers. If generosity can be a benign form of pathology, Jim and Gloria were afflicted by it, and their trustingness extended to their most disreputable servants, who were constantly ripping them off. One, an insolent Pakistani houseman whom Gloria had longed to fire but had hesitated to do so out of tenderheartedness, brought her finally to her senses when she glimpsed him one evening across the floor of a tony nightclub, bewigged and stunningly garbed in one of her newly bought Dior gowns. Episodes like that were commonplace *chez* Jones in the tumultuous sixties.

There were literary journalists of that period who enjoyed pointing to a certain decadence in the Joneses' life-style and wrote reproachful monographs about the way that Jim and Gloria (now parents of two children) comported themselves: dinners at Maxime's, after-dinner with the fat squabs at hang-outs like Castel's, vacations in Deauville and Biarritz, yachting in Greece, the races at Longchamps, the oiled and pampered sloth of Americans in moneyed exile. Much the same had been written about Fitzgerald and Hemingway. The tortured puritanism that causes Americans to mistrust their serious artists and writers, and regards it as appropriate when they are underpaid, evokes even greater mistrust when they are paid rather well and, to boot, hobnob with the Europeans. Material success is still not easily forgiven in a country that ignored Poe and abandoned Melville. There was also the complaint that in moving to France for such a long sojourn Jim Jones had cut off his roots, thus depriving himself of the rich fodder of American experience necessary to produce worthwhile work. But this would seem to be a hollow objection, quite aside from the kind of judgmental chauvinism it expresses. Most writers have stored up, by their mid-twenties, the emotional and intellectual baggage that will supply the needs of their future work, and the various environments into which they settle, while obviously not negligible as sources of material and stimulation, don't really count for all that much. Jim wrote some exceedingly inferior work during his Paris years. *Go to the Widow-Maker*, which dealt mainly with underwater adventure—a chaotic novel of immeasurable length, filled with plywood characters, implausible dialogue, and thick wedges of plain atrocious writing—spun me into despondency when I read it. There were, to be sure, some spectacular underwater scenes and moments of descriptive power almost like the Jones of *Eternity*. But in general the work was a disappointment, lacking both grace and cohesion.

Among the distressing things about it was its coming in the wake of *The Thin Red Line*, a novel of major dimensions whose rigorous integrity and disciplined art allowed Jim once again to exploit the military world he knew so well. Telling the story of GIs in combat in the Pacific, it is squarely in the gritty, no-holds-barred tradition of American realism, a genre that even in 1962, when the book was published, would have seemed oafishly out-of-date had it not been for Jim's mastery of the narrative and his grasp of the sun-baked milieu of bloody island warfare, which exerted such a compelling hold on the reader that he seemed to breathe new life into the form. Romain Gary had commented about the book: "It is essentially an epic love poem about the human predicament and like all great books it leaves one with a feeling of wonder and hope." The rhapsodic note is really not all that overblown; upon rereading, *The Thin Red Line* stands up remarkably well, one of the best novels written about American fighting men in combat. Comparing it, however, with *Go to the Widow-Maker* produced a depressing sense of retrogression and loss. It was like watching a superb diver who, after producing a triple somersault of championship caliber, leaps from the board again and splatters himself all over an empty pool. Jim's nettled response to my hesitantly negative criticism makes me glad that I never expressed my real feelings or my actual chagrin; he might have wanted to strangle me.

But it is important to point out that although *Go to the Widow-Maker* was written in Paris, so was *The Thin Red Line*. This would strongly suggest that the iniquitous life that Jim Jones had reputedly led in Paris, the years of complacent and unengaged exile, bore little relation to his work, and that if he had stayed at home, the motivations that impelled him in a particular literary direction, and that shaped his creative commitments, would probably have remained much the same. Jim loved the good life. He would have richly enjoyed himself anywhere and would have, as always, worked like hell. But a common failing of many writers is that they often choose their themes and address their subject matter as poorly as they often choose wives or houses. What is really significant is that while a book like *Go to the Widow-Maker* represents one of those misshapen artifacts that virtually every good writer, in the sad and lonely misguidedness of his calling, comes up with sooner or later, *The Thin Red Line* is a brilliant example of what happens when a novelist summons strength from the deepest wellsprings of his inspiration. In this book, along with *From Here to Eternity* and *Whistle*—a work of many powerful scenes that suffered from the fact that he was dying as he tried, unsuccessfully, to finish it—Jim obeyed his better instincts by attending to that forlorn figure whom in all the world he cared for most and understood better than any other writer alive: the common foot soldier, the grungy enlisted man.

Romain Gary wasn't too far off. There was a certain grandeur in Jones's vision of the soldier. Other writers had written of outcasts in a way that had rendered one godforsaken group or another into archetypes of suffering—Dickens's underworld, Zola's whores, Jean Genet's thieves, Steinbeck's migrant workers, Agee's white Southern sharecroppers, Richard Wright's black Southern immigrants, on and on—the list is honorable and long. Jones's soldiers were at the end of an ancestral line of fictional characters who are misfits, the misbegotten who always get the short end of the stick. But they never dissolved into a social or political blur. The individuality that he gave to his people, and the stature he endowed them with, came, I believe, from a clear-eyed view of their humanness, which included their ugliness or meanness. Sympathetic as he was to his enlisted men, he never lowered himself to the temptations of an agitprop that would limn them as mere victims. Many of his soldiers were creeps, others were outright swine, and there were enough good guys among the officers to be consonant with reality. At least part of the reason he was able to pull all this off so successfully, without illusions or sentimentality, was his sense of history, along with his familiarity with the chronicles of war that were embedded in world literature. He had read Thucydides early, and he once commented to me that no one could write well about warfare without him. He'd also linked his own emotions with those of Tolstoy's peasant soldiers, and could recite a substantial amount of *Henry V,* whose yeoman-warriors were right up his alley. But the shades of the departed with whom he most closely identified were the martyrs of the American Civil War. That pitiless and aching slaughter, which included some of his forebears, haunted him throughout his life and provided one of the chief goads to his imagination. To be a Civil War buff was not to be an admirer of the technology of battle, although campaign strategy fascinated him; it was to try to plumb the mystery and the folly of war itself.

In 1962, during one of his visits to America, I traveled with Jim to Washington. Among other things, an influential official with whom I was friendly and who was on President Kennedy's staff had invited the two of us to take a special tour of the White House. Oddly, for such a well-traveled person, Jim had never been to Washington, and the trip offered him a chance to visit the nearby battlefields. He had never seen any of the Civil War encampments. Jim went out to Antietam, in Maryland, after which we planned to go to the Lincoln Memorial before driving over to the White House. When he met me at our hotel, just after the Antietam visit, Jim was exceptionally somber. Something at the battlefield had resonated in a special troubling way within him; he seemed abstracted and out-of-sorts. It had been, he told me finally, a part of the battleground called the Bloody Lane that had so affected him when he'd seen it.

He'd read so much about the sector and the engagement and had always wondered how the terrain would appear when he viewed it firsthand. A rather innocuous-looking place now, he said, a mere declivity in the landscape, sheltered by a few trees. But there, almost exactly a century before, some of the most horrible carnage in the history of warfare had taken place, thousands of men on both sides dead within a few hours. The awful shambles was serene now, but the ghosts were still there, swarming; it had shaken him up.

Soon after this, at the Lincoln Memorial, I realized that the cavernous vault with its hushed and austere shadows, its soft footfalls and requiem whispers, might not have been the best place to take a man in such a delicate mood. Jim's face was set like a slab, his expression murky and aggrieved, as we stood on the marble reading the Gettysburg Address engraved against one lofty wall, slowly scanning those words of supreme magnanimity and conciliation and brotherhood dreamed by the fellow Illinoisian whom Jim had venerated, as almost everyone does, for transcendental reasons that needed not to be analyzed or explained in such a sacred hall. I suppose I was expecting the conventional response from Jim, the pious hum. But his reaction, soft-spoken, was loaded with savage bitterness, and for an instant it was hard to absorb. "It's just beautiful bullshit," he blurted. "They all died in vain. They all died in vain. And they always will!" His eyes were moist with fury and grief; we left abruptly, and it required some minutes of emotional readjustment before the storm had blown over and he regained his composure, apologizing quickly, then returning with good cheer and jokes to more normal concerns.

Many years went by before I happened to reflect on that day, and to consider this: that in the secret cellars of the White House, in whose corridors we were soon being shepherded around pleasantly, the ancient mischief was newly germinating. There were doubtless all sorts of precursory activities taking place which someday would confirm Jim's fierce prophecy: heavy cable traffic to Saigon, directives beefing up advisory and support groups, ominous memos on Diem and the Nhus, orders to units of the Green Berets. The shadow of Antietam, and of all those other blind upheavals, was falling on our own times. James Jones would be the last to be surprised.

[Introduction to *To Reach Eternity: The Letters of James Jones*,
New York: Random House, Inc., 1989]

Bennett Cerf

BENNETT MIGHT HAVE APPRECIATED the fact that several years ago two of his Random House writers, Philip Roth and myself, walked along a beach in East Hampton loftily pigeonholing people into three categories: the well poisoners, the lawn mowers (these are most of the people) and the life-enhancers. Needless to say, Bennett belonged to that rare and precious species called the life-enhancers, of which humankind has so much need. Being a life-enhancer, he invigorated and replenished the world he lived in, leaving the people with whom he came in touch exhilarated by his presence. The vital force in Bennett was so powerful, so seemingly indomitable, that he appeared virtually deathless, and perhaps that is one of the reasons that his passing causes us this dismay we feel. I recall one night some years ago flying on a plane with Bennett through a dark, lovely, star-crowded sky over Pennsylvania. The clear light of the cities below seemed to merge with the glittering stars, creating a wonderful radiant effect that touched us both deeply. Suddenly Bennett turned to me and said something which in another man might seem odd or even slightly bizarre but which in Bennett expressed his own quintessence. "Ah, Bill," he exclaimed, "I love being alive so much!" Perhaps this explains why he was both so rare and so valuable. Loving life with that unquenchable love of his, he imparted the very spirit of life to others—that buoyant, generous, inimitably vivacious spirit that became apparent the instant he entered a room and that no one who knew him will ever forget. He adored jokes, of course, and I think he might have appreciated it had I tried to make one up for this occasion. At the moment my own sense of loss is too keen, although I am consoled by the thought that there will come a time when memory will permit us all to re-experience, without grief, the warmth and the good cheer that were bestowed upon us by this immeasurably loving, life-enhancing man.

[Speech delivered at Memorial Service, St. Paul's Chapel,
Columbia University, August 1971]

François Mitterrand

A TRUTH WORTH REPEATING is that the quality of being intellectual does not guarantee excellence, or even competence, in a political leader. Nonetheless, it would be hypocrisy to say that, in their secret hearts, intellectuals do not wish to see authentic members of their kind ascend to seats of power. With what passion the souls of thinking men and women were stirred when John F. Kennedy became president. Kennedy, of course, was no intellectual; but he was the first American president in many years to give the impression that a book was not an alien object. Also, in fairness to the Kennedy image, which has become much tarnished in recent years, it has to be said that at least he had a touching and—for a president—perhaps unique concern for what intellectuals thought of him. During one of the two conversations I had with Kennedy he was gloomily preoccupied, and clearly much hurt, because Alfred Kazin, in an *American Scholar* article, had belittled his pretensions to a place among the intelligentsia. With real pain, like a jilted lover, he spoke of Kazin and while his somewhat callow discomfiture if anything helped validate Kazin's conclusions, it also revealed to the writer in his presence something quite appealing about the Kennedy sensibility. A president fussing about the animadversions of a literary critic: after the Eisenhower doldrums, it was fresh and a little amazing.

It was not publicized that, on the day after his inaugural, one of François Mitterrand's first official acts was to grant citizenship to Julio Cortázar of Argentina and Milan Kundera of Czechoslovakia, two exiled writers who had long and vainly petitioned the preceding administration for the right to become Frenchmen. Mitterrand's act was both symbolic and fraternal—the gesture of a politician who is also both an intellectual and a literary man. Mitterrand would doubtless object to the latter designation for, as he tells us in his remarkable book *The Wheat and the Chaff*, he always insists upon being called a politician, preferring action to words.

Yet, one feels a certain lack of commitment in this—at the very least an ambivalence—for although he says, "I could never have been an imaginative writer," he immediately adds: "I observe—and I write. I like the written word. Language, philology, grammar. I believe that real literature is born from the exact correspondence of word and thing. I was brought up in that classical school where essays in French and recitations in Latin taught me the proper order and cadence of words and phrases." This concern with literary style is very much in evidence in *The Wheat and the Chaff*, which is a free-flowing account of Mitterrand's life and thought during most of the years of the 1970s. Mitterrand calls the book a hybrid, neither diary nor chronicle; but if so it is a hybrid in other interesting ways.

Written in the days when the idea of a Socialist victory in France was a daydream, the book is in part an underdog's view of contemporary events and at the same time a blueprint for Socialist action. These passages are deft, abrasive, resolute, and (one realizes with something akin to shock) prophetic. An uncanny feeling comes over one with reflection that such matters as the nationalization of commerce—an ideal which, when Mitterrand was brooding on it, must have seemed millennial in its improbability—have begun quietly to be realized. But if the book were a mere political document it would, I suspect, despite the admirable contours of the writing, appear dated already, and could not possibly seize our attention.

What distinguishes the work, and makes it the exciting "hybrid" it is, is precisely that multifaceted literary gift that Mitterrand deprecates in himself, but which makes page after page spring into vivid life. Mitterrand may not be an "imaginative writer," but among the attractions of his book—removing it light-years from the lackluster volumes of most of the world's politicians—is the way in which so much that is observed seems filtered through the sensibility of a first-rate novelist. Whether it is nature that he is writing about, or his basset hound Titus, or encounters with such figures as Mao Tse-tung or Golda Meir or Pablo Neruda, Mitterrand has the good novelist's knack of looking past the obvious for the immanent, the particular, the revealing detail. It is relatively rare, in the writing of politicians, to experience colors and smells and the actual presence of human flesh; thus how refreshing it is to come upon this description of Mao in 1961: ". . . of medium height, wearing a gray

Sun Yat-sen uniform, with one shoulder lower than the other, slow of step, his face round and seemingly quite at peace, short of breath and soft of voice . . . his small, well-manicured hands, his laugh . . . the serenity that pervaded the room. By comparison what a bunch of marionettes our Western dictators are, with their flashy uniforms, their strident voices, their theatricality."

As one who aspired to the presidency, Mitterrand has been perhaps more than normally fascinated by power and those who wield it. His long-time position as First Secretary of the French Socialist Party allowed him propinquity to the movers and shakers of his time—both at home and abroad—and some of the most engaging passages of the book are those having to do with these figures. It must be painfully difficult for any political leader to write without rancor about his rivals, past or present, especially after years of defeat, near-misses, and repeated disappointments. It is all the more impressive, therefore, to view the large-hearted fairness with which Mitterrand treats the character and career of two whose ideals he has the most strenuously opposed: de Gaulle and Malraux. To feel a certain irony in Mitterrand's retrospective treatment of his predecessor is nonetheless to admire the civilized restraint he employed in his analysis of Gaullism, as well as the sympathy he displays for the General's faults, even extending to his chauvinism and megalomania. These Mitterrand can understand even when he cannot condone. Hating de Gaulle's ideas or, as he implies, lack of them, he can still respect the man for some ineluctable historical presence.

His experience in the Resistance during the war was plainly a pivotal perception in Mitterrand's life—just as the war, in a different way, was crucial to de Gaulle's. Mitterrand is able to vibrate sympathetically to certain aspects of de Gaulle's personality because of this shared experience; one feels that Mitterrand's love of France is as passionate as that of the General's, though mercifully shorn of its mysticism. "I live France," Mitterrand writes. "I have a deep instinctive awareness of France, of physical France, and a passion for her geography, her living body. There is no need for me to seek the soul of France—it lives in me." One feels no chauvinistic fever in these honest lines.

Again, Mitterrand's treatment of Malraux is a measure of his magnanimity and amplitude of vision. (Even as I write these words I am brought up short by the improbable idea of presidential concern with a novelist: imagine Ronald Reagan in serious meditation about the career of even so public a writer as Hemingway!) However, lest it be construed that Mitterrand is possessed of angelic forbearance, it must be said that his intellectual judgments can be as tough as rawhide. For Malraux's poorer work he has nothing but distaste, just as he loathes the grandiose posturing of his "official" life. But—having uttered his scathing observations—how warmhearted he is when, shortly after Malraux's death, he finds himself assessing that long, contradictory, and complex career. His final tribute to this man is a fine example of the generosity that seems to animate Mitterrand's private and political life. Even his detailed response to the character and vocation of Georges Pompidou, for whom he has almost unbounded contempt, is shot through with a rueful compassion. One keeps marveling at the sheer *patience* Mitterrand exhibits during these years of disappointment and waiting.

I was among several writers invited to Mitterrand's inaugural in May of 1981. After lunch on that day, as we stood in a small informal group in the bright springtime garden of the Elysée Palace, Mitterrand spoke of America. He spoke of it, I felt, with something of a feeling of mystery, alluding to it as that "vast continent, quite incomprehensible." Mitterrand has been an indefatigable traveler; America has become a frequent way station on his itinerary during recent years. Some of that same incomprehensibility and mystery which he mentioned to us will be found in this book, along with his sense of ever-renewed wonder. He has an undisguised fondness for the United States, and even in 1972—haunted by the awareness of our bombers then devastating Vietnam—he could meditate with eloquence on the land and its destiny. Like all sensible Europeans, he seems to temper his fondness with profound unease over our perpetually alarming foreign policy; but even here there is a certain philosophical patience in his point of view—his description of a long conversation with Henry Kissinger in 1975 is fascinating, both in its scope of exchanged ideas and in the sympathy (or at least lack of acrimoniousness) brought to bear on his portrayal of a statesman opposed to nearly everything socialism stands for. (In an earlier passage Mitterrand notes the appalling irony inherent in the award to Kissinger of the Nobel Peace prize; even then, however, one feels Mitterrand's justified animus is directed more against official idiocy on the part of the bestowers than against Kissinger.)

Mostly, one cannot help being beguiled by Mitterrand's reflections on the United States: perplexed and troubled, one feels, by America's collective mind, wryly aware of the mediocrity of its political leaders (Ronald Reagan, not yet elected president, has received his reputation "thanks to the qualities he revealed in the exercise of his profession as television master of ceremonies, and has seduced the old machine that produced Lincoln"), Mitterrand still regards us with affection and hope. From near the top of Rockefeller Center he notes a flight of mallard ducks ascend from the East River; in the midst of this "poetic geometry" of the city which so moves him, the wild birds are a reaffirmation of the natural order of things, even here.

There are certain passages in *The Wheat and the Chaff* that will perhaps appear less compelling to the American reader than those that I have just described. Those having to do with the aspirations and programs of the Socialist Party during the 1970's, and Mitterrand's own musings upon certain current events, may now lack the urgency they once had. But the same could be declared, let us say, for some of the meditations of George McGovern or Adlai Stevenson on the policies in their times of the Democratic Party. What finally gives this book its extraordinary savor is the range of curiosity of its author, its mirror-bright reflections on people and places, its often intense feeling for nature, and its ubiquitous and passionate concern for the destiny of human beings in a calamitous century.

In saying this I do not want to minimize Mitterrand's justifiable preoccupation with Socialist principles, which everywhere energizes the book and is, after all, the prime reason for its being. About socialism, Mitterrand is passionate, but at the same time unpretentious. He is wary of Socialist dogma, which he sees as being as potentially dangerous as any other dogma.

"Socialism does not represent values that are superior to the humble truth of facts," he writes. "Nor yet does it constitute truth in itself. It argues, seeks, approximates. It knocks down idols and taboos." Which is as modest, eloquent, and appealing a description of a political ideal as one could imagine. But as I say, *The Wheat and the Chaff* is anything but a tract. In it the play of intellect and the range of curiosity and interest constantly fascinate. Is it an ingenuous reaction on my part—the reflex of an American anaesthetized by contemplation of one chief magistrate after another who more or less thinks and looks like Gerald Ford—that I have to pinch myself from time to time to realize that the president of a great nation has written this book? Perhaps so; perhaps such a connection is in the end of little importance. Nevertheless, it is a happy surprise to come across Mitterrand's sardonic reflections on certain bizarre funeral rites beginning to be practiced in France (and imported from the USA), and his gleeful scorn modulating beautifully into this final conclusion: "A society which hides death from the eyes of the living . . . is not magnifying life but corrupting it. Birth and death are the two wings of time. How can man's spiritual search come to fulfillment if he ignores these dimensions?"

The sensibility that produced such lines is rare not alone in a politician but in anyone, and this is what helps give *The Wheat and the Chaff* its commanding vigor. It is to be expected that a man whom nature touches so poignantly, and who writes about natural things with such sensitivity and affection, should express a constant concern with the environment and the proliferation of ecological blights and horrors. But even so delicately attuned a person as Mitterrand can hardly claim to be alone in these perennial anxieties. The superb moments in the book come when the thoughts of the political creature and those of the artist (I do not think that too extravagant a word) merge together, creating insights which it may be of critical importance for the present-day reader to attend to. I am thinking not only of Mitterrand's loving appreciations of two poets who were also his friends—Theodorakis and St. John Perse—but in particular of his description of Pablo Neruda, old and dying, his own agony refracted in the murder of Salvador Allende and the terrible betrayal of Chile. It was none other than Neruda, Mitterrand tells us, who urged him to read for the first time Gabriel García Marquez's *One Hundred Years of Solitude*, that dark yet dazzling masterpiece whose pages open up so many doors of perception about Latin America and its prodigious destiny. Mitterrand remains haunted by the book, and throughout his own work there is a concern with Latin America—especially the outrages perpetrated there—that amounts almost to an obsession. But what a splendid obsession! As much an outsider to that world as, say, Alexander Haig, Mitterrand has acquired touchstones to the secrets of our southern hemisphere that may transcend the brute demands of *Realpolitik*. Neruda. Gabriel García Márquez and the tragic village of Macondo. How exhilarating it is to discover a man of politics gleaning new insights from these poetic visions. It may be naive, as I implied at the outset, to think that the world can be saved by men who respond with passion to these visions. But I for one feel cleansed, at least briefly, by the notion of such grace and tenderness dwelling together with the exigencies of power.

[Introduction to *The Wheat and the Chaff*, New York: Seaver, 1982]

LOOKING
BACK

Christchurch

Iɴ ᴅᴇᴄᴇᴍʙᴇʀ of the second of my two years at Christchurch, there occurred an event which would decisively alter my life and the lives of my friends here at school and indeed people everywhere. On that day—it was a mild and golden and cloudless Sunday—I had taken illegal leave of the campus and had gone on a gently beer-soaked automobile ride through this incomparable Virginia countryside, which was beautifully forlorn and wild-looking in those days. It was a wintry, leafless afternoon—very bright, as I say—with no hint in it of menace. My companions on the ride that afternoon were a classmate named Bill Bowman and two girls from Urbanna, who even at this late date shall remain nameless. Bowman, besides being a year older than I was, was a native of New York City, and thus I trusted him in sophisticated matters, such as beer. The beer we were drinking out of brown bottles, purchased stealthily the day before at Cooks' Corners, was a vile concoction called Atlantic, so crudely brewed that gobbets of yeast floated in it like snowflakes. I earnestly hope it is no longer being manufactured. At any rate, our car and its occupants finally ended up down the road in West Point where, inhaling the sweet fumes of the papermill's hydrogen sulfide (intense and ripe even on the Sabbath), we dismounted at a seedy little café for hamburgers. It was while we were in this dive, eating hamburgers and surreptitiously swilling the foul Atlantic, that the waitress came to the table and announced the perplexing and rather horrible radio news. I'll never forget her homely face, which was like a slab of pale pine with two small holes bored in it, nor her voice, which had all the sad languor of the upper Pamunkey River. "The Japanese," she said, "they done bombed Pearl Harbor." Her expression contained a certain real fear. "God help us," she went on, "it's so close. Imagine them gettin' all the way to South Carolina."

That woman's knowledge of geography was only a little less informed than our own, and the next day—as we sat in study hall listening to the radio and President Roosevelt's call for a declaration of war against the Axis powers—few of us sitting there could realize how irrevocably things would be changed—for us and the world—and how all of our lives thenceforth would be in one way or another determined by the existence of war.

I would not be so fatuous as to say that when I was here all was perfect bliss, that in this garden of earthly delights high above the Rappahannock a scuffed toe would not have uncovered a toad or two. But of all the schools I attended, including the three institutions of higher learning I went to subsequently in the South and North, only Christchurch ever commanded something more than mere respect—which is to say, my true and abiding affection. I think that much of the warmth and sweetness I felt and still feel for Christchurch has to do with the fact that when I was a student the place was very small and resembled a family—a sometimes tumultuous and quarrelsome, always nearly destitute but at the same time close-knit and loyal family. There were, I believe, only fifty-odd boys. We were poor. The school was poor. Many schools at the end of the Depression were poor, but the threadbare nature of Christchurch was almost Dickensian in its pathos. The library, for instance. At sixteen, I had a natural inclination for geography and I loved to pore over maps, but in the library there was only one geography book. It was not a *bad* atlas, had it been left undamaged, but it had been divested of Africa and all of Eastern Europe—something which to this day has produced significant gaps in my knowledge of the earth. The works of American literature stopped with Jack London—no Hemingway, no Fitzgerald, no Thomas Wolfe, no Theodore Dreiser; in compensation, we had that laudable work *Tom Sawyer*, but even this boy's classic palled upon perhaps the fifth reading. The *Encyclopaedia Britannica* was of such antique vintage that its information in the technological sphere alone ceased, I remember, with the invention of the telegraph and the diving bell. The pride of the entire library was a complete twenty-volume Shakespeare, but at least three volumes had been left out in the rain and the pages were stuck together, while someone else had stolen both *King Lear* and *Richard III*. Despite all this deprivation, I managed to get educated enough to pass on to college and acquit myself with at least passable honor. Our masters, good-natured and hideously underpaid drudges who possessed nonetheless high ideals and admirable patience, dispensed as much learning as was within their power. I still salute them in memory. When out of sheer exhaustion the teachers flagged and stumbled, the brotherly familylike nature of the school allowed us to teach each other. My classmate Tommy Peyton taught me all the trigonometry I ever knew. Langley Wood tutored me in chemistry, also about the girls in Richmond. It was in Jimmy Davenport's late-evening seminar that I learned how to beat the dealer at blackjack.

In later years, after leaving Christchurch and college, I became the good friend of several of those who had attended the great preparatory schools of New England. In all truth, it must be said that the potential for a good early education must have been somewhat larger at these richly endowed schools, with their splendid libraries and other resources, than it was at Christchurch; but I emphasize that word "potential" in the realization that at Christchurch, for those of us who had the determination—and most of us did—it was possible to overcome the handicaps and obtain an excellent preparation for college while in the process having a good time. Most of my friends who went to those venerable Northern institutions with names like Andover and St. Paul's did *not* seem to have a good time; so often their descriptions of school life are bleak, cold, impersonal, resembling a bearable but monotonous servitude rewarded later by glorious times at Princeton or Yale. At Christchurch I remember we worked as hard as anyone else to get our learning, but we also enjoyed ourselves. And I say that with memory uncontaminated by false nostalgia. Nothing warms my heart more than the recollection of those little sloops we sailed down on this matchless river. Certainly there are few schools in America that have proximity and access to a waterway of such magnificence. It mattered little to us that some of the boats were ancient and badly caulked and waterlogged and had been known with some frequency to sink sedately beneath the waves, even in the middle of a race; they were *our* boats and we loved them. Sailing, like the other sports, gave us ravenous appetites, and this leads to another obvious delight: the always tenderly prepared meals of Mr. Joseph Cameron, who of course is now an almost global legend. Could anything be more incongruous, more preposterous than the idea of any institution of learning where the food was consistently palatable and often superb? While my Ivy League friends still complain thinly and bitterly of soggy Swiss steaks and glutinous mashed potatoes, I recall cheese biscuits and pastries and delicately grilled fish, fresh from the river or the bay, which would have caused a French chef to salivate with envy. Christchurch may not have been in those days a well-heeled place, but it had a warm and golden ambience, and life was sweet, and we ate like kings.

[From Commencement Address at Christchurch School, May 24, 1974]

The James

I N THE EARLY 1940s, despite my mediocre record at Christchurch
School, my father set about to find a place where I might con-
summate my higher education. My wretched grades at Christchurch
—by that I mean I had, I recall, flunked trigonometry four times
in a row—made a scholarship anywhere out of the question, and
since my father was paying the ticket, he felt (with great justification, I now realize) that he could determine the school I was
going to attend. Anyplace north of the Potomac was unthinkable,
since although my father was not really an unreconstructed Southerner (having married my mother, a lady from Pennsylvania), he
was born in North Carolina only twenty-odd years after the Civil
War; until his dying day his own father, my grandfather, limped
from a knee wound obtained at Chancellorsville, and thus his mistrust of Yankee education was abiding and considerable. He resolved, then, that I should enroll in a college either in his native
state or in Virginia, which was mine. Any institution farther south
he regarded as primitive, and totally unfit for a lad of my ancestry
and upbringing.

He narrowed the choices down. The University of Virginia,
the most obvious option, was immediately cast aside; its reputation
in regard to alcohol was more horrendous then than it is now;
there were freshmen there, he had heard on good authority, who
had been apprehended wandering the streets of Charlottesville in
the throes of *delirium tremens*, and since my father sensed my own
incipient predilection for the bottle, he was not about to throw me
into the lion's den. Then there was William & Mary. So close at
hand to my hometown, William & Mary seemed another obvious
choice. But the school was eliminated on the grounds of what he

called intellectual vacuity—a condition which had prevailed there ever since the founding of Phi Beta Kappa in 1776. Likewise, Washington & Lee was rejected. He found the place effete and frivolous, lacking in depth of concern for the examined life, and with some reason: after a brief visit to Lexington, he was profoundly offended by the hundreds of uniform seersucker suits and white buckskin shoes. He called them "Lightweights!" Finally, then, my father and I traveled up here to Hampden-Sydney, whose Presbyterianism and strictures about alcohol my father regarded happily. I hope you will not take it as all loose flattery when I say that I was so totally beguiled by this serene and lovely campus (it remains so, I'm happy to say, to this very day) and by the splendid easygoingness of the place, and by so much else in the human sense that was wonderfully attractive, that I said to myself: This is where I want to be. My father, I could tell, was also not immune to the charms of the school, physical and otherwise; but he was even more of a pushover for honorifics (it was one of his venial sins), and when he was informed that this venerable institution had contributed, on a per capita basis, more biographic subjects to *Who's Who in America* than any college in the country, he had all but had me enrolled. But soon after this, fate intervened—fate in the form of those four consecutive Fs at Christchurch. To my intense disappointment I was turned down, and so I went to another Presbyterian college—Davidson, in North Carolina, which inexplicably overlooked my academic shortcomings and gained the indifferent student that Hampden-Sydney had prudently shunned. I was not a good scholar at Davidson either.

A short time ago, while brooding on this melancholy tale, I was naturally led into thoughts of Virginia. Despite my longtime residence in the North, my native state still compels a strong hold on me. If it is true that an artist's world is largely determined by the experiences of the first two decades of his life, and this is a theory held by Sigmund Freud, Ernest Hemingway and myself, then the Virginia which I so vividly and poignantly recall from my early years worked on me a lasting effect, made me in large measure the writer that I am. And so, as I cast about for a theme which might be appropriate to talk about, I hesitated, wondering if the simplicity of the idea that struck me might not, in its very simplicity, be inadequate. On the other hand, what I had in mind did seem to represent something profoundly important, even critical, in its significance not only for Virginia but for the future and the quality of all our lives.

I am speaking of a river, one that flows less than forty miles north of here. A nearby stream, the Appomattox, is its tributary, familiar to all of you. I am referring, of course, to the James. To the north, as it winds through Buckingham and Albemarle counties, and past the old plantation of Bremo in Fluvanna, the James is a modest and pleasant stream, a mere trickle of an unfledged watercourse meandering through the Piedmont. But down on the east bank of the lower Peninsula, where I was born and reared, the river is nearly six miles across at its widest, a vast and lonely expanse that makes up one of the broadest estuaries of any river in America. More than anything else, the James River was the absolute and dominating physical presence of my childhood and early youth. As I envision how a child growing up on the flanks of the Rockies or Sierras must ever afterward be enthralled to the memory of mountain peaks, or as I recollect how a writer like Willa Cather, brought up on the Nebraska prairies, was haunted for life by that majestically unending "sea of grass," so for me the sheer geographical fact of the James was central to my experience, so much a part of me that even now I wonder whether some of that salty-sweet water might not have entered my bloodstream. A good deal of this, of course, had to do with the omnipresent spell of the river's prodigious history. No river in America was ever compelled to carry such an onerous burden, and we little tykes were never allowed to forget it as we sat in our classrooms overlooking the sovereign waterway itself, informed by one schoolmarm after another that yonder—just there!—Captain John Smith sailed past on his momentous journey, while just there, too, in 1619, another ship lumbered upstream with a different cargo to make the James the mother-river of Negro slavery for the whole New World. And nearby were the great river mansions—Carter's Grove, Westover, Shirley—populated with ghosts of bygone centuries.

But if the James was the past, that past coexisted with the present—and what a vital present that was! Winter, summer, spring and fall—the river was rarely out of my sight; its presence subtly intruded on all my other senses. When I woke up on spring mornings the first thing I smelled was the river's brackish odor on the wind, a rich mingling of salt and seaweed and tidal mud, of organic matter in benign dissolution. There was the music of the river, too, diurnal sounds which wove themselves into the very fabric of village life—the cry of gulls; waves thrusting, lapping; the flapping of sails as they luffed at the pier; boat horns; and always the sing-song voice of Negro oystermen as they labored above their tongs. We swam in the river from April until October; the water—partly fresh, partly oceanic—was faintly saline on the tongue, and in July it was as warm as mother's milk, and just as reassuring. The salinity, of course, accounted for the quality of the oysters; cousins to the Lynnhaven variety, they were the size of small saucers and utterly luscious to swallow; and then there were crabs. The crabs were not simply abundant; they existed in such flabbergasting profusion as to seem almost menacing. In midsummer we netted swarms of them with absurd ease from the village pier, using hunks of gamy meat for bait. When I was eleven or twelve I was a soft-shell-crab businessman; the delicious little creatures were so numerous in the mudflats of low tide that I could fill a market basket in less than an hour and then peddle these—layered with fragrant seaweed— at the back doors of the village houses, where the ladies grumbled at my exorbitant price: three cents apiece, an inflationary penny more than the previous year. I loved this big, fecund, blowsy, beautiful, erotic river. It was erotic, and I achieved with it a penultimate intimacy by nearly drowning in it in my thirteenth year, when the little boat in which I was learning to sail capsized and sank. Still, I loved the James, and in memory its summertime shores are tangled with all that piercing delight of youthful ro-mance; recollecting the moonlight in huge quicksilver oblongs on those dark waters, and the drugstore perfume of gardenia, and boys' and girls' voices. I no longer wonder why the river had such a lasting effect on my spirit, becoming almost in itself a metaphor for the painful sweetness of life and its mystery.

[From Commencement Address at Hampden-Sydney College,
May 23, 1980]

Almost a Rhodes Scholar

IN THE WINTER OF 1947 it appeared that I was on my way to becoming a Rhodes scholar. During the period after World War II when I went back to continue my studies at Duke University, I had applied myself with considerable passion to what was then, as now, known—I think unhappily—as "creative writing," and it became about the only academic discipline in which there was descried that I had any talent at all. However, my promise was such that my late teacher, Professor William Blackburn—God bless him—determined that it might be a good idea to apply for a Rhodes scholarship on the basis of my writing ability. I was a graduating senior, an English major, impoverished, with nothing much looming on the horizon in the way of a livelihood after my midyear graduation a month or so hence. Professor Blackburn—who had himself been a Rhodes scholar—was, like most Rhodes scholars, an ardent Anglomaniac, and was able to beguile me with visions of all the delights that a year or two at Oxford might offer: studying Old Norse and Middle English in the damp and drafty rooms at Merton College—a place which, he said, one grew fond of; reading Keats and Hardy under the tutelage of Edmund Blunden; drinking sherry and eating scones, or picnicking on plovers' eggs and champagne, as the pale lads did in novels by Aldous Huxley; having one's own fag—whatever that meant; going *down* to London for weekends; enjoying summer vacations in Normandy or boating along the Rhine. Another attraction: one would be paid a reasonable stipend. Whatever its defects (and I could not see many), it mostly sounded perfectly wonderful, and so I was quite acquiescent when Professor Blackburn urged me to try out for the preliminary competition—that of the state of North Carolina, held in Chapel Hill. I was a little apprehensive; my grades had not really been outstanding throughout my academic career, and I had been under the impression that "Rhodes scholarship" and "outstanding" were virtually synonymous. No matter, said Professor Blackburn; the new policy of the Rhodes selections placed much less emphasis on scholarly achievement than previously; candidates were beginning to be chosen far more for their promise as creative talents, and therefore I stood a very good chance. Well, it turned out that he was right. I submitted the manuscripts of several short stories. To my astonishment, out of a field of more than twenty I was one of *two* students to win the competition from North Carolina. The field had been loaded with hotshots, too: straight-A scholars from Davidson and Chapel Hill, an accredited genius from Wake Forest, a magnificently proficient German linguist from Duke. What a heady and vainglorious triumph I felt—and what a victory it was for the creative spirit! I was so exhilarated that day when I heard the good news that many hours passed before sober reflection set in, and I began to wonder just how much of my success had been determined by the fact that Professor Blackburn, my beloved and idealistic mentor, had been chairman of the selection committee. Anyway . . .

The regional competition for the Southeastern states was held a few days later here in Atlanta—indeed, within the very bowels of this hotel where we are all meeting. I was twenty years old and the trip marked several "firsts" for me. The era of air travel, for instance, had not then really arrived in all of its dynamic and stupendous actuality; it was not yet really part of the matrix of our national existence. I had flown several times on military planes in the Marine Corps, but my trip to Atlanta from Durham was my first experience with a commercial aircraft. It was an Eastern DC-3, and I got slightly airsick, though my malaise may have been compounded by the truly visceral excitement which now agitated my every waking hour; I was racked with visions of Oxford in the mists of fall, of pubs and golden yards of foaming ale, of pretty Scottish lasses with that weather-rouged flush on their creamy cheeks, and of myself, winning my honors with a thrilling exegesis of *The Faerie Queene*. But then—Atlanta! Down through the clouds our plane made its descent. And here was an airport—imagine!—about the size of the Greyhound bus station in Goldsboro, North Carolina, and then, a leisurely, halting taxi drive by way of a bumpy two-lane highway through a sleepy Southern city where Peachtree Street was thronged with Negro vendors and the air was still haunted by the ghosts of Sherman's departed legions, and finally, the Atlanta Biltmore, its lobby filled with potted palms, cuspidors and salesmen from as far away as Moultrie and Al-benny.

There was also something intangibly sinister about the place—something that troubled me even as I went through the check-in proceedings—until at last I realized what the problem was: behind nearly every potted palm, at every portal and exit, there lurked a uniformed fireman. I hope that my memory of this detail does not cast a shadow over the present assembly, but the fire alert was due to a terrible catastrophe that had struck Atlanta only a week before my arrival. In one of the worst fires in Atlanta history—and the greatest conflagration in Georgia since the burning of Atlanta in 1864—the Hotel Winecoff, only a few blocks away, had been destroyed, with the loss of over a hundred lives. The presence at the Biltmore of all this fire-fighting muscle caused me to seek for a striking metaphor, but I had to settle for the homely and rather imperfect one of the barn door being shut after the horse has run away; so many firemen *should* have allayed certain basic anxieties about nocturnal safety (I'm not exaggerating too much when I say that there seemed to be firemen enough around for one to spend the night with each and every guest), but their presence inexplicably made me *more* nervous, and that night I went to bed in a deep unease, worrying about my interview the next day, and waking hourly to the smell of imagined combustion.

The next day—the day of the interviews—was nearly interminable, lasting, I recall, from very early in the morning until eight or nine in the evening. During those long hours I had time to sit and fret miserably on one of the couches on the Biltmore mezzanine, to read, to chat with a few of my thirty or so competitors, and in doing so, to take stock of my chances. I felt profoundly intimidated. These young men comprised the intellectual elite—no, the super-elite—of all the colleges and universities of the Southeast; they possessed, I was certain, staggeringly high IQs, had burnt countless gallons of midnight oil to achieve scholastic mastery. They were, in short, the flower of their generation, and win or lose, I was proud to be counted among them. Hooray for Cecil Rhodes! Hooray for Oxford! I thought. The hours dragged on. Even in some of the darkest trials of my officer candidacy in the Marine Corps I did not suffer such suspense, such spasms of anxiety, such despair mixed with forlorn hope. How sweet it would be, I thought, munching on my ham-and-cheese sandwich, to row for old Balliol, to hit a wicket or swing whatever is swung at cricket for Oriel or All Souls. I thought of the Lake Country, Cornwall, Westminster Abbey. I can recall now nothing of my own interview, only that I seem to have acquitted myself with dignity and aplomb; I think it must have lasted half an hour or more. It was long past dark when, fatigued with the bone-stiffening fatigue that only such miserable waiting can induce, we sat and watched a committee member—himself quite haggard—emerge from the conference room and slowly read the names of the dozen winners. My name was not among them. The relief—no matter how painful the under-girding of disappointment—was immediate, almost blissful. And I felt some small twitch of solace—albeit solace mixed with puzzle-ment—when, after extending routine thanks to all, the committee member singled me out, requesting that I stay behind after the other candidates had dispersed. What on earth was this? I won-dered, with a deft surge of hope. Was I to be given some secret, heretofore unrevealed and unannounced consolation prize? A watch? A Bible? A set of the *OED*?

I sat there alone for a long while on the nearly deserted, stale-smelling mezzanine, stranded in my bafflement. Finally only a single fireman shared my solitude. At last out of the conference room shambled the tired but friendly-looking chairman of the committee, a doctor of divinity who was also the distinguished chancellor of Vanderbilt University. His name was Harvie Branscomb. He was a good man. He extended his hand and offered his condolences, and then sat down beside me on the couch. As I may have known, he said, he had been a close friend of Bill Blackburn's when they both taught at Duke several years before; because of this connection it was all the more difficult for him, personally, to have had to pass me over.

"It was because of you that we took so long," he said in his fatherly, friendly voice. "We argued and argued about you for at least an hour. You see—your writing, those stories—they really were very impressive, we all thought, but—" He paused, then said, "We did want a creative person, but—" And then he halted.

"I appreciate what you tried to do," I said. "I'll always be grate-ful for that."

"I guess you know why we finally felt that we had to pass you over—"

"My grades—" I interrupted.

"Yes," he went on, "it's not that you just flunked physics. Even the Rhodes scholarship doesn't demand perfection. One or two of the winners today had rather—well, shaky areas in their academic records. It was—"

"You don't have to tell me," I put in.

The chancellor said, "Yes, to flunk physics not just once but *four* times in a row. And that final exam grade, the last semester: thirty-eight. We couldn't overlook that." He hesitated, then gave a rueful smile. "One of the committee members said that you seemed to demonstrate a 'pertinacity in the desire to fail.' We had to consider how such a trait might appear to the people at Oxford . . ."

I could say nothing. Finally, after a bit of a silence, the chancellor said, "You know, son, maybe this is really for the better. I mean, I was at Oxford over twenty-five years ago, and I've watched hundreds of Rhodes scholars come back to America and begin their careers and I'll be dogged if I can name a single writer—a single poet or playwright or short-story writer or novelist—that came out of the entire huge crowd. Oh, a lot of brilliant people and a lot of brilliant careers in many fields—but not a single writer worth the description. Funny thing, Oxford—it's a wonderful place for learning, the finest place of its kind in the world, and yet it has a way of tending to *channel* people, to fit them into a mold. If you really want to know the truth, I believe that if we had chosen you it may have been the end, once and for all, of your ambitions to be a writer. Most probably, you would have become a teacher—a dog-gone good teacher, you understand, but not a writer." He stopped and looked out over the deserted mezzanine with its potted palms and spittoons. "A *good* teacher, mind you," he insisted again, as if to stroke my bruised ego. "I'm sure you would have come back and begun teaching at Duke or the University of Virginia or Sewanee or someplace. It'd be a good life, you'd have been truly distinguished—but you surely wouldn't have become a writer."

The chancellor's eyes, glazed with a terrible tiredness, seemed to rest on a remote distance, and I have wondered recently when thinking of that moment, if in his touching and truly generous concern for me, he might have been brooding upon other possibilities in the theoretical career which my "pertinacity in a desire to fail" had caused him and his colleagues reluctantly to deny me: that is, for example, membership in the South Atlantic Modern Language Association, which, thirty-odd years later, in 1979, would bring me to this very hotel, ready for the familiar annuity of cerebral interplay, conventional tedium, painful politics and the saving balm of various sorts of fellowship.

But the chancellor and I bade each other goodbye then, and I terminated my stay in Atlanta with another dubious "first." I had been since my early adolescence an imbiber of beer and beer alone; Budweiser had always seemed to be a beverage I could handle. But this night, on my way to the train station, I bought a bottle of Old Grand-Dad bourbon; it was, I remember precisely, a full half pint, which was a prodigious amount of booze for a young man of twenty—at least, I know, for me. I got gloriously drunk on the Southern Railway local that rattled its way all night up through the Carolinas, gazing out at the bleak, moon-drenched, wintry fields and happily pondering my deliverance. The chancellor, bless his soul, had really taken most of the curse off the bitter defeat I had initially felt there at the Biltmore. It really was better for me not to go to Oxford, I told myself, throwing in various Anglophobic injunctions: the food you wouldn't feed to a starving hound dog, the men were prancing homosexuals, the women all had foul breath, it was a moribund civilization. "Screw Oxford," I remember saying aloud, and "Up yours, Cecil Rhodes!" Next year, instead of shivering to death in some library carrel, instead of—and "Get this, old fellow!" I heard myself cackling—instead of writing a paper on the hexameters of Arthur Hugh Clough, that old Victorian nanny, I would be in New York, beginning my first novel. It was with this fantasy in mind that I slipped off into a bourbon-heavy slumber, sleeping past Durham and waking up with a stupefying headache in Norlina, practically on the Virginia border, feeling (despite this dislocation and my hangover) amazingly happy.

[Speech delivered to the South Atlantic Modern Language Association, Atlanta, Georgia, December 1979]

Lie Down in Darkness

WHEN, IN THE AUTUMN OF 1947, I was fired from the first and only job I have ever held, I wanted one thing out of life: to become a writer. I left my position as manuscript reader at the McGraw-Hill Book Company with no regrets; the job had been onerous and boring. It did not occur to me that there would be many difficulties to impede my ambition; in fact, the job itself had been an impediment. All I knew was that I burned to write a novel and I could not have cared less that my bank account was close to zero, with no replenishment in sight. At the age of twenty-two I had such pure hopes in my ability to write not just a respectable first novel, but a novel that would be completely out of the ordinary, that when I left the McGraw-Hill Building for the last time I felt the exultancy of a man just released from slavery and ready to set the universe on fire.

I was at that time sharing a cheap apartment with a fellow graduate from Duke University, a Southerner like myself. It was a rather gloomy basement affair far up Lexington Avenue near Ninety-fourth Street. I was reading gluttonously and eclectically in those days—novels and poetry (ancient and modern), plays, works of history, anything—but I was also doing a certain amount of tentative, fledgling writing. The first novel had not yet revealed itself in my imagination, and so most of my energies were taken up with short stories. The short story possessed considerably more prestige then than now; certainly, largely because of an abundance of magazines, the short story had far greater readership, and I thought that I would make my mark in this less demanding art form while the novel-to-be germinated in my brain. This, of course, was a terrible delusion. The short story, whatever its handicaps, is one of the most demanding of all literary mediums and my early attempts proved to be pedestrian and uninspired. The rejection slips began to come back with burdensome regularity.

Yet plainly there was talent signaling its need to find a voice, and the voice was heard. An extremely gifted teacher, Hiram Haydn, was conducting a writing course at The New School for Social Research, and I enrolled. Haydn was a pedagogue in the older, nonpejorative sense of the word, which is to say a man who could establish a warm rapport with young students. He had a fine ear for language, and something about my efforts, groping and unformed as they were, caught his fancy and led him to an encouragement that both embarrassed and pleased me.

Hiram Haydn was also an editor in a book publishing house. He said that he felt my talents might be better suited to the novel and suggested that I start in right away, adding that his firm would underwrite my venture to the extent of a $100 option. While hardly a bonanza, this was not nearly as paltry as it might sound. One hundred dollars could last a frugal young bachelor quite a long time in 1947. More importantly, it was a note of confidence that spurred my hungry ambition to gain glory and, perhaps, even a fortune. The only drawback now—and it was a considerable one—was that I had no idea as to how I would go about starting a novel, which suddenly seemed as menacing a challenge as all the ranges and peaks of the Himalayas. What, I would ask myself, pacing my damp Lexington Avenue basement, just what in God's name am I going to write about? There can be nothing quite so painful as the doubts of a young writer, exquisitely aware of the disparity between his capabilities and his ambition—aware of the ghosts of Tolstoy, Melville, Hawthorne, Joyce, Flaubert, cautionary presences crowding around his writing table.

That winter, between Christmas and New Year's Day, a monumental blizzard engulfed New York City. The greatest snowfall in sixty years. During that snowbound time two things occurred that precipitated me into actual work on my novel, as opposed to dreaming. The first of these was my receipt of a letter from my father in my hometown in Virginia (after three days the mail had begun to arrive through the drifts), telling me of the suicide of a young girl, my age, who had been the source of my earliest and most aching infatuation. Beautiful, sweet and tortured, she had grown up in a family filled with discord and strife. I was appalled and haunted by the news of her death. I had never so much as held her hand, yet the feeling I had felt for her from a distance had from time to time verged on that lunacy which only adolescent passion can produce. The knowledge of this foreshortened life was something that burdened me painfully all through those cold post-Christmas days.

Yet I continued to read in my obsessed way, and the book which I then began—and which became the turning point in my struggle to get started—was Robert Penn Warren's *All the King's Men*. I was staggered by such talent. No work since that of Faulkner had so impressed me—impressed by its sheer marvelousness of language, its vivid characters, its narrative authority, and the sense of truly felt and realized life. It was a book that thrilled me, challenged me and filled me with hope for my own possibilities as a writer. And so it was that soon after finishing *All the King's Men*, I began to see the first imperfect outline of the novel—then untitled—which would become *Lie Down in Darkness*. I would write about a young girl of twenty-two who committed suicide. I would begin the story as the family in Virginia assembled for the funeral, awaiting the train that returned her body from the scene of her death in New York City. The locale of the book, a small city of the Virginia Tidewater, was my own birthplace, a community so familiar to me that it was like part of my bloodstream.

And so even as the book began to take shape in my brain I became excited by the story's rich possibilities—the weather and the landscape of the Tidewater, against which the characters began to define themselves: father, mother, sister, and the girl herself, all doomed by fatal hostility and misunderstanding, all helpless victims of a domestic tragedy. In writing such a story—like Flaubert in *Madame Bovary*, which I passionately admired—I would also be able to anatomize bourgeois family life of the kind that I knew so well, the WASP world of the modern urban South. It was a formidable task, I knew, for a man of my age and inexperience, but I felt up to it, and I plunged in with happy abandon, modeling my first paragraphs on—what else?—the opening chapter of *All the King's Men*. Any reader who wishes to compare the first long passage of *Lie Down in Darkness* with the rhythms and the insistent observation and the point of view of the beginning pages of Warren's book will without difficulty see the influence, which only demonstrates that it may not always be a bad thing for a young writer to emulate a master, even in an obvious way.

Lie Down in Darkness also owes an enormous debt to William

Faulkner, who is of course both the god and the demon of all Southern writers who followed him. Writers as disparate as Flannery O'Connor and Walker Percy have expressed their despair at laboring in the shadow of such a colossus, and I felt a similar measliness. Yet, although even at the outset I doubted that I could rid myself wholly of Faulkner's influence, I knew that the book could not possibly have real merit, could not accrue unto itself the lasting power and beauty I wanted it to have, unless the voice I developed in telling this story became singular, striking, somehow uniquely my own. And so then, after I had completed the first forty pages or so (all of which I was satisfied with and which remain intact in the final version), there began a wrestling match between myself and my own demon—which is to say, that part of my literary consciousness which too often has let me be indolent and imitative, false to my true vision of reality, responsive to facile echoes rather than the inner voice.

It is difficult if not impossible for a writer in his early twenties to be entirely original, to acquire a voice that is all his own, but I was plainly wise enough to know that I had to make the attempt. It was not only Faulkner. I had to deafen myself to echoes of Scott Fitzgerald, always so easy and seductive, rid my syntax of the sonorities of Conrad and Thomas Wolfe, cut out wayward moments of Hemingway attitudinizing, above all, be myself. This of course did not mean that the sounds of other writers could not and did not occasionally intrude upon the precincts of my own style— T. S. Eliot, who was also a great influence at the time, showed definitely how the resonance of other voices could be a virtue— but it did mean, nonetheless, the beginning of a quest for freshness and originality. I found the quest incredibly difficult, so completely taxing that after those forty pages I began contemplating giving up the book. There seemed no way at all that I—a man who had not even published a short story—could reconcile all the formidably complex components of my vision, all of the elements of character and prose rhythms and dialogue and revelation of character, and out of this reconciliation produce that splendid artifact called a novel. And so, after a fine start—I quit.

I went down to Durham, North Carolina, where I had gone to college, and there took a tiny back-street apartment, which I shared with a very neurotic cocker spaniel. Here I tried to write again. I toyed with the novel but it simply would not move or grow; the dispirited letters I wrote to Hiram Haydn must have told him that his one hundred dollars had gone down the drain. But plainly he was not to be discouraged, for after a whole year had gone by he wrote me from New York suggesting that my energies might be recharged if I once again moved north. It seemed a reasonable idea, and so in the summer of 1949, after transferring ownership of my spaniel to a professor of philosophy at Duke, I came back to the metropolis, still so impecunious that I had to take a cheap room far away from Manhattan's sweet dazzle, in the heart of Flatbush. (I stayed there only a month or so but it was an invaluable experience, demonstrating the serendipitous manner in which life often works to a writer's advantage: that month's residence provided the inspiration for a novel I wrote much later, *Sophie's Choice*.) In Brooklyn, too, I was unable to write a word.

But salvation from all my dammed-up torment came soon, in the form of two loving friends I had met earlier in the city. Sigrid de Lima, a writer who had also been in Haydn's class, and her mother, Agnes, recognized my plight and invited me to live in their fine old rambling house up the Hudson in the hills behind Nyack. There, in an atmosphere of faith and affection and charity (a home-like ambience which I plainly needed and whose benison I have never been able to repay), I collected my wits and with a now-or-never spirit set forth to capture the beast which had so long eluded me.

And as I began to discipline and harness myself, began for the first time to examine as coldly and as clinically as I could the tough problems which before this I had refused to face, I had a fine revelation. I realized that what had been lacking in my novelist's vision was really a sense of architecture—a symmetry, perhaps unobtrusive but always there, without which a novel sprawls, becoming a self-indulged octopus. It was a matter of form, and up until now this was an issue that out of laziness or fear, perhaps both, I had tried to avoid. I did not have to construct a diagram or a "plot"—this I have never done. I merely had to keep aware, as I progressed with the narrative in flashback after flashback (using the funeral as the framework for the entire story) that my heroine, Peyton Loftis, would always be seen as if through the minds of the other characters; never once would I enter her consciousness.

Further, she would be observed at progressive stages of her life, from childhood to early adulthood, always with certain ceremonials as a backdrop—country-club dance, a Christmas dinner, a football game, a wedding—and each of these ceremonials would not only illuminate the tensions and conflicts between Peyton and her family but provide all the atmosphere I needed to make vivid and real the upper-middle-class Virginia milieu I had set out to describe. Only at the end of the book, toward which the entire story was building—in Peyton's Molly Bloom–like monologue— would I finally enter her mind, and I hoped this passage would be all the more powerful because it was suddenly and intensely "interior," and personal. This, at any rate, was the scheme which I evolved, and from then on the writing of the book, while never easy (what writing is?), took on a brisk, self-generating quality in which I was able to command all other aspects of the story— dialogue, description, wordplay—to my own satisfaction, at least.

I completed *Lie Down in Darkness* on a spring evening in 1951 in a room on West Eighty-eighth Street in Manhattan, where I had moved after my liberating year in Rockland County. I finished Peyton's monologue last (having already written the ultimate scenes), and if to the present-day reader the passage has an added sense of doom and desperation, this may be because, a few months before, I had been called back by the Marine Corps to serve in the Korean War. Thus I think I had, like Peyton, only meager hopes for survival. I was twenty-five years old and—like Peyton—was much too young to die. But I survived, happy beyond my craziest dreams at the generally good reviews and at the fact that *Lie Down in Darkness* even reached the best-seller list. This was on the same list as two other first novels which, said *Time* magazine later on that year, expressed like mine a depressing and negative trend in American letters: *From Here to Eternity* and *The Catcher in the Rye*.

[*Hartford Courant Magazine*, January 3, 1982]

The *Paris Review*

MEMORY IS, of course, a traitor, and it is wise not to trust any memoir which lends the impression of total recall. The following account of the founding of the *Paris Review* comprises my *own* recollection of the event, highly colored by prejudice, and must not be considered any more the gospel than those frequent narratives of the twenties, which tell you the color of the shoes that Gertrude Stein wore at a certain hour on such and such a day. . . .

The *Paris Review* was born in Montparnasse in the spring of 1952. It was, as one looks back on it through nostalgia's deceptive haze, an especially warm and lovely and extravagant spring. Even in Paris, springs like that don't come too often. Everything seemed to be in premature leaf and bud, and by the middle of March there was a general great stirring. The pigeons were aloft, wheeling against a sky that stayed blue for days, tomcats prowled stealthily along rooftop balustrades, and by the first of April the girls already were sauntering on the boulevard in scanty cotton dresses, past the Dôme and the Rotonde and their vegetating loungers who, two weeks early that year, heliotrope faces turned skyward, were able to begin to shed winter's anemic cast. All sorts of things were afoot —parties, daytime excursions to Saint-Germain-en-Laye, picnics along the banks of the Marne, where, after a lunch of bread and saucissons and Brie and Evian water (the liver was a touch troubled, following a winter sourly closeted with too much wine), you could lie for hours in the grass by the quiet riverside and listen to the birds and the lazy stir and fidget of grasshoppers and understand, finally, that France could be pardoned her most snooty and magisterial pride, mistress as she was of such sweet distracting springs.

At night there was a bar called Le Chaplain, on a little dog-leg street not far from the Dôme, where a lot of people used to go; you could carve your name with an outstretched forefinger in the smoke of the place, but the refreshment was not too expensive, and in its ambience—quiet enough for conversation yet lively enough to forestall boredom, gloom, self-conscious lapses—it seemed to be a fine place to sit and work up a sweat about new magazines and other such far-fetched literary causes. Even though outside there was a kind of calm madness in the air—French boys, too, were being sent to that most futile and insane of wars, Korea—and in spite of the beatific spring, there was a subdued yet tense quality around, as of a people pushed very close to the breaking point, or as of one hysteric woman who, if you so much as dropped a pin behind her, would break out in screams. "*U.S. Go Home.*" The signs are gone now, for the moment. At that time, though, our national popularity had reached *the* nadir and in Paris there have been better times for literary ventures. But all of us had been in one war; besides, the young *patron* of Le Chaplain, named Paul, by his own proclamation loved America almost as much for "*ses littérateurs*" as for "*ses dollars*" (winks, knowing laughter, toasts in beer to two great nations), and if the *Paris Review* were to celebrate a patron saint, it would possibly have to be this wiry, tough, frenetic Algerian with the beneficent smile, who could vault over the bar and stiff-arm a drunk out into the night in less time than it takes to say Edgar Poe, and return, bland as butter, to take up where he left off about Symbolist imagery. Try starting a little magazine at Toots Shor's. *Les américains en Amérique!* indeed.

Later that spring, as the idea of a new magazine grew less far-fetched (by this time someone mentioned that he actually knew where he could raise $500), we convened in an apartment on a hidden, sleepy street behind the Gare Montparnasse called the Rue Perceval. The apartment belonged to Peter Matthiessen, to whom credit is due for having originated the idea for the magazine. No one seemed to know the obscure street, not even the shrewdest of Left Bank cabdrivers, and in this seclusion three flights up, in a huge room with a sunny terrace overlooking all of Paris, the plans went forward in euphoria, in kennel snarls of bickering, in buoyant certitude, in schism and in total despair. Though it is no doubt less complicated to organize a little magazine than to start some sort of industrial combine, it is imponderably more difficult an enterprise, I will bet, than opening a delicatessen, and in France one must multiply one's problems—well, by France; to learn successfully how to browbeat a Parisian printer, for instance, is rough schooling for a Parisian, even more so for a recent graduate of Harvard or Yale, and the bureaucratic entanglements involved in setting up a corporation known as *Société à Responsibilité Limitée au capital de 500.000 frs.* must be self-evident to anyone who has even so much as lost his passport. Yet somehow the thing was accomplished.

To be young and in Paris is often a heady experience. In America a writer not only never knows who or where he is ("Well, what I mean is, was it a best seller?" "Is this novel of yours sort of historical, or maybe what they call psychological?" "Well, I really meant, what do you do for a *living*?"), he gets so he does not *want* to know. In Paris, on this level at least, it is different, as we all know, and like that hardship case of an American writer of authenticated record whose landlady, spying his translated poem in *Les Nouvelles Littéraires* and recognizing his name, offered him out of glowing pride a two percent reduction in his rent—like this young writer, touched by the sentiment even if not by sheer largesse, we feel peculiarly at ease for a change, we know where we are, and we wish to stick around. And so we persisted.

One sunny afternoon toward the end of that spring George Plimpton, another of the founders (the others were Thomas Guinzburg, Harold Humes, William Pène du Bois and John Train), arrived at Matthiessen's apartment bearing two sinister-looking green bottles of absinthe. He burst in upon a glum gathering desultorily testing names. *Promises. Ascent. Villanelle. Tides. Weathercock. Spume. Humes.* (I think it was Matthiessen who later hit upon the perfectly exact and simple title that the magazine bears.) Everyone was at low ebb, and it is quite probable that once again the group would have broken up had it not been for Plimpton's absinthe. Here I do not wish to suggest that there was something so fortuitously creative about that afternoon as to lead us to discover right then, once and for all, what we wished the magazine to "be"; by the same token, absinthe, according to the *Britannica*, "acts powerfully upon the nerve centers, and causes delirium and hallucinations, followed in some cases by idiocy." One can make what one will out of that; for myself, I simply believe that that afternoon was the one upon which we were destined to make a breakthrough, and that Plimpton's absinthe, while it might not have aided us in our efforts to define our policy, did nothing to hinder us, either. At any rate, toward the end of that day we had discovered roughly what we wished to make of the magazine, and we were in surprising accord.

[From *Harper's Bazaar*, August 1953]

The Long March

ALTHOUGH NOT NEARLY SO LONG nor so ambitious as my other works, *The Long March* achieved within its own scope, I think, a unity and a sense of artistic inevitability which still, ten years after the writing, I rather wistfully admire. Lest I appear immodest, I would hasten to add that I do not consider the book even remotely perfect, yet certainly every novelist must have within the body of his writing a work of which he recalls everything having gone just *right* during the composition: through some stroke of luck, form and substance fuse into a single harmonious whole and it all goes down on paper with miraculous ease. For me this was true of *The Long March*, and since otherwise the process of writing has remained exceedingly painful, I cherish the memory of this brief work, often wondering why for a large part of the time I cannot recapture the sense of compulsion and necessity that dominated its creation.

Possibly much of the urgency of the book is due to factors that are extremely personal. As the reader may eventually begin to suspect, the story is autobiographical. To be sure, all writing is to some degree autobiographical, but *The Long March* is intensely and specifically so. I do not mean that the central figures are not more or less imaginary—they are; but the mortar explosion and the forced march, which are central to the entire narrative, were actual incidents in which I was involved, just as I was bound up, for a time, in the same desolating atmosphere of a military base in the midst of a fiercely hot American summer. If the story has a sense of truth and verisimilitude, it is because at the time of the writing all of these things—the terrible explosion, the heat of summer and the anguish of the march itself—still persisted in my mind with the reality of some unshakable nightmare.

Perhaps it was an even larger nightmare which I was trying to create in this book, and which lends to the work whatever symbolic power it has the fortune to possess. Because for myself (as I do believe for most thoughtful people, not only Americans but the community of peaceable men everywhere) the very idea of another war—this one in remote and strange Korea, and only five years after the most cataclysmic conflict ever to engulf mankind—possessed a kind of murky, surrealistic, half-lunatic unreality that we are mercifully spared while awake, but which we do occasionally confront in a horrible dream. Especially for those like myself who had shed their uniforms only five years before—in the blissful notion that the unspeakable orgy of war was now only a memory and safely behind—the experience of putting on that uniform again and facing anew the ritualistic death dance had an effect that can only be described as traumatic. World War II was dreadful enough, but at least the issues involved were amenable to reasonable definition. To be suddenly plunged again into war, into a war, furthermore, where the issues were fuzzy and ambiguous, if not fraudulent, a war that could not possibly be "won," a senseless conflict so unpopular that even the most sanguinary politician or war lover shrank from inciting people to a patriotic zeal, a war without slogans or ballads or heroes—to have to endure this kind of war seemed, to most of us involved in it at the time, more than we could bear. War was no longer simply a temporary madness into which human beings happily lapsed from time to time. War had at last become *the* human condition.

It was this feeling I believe I was trying to recapture when sometime later, in the summer of 1952, I found myself in Paris still unable to shake off the sense of having just recently awakened from a nightmare. My own ordeal and the ordeal of most of my Marine Corps friends (including one or two who died in Korea) was over —yet the persistent image of eight boys killed by a random mortar shell and of a long and brutal march lingered in my mind. Senseless mass slaughter and a seemingly endless march, the participants of which were faceless zeroes, were all that in retrospect appeared to me significant about this war without heroes, this war which lacked so utterly a sense of human identity, and which in so sinister a fashion presaged the faceless, soulless, pushbutton wars of the future. All right, I would write about this faceless, soulless march.

Yet, all my intentions to the contrary, I began to understand, as I wrote, that even in the midst of an ultimate process of dehumanization the human spirit cannot be utterly denied or downed: against all odds, faces emerge from the faceless aggregate of ciphers, and in the middle of the march I was creating I found Captain Mannix slogging and sweating away, tortured, beaten but indomitable. A hero in spite of himself or me, he endures, and in the midst of inhumanity retains all that which makes it worthwhile to be human. I myself cannot be sure, but possibly it is the hopeful implications derived from this mystery—this kind of indefatigable man—which are all an artist can pretend to suggest, however imperfectly, in his struggle to comprehend the agony of our violent, suicidal century.

[Introduction to the Norwegian edition of *The Long March*]

Auschwitz

SPRINGTIME AT AUSCHWITZ. The phrase itself has the echo of a bad and tasteless joke, but spring still arrives in the depths of southern Poland, even at Auschwitz. Just beyond the once electrified fences, still standing, the forsythia puts forth its yellow buds in gently rolling pastures where sheep now graze. The early songbirds chatter even here, on the nearly unending grounds of this Godforsaken place in the remote hinterland of the country. At Birkenau, that sector of the Auschwitz complex that was the extermination camp for millions, one is staggered by the sheer vastness of the enterprise stretching out acre upon acre in all directions. The wooden barracks were long ago destroyed, but dozens of the hideous brick stablelike buildings that accommodated the numberless damned are still there, sturdily impervious, made to endure a thousand years.

Last April, as this visitor stood near Crematorium II, now flattened yet preserved in broken-backed rubble, his gaze turned and lingered upon the huge pits where the overflow of the bodies from the ovens was burned; the pits were choked with weeds but among the muck and the brambles there were wildflowers beginning to bloom. He reflected that "forsythia" was one of two loan words from Western languages that he recognized amid his meager command of Polish. The other word, from the French, was *cauchemar* —"nightmare." At the beginning of spring, the two images mingle almost unbearably in this place.

At Auschwitz itself, in the original camp nearby, there is still the infamous slogan over the main gate—*Arbeit Macht Frei*—and only yards away, unbelievably, a small hotel. (What does the guest really order for breakfast? A room with *which* view does one request?) It is hardly a major world tourist attraction but Auschwitz is not unfrequented. Many of the visitors are Germans, festooned with Leicas and Hasselblads, whose presence does not seem inappropriate amid the *echt*-German architecture.

These grim warrens, too, were built to last the Hitler millennium. Hulking and Teutonic in their dun-colored brick, the rows of barracks where hundreds of thousands perished of disease and starvation, or were tortured and hanged or shot to death, now shelter the principal museum exhibits: the mountains of human hair, the piles of clothes, the wretched suitcases with crudely or neatly painted names like Stein and Mendelson, the braces and crutches, the heaps of toys and dolls and teddy bears—all of the heart-destroying detritus of the Holocaust from which one stumbles out into the blinding afternoon as if from the clutch of death itself. Even thus in repose—arrested in time, rendered a frozen memorial, purified of its seething mass murder—Auschwitz must remain the one place on earth most unyielding to meaning or definition.

I was unable to attend the recent symposium on Auschwitz at the Cathedral Church of St. John the Divine in New York City, but many of the aspects of the proceedings there, at least as reported, troubled and puzzled me, especially because of the overwhelming emphasis on anti-Semitism and Christian guilt. My interest in the meeting was deep, since although I am not nominally a Christian, my four children are half-Jewish and I claim perhaps a more personal concern with the idea of genocide than do most gentiles.

There can be no doubt that Jewish genocide became the main business of Auschwitz; the wrecked crematoria at Birkenau are graphic testimony to the horrible and efficient way in which the Nazis exterminated two and a half million Jews—mass homicide on such a stupefying scale that one understands how the event might justify speculation among theologians that it signaled the death of God.

The Holocaust is so incomprehensible and so awesomely central to our present-day consciousness—Jewish and gentile—that one almost physically shrinks with reticence from attempting to point out again what was barely touched on in certain reports on the symposium: that at Auschwitz perished not only the Jews but at least one million souls who were not Jews. Of many origins but mainly Slavs—Poles, Russians, Slovaks, other—they came from a despised people who almost certainly were fated to be butchered with the same genocidal ruthlessness as were the Jews had Hitler won the war, and they contained among them hundreds of thousands of Christians who went to their despairing deaths in the belief that *their* God, the Prince of Peace, was as dead as the God of Abraham and Moses.

Or there were the few ravaged survivors, like the once devoutly Catholic Polish girl I knew many years ago, the memory of whom impelled my visit to Auschwitz. It was she who, having lost father, husband and two children to the gas chambers, paid no longer any attention to religion, since she was certain, she told me, that Christ had turned His face away from her, as He had from all mankind.

Because of this I cannot accept anti-Semitism as the sole touchstone by which we examine the monstrous paradigm that Auschwitz has become. Nor can I regard with anything but puzzled mistrust the chorus of *mea culpas* from the Christian theologians at the symposium, rising along with the oddly self-lacerating assertion of some of them that the Holocaust came about as the result of the anti-Semitism embedded in Christian doctrine.

I am speaking as a writer whose work has often been harshly critical of Christian pretensions, hypocrisies and delusions. Certainly one would not quarrel with the premise that Christian thought has often contained much that was anti-Semitic, but to place all the blame on Christian theology is to ignore the complex secular roots of anti-Semitism as well. The outrages currently being perpetrated against the Jews by the secular, "enlightened," and anti-Christian Soviet Union should be evidence of the dark and mysterious discord that still hinders our full understanding of the reasons for this ancient animosity.

To take such a narrow view of the evil of Nazi totalitarianism is also to ignore the ecumenical nature of that evil. For although the unparalleled tragedy of the Jews may have been its most terrible single handiwork, its threat to humanity transcended even this. If it was anti-Semitic, it was also anti-Christian. And it attempted to be more final than that, for its ultimate depravity lay in the fact that it was anti-human. Anti-life.

This message was plainly written in the spring dusk at Auschwitz only short weeks ago for one observer, who fled before the setting of the sun. To linger in Auschwitz after nightfall would be unthinkable.

[*New York Times* Op-Ed page, June 25, 1974]

The MacDowell Medal

I WAS QUITE BOWLED OVER when John Updike telephoned last spring to tell me that he and the distinguished members of the committee had chosen me for the medal. I had of course heard of it and knew of its very special quality. But, in all honesty, I never thought it would come my way. I was very surprised, but gradually I cooled off and began to wonder at the reason for my intense mixed reaction. I began to feel a little troubled. I asked myself why news of such an honor—even one of the greatest prestige like the MacDowell Medal—should leave me with this sense of uneasiness. Was it because some inner voice told me that I might not really deserve it—that there were at least three or four writers whom I greatly admired whose work should have gained the accolade instead of mine? Or was it because the whole issue of medals and prizes had once more surfaced, this time beneath my nose, making me ask the question again: "Are prizes necessary, or even desirable?" Isn't satisfaction in one's work sufficient reward, and so forth? These are, of course, tiresome worries. I am a Gemini with a bifurcated ego, one branch of which delights in being stroked, while the other emits howls of dismay. I was at that moment re-reading the stories of my fellow Virginian (although born in Boston), Edgar Allan Poe, and it suddenly occurred to me that some of the distress I felt may have come from the question I abruptly asked myself: "Had Edgar Allan Poe ever won a medal?" I went to the source book (an old and rather ponderous biography by one Edmund Clarence Stedman), in which I was puzzled to discover, among other things, that Poe suffered from, and may have even died in part from, a malady described as "platonic erotomania," which baffled me for a long time because Stedman offered no explanation. I put aside, however, the search for this riddle, and was able to ascertain after diligent checking that, no, Poe had never won a medal. This fact so piqued my interest that I was led to further research on medals, especially of the nineteenth century and more particularly as they affected the culture of the United States and of Europe, and I came up with some provocative data that I want to share with you very briefly. I'm concentrating on literary artists, though I'm sure similar cases could be made in music and the visual arts.

In the 1800s, Europe rewarded its writers handsomely with medals and trophies. Victor Hugo was a major collector of laurels; he had a whole room filled with bronzes and statuettes that fed a self-esteem already swollen by public idolatry scarcely equalled in the history of literature. At the same time, the behavior of Gustave Flaubert is an example of the extreme ambivalence toward medals which artists have often displayed. There is no more crushingly contemptuous line in all of world fiction than the final sentence of *Madame Bovary*, where the narrator, simultaneously summing up his feelings for his least favorite character, the odious Monsieur Homais, and expressing his hatred of such bourgeois claptrap as the Legion of Honor, writes: "He has just been awarded the Legion of Honor." It is the put-down par excellence. Yet, a few years after *Madame Bovary* appeared, the recently reviled but now redeemed Flaubert was himself offered the Legion of Honor, a medal which one biographer described the great man as accepting with "gleeful alacrity." So much for the famous cold Flaubertian detachment. But the champion acquirer of medals has to be Henrik Ibsen. So great was the demand for Ibsen's presence at medal-giving ceremonies all over Europe that the dramatist wrote his plays for half the year and went collecting medals the other half. Departing Oslo, then known as Christiania, in the spring, he would head southward to Bonn and Leipzig, pause, then mosey on to Vienna and Budapest—at all of which places there were kings and princes to hang medallion-bedecked ribbons around his neck—and then, as summer grew ripe, he would pass on down to Torino, Milano, Rome, back up to Paris and Brussels, thence to London for a whole clutch of medals and on to Amsterdam, Dublin, and Edinburgh, returning at last, when the first chill breeze of autumn roiled the North Sea, to Norway, clanking with bronze and gold, so weighted down with the ornaments that overlaid his chest that he was actually seen to list slightly to port as he trudged down the gangplank into the arms of his cheering admirers.

Contrast, if you will, this European cornucopia of honors with the situation as it existed at the same time in our country. No one cared a fig for literature. No medals for Edgar Allan Poe, no medals for Fenimore Cooper or Hawthorne, no medals for Whitman. No medals, no prizes, no annual publishers' awards, no seals of approval from a book critics circle, no fellowships, no grants, no MacDowell Colony, nothing. It may have seemed a bleak and ungenerous society when compared with Europe, if anyone bothered to make the comparison, and certainly nineteenth-century American writers were unrewarded when likened to their present-day counterparts, yet it is hard to believe that the existence of awards and honors might have improved the quality of the work of our literary ancestors. There is something about the immense and tormented loneliness of the writers at that time—an alienation far more intense, really, than the one rather facilely attributed to our own period— that makes it plausible to think that their work might have been violated, perhaps even irreparably damaged, had that loneliness been intruded upon by anxieties over winning a prize. Like all artists, they were hungry for recognition, and this a few of them got, though most failed to receive anything like renown commensurate with their genius; it may be that at least part of the splendor of their achievement derives from the very loneliness and obscurity out of which it flowered. One thinks with relief of Emily Dickinson never having had to compound her existential dread by missing out, once again, on the Bollingen, and only horror could attend contemplation of what twentieth century book chat might have achieved back in those days, the gossip churning about Melville's stupendous, perennially-doomed quest for the Pulitzer, or a MacArthur grant going to Mark Twain, who didn't need it.

The twentieth century, however, has offered no dearth of awards in America. Only France exceeds us in the bestowal of public bouquets to flatter the artistic self (in France it is often literally nothing but a bouquet). But the trouble is that the proliferation of awards has frequently debased the very concept of honor, and laurel branches descend indiscriminately upon the brows of the journeyman and the hack. If, as in my Presbyterian childhood, every boy and girl wins a Bible, there is not much feeling of distinction. More seriously, the reputedly prestigious prizes become tainted, like virtually everything else in the nation, by commercialism or, worse, by political infighting which results in cowardly compromises and the award going to individuals of stunning me-

PRAYING
WITH
MARY

To Carol

PRAYING
WITH
MARY

A TREASURY
FOR ALL OCCASIONS

JANICE T. CONNELL

Jan Connell

HarperOne
An Imprint of HarperCollins_Publishers_

HarperOne

HarperCollins books may be purchased for educational, business, or sales
promotional use. For information please write: Special Markets Department,
HarperCollins Publishers, 10 East 53rd Street, New York, NY 10022.

HarperCollins Web site: http://www.harpercollins.com

HarperCollins®, 📖®, and HarperOne™ are trademarks of HarperCollins
Publishers.

FIRST HARPERCOLLINS PAPERBACK EDITION PUBLISHED IN 1999

Designed by Laura Lindgren

Library of Congress Cataloging-in-Publication Data
Connell, Janice T.
    Praying with Mary : a treasury for all occasions / Janice T. Connell.
      p. cm.
    ISBN 978–0–06–061521–5
    1. Mary, Blessed Virgin, Saint—Prayer books and devotions—English.
I. Title.
BX2160.2.C536   1997
242'.74—dc21   97–41337

09 10 11 12 RRD(H) 10 9

DECLARATION

CONSECRATION, SPECIAL BLESSING, DEDICATION

This book was consecrated to the Holy Trinity in thanksgiving for the gift of the Incarnation through the Blessed Virgin Mary during a Mass concelebrated with His Holiness, Pope John Paul II, at the Vatican, by His Excellency, Roman Danylak, Titular Bishop of Nyssa, Apostolic Administrator, Eparchy of Toronto, Canada, on November 24, 1995.

Father Thomas King, S.J., invoked a special blessing during a Mass at Georgetown University, Washington, D.C., upon all those who read this book, all who prepare it, all who handle it. He placed each under the protection of the Lord Jesus Christ and His entire Nine Choirs of Angels.

Praying with Mary is dedicated to the Children of Mary, Mother of God, everywhere, living, deceased, and yet to be born, with great love and gratitude to the Eternal Father, the Lord Jesus Christ, and the Holy Spirit for the gift of Mary. May it bear sweet fruit for the Kingdom of Mary's Son.

Praying with Mary contains a collection of prayers and quotations from Liturgies, Doctors of the Church, Saints, Popes, and Councils from the public domain of the documents of history. In some instances, the prayers have been slightly adapted in conformity with modern linguistic usage.

Certain prayers to Mary are used with the gracious permission of the Sovereign Military and Hospitaller Order of Malta, British Association, London, through the courtesy of Julian Allason, Knight of Obedience, Editor, *Prayers of the Sovereign Military and Hospitaller Order of Malta*.

Certain prayers to Mary are used with the gracious permission of Ravengate Press Publishers, Still River, MA, from the text *Virgin Wholly Marvelous*, edited by David Supple, O.S.B.

A prayer from *The Diary of Sister M. Faustina Kowalska, Divine Mercy in My Soul*, copyright © 1987. Congregation of Marians of the Immaculate Conception; all world rights reserved; printed with permission.

Certain prayers to Mary are from *Heavens Bright Queen*, compiled from approved Catholic publications by William A. Walsh, Carey-Stafford Company, New York, 1906.

The Little Compline, with the Akathist Hymn. Fort Wayne, IN: Saint John Chrysostom Antiochian Church, 1995, pp. 6, 7, 8, 12. The Very Reverend Joseph Rahal, Archpriest, Antiochian Orthodox Christian Archdiocese of North America, Translator. Slightly adapted.

Every effort has been made to identify the author of each prayer herein. Some remain unknown.

The expertise and graciousness of Fr. Thomas A. Thompson, S.M., Director of the Marian Library International Marian Research Institute, and his colleagues are reflected in this text.

Nothing in this book should be read to imply that if a certain prayer is said in a certain way, a certain result will occur.

The promises referred to herein should be regarded as manifestations of divine love and graciousness; encouragement to a life of holiness.

ACKNOWLEDGMENTS

My family, especially my husband, our children, and grand-children, whose love for Mary touch every page of this joyous book.

Archbishop Philip Hannan, Bishop Roman Danylak, Robert Faricy, S.J., Thomas King, S.J., Thomas Thompson, S.M., Adrien VanKaam, C.S.Sp., Michael Scanlan, T.O.R., Thomas Forrest, C.S.s.R., Thomas Duffy for their committed devotion to the Mother of God, and for their discernment, scholarship, and encouragement, all of which find expression in the text.

Joëlle Delbourgo, whose wisdom and courage guided this book.

Leigh Ann Sackrider for her expertise and graciousness.

The skillful staff at Harper Collins for their dedication and commitment to this project.

Children of Mary throughout the world who helped me to prepare this text.

Marcy Posner and Matthew Bialer for their assistance.

Any mistakes or errors are totally due to my inadequacies.

Contents

PRAYERS

AUTHOR'S NOTE

The original idea for this book belongs to Mother Teresa of Calcutta, Foundress of the Missionaries of Charity. She approached me as I stood in a crowd at a large reception for her in Washington, D.C. To my amazement, Mother Teresa placed her right hand over my heart, bowed her head, prayed fervently, then looked into my eyes and said: "The Blessed Mother wants me to write a prayer for your next book, *Praying with Mary.*" I did not know then that I would ever write another book, but quite obviously, Mother Teresa did.

I must admit that I probably would never have thought to compose a book such as this, but who would be so foolish as to disregard Mother Teresa's wisdom? Her prayer from Mary that Mother Teresa wrote for this book is:

— ❧ —

Mary, Mother of Jesus,
Help me to be only
All for Jesus, holy.

God bless you.

FOREWORD

God looks for us, for each of us. He calls us by name, each one by his or her own name, and He works hard to find each of us. He calls you, and me, and every one of us, to Himself.

God looks for me, and for you, so hard and so long and with such patience and love and determination that, finally, we find Him, and we continue to find Him and to grow in union with Him. We learn to know Him, to speak to Him, to be with Him, to trust Him, to depend on Him.

Here is a book that will help you to find God, a book that will help you to pray. Jan Connell has written a book that will help you to pray to God our Father, to Jesus, and also to the Mother of Jesus, Mary.

Not of course that we put Mary, Jesus' mother, on the same level with Jesus or the Father or the Holy Spirit. She is not at all, in any way, God or divine any more than you are or I am. But she is the Mother of Jesus. And so she is, in the order of the spirit, in the spiritual order, your mother and my mother. And she helps her children. She wants to, and so she does.

Jesus is Mary's child. So am I. So are you. We can turn to her, get her help. She teaches us to find God and to find Him more. She teaches us to pray. She teaches us to avoid sin. She teaches us to love, and to love more and to love better.

Mary is transparent, like the air we breathe. She does not want us to be centered on her, but on God. She leads us to Him, and that is what she is interested in. She is, after all, not just your mother and my mother; she is the Mother of God, who has become in Jesus human like us in all things except sin. She is the Mother of Jesus, and He is God, equal to the Father and one with the Father in the Holy Spirit. We are Jesus' brothers and sisters, and children of the Father. And, too, in a different but very real way, we are children of Mary.

Mary has nothing of herself, nothing her own; and she wants nothing for herself. She wants everything for her children, for you, for me, and for Jesus. Her strength is her nothingness. God has looked, and looks still, on the lowliness of Mary, his handmaid, and she magnifies the Lord and rejoices in Him, and helps us to be more united with Him.

Do not be afraid to turn to her, or to pray to her. She will lead you to Jesus. That is what she does. It is really who she is. We might say that it is her job. It is certainly what she wants to do, and can do.

This book will help you to climb the mountain of peace. It will help you to walk with God. Take your time reading it. When something you read strikes you, stop there. Pause and savor it, let it sink in. Take your time.

Do not race through this book as if it were a book on science or mathematics. What is important in this book is not the information, not the contents; it is not an almanac that you want to use to look up facts. This is a practical book, and what has importance here is not so much the content as the process. Through this book, the Lord wants to teach us the process of climbing the mountain of peace, the way to walk with Him.

The mountain is the privileged place of encountering the Lord. Moses meets God on the mountain, he receives the Ten Commandments on Mount Sinai. Mount Zion is the holy mountain of God, the special place of His presence. Jesus goes up to the mountaintop alone to pray. He calls His disciples to the top of the mountain when He chooses his twelve Apostles. The transfiguration of Jesus takes place on the mountaintop.

And the mountain is the mountain of peace. "It shall come to pass in the latter days that the mountain of the house of the LORD shall be established as the highest of the mountains, and shall be raised above the hills; and all the nations shall flow to it, and many peoples shall come, and say: 'Come, let us go up to the mountains of the Lord, to the house of the God of Jacob; that he may teach us his ways and that we may walk in his paths.' For out of Zion shall go forth the law, and the word of the Lord from Jerusalem. He shall judge between the nations, and shall decide for many peoples; and they shall beat their swords into plowshares, and their spears into pruning hooks; nation shall not lift up sword against nation, neither shall they learn war any more" (Isaiah 2:2–4; *see* Micah 4:1–3).

God leads us to the top of the mountain of peace so that we can find Him there. This book is one of God's ways of looking for us so that we can find Him and walk with Him, and find Him always more and walk with Him always more closely.

Robert Faricy, S.J.
Rome, Italy, Easter 1996

INTRODUCTION
Spiritual Mother

— ❧ —

Secrets of the Ages

Praying with Mary is about loving our way home. Why Mary? There are extraordinary secrets about her that we are slowly discovering. First, Mary was created to bring Pure Love to the love-starved human race. Second, by her decision to allow the Word to be made flesh within her and dwell among us, she welcomed Pure Love, cooperated with Pure Love, and appropriated It into every fiber of her human being. Finally, by Mary's total obedience to God's will for her, the human race has full admittance to the Heart of God forever.

When Mary became the Mother of God, she became our own Spiritual Mother too. We are her children whom she lovingly protects and nurtures. God Himself honors Mary under His own Law. He will never refuse His Mother's children entrance to His Divine Heart. God Himself formed the heart of Mary to nurture every child of His into the Kingdom of Love.

Throughout the world, I encounter people who ask me: "Why do you pray to or with Mary? I pray directly to Jesus." Others tell me they prefer to pray only to God. I truly understand this method of prayer.

When I was a child, and later a young woman, though I prayed to God, I also prayed to the Blessed Mother, asking her to intercede with her Divine Infant on my behalf. I always thought of her with the Baby Jesus in her arms. I also thought then that Heaven is only for the next life.

As blessings upon blessings were showered upon my life, I came to love Jesus more profoundly. In my prayer life, I learned to speak to Jesus as my best friend and confidant. Blessings continued to be heaped upon blessings. His Love and Goodness drew me to classes, theologians, books, and holy people. The joy of knowing Him created a longing to know Him better, to serve Him more perfectly.

During that time, my secular life thrived, as did my husband, children, and career. But lurking in the background of this lifestyle were also the painful circumstances that all people experience. One day a close friend of ours, who was our own age and a dedicated believer, was diagnosed with a terminal illness. Nine months later, after great suffering, he died. His wife and four children were numb with grief and shock. All of us who were close to the family remained in a state of stunned silence at his funeral. There were no words that comforted anyone.

During that time, my relationship with the Lord Jesus, whom I had considered my best friend, became what the experts call a "dark night of the soul." Though my faith told me that He was with me, Jesus was so silent, so unreachable that He may as well not have been there. I prayed constantly, but it was like praying into an empty box. One of my children said, "Mom, He's just better at hide-and-seek than you are. You've got to go find the Lord Jesus."

We lived in a city on the East Coast in those days. My husband and I belonged to an ecumenical sharing group sponsored by the churches in our city, and I served on a Jewish-Catholic dialogue committee. Everyone knew everyone else. We had shared our joys, and now we were called to share some inexplicable sorrow. Our friend's death made no sense. The Christians in our group spoke of the Lord Jesus on the cross as an explanation of "why bad things happen to good people." Everyone spoke of Good Fridays turning into Easter Sundays. Our friend, however, was never going to be there for his bereaved wife and shocked children. There would never be another Easter Sunday for them with their husband and father in this life.

Then someone on the dialogue committee handed me a book by a famous rabbi. It was called *Why Bad Things Happen to Good People*, the same phrase many of my Christian friends had used. I quickly scanned the book and almost instantly experienced an inward answer to my crisis of faith. I realized I truly did not know the Lord Jesus Christ. I mentioned this, and all of us bowed our heads and prayed fervently to awaken to Truth and know the One True God.

That night, I had a strange dream. I was living in Biblical times, when Jesus walked the earth. My heart was filled with that detachment we hear about from the great spiritual teachers. Jesus was everything to me. He lived in all my thoughts, my hopes. His Word was my life's road map, the only language I wanted to understand. I saw myself walking with Him. He was Pure Love and I was part of it. Never had I known such ecstatic joy. I knew then why Peter wanted to build a tent on the Mountain of Transfiguration. I saw Moses, and Elijah too, in the dream. They were filled with the same pure love, the same pure joy. I really have no words to explain the experience, except to say that a hymn began to resonate in my heart. I recognized that the blades of grass upon which we walked and each of us are one in Jesus. All creation and we are one in Jesus. All creation is one in praising and adoring God. My being was so full of love that, for only a moment, I melted into all creation, through Jesus, for Jesus, and in Jesus.

Then the hymn was no longer in my soul, and Jesus and I were walking alone. At that moment, He seemed very much a man with a mission and a destination. There was no mystical splendor now. The scenery was not lush and beautiful. Rather, the area was arid, parched. The high grasses looked heavy in the oppressive heat of a desert summer. Jesus walked faster. I hurried to keep up with Him. Then we turned into a glen hidden behind tall cedar trees. A small shelter there, protected from the heat of the sun, contained a wooden table and several simple seats. Mary, His Blessed Mother, was seated on one of them. She was busy arranging flowers. Jesus literally handed me over to His Mother with the words: "Here—prepare her to dine at our table." And without even a glance, He turned and walked away. I was devastated. Part of me was dying. Truth showed me that to lose the Presence of Jesus is to be extinguished.

Then I realized that Mary was looking at me. I knew she could read my heart and my thoughts. I also knew she could feel my abject sorrow. In the blink of an eye, I understood the words of the hymn that once again flooded my being. "Praise the Holy Trinity. Undivided Unity. Holy God. Mighty God. God Immortal, be adored!" And in that instant, I knew (on a level that includes the intellect but is not restricted to it) the Lord Jesus as God, the Second Person of the Holy Trinity, and Jesus, the glorified man, one in being with the Father, through whom all things are made, God from God, Light from Light, True God from True God and true man. In that moment of graced understanding, I experienced the embrace of my Real Mother, the Blessed Mother of the Lord Jesus Christ. God allowed me to know how Mary has been assigned from all eternity to nurture the human race into the Heart of God. In those precious moments, I received a new heart. That is His Plan for everyone.

Whether we know our Blessed Mother or her Son by name, we all know them in the depths of our longings and the heights of our dreams, and we belong to them. We are one family, you and I, and all creation. We are the Family of God. Our Mother has come to earth to gather her Son's Sheep and prepare us well to dine at the Wedding Feast of the Lamb.

Mary is the "goddess" all people dream of, yet she is not, nor has she ever been, divine. Every grace Mary possesses is a gift from God, not only for her but for everyone, so that His Kingdom may reign throughout the world and ever after.

During the thirty years of silence that preceded His public life, Jesus allowed His Blessed Mother to love, nurture, and serve Him. Yet God was also loving, serving, and nurturing her. The relationship of Jesus, the God-man, and His mortal mother Mary unveils the mystery of reciprocal Divine Love and human love. The love between Jesus and Mary is the prototype of the Pure Love between God and humanity. Mary can help us enter into that reciprocity of Love.

There is an easy way to live and a hard way. Mary wants to make our journey easier. She is the perfect prayer partner who holds our hand as we travel life's path, and because the journey is difficult, she nurtures us nearer God. Our Blessed Mother shall drink the bitterest dregs of our cup of sorrow for us; she will pick us up when we are tired and carry us where we long to go, into the Heart of Pure Love. As our Spiritual Mother, she presents our wounded hearts to God in her own stainless hands. And because she is also the Mother of God, He will never refuse what we ask through her.

I have been collecting the prayers in this book for many years. Some come from family members. In my travels, gracious people have shared prayers to our Blessed Mother that have sustained them and their families for countless generations. For two thousand years, such prayers have revealed the inherent dignity with which God has endowed the human race. Each one is a light, a beacon that unveils the glories of humanity and especially the great blessing of motherhood.

Unfortunately, many people today have lost touch with these once ubiquitous prayers. Since families have become smaller units, with grandparents and other relatives often living apart from younger generations, many people have grown up without learning or even hearing some of the most famous Marian prayers. There is a universal hunger to reclaim our knowledge of these prayers. I receive countless calls and letters from people all over the world who want to know how to pray the Rosary, for example, or who need an especially powerful prayer in a time of personal or family crisis.

This book can be used in whatever way feels right for you. Some will want to read it from beginning to end in sequence, perhaps savoring favorite prayers they recognize from child-hood or know from daily use. Others will want to go directly to the chapter that suits their particular need at the time—for example, a person who feels a need to strengthen his or her faith may want to focus on "Prayers for Daily Inspiration." Still others will skim through the book, and some may want simply to set the book aside for use in an emergency.

Perhaps you've never prayed before, or it's been quite some time since you've prayed. If this is the case, the very fact that you've picked up this book is a call to come closer to the Lord Jesus. He wants to invite you into His Family, to know and trust His Mother. After all, if we desire to dwell with Jesus in His Home in Heaven, it is wise to draw near His Mother now as the opportunity presents itself. Perhaps you would like to begin by finding a quiet place where you can be alone. As you hold the book, you might say a short prayer, asking God to reveal to you whatever you need right now. Then find a prayer that for any reason seems the right one for you. Read it silently or aloud. You can say it once or many times. Leave the book beside your bed and pray from it every day. Carry it with you when you are far from home. Hold it in times of sorrow or confusion. Follow whatever your heart tells you to do.

How do any of us who pray know if a prayer is effective? We will know if our prayer has been directly answered, but if it seems that it isn't working, there are several questions to ask: Have I offended the Lord or one of His people? Did I get off the right path? You may ask the Blessed Mother to bring the wisdom of her motherly love and show you how to be more pleasing to God. Perhaps we need to ask the Lord what it is He's trying to teach us by not giving us that for which we pray. If you do not receive exactly what you ask for in prayer, know for certain that God will give you something better. God does answer all prayers, and God can never be outdone in generosity.

There are many ways to journey to God, perhaps as many as every human being ever created. Pray as you desire. Pure Love awaits you.

CHAPTER I

MOTHER OF GOD

Prayers of Early Believers

Human beings are born with a broken heart. There is a solution, however, for all of us, and it is not by chance that you have found this book.

There is only one way to heal our broken hearts, and that is through God's Pure Love. Pure Love flows from God, and all Love leads back to God. We need that Pure Love to live; nothing else satisfies us. By its very nature, Pure Love is unconditional. Anything less is mere conditional love, which tells us that we are not intrinsically worthy of being loved just for who we most deeply are. Pure Love, however, loved us into being, sustains us in being, and patiently awaits us day and night. Each of us was breathed out of the Heart of God into our mother's womb, and if we follow our deepest longings, they will lead us back to the Heart of God Who is Pure Love. Nothing in life is worth so much as finding Pure Love. Once that gift is ours, we possess the secret of the ages.

Pure Love is also pure grace. Grace, which is love between God and a human soul, is something no one can earn. No one can buy it either, and no one can deserve it, because Pure Love is not about deserving. The fact that we exist is proof that we are loved. God created, sustains, and nurtures us on this earth because of His Faith in us and His Hope that each of us will freely choose to love our way back to the Divine Heart whence we came.

Praying with Mary is a tradition as old as Christianity itself. Jesus certainly prayed with His Mother, and so did the Apostles. On the night of Pentecost, Mary was present with Jesus' disciples as the group prayed and experienced the Holy Spirit. And Scripture offers us a perfect example of Mary's intercessory power in Saint John's scene of the wedding feast at Cana. Although Jesus said to His Mother that His hour for performing public miracles had not yet arrived, Mary, knowing that the hosts would need more wine, simply pointed to Jesus and told the wedding attendants, "Do whatever He tells you." Jesus, of course, went on to perform a miracle, changing the water to wine. Mary's faith in Jesus' Pure Love was so great that she knew He would not refuse her request to take care of the people; today, she still presents our requests to God with the same perfect faith and compassion.

Each of us who seeks a full prayer life should know the powerful story of Mary's Dormition. Here is how Saint John Damascene wrote about it early in the eighth century:

It has been handed down to us from of old, that at the time of the glorious passing of our Lady, all the Holy Apostles who were then toiling in various parts of the world for the salvation of mankind were in an instant caught up into the air, and borne together to Jerusalem. There a vision of angels appeared to them, and they heard the Chant of Angelic Powers. And thus, with glory to God, she yielded up her blessed soul into the hands of her Maker. As for her body, which in an ineffable manner had harbored God, it was carried out for burial amid the hymns of angels and the apostles, and was laid in a tomb at Gethsemane, and for three days the songs of angels continued without ceasing. At the end of the three days the melody of the angels ceased, and Thomas, who alone had been absent, having come on the third day, and desiring to pay homage to that body which had harbored God, the apostles opened the tomb, but search as they would, nowhere could they discover the sacred body. They found only the clothes in which it had been enshrouded and being refreshed with the ineffable fragrance which proceeded from them, they once more closed the tomb. Astounded at the extraordinary and mysterious event, they could but conclude, that He Whom it had pleased to take flesh of the Virgin Mary, and of her to be made Man and to be born—though He was God the Word and the Lord of glory—and Who had kept her virginity unimpaired even after childbirth, had also been pleased, upon her departure hence, to shield her sinless body from decay, and to honor it by removal hence from the common and universal resurrection.

According to Holy Land lore, one of the most important and beloved prayers to Mary traces its origins to this glorious scene. Legend tells us that Mary appeared to the apostles gathered there, surrounded by brilliant Light and angels of celestial splendor. She wore a crown of twelve stars that seemed to join heaven and earth; the awestruck mourners swooned as the divine Light illuminated their human understanding. Filled with the Holy Spirit, they greeted her with the following salutation:

— ❧ —

Hail Mary, full of grace,
the Lord is with thee.
Blessed art thou amongst women
and blessed is the fruit of thy womb,
Jesus.
Holy Mary, Mother of God,
pray for us sinners,
now and at the hour of our death.
Amen.

— ❧ —

This prayer—which can also be found in chapter 9—sometimes called the "angelic-apostolic salutation," is the famous Hail Mary. It can be prayed on its own (it is often repeated three times) but also frequently makes up a part of other prayers, such as the Angelus (this chapter) and, of course, the Rosary (chapter 9).

Early believers knew about and understood the importance of Mary's apparition to the Apostles and disciples. No one doubted that Mary lives on in her Son, the Resurrected Christ. And so it was only natural that people of faith would begin to spend time each day in dialogue with Mary. Holding their Spiritual Mother's hand in prayer, people began to climb the spiritual staircase out of human helplessness, poverty, defeat, sickness, and even death. People of all classes—rulers, nobles, merchants, peasants, slaves, and citizens—found solace in Mary's tender compassion. Great leaders such as Saint Irenaeus, Saint Epiphanius, Saint Ambrose, Saint Jerome, and Saint Augustine taught that our spiritual regeneration is rooted in our relationship to Mary. They themselves prayed to her as most loving, most faithful, most gracious Spiritual Mother. Today, Mary still speaks to us in the sacred silence of our hearts, always leading us to God.

Although early prayers with and to Mary come to us from antiquity, each one attests to truths about the love, help, and power of our Blessed Mother to guide, protect, enrich, and nurture us today. In this chapter are gathered some wonderful ancient prayers to Mary by spiritual giants. As you pray them, I trust you will discover this sublime secret of the ages: these prayers to Mary are as powerful today as they were almost two thousand years ago.

The Hail Mary prayer is beloved throughout the world. Its origins are rooted in the words of the Archangel Gabriel to Mary at the Annunciation (Luke 26–38) and the words of Elizabeth at the Visitation (Luke 1:42). In about A.D. 411, Saint Jerome said the truths contained in the Hail Mary are so sublime, so amazing that no human being or angel can fully understand them. Even quarterbacks of championship football teams have been known to throw "Hail Mary" passes with high hopes that Saint Jerome was correct.

— ⌘ —

HAIL MARY

Hail Mary, full of grace,
the Lord is with thee.
Blessed art thou amongst women
and blessed is the fruit of thy womb,
Jesus.
Holy Mary, Mother of God,
pray for us sinners,
now and at the hour of our death.
Amen.

— ⌘ —

HAIL MARY, OLD SLAVONIC
(BYZANTINE) RITE

Hail, Mother of God, Virgin Mary, full of grace, the Lord is with you; blessed are you among women, and blessed is the fruit of your womb. For you have borne Christ, the Savior and Deliverer of our souls.

A prayer and custom from the early days of Christianity continues throughout the world. Church bells ring out at 6:00 A.M., at noon, and at 6:00 P.M., reminding people to pray the Angelus.

THE ANGELUS

The Angel of the Lord declared unto Mary.
And she conceived by the Holy Spirit.
(*Recite the Hail Mary.*)

Behold the servant of the Lord.
May it be done unto me according to thy Word.
(*Recite the Hail Mary.*)

And the Word was made flesh
And dwelt amongst us.
(*Recite the Hail Mary.*)

Pray for us, O Holy Mother of God
That we may be made worthy of the promises of
    Christ.
Let Us Pray
Pour forth, we beseech Thee, O Lord, Thy grace
    into our hearts, that we, to whom the Incarnation
    of Christ, Thy Son, was made known by the mes-
    sage of an angel, may by His passion and cross, be
    brought to the glory of His Resurrection. We ask
    this through the same Christ our Lord. Amen.[1]

THE MIRACLE PRAYER

Since at least the third century the faithful have recited the following prayer in times of dire emergency. The prayer possibly dates to the actual time of Christ and may have been spoken directly to Mary during her life on earth.

This prayer is extraordinarily effective. When my children were growing up, they always prayed it in times of great need. It is lovingly known as our family's "Emergency Prayer," and we have never known it to fail.

MEMORARE OF
THE BLESSED VIRGIN MARY

Remember O most loving Virgin Mary that it is
    unheard of that anyone who has ever had
    recourse to your protection, implored your help,
    or sought your intercession, was left forsaken.
Inspired therefore by this confidence in your good-
    ness, I fly unto you my Mother,
O Virgin of virgins.
To you do I come, before you I stand,
a sorrowful sinner. Despise not my poor words,
O Mother of the Word Incarnate,
but graciously hear and grant my prayer.
Amen.

Saint Ephraem (c. 306–373), a revered Doctor of the Church, was never ordained to the priesthood, though he received Holy Orders as a Deacon. So sublime were his prayers and revelations of God's Loving Plan for the human race that he is known as the Harp of the Holy Spirit.

———— ❧ ————

O Virgin Immaculate, Mother of God and my Mother, from your sublime heights turn your eyes of pity upon me. Filled with confidence in your goodness and knowing full well your power, I beg you to extend to me your assistance in the journey of life, which is so full of dangers for my soul. In order that I may never be a slave of the devil through sin, but may ever live with my heart humble and pure, I entrust myself wholly to you. I consecrate my heart to you forever, my only desire being to love your divine Son, Jesus. Mary, none of your devout servants has ever perished; may I, too, be saved. Amen.

Saint Ephraem of Edessa

———— ❧ ————

Saint John Chrysostom (c. 347–407), Doctor of the Church and considered the greatest of the Greek Fathers, gave us this prayer.

— ❧ —

Would you know how far our Mother Mary surpasses in dignity the citizens of Heaven? They with
fear and trembling stand before God covering
their faces with their wings; she offers up the
human race to Him to Whom she gave birth.
Through her, we may obtain pardon for our sins.
Hail then O Mother heavenly being, Virgin-
throne of God, the glory and bulwark of the
Church; pray for us constantly to Jesus your Son,
our Lord, that through you, we may find mercy in
the day of judgment, and attain to the good things
laid up for those who love God.

Saint John Chrysostom

— ❧ —

The conversion writings of Saint Augustine (354–430) rank
among the greatest spiritual literature in the world. A rich playboy, Augustine set out to taste the earth's finest pleasures. At
the height of his journey, he heard a voice direct him to read
the Scriptures with special attention to Romans 13:13–14. The
Sacred Word so touched his spirit that he abandoned his former way of life and thereafter sought sanctity as zealously as he
had pursued his youthful philanderings. Saint Augustine is
regarded as one of the most extraordinary Doctors of the
Church and is known as the Doctor of God's Grace.

O Blessed Mary, who can return to you sufficient
thanks, or adequately celebrate your praises, for
having by your consent succored a ruined world?
What praise can human weakness offer to you,
which by your means has found the port of salvation? . . . Holy Mary! succor the miserable, help
the fainthearted, comfort the mournful, pray for
the people, intercede for consecrated souls, pray
for devoted souls and let all experience your intercession who celebrate you. Amen.

Saint Augustine

Saint Cyril of Alexandria (376–444), a great Marian Theologian and Doctor of the Church, presided at the Council of
Ephesus, at which the Dogma of Mary, Mother of God was
officially proclaimed.

Hail, Mother and Virgin, Eternal Temple of the
Godhead, Venerable Treasure of Creation, crown
of virginity, support of the true faith, on which the
Church is founded throughout the whole world.
Mother of God, who contained the Infinite God
under your heart, whom no space can contain:
through you the Most Holy Trinity is revealed,

adored and glorified, demons are vanquished,
Satan cast down from heaven into hell and our
fallen nature again assumed into heaven.

Through you the human race, held captive in
the bonds of idolatry, arrives at the knowledge of
Truth. What more shall I say of you? Hail,
through whom kings rule, through whom the
Only-begotten Son of God has become the Star of
Light to those sitting in darkness and in the
shadow of death. Amen.

Saint Cyril of Alexandria, c. A.D. 444

The following Cradle Song of the Virgin shows us Mary's
tender love for God that forever changes our relationship with
our Creator. The prophets prayed and dreamed and spoke of
that love.

CRADLE SONG OF THE VIRGIN
Angels! ye holy
Who fly through the palm groves,
Hold quiet the branches,
My Baby is asleep.

Palm-groves of Bethlehem
That sway in the tempest,

the winds are loud moaning
As through you they sweep;
Restrain your wild fury,
Move gently above us;
Hold quiet your branches,
My Baby is asleep.

My Child, my divine One,
Who came down from Heaven,
What pangs He must suffer!
What tears He must weep!
O let Him one moment
Forget all His anguish,
Hold quiet your branches,
My Baby is asleep.

The tempests blow 'round Him;
Ye see that I have not
Wherewith from My Darling
The cold blasts to keep.
O angels, ye holy,
Who o'er us are flying,
Hold quiet the branches—
My Baby is asleep.[2]

——— ⊷ ———

CHAPTER 2

MOTHER OF DIVINE GRACE

Prayers of Praise and Gratitude

The prayers collected in this chapter are not prayers for earthly favors or intercession (although quite efficacious prayers for help in times of trouble do exist and can be found later in this book). Rather, these prayers are devoted to praising God with the help of Mary, or to Mary herself. Great heavenly favors flow to earth from these prayers. People who are aware of the mystery of the Incarnation of Jesus Christ, that God so loved us and so trusted Mary that the Second Person of the Holy Trinity was willing to become a baby in her womb, are truly able to praise Mary and thank God for her. To praise Mary is to praise the way God chose to redeem the human race.

Praising God and Mary is one way of demonstrating and cultivating gratitude for all we have. We each have unique and exquisite gifts from God, including our joys, our sorrows, our families, our work, even our recreation and exercise, but we are not using them properly if we don't offer prayers of praise in a spirit of humble thankfulness.

We are stewards of all we possess. Those who live comfortable lives or have great opportunities cannot sink into complacency; instead, from those with much, much is expected. In the widest sense, each gift we have belongs to everyone throughout the world, especially to those who do not yet possess such blessings. To realize this is to acknowledge God as our Gift-Giver and praise and thank Him for entrusting us with His gifts. We bring God joy when we praise and thank Him for His Blessed Mother, His saints and angels, and one another. Even our most meager prayer of praise and thanksgiving spills God's joy at our prayer upon the whole world.

Mary's life teaches us that it is pleasing to God when we use His gifts with love, gratitude, and petitions for our brothers and sisters. She herself offers the use of everything she touches for God's honor and glory. Wisdom teaches us to offer Mary our praise, for no one is closer to God than she, and no one has ever imitated Him so perfectly. In Heaven with Jesus, Mary always offers our imperfect praise to God mingled with her perfect love, thanksgiving, and obedience to His will.

God's love for us and Mary's glory shine in His Plan for the human race. This Plan, which no one of us fully comprehends, often seems wholly hidden to our human minds; it manifests itself only in God's ways and in God's time. And sometimes, as part of the Plan, difficult situations or events seem overwhelming. But even when they do, when we feel abandoned, betrayed, or unloved, Mary's example leads us to praise God and thank Him for His Son, Jesus, who came to us through Mary. Sometimes it is almost impossible to say "thank you" when everything seems wrong. But if we have already practiced praising God in good times, for the good things we have, offering prayers of praise and gratitude in bad times becomes easier. And in all times, good, bad, and uncertain, those who praise Mary praise the Mother whose Son is the Savior of the World, the Divine Architect whose name is Beauty. Jesus, the Light of our hearts, quenches our burning thirst: Beauty, so ancient and so new, honors those who honor His Mother, for God can never be outdone in generosity.

The following prayer was given in 1917 to three shepherd children, Blessed Jacinta, Blessed Francisco, and Lucia, at Fátima, Portugal, by the Angel of Peace, who identified himself as the Guardian Angel of Portugal. The great Angel of Peace requested that the children make this prayer known to all people on earth. Shortly thereafter, the Blessed Mother appeared to the children and encouraged them to say this prayer. It is such a powerful prayer that the children of Fátima lost all sense of earthly time as they prayed it with their heads bowed to the earth and became caught up in the depths of the mysteries of God.

PRAYER WITH THE QUEEN OF ANGELS

Presented to the world by
the Angel of Peace at Fátima, Portugal, 1917.

O Most Holy Trinity,
Father, Son and Holy Spirit,
I adore Thee profoundly.
I offer Thee the Most Precious
Body, Blood, Soul and Divinity
Of Jesus Christ, present in all
The Tabernacles of the world,
In reparation for the outrages,
Sacrileges and indifference by which
He is offended.
By the infinite merits of
The most Sacred Heart of Jesus
And the Immaculate Heart of Mary,
I beg the conversion of poor sinners.
Amen.
(*Recite three times.*)

The next prayer to Mary belongs to the mystical Saint Catherine of Siena, who was born on the feast of the Annunciation, 1347, and lived only thirty-three years. Saint Catherine of Siena, one of only three women Doctors of the Church, is a giant in the faith; her devotion to Mary is a light for all generations. The following prayer illumines Mary's place in the human family.

If I consider your own great counsel, eternal
  Trinity,
I see that in your light you saw the dignity and
  nobility of the human race.
So, just as love compelled you to draw us out of
  yourself,
so that same love compelled you to buy us back
  when we were lost.
In fact, you showed that you loved us before we
  existed,
when you chose to draw us out of yourself only for
  love.
But you have shown us greater love still by giving
  us yourself,
shutting yourself up today in the pouch of our
  humanity.
And what more could you have given us
than to give us your very self?
So you can truly ask us,
"What should I or could I have done for you that
  I have not done?"
I see, then, that whatever your wisdom saw,
in that great eternal council of yours,
as best for our salvation,
is what your mercy willed,
and what your power has today accomplished.
So in that council your power, your wisdom, and
  your mercy

agreed on our salvation
O eternal Trinity.
In that council your great mercy
chose to be merciful to your creature,
and you, O eternal Trinity, chose to fulfill your
   truth in us
by giving us eternal life.
For this you had created us, that we might share
and be glad in you.
But your justice disagreed with this, protesting in
   the great council
that justice, which lasts forever,
is just as much your hallmark as is mercy.
Therefore, since your justice leaves no evil
   unpunished
nor any good unrewarded,
we could not be saved
because we could not make satisfaction to you for
   our sin.

So what do you do?
What way did your eternal unfathomable wisdom
   find
to fulfill your truth and be merciful,
and to satisfy your justice as well?
What remedy did you give us?
O see what a fitting remedy!
You arranged to give us the Word, your only-
   begotten Son.

He would take on the clay of our flesh which had
    offended you
so that when he suffered in that humanity
your justice would be satisfied—
not by humanity's power,
but by the power of divinity united with that
    humanity.
And so your truth was fulfilled,
and both justice and mercy were satisfied.

O Mary, I see this Word given to you, living in
    you
yet not separated from the Father—
just as the word one has in one's mind does not
    leave one's heart
or become separated from it
even though that word is externalized and com-
    municated to others.
In these things our human dignity is revealed—
that God should have done such and so great
    things for us.

And even more: in you, O Mary,
our human strength and freedom are today
    revealed,
for after the deliberation of such and so great a
    council,
the angel was sent to you to announce to you the
    mystery of the divine counsel

and to seek to know your will,
and God's Son did not come down to your womb
until you had given your will's consent.
He waited at the door of your will for you to open
   to him;
for he wanted to come into you, but he would
   never have entered
unless you had opened to him, saying,
"Here I am, God's servant; let it be done to me as
   you have said."

The strength and freedom of the will is clearly
   revealed, then,
for no good nor any evil can be done without that
   will.
Nor is there any devil or any other creature that
   can
drive it to the guilt of deadly sin without its consent.
Nor, on the other hand, can it be driven to do
   anything good
unless it so chooses.
So the human will is free, for nothing can drive it
   to evil
or to good unless it so chooses.
The eternal Godhead, O Mary, was knocking at
   your door,
but unless you had opened that door of your will,
God would not have taken flesh in you.

Blush, my soul, when you see that
today God has become your relative in Mary.
Today you have been shown that even though
you were made without your help,
you will not be saved without your help.
For today God is knocking at the door of Mary's
    will and
waiting for her to open to Him.

O Mary, my tenderest love!
In you is written the Word from whom we have
    the teaching of life.
You are the tablet that sets this teaching before us.
I see that this Word, once written in you,
was never without the cross of holy desire.
Even as He was conceived within you,
desire to die for the salvation of humankind
was engrafted and bound into Him.
This is why He had been made flesh.
So it was a great cross for Him to carry for such a
    long time
that desire, when He would have liked to see it
    realized at once.
In fact, the Godhead was united even with Christ's
    body in the tomb
and with His soul in limbo,
and afterwards with both His soul and body.
The relationship was so entered into and sealed
that it will never be dissolved,

any more than it has been broken up to now.
Amen.

Saint Catherine of Siena, c. 1370

Saint John Eudes (1601–1680) was a Christian feminist long before the word entered human consciousness. He founded the women's congregation of the Sisters of Our Lady of Charity of the Refuge, which later became known as the Good Shepherd Nuns. This group was consecrated to the charism of helping women in need. He also founded seminaries and published spiritual literature that includes devotions to the Sacred Heart of Jesus. Saint John Eudes encouraged others to say the following prayer.

Hail Mary! Daughter of God the Father.
Hail Mary! Mother of God the Son.
Hail Mary! Spouse of the Holy Spirit.
Hail Mary! Temple of the Most Blessed Trinity.
Hail Mary! Pure Lily of the Effulgent Trinity.
Hail Mary! Celestial Rose of the ineffable Love of
    God.
Hail Mary! Virgin pure and humble, of whom the
    King of heaven willed to be born and with thy
    milk to be nourished.

Hail Mary! Virgin of Virgins,

Hail Mary! Queen of Martyrs, whose soul a sword
transfixed,

Hail Mary! Lady most blessed! unto whom all
power in heaven and earth is given.

Hail Mary! My Queen and my Mother! my Life,
my Sweetness and my Hope,

Hail Mary! Mother Most Amiable,

Hail Mary! Mother Most Admirable,

Hail Mary! Mother of Divine Love,

Hail Mary! Immaculate! Conceived Without
Sin!

Hail Mary! Full of Grace! The Lord is with
Thee!

Blessed art thou among women! And blessed is
the Fruit of thy womb, Jesus!

Blessed be thy spouse, Saint Joseph,

Blessed be thy father, Saint Joachim,

Blessed be thy mother, Saint Anne,

Blessed be thy guardian, Saint John,

Blessed be thy holy angel, Saint Gabriel,

Glory be to God the Father, Who chose thee,

Glory be to God the Son, Who loved thee,

Glory be to God the Holy Spirit, Who espoused
thee.

O Glorious Virgin Mary, may all people love and
praise thee.

Mary, Mother of God! pray for us and bless us,
now and at death in the Name of Jesus, thy
Divine Son. Amen.

Attributed to Saint John Eudes

— ❧ —

Saint Bernardino of Siena (1380–1444) was a great missionary who was deeply devoted to the Mother of God, with whom he shared a birthday. His parents died when he was seven years old, and the saint turned to the Mother of Jesus for his consolations. He found in Mary a profoundly loving prayer partner and confidante for the rest of his life.

— ❧ —

O WOMAN

O Woman,
filled with blessings above all creatures,
You are the only Mother of God.
You are the Queen of the Universe.
You are the dispenser of all graces.
You are the ornament of the Church.
In you is contained the incomprehensible
   greatness of all virtue, and all gifts.
You are the temple of God,
the paradise of delight,
the model of all the just,
the consolation of your children,

the glory and source of our salvation.
You are the gate of heaven, the joy of the elect,
the object of God's great Plan for His holy people.
Though we only imperfectly celebrate your
    praises,
your love for us overcomes all our deficiencies.
May we worthily praise you,
our Mother in God,
for all eternity. Amen.

Saint Bernardino of Siena

———— ⌇ ————

Saint Basil the Great (c. 329–379), Doctor of the Church, is the Patron Saint of Russia and the Patriarch of Eastern Monasticism. He was born into a family of saints, all of whom were deeply devoted to Mary, including his father, Saint Basil the Elder, his mother, Saint Emmelia, his brother, Saint Gregory of Nyssa, his sister, Saint Macrina the Younger, and his grandmother, Saint Macrina. Though the family was wealthy and influential, Basil felt a call to live in voluntary poverty and led his prayerful family in understanding the place of created things in God's Plan for the human race. His principles and rules continue to guide monasteries of the Eastern Church.

ALL CREATION REJOICES

O you who are full of grace, all creation rejoices in
  you!
The hierarchies of the angels and the race of men
  rejoice.
O sanctified temple and rational paradise, virginal
  glory, of whom God took flesh!
He who is God before all ages, became a child.
Your womb He made His Throne,
and your lap He made greater than the heavens.
Indeed all creation exults in you.
Glory be to you!

From the Byzantine Liturgy of Saint Basil

Saint Bonaventure (c. 1221–1274), Doctor of the Church,
was an Italian Franciscan who studied and taught Scripture and
theology in Paris. He was a contemporary of Saint Thomas
Aquinas and is revered as one of the great medieval Fathers. He
was a man capable of extraordinary prayer. Humble and always
available to anyone who sought his time, Saint Bonaventure
was guided in his earthly path to the Heart of God by his love
for the Blessed Virgin Mary. He is known as the Seraphic Doctor of the Church because his many works illumine God's
unfathomable love for the human race.

O MARY, LET ME ALWAYS REMEMBER

O Mary, let me always remember when you com-
    prehended the depths of the love of the Eternal
    Father toward the human race to be so great that,
in order to save them, He willed the death of His Son;
and on the other hand,
seeing the love of the Son in wishing to honor His
    Father perfectly
and therefore to die for us:
in order to conform yourself,
who was always and in all things united to the will
    of God
to this excessive love of both the Father and the
    Son towards the human race,
you also, with your entire will offered,
and consented to the death of your Son,
in order that we might be saved.

Saint Bonaventure, c. 1274

Saint Francis of Assisi (c. 1181–1226) is renowned throughout the world for his spirit of voluntary poverty, for founding
the Franciscan Order of Priests, Brothers, and Sisters, for bearing the wounds of Christ in his own body, and for bequeathing
to future generations a joy-filled love for God, the Blessed
Virgin Mary, the angels and saints, all people, animals, and
things throughout God's creation.

HAIL, HOLY LADY

Hail, holy Lady,
Most holy Queen,
Mary, Mother of God,
Ever Virgin;
Chosen by the most holy Father in heaven,
Consecrated by Him,
With His most holy, beloved Son
And the Holy Spirit, the Comforter.
On you descended, and in you still remains
All the fullness of grace
And every good.
Hail, His Palace.
Hail, His Tabernacle.
Hail, His Robe.
Hail, His Handmaid.
Hail, His Mother.
And hail, all holy virtues,
Who, by the grace
And inspiration of the Holy Spirit,
Are poured into the hearts of the faithful
So that, faithless no longer,
They may be made faithful servants of God
through you.

Saint Francis of Assisi

HAIL TO THE MOTHER OF GOD

The title Mother of God,
Theotokos, or God-bearer, was sanctioned at
the Council of Ephesus in 431.

Hail to the Mother of God,
Hail to the Spouse of God Almighty,
Hail to the Flower of Grace Divine!
Hail to the heir of David's line!
Hail to the world's great Heroine!
Hail to the Virgin pre-elect!
Hail to the Work without defect
Of the Supernal Architect!
Hail to the Maid ordained of old,
Deep in eternities untold,
Ere the blue waves of ocean rolled!
Ere the perennial founts had sprung,
Ere in either the globe was hung,
Ere the morning stars had sung.
Welcome the beatific morn
When the Mother of Life was born—
Only hope of a world forlorn!
What a thrill of ecstatic mirth
Danced along through Heaven and Earth
At the tiding of Mary's birth!
Happy, happy the angel band
Chosen by Mary's side to stand,
As her defense on either hand!
Safe beneath our viewless wings,

Mother elect of the King of kings,
Fear no harm from hurtful things.
What though Eden vanished be,
More than Eden we find in thee!
Thou our joy and jubilee!

Edward Caswell, c. 1900

— ❧ —

O MOTHER-MAIDEN

O Mother-Maiden! O Maid and Mother free!
O bust unburnt, burning in Moses' sight!
That down didst ravish from the Deity,
Through humbleness, the Spirit that did alight,
upon thy heart, whence, through that glory's
   might,
conceived was thy father's sapience!

Lady, thy goodness, thy magnificence,
Thy virtue, and thy great humility,
Surpass all science and all utterances;
For sometimes, Lady! ere men pray to thee,
Thou goest before in thy benignity,
The light to us vouchsafing to our prayer,
To be our guide unto thy Son so dear.

My knowledge is so weak, O blissful Queen,
To tell abroad thy mighty worthiness,
That I the weight of it may not sustain;

But as a child of twelve months old, or less,
That laboreth his language to express;
Even so fare I; and therefore, I thee pray,
Guide thou my song, which I of thee shall say.

Geoffrey Chaucer (c. 1342–1400)
(modernized by William Wordsworth)

—— ❧ ——

VIRGIN AND MOTHER
OF OUR DEAR REDEEMER

Virgin and Mother of our dear Redeemer,
All hearts are touched and softened at your name;
Alike the bandit, with the blood-stained hand,
The priest, the prince, the scholar and the peasant,
The man of deeds, the visionary dreamer,
Pay homage to you as one ever present,
And even as children, who have much offended
A too indulgent father, in great shame,
Penitent, and yet not daring unattended
To go into his presence, at the gate
Speak with their sister, and confiding wait
Till she goes in before and intercedes:
So men, repenting of their evil deeds,
And yet not venturing rashly to draw near
With their requests an angry father's ear,
Offer to you their prayers and their confession,
And you for them in heaven make intercession.
And if our faith had given us nothing more,

Than this example of all Womanhood,
So mild, so merciful, so strong, so good,
So patient, so peaceful, loyal, loving, pure—
This were enough to prove it higher and truer
Than all the creeds the world had ever known before.
        Henry Wadsworth Longfellow (1807–1882)

— ❧ —

AVE MARIA

Ave Maria! o'er the earth and sea,
That heavenliest hour of heaven is worthiest thee!
Ave Maria! blessed be the hour
The time, the chime, the spot, where I so oft
Have felt that moment in its fullest power
Sink o'er the earth so beautiful and soft
While swung the deep bell in the distant tower,
Or the faint dying day hymn stole aloft,
And not a breath crept through the rosy air,
And yet the forest leaves seem'd stirr'd with prayer.

Ave Maria! 'tis the hour of prayer;
Ave Maria! 'tis the hour of love;
Ave Maria! may our spirits dare
Look up to thine and to thy Son's above.
Ave Maria! oh, that face so fair,
Those downcast eyes beneath the Almighty Dove!
        Lord George Noel Gordon Byron (1788–1824)

ONE SIGH OF RAPTURE

The wandering shepherds told their breathless tale,
Of the bright choir that woke the sleeping vale;
Told how the shining multitude proclaimed;
They spoke with hurried words and accents wild;
Calm in His cradle slept the heavenly Child.
No trembling word your Motherly joy revealed,—
One sigh of rapture, and your lips were sealed.

Oliver Wendell Holmes (1809–1894)

CHAPTER 3

MOTHER MOST POWERFUL

Prayers of Consecration

Our Blessed Mother invites us to consecrate our hearts, our families, our yesterdays, and our tomorrows to her Immaculate Heart so that she may present them all to her Son on our behalf. By consecrating ourselves to God through Mary, we are entrusting ourselves to her; by prayerful commitment, we place everything we have in her hands. Mary becomes our advocate with God. She knows Him well: she knows what He likes, and how He likes to receive everything human.

Saint Bernard of Clairvaux (1090–1153) had the privilege of seeing our Blessed Mother. This is what the great French Doctor of the Church taught regarding all gifts to God, including the gift of ourselves:

If you wish to offer anything to God, do not forget to present it through Mary, in order that Grace may return to its Author through the same channel by which it came to you; for God, no doubt could have bestowed His graces without her mediation, but He wished to provide you with a pure means of returning to Him. Perhaps your hands are stained with blood, or soiled by things you should have rejected. Therefore it is that the little you desire to offer should be presented by the pure and worthy hands of Mary. You may then be secure that your offering will not be despised. Her hands are like the pure and spotless lily, and He who loves the lily will be pleased to see among the lilies the modest gift which you present to Him through the hands of Mary.

Six hundred years later, Saint Louis Marie Grignon de Montfort bequeathed us his reflections concerning consecration to Mary:

All our perfection consists in being conformed, united, and consecrated to Jesus Christ: and therefore, the most perfect of all devotions is, without any doubt, that which perfectly conforms, unites and consecrates us to Christ. Now, Mary being the most conformed of all creatures to Jesus Christ, that which most consecrates and conforms the soul to Our Lord is devotion to His Holy Mother, and the more a soul is consecrated to Mary, the more it is consecrated to Jesus.

Hence it comes to pass that the most perfect consecration to Jesus Christ is nothing less than a perfect and entire consecration of ourselves to the Blessed Virgin, and this is the devotion I teach; a perfect renewal of the vows and promises of Baptism.

This devotion consists in giving ourselves entirely to Mary, in order to belong entirely to Jesus through her. We must give her:

1. our body, with all its senses and members;
2. our soul, with all its powers;
3. our exterior goods of fortune, whether present or to come
4. our interior and spiritual goods, which are our merits and our virtues, and our good works, past, present and future. . . .

We give to her all our merits, graces and virtues—not to communicate them to others, for our merits, graces and virtues are, properly speaking, incommunicable, and it is only Jesus Christ Who, in making Himself our surety with His Father, is able to communicate His merits—but we give her them to keep them, augment them and embellish them for us.

Our satisfactions, however, we give her, to communicate to whom she likes, and for the greatest glory of God. . . . By this devotion, we give to Jesus Christ in the most perfect manner, by Mary's hands, all we can give to Him. . . . Here, everything is given and consecrated to

Him, even the right of disposing of our interior goods, and of the satisfactions which we gain by our good works day after day. . . .

We consecrate ourselves at one and the same time to the most Holy Virgin and to Jesus Christ: to the most Holy Virgin as to the perfect means which Jesus Christ has chosen whereby to unite Himself to us, and us to Him; and to Our Lord as to our last end, to Whom as our Redeemer and our God we owe all.

The value of family consecrations was disclosed to our family in a highly unusual and blessed way. Before our children were born, my husband and I consecrated them to the Immaculate Heart of Mary and to the Sacred Heart of Jesus, in accordance with our faith. As our children grew into adulthood, we were concerned about their level of commitment to our family beliefs. After our youngest child finished high school, the entire family journeyed to a Marian Shrine far from home. Each of us fasted in preparation for the trip, and we increased our prayer life.

On the first morning of our visit to the Shrine, my husband and I climbed a tall mountain and knelt before a huge cross in quiet prayer. There, as we prayed, we reconsecrated our children to the Immaculate Heart of Mary for her Son. No one was near us, and no one heard us. But several hours later a young villager, whom we did not know at the time, approached us. Though she does not speak English, she said these exact English words: "The Blessed Mother asked me to thank you for giving your children back to her and to tell you they are better off with her." We were stunned. We also learned the value of reconsecration.

Only in deepest faith and trust are we able to hand over to Mary what we hold most dear. Yet God had such great faith in her, and so profoundly trusted her, that He became Mary's helpless Infant, allowing Himself to be totally dependent on her for every human need. If God so entrusts Himself to Mary, why shouldn't we?

MARY'S PROMISE

A famous nun from long ago, Saint Gertrude the Great (c. 1256–c. 1302), lives on powerfully in our collective memory. On one occasion, the Blessed Mother appeared to the German Benedictine Sister with the following promise that is as blessed today as it was in Saint Gertrude's lifetime:

> I will appear at the hour of death to those who pray to me as the *White Lily of the Ever Peaceful and Glorious Trinity* with such glory that they will experience the very joys of Heaven.

In response, the saint composed this prayer of consecration that binds us to Mary's great promise:

— ❧ —

CONSECRATION PRAYER TO MARY

Hail, White Lily of the ever peaceful and glorious Trinity!
Hail Vermilion Rose, the Delight of Heaven,

Of whom, the King of Heaven was born,
And by whose milk He was nourished!
Do thou forever feed our souls by the effusions of
    your divine influences.
Amen.

Saint Gertrude the Great

On the mountain of Jasna Gora, overlooking the city of Czestochowa, Poland, stands the famous Shrine of Our Lady of Czestochowa, considered by many to be one of the holiest places in the world. Contained in the Shrine is the ancient and greatly venerated image of the "Black Madonna."

Pope John Paul II has led the world in consecration before the Holy Image of the Black Madonna. This prayer is recommended to be said each day upon arising.

CONSECRATION TO
THE BLACK MADONNA,
OUR LADY OF CZESTOCHOWA

Holy Mother of Czestochowa, you are full of
    grace,
goodness and mercy.
I consecrate to you all my thoughts, words and
    actions,
my soul and body.

I beseech your blessings and especially prayers
for my salvation.
Today I consecrate myself to you,
Good Mother, totally
with body and soul amid joy and
sufferings to obtain for myself and others
your blessings on this earth
and eternal life in heaven. Amen.

— ❧ —

Few men of such eminence extol the virtues and glories of
the Blessed Virgin Mary as does Pope John Paul II, who has
entrusted world peace to Mary and encourages others to do
likewise. The following is a personal consecration to Jesus
through Mary used daily by His Holiness:

— ❧ —

In the presence of all the heavenly court I choose
thee this day for my Mother and mistress. I deliver
and consecrate to thee, as thy slave, my body and
soul, my goods, both interior and exterior, and
even the value of all my good actions, past, present
and future; leaving to thee the entire and full right
of disposing of me, and all that belongs to me,
without exception, according to thy good pleasure,
for the greater glory of God in time and eternity.

Saint Louis Marie Grignon de Montfort, c. 1713

Another well-known daily consecration:

— ❧ —

MORNING OFFERING OF REPARATION
O Jesus, through the Immaculate Heart of Mary,
and in union with the Holy Sacrifice of the Mass
being offered throughout the world, I offer You all
my prayers, works, joys and sufferings of this day
in reparation for offenses committed against Your
Sovereignty, against the Immaculate Heart of
Mary, for my sins and the sins of the whole world.
Amen.

— ❧ —

For those who may not have known about the Consecration
Life Offering until now, various versions of the following prayer,
taught in Catholic schools for generations, may be helpful.

— ❧ —

CONSECRATION LIFE OFFERING
O my God, in union with the Lord Jesus Christ,
through the Immaculate Heart of Mary,
I offer to you my entire life, just as it is,
from the moment You breathed me out of Your
    Infinite Heart of Love
into my mother's womb,

until that moment we are reunited when my life
  on earth is spent.
I offer to You all my handicaps and weaknesses,
past mistakes and failures, talents and abilities;
all the joys, sorrows, blessings, disappointments
and victories of my entire life.
I entrust to Your mercy my past and my future.
I place in Your Hands my family and loved ones;
those who are living now on earth, those who preceded me and those yet to be born.
I offer to You all that happens to me
this day and every day of my life,
together with all my thoughts, words and deeds,
for Your honor and glory
and for the salvation of souls.
May Your Perfect Will be realized in my life.
  Amen.

— ☙ —

FÁTIMA ACT OF CONSECRATION TO
THE IMMACULATE HEART OF MARY

O Virgin of Fátima, Mother of Mercy, Queen of
  Heaven and earth, Refuge of Sinners,
we consecrate ourselves to your Immaculate Heart
in order to enter into a more intimate relationship
  with your Divine Son, Jesus Christ.
To you we consecrate our hearts, our families and
  all that we have.

So that this consecration may be effective and lasting,
we renew today, and every day, the promises of our
    Baptism:
we promise to live as faithful Christians, to read
    the sacred Scriptures,
to pray, especially the Rosary of your Son, to
    partake of the Holy Eucharist, to observe the
    First Saturdays of Reparation each month,
and to work and sacrifice for the conversion of
    sinners, especially ourselves.
We pray that through your intercession
the coming of the Kingdom of Christ may be
    hastened. Amen.

— ❧ —

DAILY OFFERING

O Jesus, through the Immaculate Heart of Mary,
I offer You all my prayers, works, joys and
    sufferings,
all that this day may bring,
be they good or bad:
for the love of God,
for the conversion of sinners,
and in reparation for all the sins committed
against the Sacred Heart of Jesus
and
the Immaculate Heart of Mary.
Amen.

THREE HIGHLY BLESSED PRAYERS OF
CONSECRATION TO MARY

Most Holy Virgin, I venerate you with my whole
   heart,
above all the angels and saints in Paradise,
as the Daughter of the Eternal Father,
and I consecrate to you my soul with all its
   powers.
(*Pray the Hail Mary.*)

Most Holy Virgin, I venerate you with my whole
   heart,
above all the angels and saints in Paradise,
as the Mother of the only-begotten Son,
and I consecrate to you my body with all its
   senses.
(*Pray the Hail Mary.*)

Most Holy Virgin, I venerate you with my whole
   heart,
above all the angels and saints in Paradise,
as the Spouse of the Holy Spirit,
and I consecrate to you my whole heart and all its
   affections,
praying you to obtain for me,
from the ever-blessed Trinity,
all that is necessary for my salvation.
(*Pray the Hail Mary.*)

This following prayer is a special consecration to Our Lady of Guadalupe, the title under which Mary appeared to native American Juan Diego in Mexico City in 1531.

— ❧ —

CONSECRATION TO
OUR LADY OF GUADALUPE

O Most Holy Virgin Mary, Mother of God,
I (*mention name*), although most unworthy of
    being your servant,
Yet touched by your wonderful mercy and by the
    desire to serve,
consecrate myself to your Immaculate Heart, and
    choose you today,
in the presence of my Guardian Angel and the
    whole heavenly court, for my special Mother,
    Lady, and Advocate, under the title of
Our Lady of Guadalupe, the name given to the
    heavenly image,
left to us as a pledge of your motherly kindness.
I firmly resolve that I will love and serve you
    always,
and do whatever I can to induce others to love and
    serve you.
I pray to you Mother of God, and my most kind
    and amiable Mother,
that you receive me into your family,
and keep me as your special child forever.

Assist me in all thoughts, words and actions at
    every moment of my life,
that every step and breath may be directed to the
    greater glory of God;
and through your most powerful intercession,
    obtain for me that
I may never more offend my Lord Jesus, that I
    may glorify Him
in this life, and that I may also love you, and be
    with you,
in the company of the Blessed Trinity throughout
    eternity in holy Paradise.
In order to live this consecration as did Juan Diego,
I promise to renew it frequently,
especially on the twelfth day of each month;
and mindful of your messages to us at Lourdes and
    Fatima and Akita,
I will strive to lead a life of prayer and sacrifice, of
    fidelity to the Rosary
and of reparation to your Immaculate Heart.
    Amen.[1]

Jesuit John Carroll was the first Archbishop of the United
States. His family risked everything to sign the Declaration of
Independence. In 1792 Archbishop John Carroll publicly
implored the Lord God to forever safeguard the young nation
under the gracious, maternal protection of Mary.

CONSECRATION OF THE
UNITED STATES OF AMERICA TO MARY

Most Holy Trinity, Our Father in Heaven,
Who chose Mary as the fairest of Your daughters;
Holy Spirit Who chose Mary as Your Spouse;
God the Son Who chose Mary as Your Mother,
In union with Mary, we adore Your Majesty
And acknowledge Your supreme, eternal dominion
    and authority.

Most Holy Trinity, we place the United States of
    America
Into the hands of Mary Immaculate
In order that she may present the country
To You.
Through her we wish to thank You for the great
    resources of this land
And for the freedom which has been its heritage.

Through the intercession of Mary, have mercy on
    the catholic church in America.
Grant us peace.
Have mercy on our President
And on all the officers of our government.

Grant us a fruitful economy, born of justice and
    labor.
Protect the family life of the nation.

Guard the precious gift of many religious vocations.
Through the intercession of Mary Our Mother,
   have mercy on the sick,
The tempted, sinners . . . on all who are in need.

Mary, Immaculate Virgin, Our Mother,
Patroness of our land, we praise and honor you
And give ourselves to you.
Protect us from every harm.
Pray for us, that acting always according to your
   will
And the will of your Divine Son,
We may live and die pleasing to God. Amen.[2]

John Carroll

— ❧ —

CONSECRATION PRAYER
FOR THE UNITED STATES

God our Father, Giver of life,
we entrust the United States of America to
Your loving care.
You are the rock on which this nation was
   founded.
You alone are the true source of
our cherished rights to life, liberty
and the pursuit of happiness.
Reclaim this land for Your glory
and dwell among Your people.

Send Your Spirit to touch the hearts of
our nation's leaders.
Open their minds to the great worth
of human life and the responsibilities
that accompany human freedom.

Remind Your people that true happiness
is rooted in seeking and doing Your will.

Through the intercession of Mary
Immaculate, Patroness of our land,
grant us the courage to reject
the "culture of death."
Lead us into a new millennium of life.
We ask this through Christ our Lord. Amen.[3]

CONSECRATION OF
THE ENTIRE WORLD
THE NEW HEAVEN AND NEW EARTH

O Divine Eternal Unchanging Creator of the
   World
How great is Thy Love. How great is Thy Mercy.

O True God, Thou Alone art Perfection.
O True God, Thou Alone needeth Nothing.
Yet, in Thine Infinite Perfection,

Thou Alone allowest every prayer we pray
To draw down upon each of us and Thine earth
The healing measures of Thine Infinite Perfection.

O Divine Eternal Unchanging Creator of the World
Thou hast freely willed to need us.
In Mary, Mother Maiden Most Pure, Thy Word
Embraced us in Mystery to dwell among Thy
    sinners.

To Thee, to Thy Plan O Great Mystery of the
    Incarnation,
We sinners do freely surrender and abandon
    ourselves,
Our families, our possessions, our earth, our lives,
Our sun and seas and streams and stars and skies.

Image and likeness of Thee are we
Who freely present to Thee all these
Of Mary, Thy Mother Maiden Most Pure
Who hovers over Thee Who rules all these.

Infinite Babe of Thy Mother Maiden Most Pure,
From Mary's heart alone flows earth to Thee to
    please,
Thy Mother Maiden Most Pure, forever the New
    Earth,
Thee, Mary's Babe, Divine Eternal Unchanging
Source of the World, forever the New Heaven.

Sing and dance and play on the New Earth
For the old has passed away in the blink of an eye.
Dwell now in the Immaculate Heart of the New
    Earth,
Mary, God's Mother Maiden Most Pure.

There eternally is the New Heaven,
Mary's Babe, Divine Eternal Unchanging
Source of the World: the Lord Jesus Christ forever.
Amen.

CHAPTER 4

MOTHER
MOST AMIABLE

Prayers for Groups

The Lord Jesus Christ promised that wherever two or more are gathered in His name, He is present. This was one of His calls to us to form prayer groups. Such prayer groups can be as simple or as elaborate as their members desire. A prayer group can be formed anywhere by a single person and his or her guardian angel; it can also be a husband and wife, parent and child, two co-workers, or even two children on a playground who pause and pray together. A prayer group can include the hundreds of thousands of people who gather in fields and in stadiums to pray with the Pope, or with Protestant Minister Billy Graham, or even the Promise Keepers. A prayer group can meet in a church, a member's home, at work during lunch hour, or under the stars. There may be a prayer leader, perhaps a priest, minister, rabbi, or sister, or a lay member selected by the group. When there is no specific leader, members may prefer to take turns reading prayers or Scripture passages aloud. Some groups light candles in front of icons or other sacred images; other groups just like to join hands around the family dinner table. But no matter what the size or approach, prayer groups strengthen their members' faith, trust in God, and ability to make wise spiritual choices.

MARY'S PRAYER GROUPS

Marian prayer groups have a long history. The good thief hanging beside Jesus on the Cross had no choice but to see Mary, to experience her tender and compassionate love for him, and to watch her adore her Son. Involuntarily, he was included in Mary's prayer group on Calvary. He began then to trust Jesus. To emulate the good thief and trust Jesus is to know Jesus' promise to him: "Today you will be with me in Paradise" (*See* Luke 23:43).

Since that prayer group at the cross, there have been official organizations that gather to pray with Mary. The Knights and Dames of Malta worldwide pray fervently to Mary under the title "Our Lady of Palermo." In the United States, there are about 140,000 members of the Catholic Daughters of America who profess a special devotion to Mary. The Knights of Columbus are renowned as filial sons of Mary. Many ethnic societies in the United States, such as the Ancient Order of Hibernia, to name only one, have strong traditions of honoring prayer life with Mary as a group.

Four hundred and twenty-five years ago, the Sodality of Our Lady was formed to enlist Catholic men in spiritual battle to bring the Kingdom of God throughout the world. This group calls Mary the commander-in-chief of its spiritual army, for, according to Scripture, Mary is the woman whose offspring crushes the serpent's head (Gen. 3:15). Sodalists are called "Children of Mary." In 1751 women were admitted to the Sodality of Our Lady. Since that time, sodalities have spread to the entire world.

The Legion of Mary is another Marian prayer group with a global presence. Like other groups, the Legion of Mary requires its members to pray together and serve the less fortunate. The fundamental motto of all these organizations is "To Jesus with Mary."

In recent apparitions, the Blessed Mother has indicated that it is pleasing to God in these times for all people to join or form prayer groups immediately as protection against the evil in the world. As a result, the number of prayer groups has increased dramatically. The Magnificat, a new Marian prayer group formed in New Orleans just ten years ago, has grown to include forty chapters across the United States. And in those same ten years, countless informal daily Rosary groups have sprung up in homes, offices, schools, hospitals, factories, and places of worship throughout the world. A Marian prayer group at the World Bank meets every day for Mass and prayer in the World Bank chapel; similarly, a group at the Pentagon says the Rosary and attends Mass together daily.

Mary's prayer groups today are a spontaneous grassroots effort of people all over the world to meet the deepest needs of their hearts. One of the benefits of belonging is the confidence Mary instills in the group that God will bring a successful conclusion to human endeavors, as long as each person does his or her utmost in prayer and work. With enough sincere personal prayer discipline, we become capable of consciously focusing on the Presence of God in all that lives. That focus ripens into an awareness of the reciprocal love relationship that God desires and effects with His human creatures.

Marian prayer groups usually begin by invoking the Lord Jesus' presence among them and inviting the Blessed Mother and the angels and saints to join with them in prayer. Amazing experiences are reported all over the world in these times by groups who extend such heavenly invitations. The groups then often read from Scripture and pray together with Mary to her Son. Afterwards, prayer group members share fellowship, perhaps discussing their difficulties and possible solutions. The meeting may close with another reading from Scripture.

Members are asked to follow Jesus without reservation, to do acts of penance for certain holy intentions. They are asked to pray more frequently and to embrace fasting. Members do without what they enjoy most, such as alcohol, cigarettes, coffee, sweets, cinema, television, unnecessary sports: they fast or abstain from some pleasure at least twice a week as a personal sign that they love God more than that pleasure. Different groups prefer to pray and fast together in different ways. No particular way is best. The fruit of Marian prayer groups is great joy and tranquillity. Renouncing all excesses, and choosing to live a moderate life of great simplicity and peace, is an underlying theme of all Marian prayer groups.

The eminent Marian theologian René Laurentin itemized certain rules for Mary's prayer groups, based on his research of Marian apparitions throughout the centuries. Several of the more practiced prayer groups choose to follow these guidelines. For those just beginning a prayer group, feel free to follow as many of these rules as possible. Gradually, the wisdom of the rules will become evident, and with perseverance, they will become a source of Light.

1. Renounce all passions and inordinate desires. Avoid constant television, particularly evil programs, excessive sports, the unreasonable enjoyment of food and drink, alcohol, and tobacco.

2. Abandon yourselves to God without any restrictions.

3. Eliminate all anguish and worry. Whoever abandons himself to God has no place in his heart for anguish and worry. Difficulties will persist, but they will serve for spiritual growth and will bring great glory to God.

4. Love your enemies. Banish from your heart all hatred, bitterness, preconceived judgments. Pray for your enemies and call the Divine Blessing over them.

5. Fast twice a week.

6. Devote at least three hours each day to prayer: include a half hour in the morning and a half hour in the evening. Include the Holy Mass with reception of the Holy Eucharist and the prayers and meditations of the Holy Rosary in the daily

prayers. Pray with great concentration and awareness. Set aside times during the day to adore Jesus
in the Most Blessed Sacrament. Allow yourselves
to be led by the grace of God. Do not focus upon
the problems of the day. God will bring solutions
to problems if each one strives to do his utmost in
working and in praying. It is necessary to extend
the spirit of prayer to all daily work and activities.

7. Be prudent. Pray for the virtue of Prudence. The
evil one will tempt and taunt those who resolve to
consecrate themselves to God. Only as faith is
strengthened through prayer and fasting is the
power of the evil one diminished.

8. Pray fervently for the Holy Father, Bishops, and all
those responsible for the Church and the people of
God. Offer prayers and sacrifices for them.'

Mary's prayer groups are for everyone on earth. Even the
weakest and sickest of God's people, such as the dying good
thief, may call to Jesus with Mary. Her prayer groups are an
invitation to kneel with her at the foot of the cross with all
humankind.

Perhaps you already belong to one of Mary's prayer groups.
If not, are you called to begin one? The following prayers may
be an excellent start for you and your guardian angel, or a
friend or family member. The day is not so distant when all
will be members of Mary's prayer groups. Until then, every
prayer from every person or group in the world will help melt
human hearts of stone.

GROUP PRAYER FOR FAITH

How can I praise you duly, O most chaste Virgin?
For you alone among humans are all holy, and you
    give to all the help and grace they need.
All we who are on the earth put our hope in you:
strengthen our faith, shine through the dimness of
    this world,
while we, God's people, sing your praise.
Throne of the Cherubim are you
and Gate of Heaven.
Pray without ceasing for us
that we may be saved in the day of dread.
Amen.

      From the Liturgy of the Antiochene Syriac Rite

GROUP PRAYER FOR HELP

Let your intercession be with us, O Mother Most
    Pure,
and come to us in our needs, as is your wont.
We are exiles on this earth, without end ever before
    our eyes, and even now many of us perish.
Help us by your prayers, O Merciful Mother.
Be always our advocate lest we are lost through our
    own ill will.
Blessed and most holy one, plead for us before
    God

that He may be gracious to us through your
  asking. Amen.
  From the Liturgy of the Maronite (Antiochene) Rite

— ⟡ —

GROUP PRAYER FOR DELIVERANCE
FROM DISTURBING TEMPTATIONS

O Mother of God, trusting in you we shall not be
  ashamed
but saved.
Strengthened by your help and intercession,
O holy, pure and perfect one,
we shall resist our temptations and scatter them.
We take up the shelter of your aid as a strong
  shield,
and we supplicate you, O Mother of God,
that you preserve each of us through your prayers.
Lead us out of the darkness of sin to glorify the
  Almighty God Who took flesh in you. Amen.
From the Liturgy of the
Coptic Office of Sleep, Alexandrian Rite

— ⟡ —

GROUP PRAYER FOR PROTECTION

We, faithful, hold a joyful feast today, shadowed
  by your coming.
O Mother of God,

praising and looking upon your most holy image,
we reverently say:
cover us with your sacred veil
and liberate us from all evil,
beseeching your Son, Christ our God,
to save our souls.
Amen.

From the Liturgy of the
Protection of the Blessed Virgin, October 1

———— ❧ ————

The following is a powerful consecration for family prayer groups.

———— ❧ ————

FAMILY CONSECRATION
TO THE LORD JESUS CHRIST

ALL: Most kind Jesus, You alone are our Lord and
Ruler. Humbly kneeling before You, we consecrate
our family, living, deceased, and yet to be born to
You forever. In You we have total trust and confidence. May Your Spirit penetrate our thoughts,
our desires, our words and actions. Bless all our
undertakings, share in all our joys, in all our trials
and all our daily labors. Grant us to know You better, to love You more, and to serve You faithfully
without faltering.

Lord Jesus Christ, Son of the Living God, protect our family forever. Enter closely into our midst and make each of us Your own through this solemn consecration to You. By the Immaculate Heart of Your Blessed Mother, under her title "Queen of Peace," set up your kingdom of peace, love, and joy throughout the world. Grant that one cry may resound from every home on earth:

"May the Lord Jesus be everywhere loved, blessed, and glorified forever."

(*Silence for meditation*)

He promised: "[W]hoever loves me will be loved by my Father, and I will love him and reveal myself to him" (John 14:21).

ALL: Come Lord Jesus, come Lord Jesus. Come Lord Jesus. Amen.

———— �œ ————

Everyone knows someone in need of conversion. The prayer for conversion below has been prayed successfully by groups in Europe and now comes to prayer groups in the United States. This prayer is also effective when prayed by only one person.

PRAYER TO MARY FOR THE
CONVERSION OF A LOVED ONE

Your prayer group of sweet loving where I gave
    myself to you
Has filled me with a wonder that is full of
    thoughts of you.
My life is now poured out, in love and work and
    prayer
And yet, there is a sadness, for I long to help and
    share.
The one whom Heaven gave me to share this life
    on earth
Has not received your gentle kiss and does not
    know your worth.
I long to share my happiness, to talk of all your
    words,
To plan our lives around them and bring others to
    the Lord.
But "my love" views me with sorrow at all the time
    I take
In chasing after visions and praying for your sake.
O gentle Mother, hear me, please touch "my love"
    for me
That together we may journey with your Blessed
    Son and thee.
Let our family be a haven for the lonely and the weak
That we may bring your blessings when a messen-
    ger you seek.

May our home be full of laughter, may our journey be a prayer.
Let our lives reflect the beauty of your loving and
your care. Amen.

Ishbel McGilvery McGregor, Inverness, Scotland

—— ⌒≥⌐ ——

FOR HEALING OF BODY,
MIND, SPIRIT, RELATIONSHIPS

A prayer group format in honor of our Blessed Mother as Queen
of Peace, which lends itself easily to a formal place of worship,
was circulated throughout the world in 1988. Ideally, this prayer
service is conducted in front of the Blessed Sacrament.

The Apostles' Creed, the Our Father, Hail Mary, and Glory
Be to the Father, along with the Joyful, Sorrowful, and Glorious Mysteries, can all be found in chapter 9 of this book. In
addition, the Litany of Loreto can be found in chapter 7, and
the Magnificat in chapter 5.

—— ⌒≥⌐ ——

ALL: We adore you, O most holy Lord Jesus Christ
and we bless you here and in all places where two
or more are gathered in Your Holy Name throughout the world.

ALL: Blessed be the Holy Trinity, one God, now
and forever. Amen.

Glory to our Father, Who created me; glory to the Son, Who redeemed me; glory to the Holy Spirit, Who sanctifies me.

ALL (Consecration to the Sacred Heart of Jesus): Jesus, we know that You are merciful and that You have offered Your Heart for us. It is crowned with thorns and with our sins. We know that You implore us constantly so that we do not go astray. Jesus, remember us when we are in sin. By means of Your Heart, make all people love one another. Make hate disappear from among Your people. Show us Your Love. We all love You and want You to protect us with Your Shepherd's Heart and free us from every sin. Jesus, enter into every heart. Knock! Knock at the door of our hearts. Be patient and never desist. We are still closed because we have not understood Your Love. Knock continuously. O Good Jesus, make us open our hearts to You, at least in the moment we remember Your Passion suffered for us. Amen.

ALL (Consecration to the Immaculate Heart of Mary, our Mother): O Immaculate Heart of Mary, ardent with goodness, show your love to us. May the flame of your heart, O Mary, descend on all mankind. We love you so. Impress true love in our hearts so that we have a continuous desire for you. O Mary, meek and humble of heart, remember us when we are in sin. You know that all people sin. Give us, by means of your Immaculate Heart, spiritual health. Let us always see the goodness of your maternal heart, and may we be converted by means of the flames of God's love for us in your heart. Amen.

Jesus said: "Peace be with you. . . . As the Father has sent me, so I send you" (John 20:21).

ALL: Lord Jesus, fill me with Your Holy Spirit that I may live Your Word and thereby be an instrument of Your peace to the ends of the earth.

Jesus said: "[B]e like servants who await their master's return. . . . You must be prepared, for at an hour you do not expect, the Son of Man will come" (Luke 12:36, 40).

LEADER: Selected reading from Sacred Scripture
(*Short silence for meditation*)

ALL: Recitation of the Joyful Mysteries of the Holy Rosary

Recitation of the Sorrowful Mysteries of the Holy Rosary

Recitation of the Glorious Mysteries of the Holy Rosary

Litany of Loreto

Magnificat

(*In silence*)

O my God, I am heartily sorry for having offended You, and I detest all my sins because I dread the loss of Heaven and the pains of hell. But, most of all my God, because You are all good and deserving of all my love. I firmly resolve with the help of Your grace to confess my sins, do penance and amend my life. Amen.

Holy Sacrifice of the Mass (with Homily) (*Priest*)

ALL (Prayer of Saint Michael the Archangel):

Saint Michael the Archangel, defend us in battle, be our safeguard against the wickedness and snares of the devil. May God rebuke him, we humbly pray; and do you, Prince of the Heavenly Host, by the power of God, cast into hell all the evil spirits who wander through the world seeking the ruin of souls. Amen.

Apostles' Creed (*Priest leads*)

Seven Our Fathers, seven Hail Marys, seven Glory Be to the Fathers

Spontaneous Prayer and Blessing (*Priest*)

———— ⬥ ————

All are invited to socialize and share experiences after the service.

CHAPTER 5

MOTHER OF OUR CREATOR

Prayers for Holiness

The Lord Jesus commanded us to be perfect as our Heavenly Father is perfect. But because God alone is holy, we continuously strive toward the perfection of holiness. We are each created to be holy; it is something for which we hunger, consciously or perhaps unconsciously; it is our eternal quest. Jesus, who is God made man, is the Light for our journey toward the Holiness of God.

We seek holiness with truthful hearts when we receive the divine gift of Wisdom. Supernatural Wisdom is a special gift the Blessed Mother obtains from her Spouse, the Holy Spirit, for those who pray to or with her. Supernatural Wisdom allows us to experience God's unconditional Pure Love now. It gives us eyes to see God in the world, ears to hear God in the world, and hearts that beat for God alone. The prayers in this chapter can lead us along the path to this great Gift.

Humility is a virtue necessary for holiness. Only a humble heart is open to God, and the more humble a heart is, the more it is capable of knowing God. Humility is a condition of the soul; like the scent of a flower, it is known by its effects. Many of the prayers in this chapter strengthen us in the pursuit of this virtue.

There is a particular saint who is endowed by God with the power to assist us in our quest for holiness. Saint Mechtildis is a beloved Marian saint and apostle of God's tender love and mercy for the human race. The Lord has given her the great gift of helping us to holiness. Although I know of no particular prayers to Mary by Saint Mechtildis, we may call upon her as a colleague in prayer to lead us to the heart of Mary. In this way, our paths to holiness will be made easier, for Mary, Mother of Divine Providence, clothes her children in her virtues. Mary always places her children in the Heart of Jesus.

Saint Louis Marie Grignon de Montfort (1673–1716) wrote a small spiritual masterpiece, *True Devotion to Mary*, that provides insights into the wonders of Mary as a perfect prayer partner. He observed:

Oh, what a difference between a soul which has been formed in Christ by the ordinary ways of those who, like the sculptor, trust in their own skill and ingenuity, and a soul thoroughly tractable, entirely detached and well molten, which, without trusting to its own skill, casts itself into Mary, there to be molded by the Holy Spirit! How many stains and defects and illusions, how

much darkness and how much human nature is there in
the former, and oh, how pure, how heavenly and how
Christ like is the latter!

— ⤳ —

PRAYER FOR THE SPIRIT OF MARY

My powerful Queen,
you are all mine through your mercy,
and I am all yours.
Take away from me all that may displease God
and cultivate in me all that is pleasing to Him.

May the light of your faith
dispel the darkness of my mind,
your deep humility
take the place of my pride,
your continual sight of God
fill my memory with His Presence.

May the fire of the charity of your heart
inflame the lukewarmness of my own heart.
May your virtues take the place of my sins.
May your merits be my enrichment
and make up for all
that is wanting in me before God.

My beloved Mother,
grant that I may have no other spirit but your spirit,

to know Jesus Christ and His Divine will
and to praise and glorify the Lord,
that I may love God with burning love like yours.[1]
Saint Louis Marie Grignon de Montfort, c. 1716

———— ✦ ————

PRAYER OF SAINT LOUIS MARIE
GRIGNON DE MONTFORT

Hail Mary, daughter of God the Father!

Hail Mary, Mother of God the Son!

Hail Mary, Spouse of the Holy Spirit!

Hail Mary, temple of the most Holy Trinity!

Hail Mary, my mistress, my wealth, my mystic rose,

Queen of my heart, my Mother, my life, my
    sweetness

and my dearest hope. I am all yours, and all that I
    have

is yours, O Virgin blessed above all things.

May your soul be in me to magnify the Lord;

may your spirit be in me to rejoice in God.

Place yourself, O faithful Virgin, as a seal upon my
    heart,

that in you and through you, I may be found
    faithful to God.

Grant, most gracious Virgin, that I may be
    numbered among those

whom you are pleased to love, to teach and to
    guide, to favor and

protect as your children.
Grant that with the help of your love I may
   despise all earthly
consolation and cling to heavenly things, until
   through the
Holy Spirit, your faithful Spouse, and through
   you, His faithful spouse, Jesus Christ be formed
   within me for the glory of the Father. Amen.

Saint Louis Marie Grignon
de Montfort (c. 1673–1716)

———— ❧ ————

PRAYER TO MARY FOR DIVINE MERCY

Intercede for us, O Mother most pure.
Come to us now in our need.
We are exiles on this earth.
Without end, ever before our eyes,
And even now we perish.
Help us by your prayers, O Merciful Mother.
Be always our advocate lest we are lost
By our own mean spiritedness.
Blessed and most holy one,
Plead for us before God,
That Divine Mercy be ours through you.
Amen.

Maronite Antiochene Rite

In her diary, Blessed Faustina Kowalska gives this prayer
that leads to the Sacred Heart of Jesus.

O MARY

O Mary, Immaculate Virgin,
Pure crystal for my heart,
You are my strength, O sturdy anchor!
You are the weak heart's shield and protection.

O Mary, you are pure, of purity incomparable;
At once both Virgin and Mother,
You are beautiful as the sun, without blemish,
And your soul is beyond all comparison.

Your beauty has delighted the eye of the Thrice-
    Holy One.
He descended from heaven, leaving His eternal
    throne,
And took Body and Blood of your heart
And for nine months lay hidden in a Virgin's
    Heart.

O Mother, Virgin, purest of all lilies,
Your heart was Jesus' first tabernacle on earth.
Only because no humility was deeper than yours
Were you raised above the choirs of Angels and
    above all Saints.

O Mary, my sweet Mother,
I give you my soul, my body, and my poor heart.
Be the guardian of my life,
Especially at the hour of death, in the final strife.[1]

— ❧ —

PRAYER OF SAINT AMBROSE
FOR MERCIFUL AWARENESS

May the life of Blessed Mary be ever present to
  our awareness.
In her, as in a mirror, the form of virtue and
  beauty of chastity
Shine forth.
She was virgin, not only in body, but in mind and
  spirit.
She never sullied the pure affection of her heart by
  unworthy feelings.
She was humble of heart.
She was serious in her conversations.
She was prudent in her counsels.
She preferred to pray rather than to speak.
She united in her heart the prayers of the poor
And avoided the uncertainty of worldly riches.
She was ever faithful to her daily duties,
Reserved in her conversations, and always
Accustomed to recognize God as The Witness of
  her thoughts.

Blessed Be the Name of Jesus.
Amen.

Saint Ambrose, c. 397

— ❧ —

PRAYER FOR TRUE WISDOM

O Mary, Mother of God
You were foretold by the Prophets,
Foreshadowed in types and figures
By the Patriarchs,
Described by the Evangelists,
Saluted most graciously by the angels,
Lead us to wisdom of the Presence of God
Now and forever.
Amen.

Saint Sophronius, A.D. c. 640

— ❧ —

PRAYER FOR KNOWLEDGE AND VIRTUE

O Young Mother! O Girl and Mother free!
O bush unburned, burning in Moses' sight!
You came down to us from the Deity,
Through humbleness the Holy Spirit did alight
Upon your heart, whence, through God's might,
You conceived our Father's only Son.
Help me to speak of this with reverence!

Holy Lady, your goodness, your magnificence,
Your virtue, and your great humility
Surpass all science and all utterance;
For sometimes, Holy Lady,
Even before people pray to you,
You come to us in your kindness
To bring Light to our prayer,
To be our guide unto your dear Son
Who is so precious to us.

My knowledge is so weak, O blissful Queen,
To speak globally of your mighty worthiness,
That the weight of your virtue is beyond my
    capacity to articulate.
But as a child of twelve months old, or less,
Who labors her language to express;
Even so fare I; and therefore, I pray to you,
Guide my words, which I of you shall say.

Author unknown, c. 570

— ❧ —

PRAYER FOR UNION WITH
THE SACRAMENT OF LOVE
O MARY, MOTHER OF GOD

O Mary, Mother of God
The Divine Sacrament is the most powerful,
And sovereign remedy of all our spiritual miseries.

It is the Source of heavenly comfort to
Alleviate the sorrows of our mortal pilgrimage.

O Mary, Mother of God,
Give to me a deep sense of my spiritual indigence.
Grant, by the power of your motherly intercession
That I may eagerly cry out
"If I but touch the hem of His garment,
I shall be saved!"

Dare I slight the tender invitations of our
Divine Redeemer?
Dare I disobey His repeated commands,
And disdain His threats?

Show me Holy Mother of God
That I cannot love Jesus
When I do not unite myself with Him
In His Sacrament of Love.
Amen.

Author unknown, c. 1050

— ❧ —

OUR LADY OF WALSINGHAM

O alone of all women, Mother and Virgin,
Mother most happy, Virgin most pure,
We salute thee, we honor thee as how we may
With our humble offerings;

May thy Son grant us, that imitating thy most
   holy manners,
We also by the grace of the Holy Spirit
May deserve spiritually to conceive Jesus
In our inmost soul,
And once conceived, never to lose Him. Amen.
Our Lady of Walsingham, Pray for us.
                         Attributed to Erasmus

— ≈ —

PRAYER FOR HUMILITY

I come to thee, glorious Mother of God, whom
the Church of the Saints call Mother of Humility,
Mother of Mercy. Thou art she, O Mary, who has
never refused the company of anyone; whose
mercy has never failed anyone, or whose clemency
rejected any supplicant. God forbid, mediatrix of
men, and their only hope, after thy Son, that my
sins should be an obstacle to exercising towards me
thy merciful office. Ah, no; assuredly, I hope that
thou wilt deign to obtain for me the grace to expi-
ate them, to repent of them sincerely. Amen.
              Saint William of Paris (c. 1148–1203)

— ≈ —

This is the prayer Mary prayed when the Word was made
flesh and dwelt within her.

MARY'S PRAYER: THE MAGNIFICAT

My soul doth magnify the Lord;
And my spirit hath rejoiced in God my Savior,
Because he hath regarded the humility of his
    handmaid;
for behold, from henceforth all generations shall
    call me blessed.
Because he that is mighty, hath done great things
    to me;
and holy is his name.
And his mercy is from generation unto generation
to them that fear him.
He hath shewed might in his arm:
he hath scattered the proud in the conceit of their
    heart.
He hath put down the mighty from their seat,
and hath exalted the humble.
He hath filled the hungry with good things;
and the rich he has sent away empty.
He hath received Israel his servant,
being mindful of his mercy:
as he spoke to our fathers,
to Abraham and to his seed for ever.

Luke 1:46–55

CHAPTER 6

MOTHER OF PERPETUAL HELP

Prayers and a Novena for God's Divine Help and Protection

In A.D. 370, Saint Ephraem of Edessa reminded the followers of Christ that the name of Mary is the key to the Gates of Heaven. He prophesied about times when the evil one would deceive the foolish that they are so "blessed" they can enter the Holy of Holies without the key.

Praying to Mary for help and assistance is not about bypassing God. Rather, such prayer is pleasing to God and allows our petitions to be presented by Mary in the most favorable light.

No creature can get to God, manipulate God, force God. God is Perfection. God needs nothing. Every prayer of ours draws a measure of God's Perfection upon us. God has freely willed to need us. That is the mystery of the Incarnation.¹ It is

God, in His mercy, who must reach out and grasp His creature.¹ He did just this by means of the Blessed Virgin Mary who gave us Jesus. Mary is fully human: she knows all the joys and sorrows we carry. When Mary consented to Christmas Day, she also consented to Good Friday.

There is no better or more perfect Mother. Mary's heart is so filled with compassion and love for us that she freely takes much of our cup of adversity that life brings and drinks it herself, saving for us only the sweeter portion. It is God's great love for us and Mary's great love for God that draws Mary into the most difficult moments of our life. God allows Himself to be touched by His own Mother's tears on our behalf. And although Mary's children too must suffer, their suffering is different. Mary's faithful children rest in the folds of the mantle of the Queen of Heaven.

Since most of us readily admit our lack of perfection, it is wise to turn to God's Mother for help in loving God as she does. It is also natural to approach our Spiritual Mother Mary for protection and guidance. Mary gently helps us to love her Son Jesus more, to understand His words, to find and live in the joy of God's will. We are always safe and contented in God's will. There is no other safety. There is no other contentment.

I have included in this chapter two famous and powerful novenas enlisting Mary's protection. Novenas, which are prayed for many reasons, date back to the foundation of the Church as a popular practice developed to honor the nine months that Jesus spent in the womb of His Blessed Mother. Some cultures also pray special novenas to honor the nine days that the Apostles and our Blessed Mother spent in prayer in the Upper Room between the Ascension of Jesus and the Coming of the Holy Spirit at Pentecost.

A novena is a prayer or series of prayers that is said on nine consecutive occasions. Often people pray novenas once a week or once a month. Some pray once an hour.

Novenas are quite efficacious, especially when they are said in groups, whether in church or a prayer group or among family or friends. In addition to praying the novena, the faithful are encouraged to attend daily Mass and receive the Holy Eucharist or to otherwise participate in whatever worship service is appropriate and available. A powerful accompaniment to any novena is some kind of personal fasting added to our daily routine. The effects of such prayer commitment, strengthened by fasting, are oftentimes extraordinary. Consequently, novenas are popular all over the world.

Mary is the Faithful Mother. She graciously guides us to fully accept Jesus' path to God. Mary helps us to find peace and contentment in littleness and simplicity. Mary shows us how to surrender to God and allow God to dwell in us in fullness. When we desire special help and protection, all we need to do is ask in prayer with great trust in God's providential love for each of us.

— ⌇ —

PRAYER TO MARY FOR PEACE, SECURITY, AND MATERIAL NEEDS

Hail, Lady of the world, and Heaven's bright
Queen

Virgin of virgins hail,
You are serene in God.
You shine over the earth in the early morning
   Light
Filled with Celestial Grace, and Light Divine;
O Lady of God
Hasten and extend over us your loving arms.
May your Grace guard us from evil.
May your Light defend us from all our enemies.
Amen.

Adapted from the Office of the Blessed Virgin Mary

— ✥ —

PRAYER OF A PARENT FOR A CHILD
AVE MARIA! FOR A FATHER,
HEAR A CHILD

Ave Maria! maiden mild,
Listen to a maiden's prayer;
Thou canst hear, though from the wild;
Thou canst save amidst despair.
Save may we sleep beneath thy care,
Though banished, outcast, and reviled—
Maiden! hear a maiden's prayer,
Mother, hear a suppliant child! Ave Maria!

Ave Maria! undefiled!
The flinty couch we now must share,
Shall seem with down of eider piled,

If thy protection hover there.
The murky cavern's heavy air
Shall breathe of balm if thou hast smiled,
Then Maiden! hear a maiden's prayer;
Mother, list a suppliant child! Ave Maria!

Ave Maria! stainless styled,
Foul demons of the earth and air,
From this their wonted haunt exiled
Shall flee before thy presence fair.
We bow us to our lot of care
Beneath thy guidance reconciled;
Hear for a maid a maiden's prayer,
And for a father hear a child. Ave Maria!

Sir Walter Scott (1771-1832)

— ⌾ —

PRAYER FOR ANGELIC PROTECTION

August Queen of Heaven, sovereign Mistress of
   the Angels,
who did receive from the beginning the mission
   and power to crush the serpent's head,
we beseech thee to send thy holy angels, that
   under thy command,
and by thy power they may pursue the evil spirits,
encounter them on every side, resist their bold
   attacks, and drive them hence into the abyss of
   woe.

Most Holy Mother, send thy angels to defend us
and drive the cruel enemy from us.
All ye holy angels and archangels, help and defend
us. Amen.
O good and tender Mother! Thou shalt ever be
our love and hope.
Holy Angels and Archangels, keep and defend us.
Amen.'

—— ⌬ ——

PRAYER FOR PROTECTION
AGAINST DEMONS

O Mary, powerful Virgin,
You are the mighty and glorious Protector of the
Church.
You are the Marvelous Help of Christians.
You are Terrible as an Army set in Battle Array.
You alone have destroyed every heresy in the entire
Church.
In the midst of my anguish, my struggles and my
distress,
Defend me from the power of the enemy,
And at the hour of my death,
Receive my soul into Paradise.

Saint John Bosco, c. 1880

—— ⌬ ——

MOTHER OF PERPETUAL HELP

Mother dearest, mother fairest
Help of all who call on thee,
Virgin purest, brightest, rarest,
Help us, help, we cry to thee.
Free us from all sin and sadness,
Fill our hearts with peace, with gladness;
Mary Mother, help away!
Mary, Virgin, help us aye!

Lady, help in pain and sorrow
Soothe those racked on bed of pain,
May the golden light of morrow
Bring them health and joy again,
Bring them health and joy again.

Help the poor, the sad, the weary,
Comfort those whose homes are dreary.
Mary Mother, help away!
Mary, Virgin, help us aye!

Mother! Help the absent loved ones,
Ah! we miss their presence here!
Help them, guard them far and near.
Save them from all sin and danger,
Lead safe home the weary stranger,
Mary Mother, help away!
Mary, Virgin, help us aye!

Mother, help the wounded soldier,
Set the pining captive free,
Help the sailor on mid-ocean,
Help those in their agony,
From the demon's malice guard them,
In their death-pangs watch and ward them.
Mary Mother, help away!
Mary, Virgin, pray! oh pray!

Help our priests, our virgins holy,
Help our Pope—Long may he reign!
Pray that we who sing thy praises,
May in heaven all meet again.
Help us when our life grows dreary,
Thy heart too was sad and weary,
Mary Mother, help away!
Mary, Virgin, pray! oh pray!

Author unknown, c. 1890

— ⌘ —

PETITIONS TO MARY FOR
GOD'S DIVINE PROTECTION

O Mother All Merciful, thou hast come to us with
outstretched hands, overflowing with graces, in
order to attract us to thyself, and to load us with
favors. We hasten, therefore, to follow the odor of
thy perfumes, sweeter far than that of roses. Gird us

with the cord of purity and penance, cover us with
the veil of modesty, bind us to thy service with the
links of a faithful love, and lay upon our breasts the
blessed Scapular of the Heart of thy Divine Son.
May it be for us henceforth the pledge of thy most
powerful protection until the day when we shall rest
at last in the bosom of God for all eternity. Amen.

With the approbation of
His Grace the Archbishop of Bourges

— ❧ —

The following novena is extremely effective and has been
prayed by many generations of families. One should be quite
certain to truly desire that for which this novena is prayed.

Unlike most novenas, this one is repeated each day for
thirty days. If at the end of thirty days you have not received
what you are praying for, continue to say the novena. It has
never been known to fail. A great "side effect" of the novena is
personal growth in holiness.

— ❧ —

THE THIRTY DAYS' NOVENA PRAYER TO
THE BLESSED VIRGIN MARY

Commemorative of the Passion of Our Lord Jesus Christ.

Ever glorious and blessed Virgin Mary, Queen of
Virgins, Mother of Mercy, hope and comfort of
dejected and desolate souls,

through the sword of sorrow which pierced thy
tender heart, whilst thine only Son, our Lord Jesus
Christ suffered ignominy and death upon the cross;

through that filial tenderness rooted in Pure
Love that He had for thee, grieving in thy grief,
whilst from His cross He recommended thee to
the care and protection of His beloved disciple, St.
John;

have pity upon us, we beseech thee, on our
poverty and necessities; have compassion on our
anxieties;

assist and comfort us in all our infirmities and
miseries.

Thou art the Mother of Mercy, the sweet conso-
latrix and refuge of the desolate and afflicted:

look therefore with pity on us, miserable children of Eve, and hear our prayer: for since, in just
punishment for our sins, we are encompassed by
evils, whither can we fly for more secure shelter,
than to thy maternal protection?

Attend, therefore, with an ear of pity, we beseech
thee, to our humble and earnest request.

We ask it through the mercy of Jesus Christ, thy
Son, the Redeemer of the world.

We ask it through the anguish of mind wherewith thy beloved Son, our dear Savior, was overwhelmed on Mount Olivet, when He besought
His Eternal Father to remove from Him, if possible, the bitter chalice of His future Passion.

We ask it through the threefold repetition of His prayer in the garden, from whence afterwards, with mournful tears, thou didst accompany Him along the doleful Stations of His sufferings and death.

We ask it through the welts and sores of His virginal flesh, occasioned by the cords and whips wherewith He was bound and scourged when stripped of His seamless garment, for which His executioners afterwards cast lots.

We ask it through the scoffs and ignominies by which He was insulted, the false accusations, and unjust sentence by which He was condemned to death, and which He bore with heavenly patience.

We ask it through His bitter tears and sweat of blood, His silence and resignation, His sadness and grief of heart.

We ask it through the blood which trickled from His royal and sacred head, when struck with the scepter of a reed and pierced with His crown of thorns.

We ask it through the torments He endured, when His hands and feet were cruelly fastened to the tree of the cross.

We ask it through His vehement thirst and bitter potion of vinegar and gall.

We ask it through His dereliction on the cross, when He exclaimed: "My God, My God, why hast Thou forsaken Me?"

We ask it through His mercy extended to the good thief, and through His recommending His precious soul into the hands of His Eternal Father before He expired, saying: "All is consummated."

We ask it through the blood mixed with water which issued from His sacred side when pierced with a lance, and whence a flood of grace and mercy hath flowed upon us.

We ask it through His immaculate life, bitter Passion, and ignominious death upon the cross, at which nature itself was thrown into convulsions, by the bursting of rocks, rending of the veil of the Temple, the earthquake, and darkness of the sun and moon.

We ask it through His descent to the dead where He comforted the saints of the Old Law and led captivity captive.

We ask it through His glorious victory over death, His triumphant ascension into Heaven, and through the grace of the Holy Spirit, infused into the hearts of the disciples when He descended upon them in the form of fiery tongues.

We ask it through His awful appearance on the Last Day, when He shall come to judge the living and the dead.

We ask it through the compassion He bore thee, and the ineffable joy thou didst feel at thine assumption into heaven, where thou art eternally absorbed in the sweet contemplation of His Divine Perfections.

O glorious and ever blessed Virgin, comfort the hearts of thy supplicants, by obtaining for us. . . . (*Here mention your request.*)

And as we are persuaded that our Divine Savior honors thee as His beloved Mother, to whom He can refuse nothing because thou asketh nothing contrary to His Divine Will, so let us speedily experience the efficacy of thy powerful intercession, according to the tenderness of thy maternal affection, and the charity of His amiable Heart, which mercifully granteth the requests, and complieth with the desires of those who love and fear Him.

O most Blessed Virgin, besides the object of our present petition, and whatever else we may stand in need of, obtain for us of thy dear Son, our Lord and our God, lively faith, firm hope, perfect charity, true contrition, a horror of sin, love of God and our neighbor, contempt of the world, and patience and resignation under the trials and difficulties of this life.

Obtain for us, O sacred Mother of God, the gift of final perseverance, and the grace to receive the last sacraments worthily at the hour of death.

Lastly obtain, we beseech thee, for our parents, our siblings, our spouse, our children, grandchildren, relatives, forbears, progeny, all our benefactors, those we influence remotely or proximately, whether living, dead or yet to be born, life everlasting. Amen.[4]

PERPETUAL NOVENA
IN HONOR OF OUR LADY
OF THE MIRACULOUS MEDAL

The Miraculous Medal Novena, like its counterpart, the Miraculous Medal, is renowned throughout the world. Its power and graces have sustained generations of Mary's children of all nations and stations in life.

— ⁕ —

NOVENA PRAYER

O Immaculate Virgin Mary, Mother of Our Lord Jesus and our Mother, penetrated with the most lively confidence in your all-powerful and never failing intercession, manifested so often through the Miraculous Medal, we, your loving and trusting children implore you to obtain for us the graces and favors we ask during this Novena, if they be beneficial to our immortal souls, and the souls for whom we pray. (*Here privately form your petitions.*) You know, O Mary, how often our souls have been the sanctuaries of your Son who hates iniquity. Obtain for us then a deep hatred of sin and that purity of heart which will attach us to God alone so that our every thought, word and deed may tend to His greater glory. Obtain for us also a spirit of prayer and self-denial that we may recover by penance what we have lost by sin and at

length attain to that blessed abode where you are
Queen of Angels and of Saints. Amen.

— ❧ —

AN ACT OF CONSECRATION TO OUR LADY OF THE MIRACULOUS MEDAL

O Virgin Mother of God, Mary Immaculate, we
dedicate and consecrate ourselves to you under the
title of Our Lady of the Miraculous Medal. May
this medal be for each one of us a sure sign of your
affection for us and a constant reminder of our
duties toward you. Ever while wearing it, may we
be blessed by your loving protection and preserved
in the grace of your Son. O most powerful Virgin,
Mother of our Savior, keep us close to you every
moment of our lives. Obtain for us, your children,
the grace of a happy death; so that in union with
you, we may enjoy the bliss of Heaven forever.
Amen.

O Mary, conceived without sin, pray for us who
have recourse to you. Amen. (*Three times.*)

— ❧ —

CHAPTER 7

MOTHER OF GOOD COUNSEL

Prayers in Times of Stress, Sorrow, Illness, and Abandonment

As each new season brings celebrations that honor the victories of Mary's Son Jesus over the evils of the world, so each season also brings disappointments and difficulties. Who knows better how to comfort us during difficult times than Mary, who stood at the foot of the cross of her Son? Whose heart is more overflowing with love? If we ask our Blessed Mother to help us in our times of trouble, Mary takes our cup of sorrow and drinks deeply from it, spoon-feeding us only a small amount. Mary always brings her Son to help us; He is the Remedy that heals all the evils in the world.

Illness, sorrow, abandonment, and stress of all kinds bring not only grief but the opportunity to pray. Our prayers in these times need not be complex. A prayer can be a simple outpouring of love from our heart toward the person, situation, or event for whom or which a divine remedy is desired. Below is a legend about the power of one simple prayer to Mary that rescued an entire city.

During the reign of Pope Saint Gregory the Great (590–604), human hearts had grown hard and cynical. A devastating plague broke out in Rome. Vast numbers of people suffered horribly and died violently. The stench of death was everywhere. Medical science had no remedy.

The Pope turned in prayer to Mary as Mother of God and mother of the human race. In a public act of faith, and defiant of the disease that was wiping out the population of Rome, Saint Gregory the Great carried a highly sacred icon, reputedly painted by Saint Luke, in solemn procession from the Church of Saint Mary Major to Saint Peter's Basilica.

Stories survive even to these times that those who witnessed the solemn procession heard angelic choirs chanting the glorious Resurrection Hymn that acknowledges and praises God's gifts to Mary. People, stooped with sorrow, were suddenly filled with joy at the sound of angels on high. They joined their voices with the angels to cry out this prayer.

— ❦ —

PRAYER IN TIME OF DISASTER
QUEEN OF HEAVEN
(*REGINA COELI*)

O Queen of Heaven, rejoice, Alleluia,
For He Whom you were privileged to bear,

Alleluia,
Has risen, as He said, Alleluia.
Pray for us to God, Alleluia. Rejoice and be glad,
O Virgin Mary,
Alleluia.

For the Lord has risen indeed,
Alleluia.

Let us pray.
O God, Who gave joy to the world
Through the resurrection of Your Son,
Our Lord Jesus Christ;
Grant, we beseech You
That through His Mother, the Virgin Mary,
We may obtain the joys of everlasting life.
Through the same Christ our Lord.
Amen.
May the Divine Assistance remain always with us.
Amen.

—— ⟶ ——

Legend tells us that the crowds grew as sounds of the
angelic hosts on high filled the area with the music of Heaven.
Even the dying were brought to the site of the procession. Suddenly, a huge warrior angel, brandishing an avenging sword
over the population, was visible in the sky. People fell to their
knees in shock, fright, and even in disbelief. Slowly the crowds

joined their voices with the Pontiff's, who was by now reciting the Queen of Heaven prayer over and over again with profound filial devotion as he knelt before the sacred icon.

Saint Gregory the Great was demonstrating to the crowds that a person worships God by laying down his or her will at every moment so that only God's will is done. A human will is limitation at work, but God's will is Divinity at work. The avenging angel's fierce sword reminded everyone of God's Truth written upon each human heart. The human race may live in the Heart of God only by total surrender to God's Plan at every moment.

As people prayed the Queen of Heaven prayer, each came to understand, on a deeply personal level, how Jesus venerated His Blessed Mother. Such an encounter with Living Truth brought Light to see Mary created and prepared for Jesus by His Father. The crowds gained fervor in praising God's Blessed Mother. And eventually everyone saw the angel of chastisement replace his sword of vengeance in his scabbard.

The sick got well. There were no further reported cases of the plague. That generation could never forget the angel of chastisement, for they had seen him with their own eyes. They had experienced the cleansing power of God's vengeance. People spoke of God's will with renewed reverence and taught their children to obey the great Commandments. Thereafter, Mary, the most obedient of all God's creatures, was highly honored in music, art, theater, architecture, and literature. Humanity was gradually learning that to praise Mary is to praise God's holy Plan for the human race; to honor her is to imitate her virtues.

The Queen of Heaven prayer of praise continues to be prayed by the faithful, and most especially in times of great need. A chapel dedicated to Saint Michael the Archangel, who is known as the Guardian Angel of Mary, was built on the spot where Saint Gregory the Great led the population of Rome in public recitation of the Queen of Heaven prayer. The ancient figure of the avenging angel, carved in white marble, stands, even now, in the proximity of Saint Mary Major Church in Rome.

PRAYER IN TIMES OF SORROW, ILLNESS, ABANDONMENT

This great anthem of the Blessed Virgin Mary comes to us from the early days of the Church. It has a glorious history and brings wonderful blessings and miracles, especially in times of sorrow, illness, betrayal, and abandonment.

MOTHER OF CHRIST
(*ALMA REDEMPTORIS*)

Mother of Christ, hear your people's cry,
Star of the deep and portal of the sky.
Mother of the One Who made you
from nothing.
In our strivings we struggle and call to you
for aid.
O by that joy which Gabriel the Archangel

brought to you
Pure Virgin, first and last
Look on our misery.
Amen.

———— ❧ ————

PRAYER IN DISTRESS, PAIN, BETRAYAL, FAILURE, BITTERNESS

The following prayer, though of ancient origin, has a remarkable history of bringing heavenly aid in times of distress, betrayal, failure, and bitterness. It is said that the joy this prayer evokes in heaven spills over the earth in great abundance.

———— ❧ ————

HAIL QUEEN OF HEAVEN ENTHRONED
(AVE REGINA COELORUM)

Hail Queen of Heaven enthroned!
Hail Queen of all the angels!
Root of Jesse! Gate of Morning,
From whom the world's True Light
Was born:
Glorious Virgin, joy to you,
You are beautiful beyond compare!
Fairest of all God's creation
Speak on our behalf a loving prayer.

Grant that I may praise you
O Blessed Virgin,
Give me strength against our enemies.

Let us pray.
O Most Merciful God,
Grant us help in our weaknesses;
That as we celebrate the memory of the holy
    Mother of God,
So, by the help of her intercession
May we rise again from the pain of our mistakes
Through the same Christ Our Lord. Amen.[1]

The next prayer is named after its author, Saint Theresa of
Lisieux.

THE LITTLE FLOWER'S
PRAYER TO MARY

Virgin full of grace,
I know that at Nazareth you lived modestly,
without requesting anything more.
Neither ecstasies, nor miracles, nor other extraor-
    dinary deeds
enhanced your life
O Queen of the Elect.

The number of the lowly, "little ones," is
very great on earth.
They can raise their eyes to you
without any fear.
You are the incomparable Mother
who walks with them along the common way
to guide them to heaven.

Beloved Mother,
in this harsh exile,
I want to live always with you
and follow you every day.
I am enraptured by the contemplation of you
and I discover the depths of the love of your Heart.
All my fears vanish under your Motherly gaze,
which teaches me to weep and rejoice![1]

Saint Theresa of the Child Jesus
Doctor of the Church (c. 1874–1897)

— ⟨≈⟩ —

The great Litany of Loreto honors the Mother of God
under many beloved titles. Throughout the centuries it has
been recited as a stepping-stone in the journey to union with
God. Some choose a special title from this Litany for meditation each day. Others appropriate a special title as a guide for
their lives, or for a project, military campaign, building, event,
work of art or music, or as patroness of a city, state, or nation.

Each stanza, fervently prayed, deepens human humility and sows seeds of wisdom. Although this prayer is often said in churches, as a dialogue between congregation and priest or other prayer leader, it is also quite effective when said alone.

———— ⊸ ————

Lord, have mercy on us.
Lord, have mercy on us.
Christ, have mercy on us.
Christ, have mercy on us.
Lord, have mercy on us.
Lord, have mercy on us.
Christ, hear us.
Christ, graciously hear us.
God the Father of heaven, *have mercy on us.*
God the Son, Redeemer of the world, *have mercy on us.*
God the Holy Spirit, *have mercy on us.*
Holy Trinity, one God, *have mercy on us.*

Mary, *pray for us.*
Holy Mother of God, *pray for us.*
Mother of Christ, *pray for us.*
Mother of Divine Grace, *pray for us.*
Mother of the Church, *pray for us.*
Mother Most Pure, *pray for us.*
Mother Most Chaste, *pray for us.*
Mother Inviolate, *pray for us.*

Mother Undefiled, *pray for us.*
Mother Most Lovable, *pray for us.*
Mother Most Admirable, *pray for us.*
Mother of Good Counsel, *pray for us.*
Mother of Our Creator, *pray for us.*
Mother of Our Savior, *pray for us.*

Virgin Most Prudent, *pray for us.*
Virgin Most Venerable, *pray for us.*
Virgin Most Renowned, *pray for us.*
Virgin Most Powerful, *pray for us.*
Virgin Most Merciful, *pray for us.*
Virgin Most Faithful, *pray for us.*

Mirror of Justice, *pray for us.*
Seat of Wisdom, *pray for us.*
Cause of Our Joy, *pray for us.*
Spiritual Vessel, *pray for us.*
Vessel of Honor, *pray for us.*
Singular Vessel of Devotion, *pray for us.*
Mystical Rose, *pray for us.*
Tower of David, *pray for us.*
Tower of Ivory, *pray for us.*
House of Gold, *pray for us.*
Ark of the Covenant, *pray for us.*
Gate of Heaven, *pray for us.*
Morning Star, *pray for us.*
Health of the Sick, *pray for us.*
Refuge of Sinners, *pray for us.*

Comfort of the Afflicted, *pray for us.*
Help of God's People, *pray for us.*

Queen of Patriarchs, *pray for us.*
Queen of Angels, *pray for us.*
Queen of Prophets, *pray for us.*
Queen of Apostles, *pray for us.*
Queen of Martyrs, *pray for us.*
Queen of Confessors, *pray for us.*
Queen of Virgins, *pray for us.*
Queen of All Saints, *pray for us.*
Queen Conceived Without Original Sin, *pray
    for us.*
Queen Assumed into Heaven, *pray for us.*
Queen of the Most Holy Rosary, *pray for us.*
Queen of Peace, *pray for us.*

Lamb of God, You take away the sins of the world,
    spare us O Lord.
Lamb of God, You take away the sins of the world,
    graciously hear us, O Lord.
Lamb of God, You take away the sins of the world,
    have mercy on us.
Pray for us, O Holy Mother of God.
That we may be made worthy of the promises of
    Christ.

Let us pray.

Lord God, give to Your people the joy of continual health in mind, body, and spirit. With the prayers of the Blessed Virgin Mary to help us, guide us through the sorrows of this life to eternal happiness in the life to come. Grant this through our Lord, Jesus Christ, Your Son, Who lives and reigns with You and the Holy Spirit, one God, for ever and ever. Amen.

— ❧ —

PRAYER IN TIMES OF DARKNESS
MOTHER DEAR

Mother dear, O pray for me,
whilst far from heaven and thee
I wander in a fragile bark
O'er life's tempestuous sea.
O Virgin Mother, from thy throne
so bright in bliss above,
Protect thy child and cheer my path
With thy sweet smile of love.

Mother dear, remember me,
and never cease thy care,
Till in heaven eternally
Thy love and bliss I share.

Mother dear, O pray for me,
Should pleasure's siren lay

E'er tempt thy child to wander far
from virtue's path away.
When thorns beset life's devious way,
And darkling waters flow,
Then, Mary, aid thy needy child,
Thyself a mother show.

Sodality Manual

— ⌘ —

PRAYER TO ELIMINATE FEAR

O Mother of God, if I place my confidence in
   you,
I shall be saved.
If I am under your protection,
I have nothing to fear,
for the fact of being your child is the possession of
   a certainty
of salvation,
which God grants only to those He intends to
   save.

Saint John Damascene, Doctor of the Church, c. 749

— ⌘ —

PRAYER IN BETRAYAL

Virgin, gentlest of all God's creatures,
show me how you acted toward the many ungrateful people

✳ III ✳

whom Jesus taught and for whom He worked
    great miracles.
Thus I shall learn how to put up with the faults of
    my neighbor.
How often you witnessed the ingratitude and
    betrayal Jesus received in turn for the good He
    did!
Yet your thoughts and feelings toward His enemies
    were,
like His, only thoughts and feelings of peace.
You detested sin, but you loved the sinner.
It was only the offense against God that moved
    you deeply;
you let no complaint against these foolish men
    pass your lips, and you even took up their cause
    with Jesus.
You acted toward them as you now act, after so
    many years, toward me.
I am the most faithless and ungrateful of your
    servants,
yet you treat me with kindness and win ever new
    favors from God for me.
Mother of the God of peace, win for me the grace
    never again to distress anyone with unkind
    words.
Your very name and image causes me to think
    mild thoughts.
Obtain for me the virtue of gentleness and the
    spirit of peace,

so that I may merit the glorious title of "child of
    God."

Alexander De Rouvuille[1]

— ⌇ —

PRAYER IN TIME OF TRIAL

All-holy Lady,
do not abandon me to the power of human
    beings.
Hear the plea of your servant
for I am oppressed by anguish
and find it difficult to resist the pressures of evil.
I have no defense
and I do not know where to flee.
I am assailed on all sides
and I find no consolation except in you.
Queen of the world,
hope and protection of the faithful,
do not despise my petition
but grant me what I need.

Byzantine Liturgy

— ⌇ —

PRAYER FOR MERCY, PITY,
AND KINDNESS

O Virgin Mother, daughter of your Son,
humble and exalted beyond every creature,

and established term of God's eternal plan,

you are the one who ennobled human nature
to such an extent that its Divine Maker
did not disdain to become its workmanship. . . .

O Lady, you are so great and powerful
that those who seek grace without recourse to you
are expecting wishes to fly without wings.

Your loving kindness not only comes to the aid
of those who ask for it but very often
spontaneously precedes the request for it.

In you is mercy, in you is pity,
in you is magnificence, in you is found
everything that is good in God's creation.

Dante, Paradiso, *canto XXXIII*

PRAYER IN STRESS AND SORROW

Kneeling at thy feet, O gracious Queen of Heaven,
we offer thee our deepest reverence. Thou art the
daughter of the Eternal Father, the mother of the
Divine Word, and the spouse of the Holy Spirit.
Full of grace, of virtue, and of heavenly gifts, thou
art the chaste temple of God's mercies. Thy loving
heart is filled with charity, sweetness and tender

compassion for poor sinners, and we call thee
Mother of Holy Pity. With the utmost trust I
come to thee in my sorrow and distress. Give me
confidence in thy love, and grant me what I ask—
if it be God's will, and for the welfare of my soul.
Cast thine eyes of pity upon me and upon all with
whom I am in any way connected. Shield me from
the attacks of the world, the flesh and the devil.
Remember, O fondest of mothers, that I am thy
child, purchased with the precious blood of thy
Divine Son. Pray without ceasing that the
adorable Trinity may give me the grace ever to triumph over the devil, the world, and my passions. I
ask this, O most pure Virgin, through the infinite
bounty of the Most High, through the merits of
thy Divine Son, by the care with which thou didst
nourish Him, by the devotion with which thou
didst serve Him, by the love with which thou didst
cherish Him, by thy tears and anguish in the days
of thy pilgrimage. Obtain that the whole world
may be made one people and one Church, which
shall give thanks, praise and glory to the Most
Holy Trinity, and to thee who art its mediator.

May the power of the Father, the wisdom of the
Son and the virtue of the Holy Spirit grant us this
blessing. Amen.

Pope Pius IX, March 26, 1860

PRAYER TO OUR LADY
OF LOURDES FOR HEALING

O ever Immaculate Virgin, Mother of Mercy,
Health of the Sick, Refuge of Sinners, Comfort of
the Afflicted,
You know my wants, my troubles, my sufferings.
Deign to cast upon me a look of mercy.
By appearing in the Grotto of Lourdes,
You were pleased to make it a privileged sanctuary
Where you dispense your favors.
Already many sufferers have obtained the cure
of their infirmities both spiritual and corporal.
I come, therefore, with unbounded confidence to
implore
Your maternal intercession.
Obtain, O loving Mother,
the granting of my request. . . .

I will endeavor to imitate your virtues
That I may one day share your glories
and bless you in eternity.
Amen.[4]

PRAYER TO ALLEVIATE SUFFERING

O Blessed Virgin Mary, who can worthily speak
words of praise and thanksgiving to you,

for the wondrous assent of your will that rescued a
    fallen world?
What songs of praise can our weak human nature
    recite in your honor,
since it is by your intervention alone that it has
    found the way to restoration?
Accept kindly, the poor thanks as we offer to you
    now,
though insignificant in value to the gift you have
    given us.
Dear Mother, receive the commitments we make,
obtain by your prayers
the remedies for all our mistakes.
Carry our prayers within the sanctuary of your
    heavenly life with God
and bring forth to us the gift of our reconciliation.
Take our offering, grant us our requests, obtain
    pardon for what we fear,
for you are the sole hope of sinners.
Mary, our Mother, help the miserable,
strengthen the fainthearted, comfort the
    sorrowful,
pray for your people, intercede for the clergy,
for all men, women and children consecrated to
    God.
Be ever near us and assist us when we pray
Bring to us always loving answers to our prayers.
Make it your continual commitment to pray for
    the people of God,

you, who are blessed by God,
who merited to bear the Redeemer of the world
Who lives and reigns, world without end. Amen.

Saint Augustine (c. 354–430)

— ❧ —

The prayer below comforted Pope Leo XIII in his old age, when sorrow and pain surrounded him.

— ❧ —

PRAYER IN SORROW
AND PAIN OF OLD AGE

As a little child,
I loved you like a Mother.
Now that I am old,
my love for you has grown.

Receive me in heaven
as one of the blessed,
and I will proclaim
that I have obtained
such a great prize
through your patronage.

Pope Leo XIII (reigned 1810–1903)

PRAYER FOR THE DYING

O Mary, pierced with sorrow,
Remember, reach and save
The soul that goes tomorrow
Before the God that gave;
As each was born of woman,
For each, in utter need,
True comrade and brave foreman,
Madonna, intercede.
Amen.
(Recite three Our Fathers, three Hail Marys, three
  Glory Be's in gratitude for God's Divine Mercy.)
                    Rudyard Kipling (1865–1936)

SAINT THOMAS MORE'S PRAYER
TO MARY AT DEATH

When evening shades are falling
O'er Ocean's sunnt sleep,
To pilgrim hearts recalling
Their home beyond the deep;
When rest o'er all descending,
The shores with gladness smile,
And lutes their echoes blending,
Are heard from aisle to aisle,
Then, Mary, Star of the Sea,
We pray, we pray to thee.

The noonday tempest over,
Now Ocean toils no more,
And wings of halcyons hover
Where all was strife before.
Oh, thus may life, in closing
Its short tempestuous day,
Beneath Heaven's smile reposing,
Shine all its storms away:
Thus, Mary, Star of the Sea,
We pray, we pray, to thee.

On Helle's sea the light grew dim,
As the last sounds of that sweet hymn
Floated along its azure tide—
Floated in light as if the lay
Had mixed with sunset's fading ray—
And light and song together died.

Saint Thomas More (1478–1535)

— ⟐ —

CHAPTER 8

MOTHER MOST LOVABLE

Prayers for Daily Inspiration

Faith is a highly blessed gift from God's Love. If we don't exercise this gift daily, and integrate it more and more into our everyday lives, we begin to lose it. There are no static moments in the spiritual realm; God has created us to pray and exercise our faith at all times. The prayers to Mary in this chapter help strengthen our faith commitment, for those who enter the Heart of Jesus with Mary have access to these chambers reserved for intimate family members.

For those whose faith is weak or possibly nonexistent, the following prayers of inspiration present a special opportunity. The following exercise, which uses a technique called interior intellectual imaging, often obtains the gift of faith or restores it to those who have lost it. As you try this exercise, sincerely open your heart to the possibility that there is more to life than meets the eye.

Select any prayer or prayers in this chapter that interest you, or use any other prayer in this book. Find a quiet place where you will not be disturbed. Picture in your mind the joy of knowing a perfect mother, one who is capable of loving you unconditionally, just as you are. (Perhaps you will observe an icon, or other image of the Blessed Mother holding her Sacred Infant Jesus. Visualize yourself as a tiny child in the arms of your Blessed Mother.) Focus on the image in your imagination as you say these words: "God, I believe. Please help my unbelief."

Hold on to your interior, intellectual image of your own perfect spiritual mother. Allow yourself to feel comfortable that you totally belong to her. Repeat her name: "Pure Love." Allow yourself to believe she loves you unconditionally, just as you are. Ask her to help you pray for faith. Then recite the prayer you have selected.

If you persevere with this exercise daily, amazing interior images will be conveyed to your intellect. You will move along in the spiritual life as quickly as your own personal commitment to this exercise allows. The virtue of Hope will germinate in your heart. As that experience matures, notice how the sweet buds of Love begin to scent the path of your daily life. Inspiration is a Divine Invitation.

Countless people throughout the world, of all nations, pray the following prayer every day.

THE *TE DEUM LAUDAMUS*
OF SAINT BONAVENTURE

We praise thee, O Mother of God: we acknowledge thee to be the Virgin Mary.

All the earth acknowledges thee as the only daughter of the Father.

All the angels and archangels serve thee.

The cherubim and seraphim praise thee and con-
tinually cry:

Holy, Holy, Mary, Mother of God, and pure Virgin,

Heaven and earth are filled with the majesty of thy
glory;

The glorious choir of the Apostles praise thee.

The admirable company of the Prophets praise
thee.

The white-robed army of martyrs praise thee.

The whole army of Confessors praise thee.

The Holy Church throughout the world doth
acknowledge thee

An Empress of infinite majesty,

And a worthy Mother of an only Son.

Also an Immaculate Spouse of the Holy Spirit.

Thou, O most Holy Virgin, art a Queen of honor.

Thou art the chosen daughter of the Eternal
Father.

In order that man may be saved, thou hast conceived the Son of God in thy womb.

By thee, the old serpent was crushed, and Heaven
 was opened to the faithful.

Thou dost sit at the right hand of thy Son in the
 glory of the Father.

Thou art believed to be the reconciler of the future
 Judge.

Therefore we pray thee, to come to the assistance
 of thy servants whom thy Son has redeemed
 with His precious blood.

Make them to be numbered with thy saints in
 glory everlasting.

O Mary, save thy clients and bless those who
 honor thee.

Govern them: and lift them up forever.

Day by day, O Mary, we magnify thee, and we
 praise thy name forever.

Vouchsafe, O Mary, this day and always keep us
 from grievous sins.

O Mary, take pity upon us: take pity upon us.

O Mary, in thee have I hoped. Let me never be
 confounded. Amen.

— ⬧ —

LOVELY LADY DRESSED IN BLUE

Lovely Lady dressed in blue,
Teach me how to pray!
God was just your little Boy,
Tell me what to say!

Did you lift Him up sometimes,
Gently, on your knee?
Did you sing to Him the way
Mother does to me?

Did you hold His hand at night?
Did you ever try
Telling stories of the world?
O, and did he cry?

Do you really think He cares
If I tell Him things—
Little things that happen?
And do the Angels' wings

Make a noise? And
Can He hear me if I speak low?
Does He understand me now?
Tell me—for you know!

Lovely Lady dressed in blue,
Teach me how to pray!
God was just your little Boy,
And you know the way.

Author unknown

— ⌇ —

PRAYER FOR AWARENESS
OF JESUS AMONG US

O Holy Virgin Mary, Immaculate Mother of Jesus
And our mother,
We humbly invoke you under the title of
Our Lady of the Most Blessed Sacrament
because you are the Mother of our Savior who
Lives in the Holy Eucharist.
From you He took the flesh and blood He feeds us
in the Sacred Host.
We invoke you under that title because the
Grace of the Holy Eucharist comes to us through
you,
the channel through which God's Graces reach us.
Finally, we call you Our Lady of the Most Blessed
Sacrament
because you were the first to live the Eucharistic
life.
Teach us to pray the Holy Mass as you did,
to receive Holy Communion worthily and frequently,
and to visit devotedly with Our Lord Jesus in the
Blessed Sacrament.
Amen.

John Cardinal Carberry

— ⌇ —

O MOST HOLY VIRGIN

Let me praise you, O most holy Virgin!

Let me praise you at my own cost.

Let me live, work, waste away and die, for you alone.

Let me contribute to your exaltation, to your highest exaltation.

Permit that others may outdo my zeal in glorifying you, O Mary,

so that by holy rivalry your glory may grow more rapidly,

just as He wills it, who raised you above all creatures.

In you alone, God has been more adored than in all other saints,

For you God created the world, and for you He created me also.

O let me praise you, most holy Virgin Mary.

Saint Maximilian Kolbe (1894–1941)

— ⌇ —

Tradition has taught us that the devotion of remembering and honoring the Seven Sorrows of Mary will restore faith and hope to broken hearts and to ruined families. The Seven Sorrows of Mary devotion brings divine sweetness to human sorrow and is a means of repairing human destruction. This devotion draws down heavenly strength, confidence in God's power, and abandonment to the Sorrowful Heart of Mary. The prayers in honor of the Seven Sorrows of Mary were approved and promulgated by Pope Pius VII in 1815.

The Our Father, Hail Mary, and Glory Be can all be found in chapter 9.

PRAYERS OF THE SEVEN SORROWS OF MARY

O God, come to my assistance.
O Lord, make haste to help us.
Glory be to the Father, and to the Son, and to the
    Holy Spirit,
As it was in the beginning, is now, and ever shall be,
Now and forever. Amen.

1. I grieve with you, O Mary most sorrowful, in
    the affliction of your tender heart at the
    prophecy of holy and aged Simeon and Anna
    when you presented your precious Infant Jesus
    in the Temple.
Dear Mother, by your Immaculate Heart so
    afflicted, obtain for me the virtue of humility
    and the gift of holy fear of God forever.
(*Recite the Our Father, Hail Mary, and Glory Be.*)

2. I grieve with you, O Mary most sorrowful, in
    the anguish of your most loving, Immaculate

Heart, during your flight with your Infant Jesus and Saint Joseph into Egypt, and during your sojourn there.

Dear Mother, by your Immaculate Heart so troubled, obtain for me the virtue of generosity, especially toward the poor, and the gift of piety.

(*Recite the Our Father, Hail Mary, and Glory Be.*)

3. I grieve with you, O Mary most sorrowful, in those anxieties which tried your troubled Immaculate Heart at the loss of your dear Son Jesus during three days when He was an adolescent.

Dear Mother, by your Immaculate Heart so full of anguish, obtain for me the virtue of chastity and the gift of knowledge.

(*Recite the Our Father, Hail Mary, and Glory Be.*)

4. I grieve with you, O Mary most sorrowful, in the pain of your Immaculate Heart at meeting Jesus as He carried His cross.

Dear Mother, by your Immaculate Heart so troubled, obtain for me the virtue of patience and the gift of fortitude.

(*Recite the Our Father, Hail Mary, and Glory Be.*)

5. I grieve with you, O Mary most sorrowful, in the martyrdom which your generous Immaculate Heart endured as you stood near Jesus during His crucifixion.

Dear Mother, by your afflicted Immaculate Heart, obtain for me the virtue of temperance and the gift of counsel.

(*Recite the Our Father, Hail Mary, and Glory Be.*)

6. I grieve with you, O Mary most sorrowful, in the wounding of your compassionate Immaculate Heart, when the side of Jesus was struck by the lance before His body was removed from the cross.

Dear Mother, by your Immaculate Heart thus transfixed, obtain for me the virtue of fraternal charity and the gift of understanding.

(*Recite the Our Father, Hail Mary, and Glory Be.*)

7. I grieve with you, O Mary most sorrowful, for the pangs that wrenched your most loving Immaculate Heart at the burial of Jesus.

Dear Mother, by your Immaculate Heart, sunk in the bitterness of desolation, obtain for me the virtue of diligence and the gift of wisdom.

(*Recite the Our Father, Hail Mary, and Glory Be.*)

Let us pray.

May the intercession of the Blessed Virgin Mary, Your Mother,

Whose most holy soul was pierced by a sword of sorrow in the hour of Your bitter passion be made for us,

We beseech You, O Lord Jesus Christ,
Now and at the hour of our death, before the
    Throne of Your Mercy.
Through You, O Jesus Christ, Savior of the world,
Who with the Father and the Holy Spirit
Lives and reigns world without end. Amen.
                                    Author unknown

— ⤫ —

An excerpt from the Little Compline, with the Akathist
Hymn:

— ⤫ —

THEOTOKOS

It is truly right to bless you, O Theotokos, who are
    ever
blessed and all-blameless, and the Mother of our
    God.
More honorable than the Cherubim, and more
    glorious
beyond compare than the Seraphim,
You who without stain bore God the Word,
Are truly Theotokos.
We magnify you.

I shall open my mouth and it will be filled with
    the Spirit,

and I shall speak forth to the Queen and Mother.
I shall be seen joyfully singing her praises,
and I shall delight to sing of her wonders.

Glory to the Father, and to the Son and to the
    Holy Spirit:
The ends of the earth do praise and bless you:
Hail, pure Maiden, Holy Scroll on which
The Finger of God did inscribe His Word.
Implore Him now, O Theotokos,
To write down your servants in the
Book of Life now and ever,
And unto ages of ages. Amen.

Translated by the Very Reverend Joseph Rahal

———— ✑ ————

THE MYSTICAL ROSE

O virgin Mother, daughter of thy Son,
Created beings all in lowliness
Surpassing, as in height above them all,
Term by the eternal counsel pre-ordained,
Ennobler of thy nature, so advanced
In thee, that its great Maker did not scorn,
Himself, in His own work enclosed to dwell!
For in thy womb rekindling shone the love
Revealed, whose genial influence makes now
This flower to germin in eternal peace!
Here thou to us, of charity and love,

Art, as the noon-day torch; and art, beneath,
To mortal men, of hope a living spring.
So mightily art thou, lady! and so great,
That he who grace desireth, and comes not
To thee for aidance, fain would have desire
Fly without wings. Nor only him who asks,
Thy bounty succors, but doth freely oft
Forerun the asking. Whatsoever may be
Of excellence in creature, pity mild,
Relenting mercy, large munificence,
All are combined in thee.

Dante Alighieri (1265–1321)

— ❧ —

MOTHER OF GOD

At morn, at noon, at twilight dim—
Maria! thou has heard my hymn!
In joy and woe, in good and ill—
Mother of God, be with me still?

When the hours flew brightly by
And not a cloud obscured the sky,
My soul lest it should truant be,
Thy grace did guide to thine and thee.

Now, when storm of Fate o'ercast
Darkly my Present and my Past,
Let my future radiant shine,

With sweet hopes of thee and thine!
Edgar Allan Poe (1809–1849)

— ❧ —

HEAVEN'S BRIGHT QUEEN

Let us soar away from this world's dominions,
And borrow awhile the meek turtle's pinions;
Let us mount to the home of the happy and blest,
Where the Saints and Angels eternally rest,
Nor tarry our flight on the borders of Heaven,
Since this privileged entrance by faith is given:
But on, still, still on, to the golden throne
Of God the Father, Who sitteth alone;
The Father, All present, omnipotent Being,
Almighty God, the great All-seeing.
Oh! to adore You, our Heavenly King
And forever and ever Your praises to sing!
But a mortal being must hasten on
Lest the light of faith should flee and be gone.
Lo! On the right is a glorious Throne
And another Who sitteth thereon alone,
The anointed Son of His Father's Love,
Who ascended as God and man above.
But these mortal eyes must still veil Their sight
Nor glance at a Being so dazzling and bright.
How I long for the day when my soul shall adore
And gaze on these Beauties for evermore.

Near to the Throne of the Lamb that was slain
Sits His Mother, Queen of Heaven, Star of the main:
Her throne is of ivory, silver delight,
And with glittering pearls of the ocean is bright;
The diamond glows with the emerald's sheen
While the ruby and amethyst there are seen.
If such be the splendor of Mary's throne
Encircled by Angels, a peerless zone,
What must her own perfect beauty be,
Dazzling with glorified majesty?
Her robe is of azure with sapphires delight
Fringed round with a border of silvery light.
Her tunic is gleaming with cloth of gold,
While brilliants are glowing in every fold.
Her face which was ever too lovely for earth,
The Holy Spirit beautifies round her the while,
She repays all homage with humility's dear smile.
On that queenly head is a golden crown
Which presses the hair but gently down:
On its front is a star whose dazzling sheen
Befitteth the brow of God's beloved Queen,
While its rim is fringed with a wreath of Roses
Sweeter than earth's fondest vision discloses.
Fifty are crimson, and fifty are blue,
And fifty again of the lily's hue.
The sun never shone on such flowers as those
Which might tempt one to wonder if earth hath
    its rose.

This Rosary hung on its chain of gold,
And I pondered thereon until reason told
How the Queen of the Saints from that Heaven's
   sphere
Looks down on the earth each petition to hear,
And by loved intercession the meek prayer to heed
Which her children upraise in their hour of need.

John Henry Cardinal Newman (1801–1890)

— ⌘ —

CHAPTER 9

MOTHER OF CHRIST

The Holy Rosary

THE POWER OF THE HOLY ROSARY

The Holy Rosary is the Spiritual Chain that binds generations to eternal life. It is an ancient form of praying with Mary that allows us to walk through the joyful, sorrowful, and glorious mysteries of the Life of Christ with His Blessed Mother. The Meditations of the fifteen decades of the Holy Rosary show us how Jesus and Mary always lived in God's will. The Holy Rosary teaches us that through Mary, we find the path to Jesus. The path of Jesus is God's Plan for the human race. Those who live in God's will experience Heaven on earth.

In 1917, at Fátima, the Blessed Mother gave the three little children this message for everyone on earth:

"I am the Queen of the Holy Rosary. Ask my faithful children to return to the Holy Rosary at once."

As the twentieth century draws to a close, Marian apparitions requesting God's people to pray the Holy Rosary are reported all over the world. Ordinary people claim to see the Blessed Virgin Mary, or hear her. Some even claim to see and hear the Lord Jesus Christ.

People from all walks of life and many faiths have responded to the proliferation of apparitions in this century by increasing their prayer life, by fasting several times a week, many on bread and water only, by spiritual and corporal works of mercy, and by almsgiving. In these times people all over the world are once again learning the immense, yet mysterious power of the Holy Rosary.

The Holy Rosary is a school of holiness if we are willing to learn its lessons. Pope Leo XIII wrote an encyclical about the Rosary, *Laetitiae Sanctae*, in which he deplored three pernicious tendencies at work to bring society and each of us to degradation, denigration, despair, and death.

1. Distaste for a simple life with fulfillment through sanctified labor.
2. Abhorrence of suffering of any kind.
3. Forgetfulness of a future life.

The Pope suggested a remedy that brings personal and global peace. He said the solution for the world's ailments is the Holy Rosary, which consists in a fixed order of prayer com-

bined with devout meditation on the life of Christ and His
Blessed Mother.

THE ROSARY:
SAINT DOMINIC'S STORY

Saint Dominic's story gives us much insight into opportunities
we each have in these wonderful times to truly bring lasting
peace, justice, and prosperity to the entire world. Saint
Dominic was born into an aristocratic family from Calaroga,
near the Spanish Pyrenees. In spite of his family's wealth,
Dominic was attracted to prayer and fasting from an early age
because he found a clarity of thought and a degree of peace in
prayer and fasting that insulated him from the misery he recognized in those who lived only for the pleasures of the world.

Dominic was by nature frugal. He was diligently careful to
discipline himself in his use of things, ideas, or activities that
took his mind off the ever-present mystery of God, truly present in all that lives. Solitude was a highly valued treasure for
Dominic. He longed for the joy of listening to the Voice of
God in the melody of trees that swayed to the rhythm of invisible breezes. Dominic constantly searched for silence before the
all-pervading Mystery of God's Presence. He was aware of the
Divine Gaze from the time he was a small boy. This heavenly
gift he would cherish with every ounce of energy in his being.

Dominic was ordained a priest at the age of twenty-four
and chose a life of solitude in a monastery. Because he knew
God's Love so intimately, Dominic's heart became filled with
concern for souls steeped in illusion, intoxicated with things

and ideas they could not keep, who did not know the joy of awareness of God's Divine Gaze upon them night and day. He intuited God's longing for these unconscious souls. Dominic developed such a passion to awaken souls in his hunger to please God that he prayed and fasted constantly. He asked his superiors to send him on a global rescue mission for the enslaved who did not know God. Finally he obtained permission to become a missionary in France.

Everywhere Dominic went, he was highly appreciated as a simple speaker who could communicate Gospel truths. Those who heard Dominic speak experienced awe-filled wonder at the Presence of God all around him. Dominic conveyed a conscious awareness of the Divine Gaze to his hearers. People recognized the mystery of God's Unconditional Love in the person of Dominic. His reputation and his mission grew.

The fire of love in Dominic's heart was so intense that it ignited a fire in the hearts of those who came in contact with him. Dominic constantly extolled people to wake up, to see that all the goods, ideas, plans, and achievements of the earth are only passing fancies, temporary, and do not satisfy the deepest longings of the human heart. What God offers to His human creatures is eternal joy and total happiness.

Fervent men joined Dominic. Soon each was extolling God's Divine Gaze of unconditional Love shining upon His people. The group became known as the Dominican Order of Preachers.

Saint Dominic taught that the gravity of people's sins blinds them to God's Presence. He saw sin as snakes suffocating Divine Life out of God's Holy People. To those enslaved by their human appetites, Dominic was powerless to communicate Truth.

In desperation over poor souls who could not find God, Dominic withdrew into a forest near Toulouse to pray and fast. As he rested undisturbed under the Divine Gaze of Eternal Love, Dominic prayed unceasingly for three days and three nights. During this time he found himself weeping for all people past, present, and yet to be born who do not recognize God's Presence in the world. Dominic's soul was filled with anguish, for he was keenly aware of the suffering that godlessness brings to the psyche, body, and spirit of people who do not see or hear God.

At the height of his anguish, Dominic experienced the presence of Mary accompanied by three angels. Her love and compassion were like salve to his wounded heart. Dominic recognized that she was his precious Mother, his confidante and colleague in the work of caring for God's poor, suffering children.

My dear son Dominic, I bring you a weapon from the Holy Trinity to reform the world. In this kind of warfare, wherein God's people are enslaved to their appetites and lose sight of Truth, the battering ram has always been the Angelic Psalter [the Holy Rosary]. The Hail Mary is the foundation stone of the New Testament. If you want to reach hardened souls and win them over to God, preach the power of my Psalter.

Dominic's heart was on fire with a raging zeal for the conversion of all God's people. How well he knew that conversion means awakening to God's Presence in all that lives as he raced through the forest and headed straight for the cathedral. Suddenly angels only he could see rang the great cathedral bells to summon the people.

Saint Dominic spoke of the mysterious graces and glories of the Holy Rosary as crowds filled the vast church. Quite suddenly, a supernatural storm broke out. The earth shook, the sun was darkened. Exploding roars of thunder and hissing streaks of lightning terrified the people, and they were very much afraid. Young and old alike crouched low in the church, praying more and more fervently. Were the angels putting the fear of God into them? Supernatural phenomena continued to surround Saint Dominic as he preached the wonders of the Holy Rosary, so much so that devotion to this prayer spread like a raging fire throughout the towns and villages of the world.

One day when Saint Dominic was suffering greatly and least expected any consolation from heaven, our Blessed Mother again appeared to him:

> My son, do not be surprised that your sermons fail to bear the results for which you hope. You are trying to cultivate a piece of ground upon which no rain has fallen. When Almighty God planned to renew the face of the earth, He began by sending down rain from heaven. This was the Angelic Salutation (Luke 1:28) by which God remade the world. When you give a sermon, urge people to pray the Holy Rosary. In this way your words will bear much fruit for souls.

Saint Dominic was renewed with such a zeal for the Holy Rosary that his spirit has touched souls in every part of the world ever since. Where the Holy Rosary is fervently prayed, reform and renewal bring immense divine protection to families, homes, monasteries, dioceses, parishes, schools, businesses, universities, countries, nations, cities, towns, and villages.

To pray the Holy Rosary fervently is to hold tight to the hem of Mary's dress and follow her into the Heart of God. Jesus enlightened us: "Amen I say to you, unless you be converted, and become as little children, you shall not enter into the kingdom of heaven" (Matt. 18:3). May all the world live and love and prosper under the Divine Gaze, ". . . and his name shall be called, Wonderful, Counselor, God the Mighty, the Father of the world to come, the Prince of Peace" (Isa. 9:6).

THE HOLY ROSARY

The Holy Rosary is most frequently prayed by holding a rosary, which is a string of beads designed to accommodate each of the prayers. A crucifix and a medal are attached to the string of beads. A rosary can be made of the most exquisite gems or of the simplest beads (and if a rosary is unavailable, ten fingers can serve as markers for the prayers of the Rosary); as a person says a prayer from the Rosary or meditates upon a Scriptural scene, he or she holds the bead designated for that particular part of the Rosary. The bead serves as a point of meditation, a reminder to keep one's mind focused on the prayer.

The Holy Rosary is divided into the Joyful, the Sorrowful, and the Glorious Mysteries of the Life of Christ. Each mystery is made up of five decades, and each decade consists of one Our Father, ten Hail Marys, a Glory Be to the Father, and the optional Fátima prayer. The prayers and mysteries are given below.

First, with the crucifix of the Rosary, make the Sign of the Cross. Still holding the crucifix, pray the Apostles' Creed. A large bead follows the crucifix, and after that is a series of three small beads and then another large one. Pray one Our Father on the large bead, a Hail Mary on each of the three small beads, and a Glory Be to the Father on the large bead. At this point, you will have reached the medal.

Now, holding the medal, start the First Joyful Mystery by meditating on the Scriptural scene. Then, on the same medal, pray the Our Father. Ten small beads will follow the medal, and then a large bead. (This series of ten beads plus a large bead is called a decade, and there are five decades on a rosary.) Pray a Hail Mary on each of the ten small beads, and on the large bead pray Glory Be to the Father, along with the Fátima prayer if desired. Start the Second Joyful Mystery on the same large bead, and continue this pattern until you have reached the end of the Fifth Joyful Mystery and have once again returned to the medal. Conclude by praying the Hail, Holy Queen.

If desired, repeat the rosary pattern with the Sorrowful and Glorious Mysteries. Some people pray the entire Rosary every day; others prefer to pray only one Mystery per day. Many like to follow this pattern each week:

Sunday:	The Glorious Mystery
Monday:	The Joyful Mystery
Tuesday:	The Sorrowful Mystery
Wednesday:	The Glorious Mystery
Thursday:	The Joyful Mystery
Friday:	The Sorrowful Mystery
Saturday:	The Glorious Mystery

PRAYERS OF THE HOLY ROSARY

THE SIGN OF THE CROSS

In the name of the Father and the Son and the
Holy Spirit. Amen.

THE APOSTLES' CREED

I believe in God, the Father Almighty, Creator of
Heaven and earth, and in Jesus Christ, His only
Son, Our Lord; who was conceived by the Holy
Spirit, born of the Virgin Mary, suffered under
Pontius Pilate, was crucified, died, and was buried.
He descended to the dead; the third day, He rose
again; He ascended into Heaven, and is seated at
the right Hand of God, the Father Almighty; from
thence He shall come to judge the living and the
dead. I believe in the Holy Spirit, the Holy

Catholic Church, the Communion of Saints, the forgiveness of sins, the resurrection of the body, and life everlasting. Amen.

THE OUR FATHER

Our Father Who art in Heaven, hallowed be Thy Name, Thy Kingdom come, Thy will be done on earth as it is in Heaven. Give us this day our daily bread, and forgive us our trespasses as we forgive those who trespass against us, and lead us not into temptation, but deliver us from evil. Amen.

THE HAIL MARY

Hail Mary, full of grace, the Lord is with thee. Blessed art thou amongst women and blessed is the fruit of thy womb, Jesus. Holy Mary, Mother of God, pray for us sinners, now and at the hour of our death. Amen.

THE GLORY BE TO THE FATHER

Glory be to the Father, and to the Son, and to the Holy Spirit, as it was in the beginning, is now and ever shall be, world without end. Amen.

THE FÁTIMA PRAYER

O my Jesus, forgive us our sins, save us from the fires of hell. Lead all souls to Heaven, especially those who have most need of Thy Mercy. Amen.

THE HAIL, HOLY QUEEN

Hail, holy Queen, Mother of Mercy. Hail, our life, our sweetness and our hope. To thee do we cry, poor banished children of Eve; to thee do we send up our sighs, mourning, and weeping in this vale of tears. Turn then, most gracious Advocate, thine eyes of mercy towards us, and after this, our exile, show us the blessed fruit of thy womb, Jesus; O clement, O loving, O sweet Virgin Mary. Pray for us, O holy Mother of God, that we may be made worthy of the promises of Christ, thy Son. Amen.

THE JOYFUL MYSTERIES OF THE HOLY ROSARY

The first five decades, the Joyful Mysteries of the Rosary, focus on the joyful Scriptural events in the life of Jesus Christ. They are divided into five joyful scenes from the Bible.

The First Joyful Mystery: The Annunciation (Luke 1:26–38)
The angel said to her, "Mary, do not be afraid; you have won God's favor. Listen! You are to conceive and bear a Son and you must name Him Jesus."

The Second Joyful Mystery: The Visitation (Luke 1:39–45)
And Elizabeth was filled with the Holy Spirit and cried out with a loud voice, saying, "Blessed art thou among women and blessed is the fruit of thy womb."

The Third Joyful Mystery: The Nativity (Luke 2:1–7)
And she brought forth her firstborn Son, and wrapped Him in swaddling clothes and laid Him in a manger, because there was no room for them in the inn.

The Fourth Joyful Mystery: The Presentation (Luke 2:22–39)
And when the days of her purification were fulfilled according to the Law of Moses, they took Him up to Jerusalem to present Him to the Lord.

The Fifth Joyful Mystery: The Finding of the Child Jesus in the Temple (Luke 2:41–52)
And it came to pass after three days, that they found Him in the temple, sitting in the midst of the teachers, both listening to them and asking them questions.

THE SORROWFUL MYSTERIES
OF THE HOLY ROSARY

The second five decades, called the Sorrowful Mysteries of the Rosary, focus on the sorrowful Scriptural events in the life of Jesus Christ. They are divided into five sorrowful scenes from the Bible.

The First Sorrowful Mystery: The Agony in the Garden
(Luke 22:39–46; Matt. 26:40–41)
And His sweat became as drops of blood running down upon the ground. And rising from prayer, He came to the disciples and found them sleeping.

The Second Sorrowful Mystery: The Scourging of Jesus
(Luke 23:16; John 19:1)
Pilate then took Jesus and had Him scourged.

The Third Sorrowful Mystery: The Crowning with Thorns
(Mark 15:16, 17; Matt. 27:24–29; John 19:5)
And they stripped Him and put on Him a scarlet cloak; and plaiting a crown of thorns they put it on His head and a reed into His right hand.

The Fourth Sorrowful Mystery: The Carrying of the Cross
(Luke 9:23; John 19:17; Mark 15:20)
And bearing the cross for Himself, He went forth to the place called Skull, in Hebrew, Golgotha.

The Fifth Sorrowful Mystery: The Crucifixion (Luke 23:33–43; John 19:25–27)
And Jesus cried out with a loud voice and said, "Father, into Thy hands I commend My Spirit." And having said this, He expired.

THE GLORIOUS MYSTERIES OF THE HOLY ROSARY

The third five decades are the Glorious Scriptural Mysteries of the Rosary. They are divided into five glorious scenes in the life of Jesus and Mary from the Bible.

The First Glorious Mystery: The Resurrection (Matt. 28:2–8; John 11:25–26)
He has risen, He is not here. Behold the place where they laid Him.

The Second Glorious Mystery: The Ascension (Luke 24:50; Acts 1:9; Mark 16:19)
So then the Lord, after He had spoken to them, was taken up into Heaven and sits at the right hand of God.

The Third Glorious Mystery: The Descent of the Holy Spirit (Acts 2:1–4, 11)
And they were all filled with the Holy Spirit and began to speak in foreign tongues, even as the Holy Spirit prompted them to speak.

The Fourth Glorious Mystery: The Assumption (Song of Songs 2:10, 11, 14; Rev. 12:1; Psalm 45:13, 14; Jth. 15:10)
And a great sign appeared in Heaven: a Woman clothed with the sun and the moon was under her feet and upon her head a crown of twelve stars.

The Fifth Glorious Mystery: The Coronation (Song of Songs 1:1; 6:10; Ecclus. 24:4–9; Prov. 8:32–35; Jth. 15:10–11)
Thou art the glory of Jerusalem, the honor of thy people. . . . the hand of the Lord hath strengthened thee, and therefore thou shalt be blessed forever.

There are Divine Promises attached to faithful recitation of the Holy Rosary. When people of the world become aware of the Divine Promises made by the Lord Jesus to His Mother on behalf of those who pray the Holy Rosary every day, peace will reign throughout all creation. In that time, every knee will bend and every heart proclaim that Jesus Christ is Lord.

FIFTEEN DIVINE PROMISES FROM JESUS

Jesus sent His Blessed Mother Mary to Saint Dominic (and also to Saint Alanus) with fifteen Divine Promises to those who faithfully pray the Holy Rosary.

1. To all those who will recite my Rosary devotedly, I promise my special protection and immense graces.

2. Those who will persevere in the recitation of my Rosary shall receive some signal grace.

3. Praying the Rosary shall be a most powerful armor against hell; it shall destroy vice, deliver from sin, and shall dispel heresy.

4. Praying the Rosary shall make virtue and good works flourish, and shall obtain for souls the most abundant divine mercies; it shall substitute in hearts love of God for love of the world, elevate them to desire heavenly and eternal goods.

5. Those who entrust themselves to me through the Rosary shall not perish.

6. Those who pray my Rosary piously, considering its Mysteries, shall not be overwhelmed by misfortune, nor die a bad death. The sinner shall be converted; the just shall grow in grace and become worthy of eternal life.

7. Those truly devoted to my Rosary shall not die without the consolations of the Church, or without grace.

8. Those who will recite my Rosary shall find during their life and at their death the Light of God, the fullness of God's grace, and shall share in the merits of the blessed.

9. I will deliver very promptly from Purgatory the souls devoted to my Rosary.

10. The true children of my Rosary shall enjoy great glory in heaven.

11. What you ask through my Rosary you shall obtain.

12. Those who propagate my Rosary shall obtain through me aid in all their necessities.
13. I have obtained from my Son that all the children of the Rosary shall have for their friends and confidants in life and death the saints of heaven.
14. Those who recite my Rosary faithfully are all my beloved children, the brothers and sisters of Jesus Christ.
15. Devotion to my Rosary is a special sign of predestination.

The Lord Jesus taught us that the weapons of victory over all evil are prayer and fasting. Jesus loves His Rosary. It is His life on earth. When we walk with Jesus on the path of His life on earth, we learn how to follow Him to Paradise.

The Holy Rosary is the chain that binds us to God's Ways, God's Will, God's Life. In these times, all people on earth are called to become like little children who approach God with the Chain of Eternal Life in our hands and in our hearts.

When we are able to live Christ's life on earth, we become His life on earth.

God's Love for all of us remains beyond our collective capacity yet to comprehend. God's world is a rich playground for His children. Soon there will be no evil hearts left on His playground. Though God's children weep in their suffering today, by His Love, by His Ways, all shall laugh and play before His Face tomorrow. God is Beauty. God is Love. God is.

Late have we loved You, O Beauty so ancient and
  so new;
late have we loved You!
For behold, You are within us, and we outside;
and we sought You outside and in our ugliness
fell upon those lovely things that You have made.
You were within us and we were not with You.
We were kept from You by those things,
yet had they not been in You,
they would not have been at all.
You call and cry to us and break open our deaf-
  ness:
and You send forth Your beams and shine upon us,
and chase away our blindness:
You breathe fragrance upon us and we draw in our
  breath
and do now pant for You:
we taste You, and now hunger and thirst for You:
You touched us, and we have burned for Your
  Peace.
Late have we loved You, O Beauty so ancient and
  so new;
late have we loved You! Amen.¹

NOTES

CHAPTER 1

1. Julian Allason, ed., *Prayers of the Sovereign Military and Hospitaller Order of Malta* (London: Sovereign Military Order of Malta, British Association, 1989), p. 45.

2. From Lope de Vega, as quoted in William A. Walsh, ed., *Heavens Bright Queen* (New York: Carey-Stafford, 1906), p. 84.

CHAPTER 2

1. Suzanne Noffke, O.P., ed., *The Prayers of Catherine of Siena* (New York: Paulist Press, 1993), pp. 157–65, selected excerpts. The author wishes to acknowledge the graciousness of Rev. Thomas King, S.J., Department of Theology, Georgetown University, for obtaining this prayer.

CHAPTER 3

1. *Nihil obstat:* Jerome Curtin, D.C.L.; *Imprini Potest:* Keven, Archbishop of Dublin, December 12, 1985.

2. From the Basilica of the National Shrine of the Assumption of the Blessed Virgin Mary, Baltimore, Maryland. The

author extends heartfelt thanks to Rosemary and Charles Carroll Carter for their graciousness in making available their family's historical data concerning Archbishop John Carroll.

3. From a prayer card circulated in Catholic churches.

CHAPTER 4

1. From the author's interview with Dr. René Laurentin.

CHAPTER 5

1. Anthony M. Buono, *Favorite Prayers to Our Lady* (New York: Catholic Book Publishing, 1991), p. 71.
2. Blessed M. Faustina Kowalska, *The Diary of Sister M. Faustina Kowalska, Divine Mercy in My Soul* (Stockbridge, MA: Marian Press, 1987), pp. 89–90, n. 161.

CHAPTER 6

1. Author's interview with Robert Faricy, S.J., S.T.D., Rome, October 1989.
2. The writings of Saint John of the Cross, especially *The Ascent of Mount Carmel,* explain the process.
3. *Imprimatur:* Patrick Cardinal Hayes, Archbishop of New York, September 5, 1936.
4. Author unknown. Text of prayer from F. X. Lasance, *With God* (New York: Benziger Bros., 1911), pp. 720–23.

CHAPTER 7

1. *Ave Regina Coelorum tr.* Roman Hymnal, 1884. Slightly adapted.

2. Buono, *Favorite Prayers to Our Lady*, p. 73.

3. In Matthew J. O'Connell, ed., *The Imitation of Mary* (New York: Catholic Book Publishing, 1977), pp. 193–94.

4. Adapted from *Prayers to Our Lady of Lourdes*, from approved sources. National Shrine of Our Lady of Lourdes, oldest in America, through the courtesy of Rev. Msgr. Hugh J. Phillips, Chaplain of the Grotto, Mount Saint Mary's College, Emmitsburg, MD.

CHAPTER 9

1. Adapted from Saint Augustine, *Confessions,* VII, 10, 18.

If you have information about Mary, the prayers in this book, or special prayers to Mary that you would like to share, please write to the author:

Janice T. Connell
Two Gateway Center #620
Pittsburgh, PA 15222

Kindly include a self-addressed envelope and adequate postage if you desire a response.

A portion of the proceeds of this book is dedicated to the world's sick and poor through the Missionaries of Charity and the Order of Saint John of Jerusalem.

If you desire to assist further, please identify each tax-deductible charitable gift with the memo: Praying With Mary. Kindly direct all gifts to the Missionaries of Charity *or* the Order of Saint John of Jerusalem. Include your name, address, and appropriate postage or self-addressed, stamped envelope to receive a letter of appreciation and mail to:

Missionaries of Charity
In Memory of Mother Teresa of Calcutta
335 East 145th Street
Bronx, NY 10451 USA

or

The Order of Saint John of Jerusalem
for the Infant Hospital at Bethlehem
1730 M Street NW, Suite 403
Washington, DC 20036 USA